KEY
ISSUES
in the
Afro-American
Experience

Under the General Editorship of

JOHN MORTON BLUM   *Yale University*

VOLUME SINCE 1865

KEY ISSUES in the Afro-American Experience

Edited by

NATHAN I. HUGGINS   *Columbia University*

MARTIN KILSON   *Harvard University*

DANIEL M. FOX   *Harvard University*

HARCOURT BRACE JOVANOVICH, PUBLISHERS
San Diego   New York   Chicago   Atlanta   Washington, D.C.
London   Sydney   Toronto

COVER:

Detail from the painting *Ambulance Call* by the Afro-American artist Jacob Lawrence. Courtesy of Dr. Bernard Ronis, Philadelphia. Photo by Robert F. Crandall.

SECTION OPENING PHOTOGRAPHS:

Pages   2   A black family working their farm. Courtesy of the Picture Collection, New York Public Library.

            3   A meeting of the South Carolina Legislature of 1873. Courtesy of Negro History Associates.

    44–45   Black dock workers unloading freight from a steamboat at Dog Tooth Cutoff, near St. Louis, Missouri. Courtesy of the Library of Congress.

      90   Silent Protest Parade, New York City, 28 July 1917. Courtesy of the Schomburg Collection, New York Public Library.

      91   Black Americans boarding a ship in Savannah, Georgia, for voyage to Liberia, 1 March 1896. Courtesy of Historical Pictures Service, Chicago.

   150–51   *Song of the Towers*, mural by Aaron Douglas. Courtesy of the Countee Cullen Branch of the New York Public Library.

    230   Boy looking through glass ball. Photo by Douglas Harris.

    230   Mother and child watching Yoruba wedding ceremony in Douglas Park, Chicago. Photo by Lloyd E. Sanders.

    231   Black student protest. Courtesy of Johnson Publishing Co., Chicago.

© 1971 by Harcourt Brace Jovanovich, Inc.

Paperbound ISBN: 0-15-548372-2

Clothbound ISBN: 0-15-146890-7

Library of Congress Catalog Card Number: 76-141607

Printed in the United States of America

Dedicated to four scholars of the American Negro:

Carter G. Woodson

Horace Mann Bond

Ralph J. Bunche

John Hope Franklin

Preface

New World Africans, from their first awareness of themselves as Americans, have wanted to assert the uniqueness and importance of their experience. They have called on the poetic muse: Phillis Wheatley, Jupiter Hammon, and Alberry Allson Whitman were among the early classic voices that sang the black consciousness in lyric and epic form. Polemicists and activists like Frederick Douglass, Martin R. Delany, and David Walker hammered out prose designed to awaken black men and women to their moral obligation. And from at least 1841, with J. W. C. Pennington's efforts, black Americans have had a keen sense that their story needed to be told as part of the history of America. For most blacks, there has never been any doubt that their identity is embedded in the general American history, and that they will never know themselves until they mine and refine that history themselves.

So it is only a trick of ego—a sleight of mind—that permits some observers to imply that the discovery of the Negro's place in American history and American studies is a recent event. It is arrogance to ignore or deprecate men who began their work near the beginning of this century, men like Carter G. Woodson and W. E. B. Du Bois. Many important black scholars followed, some of whom—J. Saunders Redding, John Hope Franklin, Benjamin Quarles—continue their work into this day. These men labored in a discouraging scholarly environment; indifference to their work kept the highest honors and acclaim just beyond their grasp. That they persisted despite the many obstacles was nothing short of heroic, and we are much the richer for their dedication. Consider, for instance, Carter Woodson's commitment and sense of purpose in starting, in 1915, and sustaining the Association for the Study of Negro Life and History. Because of his effort, we have had ever since the *Journal of Negro History* and the *Negro History Bulletin,* which have welcomed the essays of black and white scholars often thought too ethnic and too narrow in scope for the standard journals.

Thus formal and informal study of the Afro-American experience has existed for a long time. Nevertheless, there is something new about contemporary efforts to study Negro life and history. For the first time, Negro history has become a central concern of the general academic world. Indeed, concern has often been forced on colleges by student pressure. Growing numbers of black students found that the standard studies of "our" past—Western civilization no less than American history—failed to sound true to their lives and experience. Many white students, perplexed and annoyed by the disparity between officially stated ideals and sensed reality, suspected with good reason that a better perception of the irony and paradox that defined their present might well be achieved through an understanding of the Afro-American experience. That experience challenges conventional rhetoric on uninterrupted national progress and the success of the American Dream and is itself the essence of irony and paradox. But the new concern goes even beyond students' demands for relevance. White and black scholars have begun to see study of the Afro-American experience as a way to illuminate and reconsider perplexing problems in the American past.

The two volumes of *Key Issues in the Afro-American Experience* are designed to bring the specialist's interest and knowledge to the service of students, instructors, and general readers. We wanted to direct the energy, intelligence, and training of academicians to the creation of a collection of sharply focused essays that would both capture interest and demonstrate disciplined analysis. We wanted to choose topics that were central and essential to an understanding of the Afro-American experience. And we wanted the best people available to address themselves to those topics. These could not be essays already printed in scholarly journals—they presume a different audience.

Of the twenty-seven essays in these volumes, all but three—those by Philip Curtin, Kenneth Stampp, and Stanley Elkins—were written expressly for this collection. All other essays are fresh statements of principal issues by specialists in the field. For each essay we have provided a headnote that includes a brief biographical sketch of the author. For each section of the volumes, we have supplied a list of suggestions for further reading.

Defining relevance was a major problem in choosing the topics to be treated. Some issues that seemed urgent also seemed likely to be transformed by changes in national policy or economic conditions. We tried to make distinctions between the transient and the enduring. The definition of an Afro-American history, a black culture; the influence of Africa and the impact of slavery; black efforts at organization and resistance; the economic and social realities of Jim Crow and racism—these issues are central: relevant to the past, the present, and the foreseeable future.

It is from among these enduring issues that we have drawn the topics of these essays. We have not attempted to present a unified point of view—except for the feeling that the Afro-American experience is important to us all and deserves serious treatment. Nor have we attempted to create dispute for its own sake, though we realized that these topics and these authors would provide spirited, sometimes conflicting, statements. That is as it should be. We hope that this conflict and tension will be amplified and extended as readers talk with one another in the classroom and informally. None of these essays are thought to be definitive or to close the issue. If the essays help point the way to a meaningful perception of the Afro-American experience, if they offer some suggestions of how to probe more deeply and how to ask new questions, then we will have done something of what we set out to do.

We are indebted to Frank Freidel, from whose course on the Afro-American experience, given at Harvard College in the 1968–1969 school year, the idea for these volumes emerged. We gratefully acknowledge the constructive comments made by the following specialists who reviewed and commented on our original plan for the work: Jacob U. Gordon, University of Kansas; Peter Wood, Harvard University; Arthur Tuden, University of Pittsburgh; and James M. McPherson, Princeton University. We also thank Lenworth A. Gunther for his help on the volumes.

Nathan I. Huggins
Martin Kilson
Daniel M. Fox

Contents

2

Black Workers and Jim Crow   45

3

Resistance and Accommodation in Black Thought 91

4

The Urban Setting   151

5

Toward a New Identity 231

KEY
ISSUES
in the
Afro-American
Experience

1
Reconstruction

Unfinished Business: The Freedmen's Bureau and Federal Action in Race Relations

WILLIAM S. McFEELY

William McFeely is dean of the faculty and professor of history at Mount Holyoke College. He is the author of *Yankee Stepfather: General O. O. Howard and the Freedmen* (Yale University Press, 1968) and, with Thomas J. Ladenburg, *The Black Man in the Land of Equality* (Hayden Books, 1969). In the following essay, Mr. McFeely analyzes the difference between the promise and the performance of the Freedmen's Bureau. Bringing into focus a conflict between the law of the land and national will, he delineates the ways in which the Bureau was undermined and failed to implement social, political, and economic reconstruction. Mr. McFeely argues that the Freedmen's Bureau never exercised its potential as a federal agency and affirms the ability of the federal government to prompt a change in race relations.

Ready for Freedom

The Americans who ceased being slaves at the end of the Civil War were ready for freedom. They were, despite the fact that their ancestors (and a few of the freedmen as well) had endured the undeniable horror of the middle passage across the Atlantic. Once in America, slaves were held in bondage by a complex system of discipline that included not only the pain of whippings but the often executed threat of sale and separation from family and familiar surroundings. They also were forced to endure the deeply pervasive humiliation and tedium of heavy labor and constant surveillance. In the long history of the world far more of its population has lived as dependent people than in a state that could be called freedom, and, like others surviving subserviency, the black slaves of the South had adapted their minds to the grim situation.

But despite this discouraging American past, these black Southerners brought to freedom considerable assets for its enjoyment. One fundamental advantage was the fact that they were a physically flourishing and increasing population. From 1619 until the Civil War, 427,000 Africans were brought to English-speaking North America, most of whom were taken to the Southern states.[1] By natural reproduction, the number of black Americans in the South rose to approximately four million by 1865.

This growth in the black population of the American South was not the result of constant replenishment from Africa. Philip D. Curtin estimates that in the half-century after 1808, when the importation of slaves into the United States became illegal, only 50,000 more blacks were smuggled in.[2] The mid-eighteenth century had been the time when the largest number of slaves were brought to British North America, and therefore in 1865 most of the freedmen were fourth-, fifth-, or sixth-generation Americans.[3]

Slavery as a School

Although the blacks' long experience in the land had been as slaves, they had developed two resources valuable to them when Emancipation came: a culture of their own that had sustained them in their oppression and an education gained by observation of the mores and concerns of the dominant white culture. In the unique plantation system of the South, many resident planters and an even larger number of independent nonslaveholding farmers lived in close proximity to the slaves, and thus there was constant opportunity for such observation.[4] For example, there is no reason to think that the American tendency to talk politics was greatly impeded among planters by the presence of their slaves. White masters talked politics at dinner with little inhibition, even though their political discussions were inevitably discussions of slavery as well.

It is unfortunate in the extreme that we have virtually no primary sources that record immediately after such conversations were held how the Negroes in the room felt about them. However, we do have the diary of one white aristocrat who lived surrounded by slaves of whom she was a sharp if perplexed observer. In her April 13, 1861, entry, Mary Boykin Chesnut writes, "People talk before them as if they were chairs and tables and they make no sign." Curious about this, Mrs. Chesnut asks herself, "Are they stolidly stupid, or wiser than we are, silent and strong, biding their time."[5]

Not all the learning took place in fine dining rooms. Robert Smalls, a slave

---

[1] Philip D. Curtin, *The Atlantic Slave Trade: A Census* (Madison: University of Wisconsin Press, 1969), p. 88.

[2] Curtin, *Atlantic Slave Trade,* p. 234.

[3] Ibid., p. 216.

[4] Frank Lawrence Owsley, *Plain Folk of the Old South* (Baton Rouge: Louisiana State University Press, 1949), p. 8.

[5] Mary Boykin Chesnut, *A Diary from Dixie,* ed. Ben Ames Williams (Boston: Houghton Mifflin, 1961), p. 38.

who made a spectacular escape during the war, recorded that he first heard of Frederick Douglass' escape and subsequent leadership role in the antislavery campaign not in his master's Beaufort house, where he lived, but when he was visiting a remote plantation which had an absentee landlord.[6] Douglass' story was known in a part of the South where such communication among slaves might have been thought to be virtually impossible. Mysterious though its workings remain, an informal underground communication system effectively passed along information and made possible the discussion not only of how to escape but also of what to do once free.

These discussions did not reach Mrs. Chesnut's ears, but she wondered about them a good deal. Black and white Southerners had lived together for a long time, and when the Civil War came both groups realized that it would probably change the patterns of life they had always known. But the slaves kept the masters guessing as to how. The diarist relates in her entry of June 22, 1861: "Yesterday, some of the Negro men on the plantation were found with pistols. I have never seen aught about any Negro to show that they knew we had a war on hand, in which they had an interest."[7] However, she gives evidence that the mask of disinterest could be lifted if the moment were propitious: a friend, she says in her entry of November 11, 1861, "was in a state of abject fright because the Negroes show such exultation at the enemy's making good their entrance at Port Royal."[8]

By October 1863, Mrs. Chesnut was alert to change. Referring to her family's butler, she writes: "I taught him to read . . . but he won't look at me now. He looks over my head, he scents freedom in the air. He was always very ambitious. I do not think he ever troubled with books much, but then my father always said that Dick, standing in front of his sideboard, had heard all the subjects of earth or Heaven discussed, and by the best heads in our world."[9]

Fifty years ago, historian Ulrich B. Phillips and other friends of the antebellum way of life of the South wrote of slavery as a benign "school, constantly training and controlling pupils who were in a backward state of civilization."[10] The concept of racial inferiority implicit in the work of these writers has made some present-day historians cautious about accepting any of this group's interpretations, but their school metaphor is not entirely off the mark. Although the white teachers were undoubtedly uneasy about the world their black pupils might make, preparation for freedom was underway as the slaves watched,

---

[6] Dorothy Sterling, *Captain of the Planter: The Story of Robert Smalls* (New York: Doubleday, 1958), p. 32.

[7] Chesnut, *Diary,* p. 64.

[8] Ibid., p. 158.

[9] Ibid., p. 292.

[10] Ulrich B. Phillips, *American Negro Slavery* (New York: Appleton, 1918), p. 342.

listened, talked in private, and bided their time. Perhaps the old-fashioned concept of slavery as a school for a peculiarly American civilization has been discarded too hastily.

A Different School

The Freedmen's Bureau was a more experimental school for black Southerners. It was created by the federal government immediately after the Civil War, a time when neither the freedmen nor the twenty-seven million white Americans with whom they shared the land could tell what the new way of life would be like. Making that definition was the job of the Freedmen's Bureau.

It failed its assignment. Although it remained in existence until 1872, the agency's power lasted scarcely two years. It did not succeed in establishing a pattern of life satisfactory both to black and to white Southerners nor, more basically still, in protecting the lives of freedmen in times of violent confrontation. Many men contributed to the failure, but, setting aside questions of individual responsibility, present-day observers of our racial past offer two partially contradictory explanations for the failure of the Freedmen's Bureau. The first is that racism is a tragic flaw in the national character that cannot be expunged. The second explanation of failure contends that a national policy executed by a federal agency is an inappropriate way to approach what is either a local or a personal problem. This position is argued for both in the rhetoric of guilt indulged in by oppressors and in stern accusations expressed by the oppressed. The present-day determination of many men at the federal level to abandon work begun so well less than a generation ago has indeed strengthened the case for the latter. But despite the wide currency of these two positions on racial matters, they are not necessarily the conclusions to be drawn from the failure of the Freedmen's Bureau and other post–Civil War attempts to reconstruct the nation and provide a satisfactory way of life for the ex-slaves.

And failure it was. Even after the establishment of the Freedmen's Bureau, after the participation of black politicians in state constitutional conventions and legislatures as well as in the national Congress, and after the ratification of three amendments to the federal Constitution (ending involuntary servitude, delineating equal protection for citizens under the law, and granting the vote), black Americans still lost the future that these immense gains promised. The amendments were not enforced; the black voter was coerced and later disfranchised; the black citizen was systematically denied the protection of the law; and the black farmer was reduced to the dependent status of a sharecropper by a debt system so permanent as to effect involuntary servitude. And long before these setbacks the Freedmen's Bureau had been abandoned.

These bleak reversals of earlier advances were events of the 1870's, and indeed they hint that, even in matters of race, things do change—if only for the worse. What about the hopeful days of 1865 when people who had been slaves were suddenly free? Surely that was change and, as most of those freed probably would have agreed, change for the better. Although the freedmen began their lives in freedom somewhat wary of all white men, they came to their new positions with great expectations. They hoped that the government of the reunited nation would see to it that theirs was a better way of life than black Americans had previously known. It was encouraging when the government established an agency for this purpose. So long possessed, they liked the possessive in the agency's name. Officially it was the Bureau of Refugees, Freedmen and Abandoned Lands, but everyone called it the Freedmen's Bureau. Some white people meant the reference to be derogatory, but to the freedmen it was not.

But the Bureau let them down. In another work, I have inquired into the social philosophy and personal concerns of General Oliver Otis Howard in an attempt to determine whether he and the Freedmen's Bureau he headed were the victims of antagonistic outside forces or whether there were weaknesses in Howard's leadership that made him more directly responsible for the agency's failure.[11] The present inquiry asks a different question: Is there anything in the story of the Freedmen's Bureau to indicate that a federal agency can effect significant, useful changes in race relations?

A Federal Agency

On March 3, 1865, Congress passed a bill creating the Freedmen's Bureau. The legislation signed by President Lincoln was wide in scope. To the Bureau was "committed . . . the supervision and management of all abandoned lands, and the control of all subjects relating to refugees and freedmen from rebel states."[12] The agency was a public one; the assisting of freedmen was no longer left to the numerous church-related, private freedmen's aid societies. Throughout the war, men and women from these organizations had been working with freedmen in areas of the South captured by Union forces, and they had always argued that a public agency was needed. They foresaw that emancipation of the entire slave population would require an agency of national scope to provide for the freedmen.

Except for the less than satisfactory model of the Bureau of Indian Affairs, in 1865 no welfare branch of the federal government existed to serve as a framework for such an agency. Senator Charles Sumner urged the creation of a cabinet post for freedmen's affairs, which would have given a much-needed permanence to the endeavor. Sumner did not succeed in his effort to establish the work at the departmental level, but he did convince his congressional colleagues not to divorce attention to the problems of the freedmen from authority

---

[11] William S. McFeely, *Yankee Stepfather: General O. O. Howard and the Freedmen* (New Haven: Yale University Press, 1968).

[12] 13 U.S. Stat. 507–09, 507.

over distribution of lands on which they could sustain themselves. As long as the Treasury Department was the trustee of lands abandoned to Union armies, Sumner contended, it should also administer the affairs of the freedmen. When the Army won a jurisdictional battle and took control of those lands, Sumner successfully argued that the Freedmen's Bureau belonged in the War Department.[13]

Thus one of the nation's most ambitious experiments in social welfare was put in the unlikely hands of army officers. Initially, the officers chosen for this strange military duty were expected to have some humanitarian qualifications as well as a record of administrative ability. General Oliver Otis Howard was named commissioner of the Bureau, not only because he was a successful wartime commander but also because this officer, who prayed with his encamped soldiers as though they were his Sabbath school scholars, was known as "the Christian General." He had not been an abolitionist, but before the war had considered entering the ministry. During his extensive wartime service in the South, he came to view the problems of ex-slaves as a great challenge and an opportunity for evangelical and charitable service. He was almost unanimously regarded as a good choice for the position. As one future Bureau agent, who during the war had demonstrated his concern for freedmen, put it in 1865: "It seems as if success would always follow the 'Christian Howard.'"[14]

Howard established the headquarters of the Freedmen's Bureau in Washington and organized its work along state lines. He selected an assistant commissioner for each of the states of the former Confederacy and, because they had large populations of freedmen, also for Kentucky, the District of Columbia, and later Maryland as well. The assistant commissioners were stationed in the states to which they were assigned, and they had under them sub–assistant commissioners and other lower-ranking men, all of whom came to be known by the general term "Freedmen's Bureau agents."

The agents were the representatives with whom the freedmen came in direct contact, and the culture shock on both sides was considerable. When a young Union army officer arrived in a Southern town to set up a Bureau office, he often found that not all the plantation sense of community had disappeared. His black clients had been warned not to trust him by other white men from whom they were more used to hearing advice. On the other hand, he probably found the freedmen had heard not only of such formal matters as the Emancipation Proclamation but also of the promise of land in the congressional legislation creating the Bureau. It is likely that the agent was greeted with skepticism by people not versed in having their hopes fulfilled—and yet hopeful.

The agent was a stranger in the town. Very likely he had been attracted to the Bureau not only because it was thought to be a promising new branch

[13] McFeely, *Yankee Stepfather,* pp. 21–22.
[14] Ibid., p. 63.

of the Army in which to continue a service career but also because of a humanitarian concern for the freedmen; and yet he probably had no first-hand experience in working with black people. In his home town in the North there was nothing to compare with the intimacy of contact that had breached Southern racial and class lines under slavery. The former slaves seemed frighteningly alien to the agent as he began to listen to them relate their expectations and their complaints.

Indeed, for the agent it was a world turned upside down. His clients were people he literally could not understand and who had no better luck understanding his alien voice. The freedmen seemed foreign, and his recent enemies, local white Confederates, looked familiar. He soon discovered he had much in common with the latter group—a similar church experience, perhaps someone in town who had attended his college, or even mutual friends or relatives. The local white men quickly learned how to set the world right side up in a manner to their satisfaction. Much has been made of the hatred of white Southerners for Bureau agents (and there were few regrets when the meddlers left), but often the two groups got on well. If the agent could not comprehend the black people who came in to complain, he soon received offers of help from the very white men being complained about. The old contention of white Southerners that they "knew their people best" was used to win the Freedmen's Bureau agents over to a paternalistic view of the welfare needs of the freedmen.

Skeptical freedmen were aware that their Bureau might come to represent the planters instead of them. Originally Howard named agents who had sympathy for the freedmen. Commissions were found for civilians who had experience working with the freedmen during the war, but soon the fact that the only payroll available to Howard was that of the Army worked to the freedmen's disadvantage. Drastic reduction in the size of the Army eliminated some Bureau friends of the freedmen, and complaints from white planters to the White House concerning agents who were siding with black clients almost invariably resulted in their being either mustered out of the Army (and hence the Bureau) or transferred to duties in the educational branch of the agency or its Washington headquarters, where they would have less opportunity to intervene in controversies on behalf of the freedmen.

Forty Acres

Whether he took a partisan line or not, the basic job of the agent was to see to it that the black people had some way of subsisting now that they were no longer part of a slave system. The question was whether their carrying out of this assignment would prove congruent with the expectations of the former slaves. The freedmen's best hope for a new, satisfactory way of life lay in the wording of the bill creating the Freedmen's Bureau. Howard was explicitly instructed to "set apart for the loyal refugees or freedmen, such tracts of land . . . as shall have been abandoned" in lots of "not more than forty acres" and rent them, at a modest percent of their value, to freedmen and their families.[15] By July 1865 Howard had devised a system under which freedmen could apply for such tracts. To be sure, there were only enough acres in federal hands for 20,000 families to obtain farms of their own, but Howard and others expressed hope that the yeoman farmer concept would prove workable and that a precedent would be established for further land redistribution.[16]

On July 28, 1865, instructions were sent to the assistant commissioners in all the states of the old Confederacy save Texas (in which the Bureau was not yet established), ordering them to advertise the availability of the land and to tell the freedmen how to apply for it. All through the fall of 1865, the *New Orleans Tribune* carried advertisements of land accession, and the aggressive assistant commissioner in Louisiana, Thomas Conway, was eager to make the land grants.[17]

Almost no grants were made. Howard was on vacation in August 1865, the critical first month of his land redistribution program, and while he was away, President Andrew Johnson seized the opportunity to undercut the congressionally authorized enterprise. Earlier, in May, Johnson had issued his Amnesty Proclamation pardoning most former Confederates and allowing those remaining who had property worth at least $20,000 to request a pardon. This latter group of former leaders of the South quickly requested pardons, which were granted, and returned to their states prepared to cooperate with Johnson's plan for entrusting "home rule" to them. This process soon conflicted with the forty acres plan, because the pardoned Southerners wanted the restoration not only of their political power but also, if they had abandoned it, of their land.

On August 16, 1865, President Johnson ordered General Clinton B. Fisk, the assistant commissioner of his home state of Tennessee, to restore the lands of one B. B. Leake, whose aunt had come to Washington to plead the case at the White House. On the back of correspondence concerning the matter, the President added in his own hand, "The same action will be had in all similar cases."[18] In this simple way, Johnson destroyed the first program for providing a firm economic base for black Americans ever undertaken by the government.

When informed of the President's action, Howard did not rush to Washington to try to reverse it, and when he did return to the capital in September, he accepted an assignment from Johnson that the freedmen found hard to understand. The commissioner went on a tour across the South to convince the white men of the South that the Freedmen's Bureau stood for a

---

[15] 13 U.S. Stat. 508.

[16] McFeely, *Yankee Stepfather,* p. 105.

[17] *New Orleans Tribune,* 19 October 1865.

[18] McFeely, *Yankee Stepfather,* p. 114.

stable labor system and would not interfere with the reconstituted state governments (which were soon to pass the Black Codes restricting the mobility of the freedmen). Mississippi flatly contradicted the whole concept of freedmen gaining farms of their own by making it illegal for Negroes to own property outside a town.[19] The white Mississippians whom Johnson allowed to regain power not only were anxious to get back lands they had lost but were equally determined to prevent the freedmen from moving upward, as they would be able to do if they could establish prosperous farms. And this Mississippi law was written when the white citizens were confident that the Freedmen's Bureau would not be enforcing a contradictory federal policy on land. On his trip, Howard had made it clear that all the government would require of the slaves' former owners was that they be kind to the freedmen and obey contracts they signed with black workers.

The disappointment of the freedmen was great. Indeed, it may be conjectured that the loss of the expectation of gaining a farm of their own on the land they had so long worked had a profound effect on a whole generation of black Southerners. Their schooling as slaves had taught them what out of their slave past they should want to discard and what they should choose to retain. Chief among the discards was the discipline of gang labor in the fields, but the intense dislike of the degrading discipline of that system was not accompanied by hatred for the land on which they had worked. In their cabins at night they achieved times of privacy; they raised chickens and food crops on the patch of land around them. They did not want to lose their sustaining home place when freedom came. The wandering of freedmen the moment they learned of their emancipation has been greatly exaggerated, and much of it that did take place had as its object the seeking out of lost family members in order to bring them home. The former slaves hoped the government that had set them free would not allow freedom to mean deprivation of the thing they valued most—their own cabins and the patches of land around them.

The explicit wording of the Freedmen's Bureau bill, the American faith in the yeoman farmer ideal, the recommendation of friends who had seen such independent farms work in the Port Royal experiment, had planted in the freedmen the hope that they could stay home and farm land that would be their own. Now, only months after the end of the war freeing them, they heard the head of their Bureau denying it. In Charleston, on the Sea Islands, wherever he went, Howard found the freedmen incredulous: they could not believe that General Howard, whom they trusted as they had no man since Lincoln, would take away the farms he had promised them. When the General arrived in Jacksonville, for example, he found himself surrounded by freedmen

---

[19] *Constitution of the State of Mississippi, as Amended with Ordinances and Resolutions Adopted by the Constitutional Convention, August, 1865* (Jackson, 1865). See also Theodore Brantner Wilson, *The Black Codes of the South* (Tuscaloosa: University of Alabama Press, 1965).

certain that they were going to have farms and ready to argue with Howard's attempts to convince them that it did not matter that they would not. He climbed on a carpenter's bench and for an hour tried to make those freedmen believe that working for their former masters for wages was just as good a way of making a living as having one's own farm. Howard's brother, watching him make his plea, realized that similar disappointment would be met all across the South and that the winning of the blacks to this alternative plan would be "a super human task."[20]

The Contract System

The contract system (which Howard insisted was as beneficial to the freedmen as his forty acres plan) had started during the war. It was begun not only to protect the freedmen from the abuses of speculators who sought to obtain gang labor to raise cotton on seized lands but also to organize the labor of the freedmen efficiently. And it was the latter aspect that caught the freedmen's suspicious eye. Whatever the protection provided, the contract system served to perpetuate the basic work force structure of the slave system. The planters agreed to provide food, shelter, and care for the freedmen's families. The male head of a family, often signing with an *X,* agreed to supply the labor of the able-bodied members of his family. The work was done in field gangs under supervision. Some of the early contracts signed in the presence of Union officers during the immediate postwar weeks called for no wages, and some went so far as to use the term "in the usual way" to describe how the black workers and the white planters were to conduct themselves under the contracts.[21]

When the Freedmen's Bureau had contract forms printed, a clause calling for wages was included. The Freedmen's Bureau sought to convince itself and the freedmen that wages were wages. It would not recognize the fact that the contract did not call for the payment of an agreed-upon sum for work done by the hour or day, irrespective of the value of the product of that labor. The written contract is a fundamental concept of industrialized society, but, to the disadvantage of the freedmen, it was used to continue in effect the production and marketing concepts of agricultural slavery. The document was a promise of monetary return to the laborer only if the production (over which he had some control) was sufficient and the price it brought (over which he had no control) was high. To prevent nonpayment of wages after the crop was sold, the contract included a provision that a lien would exist on the crop to give the workers a legal claim to their pay.

---

[20] McFeely, *Yankee Stepfather,* p. 163.

[21] William S. McFeely, "The Hidden Freedmen: Five Myths in the Reconstruction Era," in James C. Curtis and Lewis L. Gould, eds., *The Black Experience in America: Selected Essays* (Austin: University of Texas Press, 1970), p. 74.

Frequently, however, the lien clause was struck from the contract by a stroke of a pen as the planter signed his name, and not infrequently the workers were told at the end of the season that the crop had not produced enough profit for their wages to be paid. Complaints to the Freedmen's Bureau agents about such practices were numerous, but even those agents willing to side with the workers' plight—rather than accept the landowners' account of his difficulty in making ends meet—could do little to help their clients. As the reports came in to headquarters in Washington, Howard learned that he could not prevent abuses of a system he had extolled to the freedmen as equal in value to his abandoned forty acres program.

In this dilemma, the freedmen were left on their own. We still do not have a thorough study of the transition in the South after slavery from the contract system to sharecropping, but it is possible that when we do, it will appear that much of the impetus for the establishment of the tenant farmer and sharecropper systems came from former slaves themselves. Work in a field gang had been one of the most hated aspects of slavery. When the white planters' lands were restored to them, freedmen who had temporarily escaped gang labor by independently working abandoned lands sometimes did as the farmers of one Sea Island community did: they left their fields without even harvesting their crops and moved to Savannah rather than resubmit to the gang system.[22] Freedmen who did not have that opportunity had to devise their own way to avoid the humility of the grinding constancy of the dawn-to-dusk discipline of the gang system. In exchange for agreeing to care for their own dependents—old people and children—for whom the planters had been responsible under both the contract and slave systems, the freedman farmer obtained from the planter a plot of land he would work on his own. Even if there were production costs or loss of security for dependents, this system, in which a farmer could be his own boss in the field, was preferable to many freedmen. Sharecropping provided a release from gang labor. As a sharecropper, a freedman could at least simulate having a farm of his own.

At the end of a crop year, the freedman turned over his produce to the landowner, who sold it and returned a share, usually a third, to the black sharecropper. No doubt many a freedman hoped this share would in time enable him to buy the land and make the farm truly his own. Neither he nor the landowner (nor for that matter the white sharecropper living under a similar arrangement) knew when sharecropping was developing that he would soon be caught in the almost perpetual debt of the lien system.[23] Debts were incurred for seed and equipment to grow the crops and for staples for the family to eat; when the crop was sold these debts often exceeded the profits, and the constricting process began over again for another year.

[22] *New Orleans Times,* 20 November 1865.

[23] C. Vann Woodward, *The Origins of the New South: 1877–1913* (Baton Rouge: Louisiana State University Press, 1951), pp. 180–85.

Protests and Politics

The slow but steady reinforcement of the economically dependent status of the black farmer in the South went on for decades. But before it set into place, the freedmen protested and asked for something other than a dependent existence. The Jacksonville farmers protested to Howard, and others petitioned the President and Congress. The entrance into politics brought results. Congress was out of session through the critical months of the spring, summer, and fall of 1865, but Republican congressmen were unhappy at the prospect of the creation by President Johnson, a former Democrat, of a conservative coalition of Southerners and Northerners (both Whigs and Democrats) who agreed with his program of political and economic restoration in the South and the maintenance nationwide of white supremacy. The Republicans began to see that only by excluding representatives from the restored Southern states could they keep their majority in Congress.

The Constitution permits Congress to determine whom it will admit, and the Southerners were refused admission in December 1865; in January, the seated members passed a bill enlarging the scope of the Freedmen's Bureau and specifying that the agency should devote itself to the enforcement of the companion legislation, the Civil Rights Bill of 1866. President Johnson's veto of the Freedmen's Bureau bill was sustained, but the Bureau continued under its original grant of authority. The companion civil rights bill was passed over the President's veto. On July 16, 1866, Congress passed a new Freedmen's Bureau bill, and this time the President's veto was overriden.[24] Howard immediately called together a commission to set up machinery for county-by-county coverage of the South and for other extensive expansions of the organization's scope. But the strengthening of the agency took place only on paper; events were rushing past the Freedmen's Bureau. Both its friends and its enemies were turning elsewhere in their efforts to influence race relations.

Black Southerners were beginning to move into politics in order to gain a better way of life for themselves. They demanded the vote. In New Orleans in 1865 they held a mock election, and their candidate received more votes than did the regularly elected governor in that city. Taking encouragement from this demonstration of effective political organization, they backed a move to reconvene a constitutional convention which had been held when the city was in Union hands in 1864. The morning the convention was to open, the black advocates of enfranchisement marched behind a band and flags to demonstrate for their cause. In front of the hall where the convention was about to meet, they encountered a group of armed white citizens. Among them, conspicuous in leadership, were members of the city police and fire departments. The black demonstrators were fired on and dispersed, and the white group then entered the convention room and killed several delegates. That night, attacks were made on the houses of black citizens; many buildings were burned and residents killed.

---

[24] 14 U.S. Stat. 173–77.

The Freedmen's Bureau had been unable to prevent this loss of life. The head of the Bureau in the city, General Absalom Baird, was aware that the President of the United States did not want him to use federal troops to protect the convention even though he had warned Bureau headquarters in Washington that violence might occur. The attackers knew that Baird's troops were an hour out of town. When they were summoned into town, they were too late to save the convention members and were unable to prevent the burnings and killings in the residential areas of the city that night.

When Congress investigated this "riot" and an earlier one in Memphis, its response was not to strengthen the Freedmen's Bureau but to move to a different approach. The agency had but one last critical act to perform: to register blacks to vote under the Reconstruction Acts of 1867. With this series of bills, the Republican Congress, seeking a new way to protect the lives of the freedmen and to hold the Republican majority, made the black Southerners voters. But this award of political participation carried with it the generally unnoticed assumption that thereafter the freedmen must look out for themselves. Though radical in their inclusion of black people in the body politic, the Reconstruction acts were retrogressive in an important sense. They enabled the federal government to abdicate its responsibility to the freedmen under the guise of giving the freedmen power enough to make the assumption of federal responsibility unnecessary. The job of defining the mores of the people of the South was turned over to the states, and when the white supremacists of the South discovered how to "redeem" their region with political guile and blatant physical violence, there was no federal Freedmen's Bureau for the blacks to turn to.

Had it still existed, it probably would not have been equal to the task of preserving the freedmen's gains. The agency, seemingly so well organized and powerful after its revalidation by Congress in 1866, had proved impotent. During the transferral of jurisdiction to the states in 1867, the assistant commissionerships of the Bureau were taken over by the regular army commanders in charge of the military districts into which the South was temporarily divided. Complaints to General Howard could not be acted on by him; he could only go to still another general and urge a lessening of the harsh treatment freedmen continued to receive. The Bureau limped along until 1872, but it was an office of only a handful of clerks largely engaged in encouraging private donors to assist the valuable schools and colleges that the Bureau had helped to start. Those colleges—Hampton, Fisk, and many others—were a valuable legacy of the days of the Bureau's great promise. But a strong federal agency that could work for the freedmen, and for a brief moment had done so, was gone.

An Assessment of the Freedmen's Bureau

The first lesson that one is tempted to draw from this short account of the Bureau's failure is that federal action in racial matters is either detrimental to the interests of the minority race or, at best, futile. Perhaps it would be wiser, however, to note the assessment of the agency by W. E. B. Du Bois in his 1901 essay "The Freedmen's Bureau." He argues that Howard's agency was both necessary and useful, and, commenting on its failure, speaks not of futility but of unfinished business: "The passing of a great human institution before its work is done . . . but leaves a legacy of striving for other men."[25] He feels that the freedmen were ready for freedom; but he realizes that they needed help in making the change from slavery. Offering them assistance in securing the economic base necessary for survival and development as free men was the Bureau's business. A look at ways the Bureau might have gone about its business successfully suggests that, with the earnest participation of the federal government, basic improvements might have been made in this nation's racial tapestry.

First, the Army was the wrong institution for the job of socially restructuring the South. The American Army had performed well in some essentially nonmilitary activities such as the exploration of the West, but nothing in its experience or tradition equipped it for the social welfare assignment that Congress had given the Freedmen's Bureau. When the agency began, the Army was immense and included men of varied talents who had become soldiers because of the war and could be easily tapped for this special postwar social enterprise. But when the Army was drastically reduced in size, the old-line army men reasserted their dominance. A career officer himself, Howard realized that humanitarian concerns were a liability in the eyes of the regular army generals who reasserted their supremacy under President Grant's second Secretary of War, William W. Belknap. These men, Howard charged, "hate the blacks."[26]

The awkwardness of utilizing the Army for the job does not argue that the job should have been relinquished by a public agency and given to a private one. The record of the private freedmen's aid societies, with their rapid loss of interest in the freedmen, and, as George M. Fredrickson has pointed out, the often conservative philosophy of such organizations suggest that the freedmen needed more than private charity.[27] In the public realm, the treatment of the Indians in the Department of the Interior did not suggest consigning the freedmen there. Charles Sumner's suggestion of a cabinet department created specifically to improve race relations would have served best, had it been properly staffed by realistic men.

The Freedmen's Bureau needed to be liberated from the uncritical American faith in the inevitable triumph of goodness. Indeed, many Americans thought that their full responsibility to the ex-slaves had been discharged by winning the war that freed them, and that the creation of the Freedmen's Bureau was merely further evidence of the nation's benevolence. The way around the

---

[25] W. E. B. Du Bois, *The Souls of Black Folk* (New York: Fawcett, 1968), p. 40.

[26] O. O. Howard to S. P. Lee, 29 December 1873, O. O. Howard Papers, Bowdoin College Library, Brunswick, Maine.

[27] George M. Fredrickson, *The Inner Civil War: Northern Intellectuals and the Crisis of the Union* (New York: Harper, 1965), pp. 98–112.

deficiencies of putting the agency in the hands of the Army was, to men of this persuasion, to pick the least military man in the Army to run the agency. That Howard was "the Christian General" was enough for most people; this sobriquet alone permitted many Americans to avoid the responsibility of critically analyzing how he performed his assignment.

Howard showed the same blind faith both in his selection of men for the Bureau and in his approach to the alternatives open to him with respect to programs for the freedmen. Thus he could view the contract system as the equal of the forty acres plan and could bury any skepticism he might have had about the trustworthiness of the upper-class leaders of the Johnsonian governments established in the fall of 1865. His appeal was to their sense of Christian charity, which his freedmen clients soon found wanting. Howard reasoned that the white Southerners would be persuaded by their own consciences if they were given to understand that he would not insist on adherence to the provisions of an act of Congress. In this appeal to a law of conscience, Howard gave credence to those who held that prescriptions for racial justice had no place in the law of the land. However, contrary to popular belief, the latter is often easier to live with. Indeed, a law might be said to be a reflection of a nation's collective conscience. A man who cannot of his own persuasion bring himself to do some socially desirable act may do it—grumbling, perhaps—if the law says he must.[28]

The Freedmen's Bureau needed to remember to whom it belonged. Conceived in paternalistic terms and designed to protect the freedmen, partially out of the fear that if they were not protected they might prove dangerous, the agency, nevertheless, began with a clear idea that the freedmen were its clients. President Andrew Johnson skillfully turned this around by replacing personnel, changing programs, and converting the Bureau into an agency to enable the planters to control their labor force. This reversal foreshadowed the dilemmas that arose in the regulatory agencies established during the Progressive era. Then too, agencies designed to protect the interest of one group by regulating the activities of another often found themselves passing under the control of those they were designed to regulate.

The key to effectiveness was in leadership and personnel. Perhaps the most obvious source of staff for the Freedmen's Bureau was the freedmen themselves. Men like Robert Smalls might have been recruited. Some black leaders did serve in the Bureau, like free-born Martin R. Delany.[29] He had advocated

---

[28] The power of the law to effect change in race relations is an underlying theme of C. Vann Woodward's *The Strange Career of Jim Crow* (New York: Oxford University Press, 1966). That the law of the land can work to worsen race relations quite as readily as to better them is the lesson of Dred Scott v. Sandford, 19 Howard 393 (1857), and Plessy v. Ferguson, 163 U.S. 537 (1896). That such law can be changed is taught by the Fourteenth Amendment and Brown v. Board of Education of Topeka, 347 U.S. 483 (1954).

[29] See the biography of Robert Smalls by Dorothy Sterling, *Captain of the Planter* (cited above), written for young people. Over Martin R. Delany, Theodore Draper raised a hornet's nest with "The Father of Black Nationalism," *New York Review of Books,* 12 March 1970; awaited is Floyd Miller's University of Minnesota Ph.D. dissertation.

emigration to Africa during the bleak days following the Compromise of 1850, but returned to the United States to fight in the Civil War when there appeared to be a chance to better his people's condition within this country. While serving as a sub–assistant commissioner of the Bureau in Charleston, Delany told a public protest meeting attended largely but not exclusively by black citizens that the lands that they had been working upon belonged to them.[30] For his vigorous participation in the fight to hold the farms and for other political reasons, Martin Delany was removed to a relatively unprovocative post in the Bureau's educational division; and he was not the only nonwhite agent who was reassigned because he "too thoroughly identified with the blacks."[31]

Merely being black was not enough, however, to insure wise response to the freedmen's needs. Some of the black missionaries sent south by the private freedmen's aid societies discovered themselves to be as much aliens in a foreign field as did their white brothers. Amos Beman,[32] the New Haven Congregationalist minister who opened a freedmen's school in east Tennessee, reported: "My first object has been to study them ['the Colored People'] thoroughly, to learn their inner life—their past history, their present wants—their future prospects, their hopes." He found the aged "dependent upon some poor relatives for a pittance of bread." Those in better condition were "young persons—men with interesting and promising families—industrious and frugal—striving right nobly to better their condition—they are mostly farmers—there are a few mechanics among this people, who find plenty of work to do."[33]

The Connecticut-born minister did not recommend that the freedmen look among themselves for leaders but, instead, that they pattern their lives on "those . . . 'bone of their bone, flesh of their flesh,' who have been elevated and improved." He mentioned as models respected leaders of Northern Negro communities: "the Garnetts [*sic*]—the Delaneys [*sic*]—the Alexander Crummells."[34]

In his report to the white secretary of the American Missionary Association, Beman made some exceedingly acute observations about white men in the region—"the Union men who loved the '*Union*' with slavery"—and, though on the side of the victor, now felt cheated by the war's outcome. Significantly, he was capable of no such insight into the attitudes of the freedmen. In dis-

---

[30] J. S. Fullerton to O. O. Howard, 20 July 1865, O. O. Howard Papers, Bowdoin College Library, Brunswick, Maine.

[31] Max Woodhull to W. H. Day, 20 September 1865, Records of the Bureau of Refugees, Freedmen and Abandoned Lands (Record Group 105), National Archives, Washington, D.C.

[32] On Amos Beman see Robert A. Warren, "Amos Gerry Beman—1812–1874: A Memoir on a Forgotten Leader," *Journal of Negro History* 22, no. 2 (1937): 200–21.

[33] Amos Beman to George Whipple, Greenville, Tenn., 25 February 1867, Amos Beman Papers, Beinecke Library, Yale University, New Haven, Conn.

[34] Amos Beman to George Whipple, 25 February 1867.

cussing their problems, he took refuge in metaphor: "They find themselves
invested with all the responsibilities of *manhood* and . . . while tempest tossed
by the storm which yet lingers, [the freedman] putters around . . . for chart
and compass—knowledge to guide him to a haven of peace and security."
Beman gave no clues about the freedmen's feelings; the minister's advice to
them was what he had taught his New Haven parishioners: temperance, marital fidelity, and frugality.[35]

If the education black Southerners had acquired while they were enslaved
had been incorporated into the Freedmen's Bureau along with the formal training and administrative experience of Northerners, both blacks and whites, that
federal agency would have been more attuned to the needs of freedmen and to
the subtleties of the South. Building on this education, the Bureau might have
been the training ground for a leadership group from among the former slaves
and might have successfully initiated both an economic and a social reconstruction.

There is evidence that white Southerners expected immense change at the
end of the war and expected and were willing to countenance the development
of black leaders. This white aristocrats preferred to anarchy. Mrs. Chesnut,
apprehensive of social disintegration, thought on June 12, 1865, that it would
be wise to "teach the Negroes to stand alone."[36] It was not long before her
class found that President Johnson would welcome reassertion of its old dominion over the blacks. But the instant the war ended there might have been
a chance to firmly establish freedmen in posts in the Bureau. No doubt both
Northern and Southern whites would have been startled by the spectacle of
black bureaucrats, but if they had been backed determinedly by the national
government, there would have been a chance for the development of a stable
class of civil servants. This group would have been of little use if it had existed
only to still agitation from beneath. The test of its value would have come not
in the restraint of black expectations but in the leadership provided for their
attainment.

The Freedmen's Bureau would have had a better chance of achieving its
task if it had held to the original conception of that task. The granting of
jurisdiction over abandoned lands to the freedmen's agency in the bill creating
the Bureau (which unequivocally called for the division of the land into small
farms for freedmen's families) was supposed to provide new black citizens
with a firm economic base. Even the possibility that speculators might have
gotten many of these farms away from the freedmen does not destroy the
validity of the premise that release from the dependent labor status of slavery,
of the contract labor system, or of subsequent debt-bound sharecropping was

[35] Amos Beman to George Whipple, 25 February 1867. See also Frederick Cooper, "Negro
Social and Political Thought, 1827–1850" (Seminar paper, Department of History, Yale
University, 1970).

[36] Chesnut, *Diary,* p. 539.

the greatest need of black Southerners. It is possible that a freedman who obtained a farm on land on which he and his family had always lived might have held on to it with greater tenacity than would the homesteader who was a newcomer.[37] A farm of his own gave a nineteenth-century American standing in his community. It even bestowed on him the right to mobility without the stigma of vagrancy. When a farmer moved, he was coming from someplace that was his. The white authors of the Mississippi Black Code, which forbade the ownership by blacks of land outside of towns—thus denying them farms—and made strict laws against vagrancy, understood this principle. Given an economic inch, the black man/poor man might have achieved a mile toward equality.

To go this distance, the freedmen would have had to breach caste and class lines in the postslavery South. Rich whites in the South fought the land redistribution program in order to keep their black labor supply available to them and not have it lured off toward a more attractive economic activity. And they fought also to regain their assets and to re-establish their position as a ruling class to which white farmers without extensive landholdings would defer. Those white Southerners who were poor and in a state of economic dependency joined on their own the opposition to the establishment of freedmen as yeomen farmers in order to preserve what they considered to be the only superiority available to them. They diverted to the maintenance of the racially drawn caste line energy that might have enabled them to break the economic class line that so severely confined them.

To be sure, it would have been asking a great deal of a nineteenth-century federal agency to break the headlock in which the South was held. The Bureau would have had to act fast. One of the most exciting ideas in Eric McKitrick's *Andrew Johnson and Reconstruction* is McKitrick's radical sense of time.[38] The moment to achieve lasting change in a conquered society is not after much time has passed and former enemies have become more reasonable, but at the instant of victory. Peace without resolution of social problems, rather than the memory of war, is what breeds lasting resentment and hatred. The beaten are more willing to accept what is decreed by the victor if it comes at the moment of defeat.

---

[37] Paul W. Gates is the foremost authority on land usage in the West. He turned his attention to the South in "Federal Land Policy in the South, 1866–1888," *Journal of Southern History* 6 (1940): 303–30, and *Agriculture and the Civil War* (New York: Alfred A. Knopf, 1965). An important new study of the continuation of the attempt of South Carolina freedmen to gain farms of their own is Carol K. Rothrock Blesser, *The Promised Land: The History of the South Carolina Land Commission, 1869–1890* (Columbia: University of South Carolina Press, 1969). For the wartime period see Willie Lee Rose, *Rehearsal for Reconstruction: The Port Royal Experiment* (Indianapolis: Bobbs-Merrill, 1964).

[38] Eric L. McKitrick, *Andrew Johnson and Reconstruction* (Chicago: University of Chicago Press, 1960), pp. 21–41.

The spring of 1865 was when the Freedmen's Bureau had its chance to make the changes that would have enabled freedmen to break past the color line. The forty acres program was the right start. An idea of Howard's that Congress rejected might have been the best second step. It called for the government to sell bonds and buy lands from cash-poor planters. The lands would then be sold to poor farmers who would pay for them over a period of time, making payment out of profits from crops. The payments would be used to retire the bonds.

How to Use the Color Line

Perhaps the secret to the success of this most basic might-have-been lay in an effort by the Freedmen's Bureau to show truly the way to use the color line.[39] During periods of actual starvation in the South due to crop failures in 1866–1867, the Bureau distributed emergency rations, and it did so with an even hand. Local agents, with plain common sense, fed both black and white people who needed feeding. Had they behaved similarly when carrying out the land redistribution program in 1865, they might have accomplished a basic reconstruction by enabling the economically dependent white Southerner to break the class line that confined him. Able to move upward, he might have felt less of a need to hold the racial caste line which so long doomed blacks to a frustration of their expectations of freedom.

But none of these might-have-beens were. A strong, permanent, well-staffed federal agency was not created. The nation moved toward Social Darwinism instead of toward a change in modes of thought helpful in meeting the problems of race. The majority of white Americans were not willing to recognize the Freedmen's Bureau as the freedmen's. The Bureau missed the chance to give the ex-slave a firm economic base from which to work for equality. And, above all, it did not effect a broad reconstruction of the South that would have allowed class mobility for poor Southerners of both colors and thereby loosened the caste line of race.

The basic reason the Freedmen's Bureau did not do so was not so much that Southerners would have refused the imposition of such change in the South in 1865 as it was that Northerners were not willing to prescribe similarly for the nation as a whole. Therein lie both the weakness and the strength of the federal agency approach to social reconstruction. The weakness is that the whole nation has to be willing to accept the change; the strength is that

---

[39] "The problem of the twentieth century is the problem of the color-line" is the famous first and last line of W. E. B. Du Bois' article "The Freedmen's Bureau," *Atlantic Monthly* 87 (March 1901): 354–65, retitled "Of the Dawn of Freedom" in 1903 in *The Souls of Black Folk* (New York: Fawcett, 1968), pp. 23–41.

acceptance of change is easier to obtain when the change is viewed not as localized punishment but as the law of the land.

During the first reconstruction and again in the second—the twentieth-century Civil Rights movement—the North gave expression to a demand for racial justice—but only in someone else's back yard. True, the Northerners, with a civil war, ended slavery and provided the freedmen with a welfare agency; but when the old ruling class of the South was restored to power by Andrew Johnson, Southerners successfully pointed out to Northerners that they should not be asked to do for the freedmen what Northerners surely would not be willing to do for the black people (or indeed white people who were poor) living in their own region. For a time the Radical Republicans in Congress worked on a strategy of building their party in the South on black votes, but this never extended to allowing real political power to be developed among the blacks, and it was not accompanied by a commitment to support the kind of economic change that would have required the services of a federal agency like a reconstructed Freedmen's Bureau.

Racial Problems Are National Problems

The problems the Freedmen's Bureau did not solve are still with us. But now there is no pretending that they face only one region of the nation. They are national, and attempts to solve them will have to fit the national realities of the twentieth century. Surely a forty-acre farm will not do, and perhaps a job alone does not give a man enough assurance to cope with the pressures of our times—although being able to depend on a steady income would certainly help. Both the major attempts at reconstruction, the Civil Rights movement of the 1950's and 1960's and the period right after the Civil War, were essentially Southern phenomena. The next try will have to be a national effort. As one nation, we will have to require that our national government finish the unfinished business of the Freedmen's Bureau.

Having disposed of the supposed inappropriateness of national action as an explanation of why the business remains unfinished and made a case for the usefulness of a federal agency in achieving social reconstruction, we must yet consider the other explanation of the failure of the Freedmen's Bureau. What about racism as a national tragic flaw? Will it ever yield to any kind of effort?

Race—color—is a facile basis for considering oneself superior to others and a way of disguising gnawing self-doubts. So handy a concept is race, so visible are racial differences, that we have come to accord them a status they do not merit. We call the acts of division done in its name racist, and we allow racism to be regarded as a basic causal factor in human behavior. Perhaps racism is not a finite or fixed cause but a mutable manifestation of man's unwillingness to look at himself honestly and critically. In our society, as Andrew Johnson's presidency so adroitly demonstrated, race can be used by one class to strengthen its political dominance over another. It has also been used by individuals who, though unwilling to acknowledge it, find racial competition the only game they can win. The American people are capable of better than that. As at the end of the Civil War, the great human resources necessary to meet the problem of the color line are available. All that is needed is to make that line one that describes but does not divide. If we look unflinchingly at the past and critically at the present, we will find that even race relations can change. Grasping this, there is just a chance that we can understand, and thus resolve, the paradox of a people allowing itself to be divided by an abstraction called race.

The Black Family During Reconstruction

ROBERT H. ABZUG

Robert Abzug is a doctoral candidate in history at the University of California, Berkeley. He has written articles for the *Journal of Negro History* and the *Indiana Magazine of History* and is currently preparing a biography of the American abolitionist Theodore Dwight Weld. In the following essay, Mr. Abzug asserts the quality of black family life in the post-Emancipation years, suggesting that many racist accounts of black mores have been allowed to prevail. In direct opposition to the view endorsed by many historians, Mr. Abzug argues that a moral and emotional commitment to family not only survived within blacks during slavery but remained a primary concern in their first years of freedom.

The study of black family life during Reconstruction can tell us much that needs to be known about the Negro's transition from slavery to freedom. It brings historical fact to bear on controversial theories concerning slavery's lasting effects on the mind and heart of the slave. In addition, by studying the freedman's attitude toward his family, one gains some insight into his changing feelings about the possibilities of life in free society. Unfortunately, in their quest for an undistorted account of the Negro during Reconstruction, historians have largely ignored the black man's private life in favor of rehabilitating his image in public affairs. As a result, the outworn, sometimes boldly racist pictures of black family life remain.

Practically from the time of Reconstruction itself, popular writers and scholars have seen the immediate post-Emancipation years as a period of anarchy, licentiousness, and tragedy for Negro families. Racist propagandists reported widespread sexual looseness and adultery, neglect of children, and general barbarity in family relations. They blamed such behavior on the Negro's inherent inferiority or on what they believed to be a reversion to primitive African customs. More modern sociologists and psychologists, while assigning them less ridiculous causes, have generally accepted the descriptive elements of the racist view. Instead of postulating racial inferiority or views based on misconceptions of African culture, modern scholars who hold a dim view of the post-Emancipation black family have usually pointed to the psychological and institutional deprivations of slavery. Yet there is much evidence to indicate that blacks were far more successful in their family lives than the old image allows. Such evidence also points to revision of our concept of what happened to the black family under slavery.

The Family Under Slavery

As many have recognized, the study of the freedman's family life must begin in slavery itself, for it was from the slave experience that blacks gained knowledge and aspirations with regard to family. It is true that slavery put great destructive pressures on black family life. Legal nonrecognition, the separation of man and wife, mother and child, sexual exploitation of slave women by the master class, and a general insecurity about any familial relationship were only a few of the objective realities that put the slave family in jeopardy.

But countering such pressures was the fact that, by practice and example, slaves learned of the commitments and satisfactions of normal family life. Whether it was through observation of the master's family or that of a local free Negro, or through entering into emotional, subsequently informal marital commitments with slave spouses, black men and women in bondage gained insight into rewards slavery denied them. They idealized the family life freedom would bring them. It mattered little whether that dream of freedom expressed itself in religion, in working to buy one's own and one's family's freedom, or in running away; the power of that dream was almost as forceful as slavery itself. When freedom came, slaves implemented the dreams of family life which previously had had such marginal reality. It was, indeed, the creative tension between that marginal reality and the idealization of family that provided the true heritage of slavery in terms of the family.

This view of the slave family experience and its meaning to the freedman runs counter to the deeply pessimistic view most commonly held, which has been best expressed in the work of E. Franklin Frazier and Stanley Elkins. To both Frazier and Elkins, slavery was a system that severely warped or completely destroyed the average black man's moral and emotional commitment to family. Frazier contended basically that slavery fostered sexual licentiousness and an indifference to matters of family that carried over into the postwar era. He concluded that only ante-bellum free Negroes and the exceptional slave had the motivation and knowledge to create stable families during Reconstruction.[1] Elkins, for his part, dismissed the importance of informal

---

[1] E. Franklin Frazier, *The Negro Family in the United States* (Chicago: University of Chicago Press, 1939), pp. 89–107.

slave families by stating that the slave family had been "destroyed" by the law.[2] Elkins also ruled out the psychic reality of aspirations for family through his conception of slavery as a closed society that offered slaves no experiences for thinking about an alternative existence. He thus limited the possibilities of slave hopes and fantasies to the level of "catfish and watermelon."[3] This view of the slave's mind leaves little doubt that Emancipation had to meet with initial failure and anarchy in the attempt at creation of families.

Such a theory of slavery's effect on the idea and institution of the family, however, does not correlate to the realities of the slave system. Slavery was not a society closed to the extent that Elkins claimed. Bondsmen had contact with whites, free Negroes, and slaves owned by other masters. Though it was true that legal nonrecognition of the slave family caused great vulnerability, it could hardly be said to have destroyed the family, nor could sexual exploitation and economically or punitively dictated separation of family members. Even without legal security or any means of self-protection, black families did exist in the slave quarters as functioning institutions and as models for others. Their familial situation created much pain and disillusionment for the slaves, but it also inspired among them an aspiration for something better.

The importance of viewing the slave family situation as a dialectic between the reality of insecurity and the aspiration of protection and self-direction becomes clear by turning to the imperfect but revealing insights afforded us into the slave's mind. Slave narratives collected during the 1920's and 1930's and slave religion as expressed in spirituals attest to the importance of family relations under slavery and the fervor of the slave's belief in freedom, whether otherworldly or earthly, as a hoped-for alternative. They refute the exceedingly dim view Elkins, Frazier, and others took toward the capacity of slaves to transcend in thought their miserable condition. They also provide a reasonable view of the slave experience as a background for what actually happened to the Negro family in freedom.

Ex-slaves remembered emotional courtship experiences and the informal marriage ceremonies which were tolerated or encouraged by the masters. But they also recalled the forced mating of slaves and the rejection of slaves' plans for marriage by the master because one slave was not healthy enough or big enough. Slaves understood what marriage and family should have meant and that slavery prevented that fulfillment. In reflecting on a typical slave marriage ceremony, one ex-slave put her finger on the difficulty. "Don't mean nothin' lessen you say 'What God jined, cain't no man pull asunder,'" she noted. "But dey never would say dat."[4] Another elderly black made clear the con-

---

[2] Stanley Elkins, *Slavery: A Problem in American Institutional and Intellectual Life* (Chicago: University of Chicago Press, 1959), pp. 53–55.

[3] Elkins, *Slavery,* pp. 81–139.

[4] Virginia Writers Project, *The Negro in Virginia* (New York: Hastings House, 1940), p. 80.

trast between the ideal and the real under slavery: "God made marriage, but de white man made de law."[5]

Since the white man made the law in every way, it has been assumed that the black man's role in the slave family relationship was absolutely destroyed. Yet the father's role was not necessarily negligible. Slave couples and their children often lived together in cabins separate from the common slave quarters, and no doubt there developed between them meaningful, close relationships. Sometimes ex-slaves spoke of their affection for their fathers, and the pain of separation: "'Course we wasn't far away from pappy," one black remembered, "but, you know, far enough so he couldn't come to us, and we cried and cried, and when any of the white people went down that way they would see pappy and he would send messages to us by them."[6] Perhaps the most damaging aspect of slavery to the black male was the violation of black women by masters and other white men. In the cause of survival, male slaves rarely tried to interfere. But it is significant that legends of their intervention were common and kept alive the spirit of manhood. One story told of Sam Watkins, a master who "would ship their husbands out of bed and get in with their wives." One slave could no longer stand such humiliation and choked Watkins to death: "He said he knew it was death, but it was death anyhow; so he just killed him."[7]

It was through reassuring legends and the cleansing hopes of slave religion that blacks retained their human dignity. To deal with the inner turmoil created by family life in all its ambiguity and instability (as well as other aspects of their troubled existence), some slaves developed a strong religious faith in an idealized, master-free afterlife. This genuine folk belief used the vocabulary of the Judaeo-Christian tradition but stressed otherworldly deliverance almost to the exclusion of other ideas. Important to the slave's concept of the next world, his sense of an alternative in the human experience, was the hope of "goin' home." The family life that had been denied him in slavery would finally be his in the world "over Jordan," where, according to the spirituals, brothers, sisters, mothers, and fathers would come together once again.[8] Reminiscences of former slaves reveal the importance of this religious belief in an afterlife to the inward survival of the slave version of family. Some tell of informally married couples who would hold hands beneath the night sky, hoping that

---

[5] Virginia Writers, *The Negro in Virginia*, p. 86.

[6] Fisk University Social Science Institute, *The Unwritten History of Slavery: Autobiographical Accounts of Negro Ex-Slaves* (Nashville: Fisk University, 1945), p. 2.

[7] Fisk University, *Unwritten History of Slavery*, p. 62.

[8] Howard Thurman, *The Negro Spiritual Speaks of Life and Death* (New York: Harper, 1947), p. 16. Paul Radin, "Note," in Fisk University Social Science Institute, *God Struck Me Dead: Religious Conversion Experiences and Autobiographies of Negro Ex-Slaves* (Nashville: Fisk University, 1945), pp. iv–v.

God would make their union sacred.[9] Another explains the reactions of some slaves to their master's transgressions: "Neither the men nor the women could help themselves. They submitted to it but kept praying to God."[10] And on the day of one slave's being sold away from his mother, he reported that "she just cried out, 'Good-bye son! Meet me in Glory.'"[11]

Life in the Contraband Camps

Until the coming of the Civil War, Glory Land lay beyond death for most slaves. Then, in as sudden a change of prospect as any people has undergone, slaves began to see the possibility of freedom's glory on earth. Booker T. Washington, for instance, remembered being awakened before dawn by his mother, "kneeling over her children and fervently praying that Lincoln and his armies might be successful, and that one day she and her children might be free."[12] When Emancipation came, it was to many slaves the deliverance for which they had ardently prayed. It was a sign from the heavens and inspiration for the task ahead. Though the difficulties of adjustment to freedom might have inspired "deep gloom" at times, a naive but fervent optimism prevailed among most of the blacks, one that saw the slave South transformed. An old Negro remembered singing:

> Old master's gone away and the darkies stayed at home;
> Must be now that the kingdom's come and the year for jubilee.[13]

The first signs that this enthusiasm touched black family life began to appear even before the Emancipation Proclamation in the Union army's "contraband camps" for slaves within Union lines. In 1861 three field slaves slipped across the lines near Hampton, Virginia, and asked for asylum. Acting as an advance guard for their families and other slaves, they sought to test the sympathies of the Yankees. They were the first of thousands of slaves to become "contraband of war" and to undergo a sometimes trying baptism of freedom in the camps that became their temporary homes. Though the physical conditions at the camps and the attitudes of many Northern soldiers hardly provided fertile soil for family life, blacks responded enthusiastically to the new basic rights they were granted. The will of the contrabands and the aid of Northern missionaries combined to bring about great progress in the stabilization of marriages and families. Contraband camps like Fortress Monroe, Craney

---

[9] Virginia Writers, *The Negro in Virginia,* p. 80.

[10] Fisk University, *God Struck Me Dead,* pp. 174–75.

[11] Ibid., p. 150.

[12] Booker T. Washington, *Up from Slavery,* ed. Louis Lomax (New York: Dell Publishing, 1965), pp. 18–19.

[13] Fisk University, *Unwritten History of Slavery,* p. 232.

Island, and City Point, all in Virginia, became proving grounds for family life in freedom.

The contrabands saw sanctification and legalization of their marriages as the first most important step in building proper families. So large were the numbers of contraband couples who wished to start new marriages or reaffirm old ones that mass ceremonies had to be instituted. As early as September 1861, the Reverend Lewis G. Lockwood performed mass marriages for hundreds of Negroes at Fortress Monroe. The missionaries, in typically paternalistic fashion, shared their wards' enthusiasm for such ceremonies. Reverend Lockwood saw his task as that of taking the Negro out of the sin of concubinage and into the bliss of marriage before God.[14] Other white officials concurred. "It was to teach and reform a people inured to [slave morals]," explained one official in Tennessee, "that the institution of lawful marriage was directed."[15]

The paternalistic assumptions of the whites in charge must have been continually jolted, however, as blacks showed their decisive commitment to stable marriages. One army chaplain concluded that Negroes did not treat marriage lightly. "In only a few cases," he noted, "was the relation broken up by fickleness and inconstancy."[16] Indicative of their almost puritanical approach to marriage and the family was the support in one camp for the expulsion of a black minister who refused to marry his mistress. Not long after his expulsion, both the minister and his mistress died of smallpox. The news of their demise, observed the officer in charge, "was looked upon by the Negroes as a direct and swift application of retributive justice, and so salutary was the effect that no other apostles of the doctrine of free love disturbed the settlement's morality."[17] Reports from Virginia suggested a similar picture. "In all this region," wrote C. B. Wilder, an officer at Fortress Monroe, "we find very few bastards, or women who are not wives and mothers." The administrator on Craney Island reported that blacks in his charge were neither "profane nor licentious."[18]

Thus, whatever finishing touches missionary efforts added in the way of ceremony, the basic force propelling Negroes toward a stable family life was their own desire for it. Those who came into the camps already "married" saw the mass ceremonies as symbolic of slavery's end. "They usually regard it as a privilege appertaining to emancipation," reported the American Freedmen's

[14] Virginia Writers, *The Negro in Virginia*, p. 190.

[15] *Report of the General Superintendent of Freedmen, Department of the Tennessee and State of Arkansas, for 1864* (Memphis, 1864), p. 94.

[16] John Eaton, *Grant, Lincoln, and the Freedmen; Reminiscences of the Civil War* (London: Longmans, 1907), pp. 211–12.

[17] Eaton, *Grant, Lincoln, and the Freedmen*, pp. 35–36.

[18] *Facts Concerning the Freedmen, Their Capacity and Their Destiny* (Boston: Commercial Printing House, 1863), pp. 5–6.

Commission, "to be married 'as the white folks are.'"[19] Slaves who came to the contraband camps single or separated from old spouses found there an opportunity to make a new start in freedom. The depth of the contrabands' emotional commitment to loved ones revealed itself most vividly when unforeseen reunions occurred. Thus did the black friend of one missionary locate her first husband at Craney Island. "'Twas like a stroke of death to me," the black woman remembered. "We threw ourselves into each others arms and cried. His wife looked and was jealous, but she needn't have been. My [present] husband is so kind, I shouldn't leave him if he [her first husband] hadn't another wife, and of course I shouldn't now."[20]

Reunions also occurred between parent and child. One little girl at Craney Island wandered down to the wharf and found her father on the crew of a docked steamer.[21] Most parents were not so fortunate, however, and they often cursed slavery and its perpetrators. "White folks got a heap to answer for the way they've done to colored folks," an angry mother complained.[22] The essential mood of the contrabands, however, even among those searching for loved ones, remained optimistic:

> I've got a wife, and she's got a baby
> Way up North in Lower Canady—
> Won't dey shout when dey see Ole Shady
>   Comin', Comin'! Hail, mighty day.
> Den away, Den away, for I can't stay any longer:
> Hurrah, Hurrah! for I am going home.[23]

First Tasks in Freedom

When the war finally ended and all slaves were free, it was not surprising that many made the reuniting of their scattered families the first order of business. "Ask almost any one what they are going to do this winter," a white traveler reported from South Carolina in 1865, "and they will answer you, 'I'se got a sister'—a wife or mother, as the case might be—'in Virginia, and I'm going to look her up and fetch her home.'"[24] Methods of reuniting

---

[19] *Preliminary Report of the American Freedmen's Inquiry Commission, June 30, 1863,* Senate Executive Document no. 53, vol. 2 (Washington, D.C.: 38th Congress, 1st Session, 1864), pp. 3–4.

[20] Lucy Chase to her family, 1 July 1864, in Henry L. Swint, ed., *Dear Ones at Home: Letters from Contraband Camps* (Nashville: Vanderbilt University Press, 1966), pp. 121–22.

[21] Lucy Chase to her family, 1 July 1864, in Swint, *Dear Ones at Home,* p. 96.

[22] Lucy Chase to her family, 2 October 1863, in Swint, *Dear Ones at Home,* pp. 59–60.

[23] Frank Moore, ed., *The Rebellion Record: A Diary of American Events, with Documents, Narratives, Illustrative Incidents, Poetry, Etc.,* 11 vols. (New York: G. P. Putnam, 1862–64; D. Van Nostrand, 1864–68), 8:63.

[24] *Nation* 1 (1865): 393.

families varied. One could place an "Information Wanted" advertisement in the newspapers of localities where the relative might be. Every issue of Negro newspapers during this period usually carried several such plaintive appeals:

INFORMATION WANTED

Of Stephen Harthor, who formerly belonged to Mrs. James Gardiner of this city—was sold in August, 1864, to a gentleman living near Wilmington, N.C. Any information of his whereabouts will be thankfully received by his father at this office.

Ruben Harthor[25]

In places where Negro newspapers did not exist, blacks found other means of reunion, including the arduous method of personal searching. One ex-slave recalled the moment his mother found him after the war. He couldn't believe it was she: "Then she took the bundle off her hand [*sic*] and took off her hat, and I saw that scar on her face. Child, look like I had wings!"[26] While traveling through the South, a correspondent for the *Nation* came upon a freedman who perhaps had more energy than most. He had walked nearly six hundred miles and had been on the road for almost two months. "[The Negro] had been sold and sent South four years before," explained the newspaperman, "and as soon as he learned he was free, [he was] determined to return to North Carolina and to try to find his wife and children."[27] Those unable or unwilling to make such an effort could only wait and grieve, as did the old slave woman of Poplar Grove, Virginia, who had had twelve children in bondage: "I don't know what has become of one of 'em. It hurts me mightily to think of 'em."[28]

But, as in the contraband camps, the optimism of the young and renewal of the old countered the tragedies of slavery. Even those who had spent the better years of their lives as slaves were willing to start again in freedom. "My husband and I have lived together fifteen years," said one mother of a large family, "and we wants to be married over again."[29] For the younger freedmen, freedom meant courtship and marriage without the old fears of eventual exploitation and separation. As in families in the rest of American society, black youths were impetuous and black mothers protective. "After we got big enough to have a big time," complained one old ex-slave who had reached puberty in freedom, "mother wouldn't let us go nowhere 'thout an old woman was with us."[30] Another remarked on the frustrating veto her

---

[25] *Augusta Loyal Georgian,* 17 March 1866.

[26] Fisk University, *Unwritten History of Slavery,* p. 274.

[27] Richard C. Dennett, "The South As It Is," Part 12, *Nation* 1 (1865): 427.

[28] *New York National Freedman,* 15 January 1866.

[29] *National Freedman* 2 (1866): 143–44.

[30] Fisk University, *Unwritten History of Slavery,* pp. 195–96.

mother had held over marriage plans. "My first husband courted me seven years," she related, "and then liked to have steadled me for my mother never did say 'Yes.'"[31] The ardent lover might have taken his cue from another freedman's rhymed letter: "If you love me as I love you, nothing shall cut our love in two. . . . Your feshionate Aaron Humfrey."[32]

Whatever the finer details of courtship, blacks married in great numbers during the early days of Reconstruction and attempted to build stable households. The freedmen seemed to grasp the essential tasks necessary to such an endeavor. One observer noted that the "sole ambition" of Negroes in 1865 was to be "owner[s] of a little piece of land, there to erect an humble home, and to dwell in peace and security at [their] own free will and pleasure."[33] The *Nation* also reported a black people's petition to the state of North Carolina asking for the right "to work with the assurance of good faith and fair treatment, to educate their children, to sanctify the family relation, to reunite scattered families, and to provide for the orphan and infirm."[34]

Bolstering these basic aspirations was the advice, at times gratuitous, of black community leaders and white missionaries. Tracts from Northerners urged the Negro to be chaste, get a job, get some education, and purchase a home if at all possible. One widely circulated pamphlet morally counseled different groups among the blacks under headings such as "To Young Men," "To Young Women," and "To Married Folks."[35] Negro newspapers and conventions emphasized the need to get settled. One editor rated getting a home as the first priority for every black man. "A home will be a glad place for the children to grow up in," he advised; "it will promote virtue and build up strong family ties."[36] For rural freedmen especially, land ownership had almost the same importance as home ownership. Recognizing this fact, a Norfolk freedmen's convention asserted that "the surest guarantee for the independence and ultimate elevation of the colored people will be found in their becoming the owners of the soil on which they live and labor."[37] A reporter in City Point, Virginia, confirmed that such advice reflected the innate wishes of the masses of blacks. He observed that the freedmen's "great anxiety is to own enough land to make them a home. The matter of home just now is of more importance to them than suffrage."[38]

---

[31] Ibid., p. 280.

[32] Mary Allan-Olney, *The New Virginians,* 2 vols. (London: W. Blackwood, 1880), 2:76.

[33] *Nation* 1 (1865): 393.

[34] *Nation* 1 (1865): 481.

[35] Brevet Major-General Clinton B. Fisk, *Plain Counsels for Freedmen in Sixteen Brief Lectures* (Boston: American Tract Society, 1866), pp. 19–35, 59–64.

[36] *Austin* [Texas] *Free Man's Press,* 1 August 1868.

[37] *Equal Suffrage: Address from the Colored Citizens of Norfolk, Va. to the People of the United States* (New Bedford, Mass., 1865), p. 8.

[38] *New York National Freedman,* 15 January 1866.

The Rural Scene

Land, at least for the rural freedman, played a crucial role in the maintenance of stable families in two important ways. First of all, it was economically easier to get along by farming one's own land than it was to manage by working for meager wages in the white man's field. It was also true that the running of a farm, with its many chores and its division of labor, provided a day-to-day *raison d'être* for a stable family life. Secondly, but just as importantly, land was a symbolic goal of freedom, one that made the discipline inherent in keeping a marriage and family together a necessary and complementary part of becoming equal in free society. Working toward the purchase of land, then, as much as the actual ownership of land, had immense power in keeping families together.

When seen as a function of both strong material and spiritual aspirations and as a factor intimately tied with preservation of the family, the black's struggle for land becomes of crucial importance. Before the war was over, it seemed that blacks would be able to partake of confiscated land. But with the end of the war and the onset of Johnson's Reconstruction policies, most of that land returned to the original owners. The black man had to turn to the open market with virtually no capital at his command. The freedmen sometimes responded by attempting to pool capital and were occasionally successful in purchasing large plots and then subdividing them among the contributors. For the most part, however, whites were reluctant to sell land to blacks even when they had the money, as was revealed before the Joint Committee on Reconstruction.[39] One witness, among many, testified to "a great unwillingness on the part of the people to allow [the Negroes] to own property."[40] Another witness attested to intimidation against even renting to blacks and stated that "a great many houses were burned down in my neighborhood, which it was feared would be rented to negroes."[41]

Yet through all such difficulties, many of the freedmen tenaciously exploited whatever opportunities came their way with a hardheaded optimism. One forty-year-old black with a wife and two children had been a slave all his life and wanted "to strike out for himself and see what he could do in a state of freedom." His old master refused to sell him land, but he was finally able to purchase a worn-out plot in the corner of a neighboring estate. He then bought a wretched horse from the government corral for $15. For labor, there were himself, his wife, and their two children. Even with such a marginal beginning the farmer had hope for the future of his family and his venture, "if God spared his life."[42]

---

[39] *Report of the Joint Committee on Reconstruction at the First Session, 39th Congress,* 4 vols. (Washington, D.C., 1866), 2:21.

[40] *Report of the Joint Committee on Reconstruction,* 2:48–49.

[41] Ibid., 2:154.

[42] Dennett, "The South As It Is," Part 10, *Nation* 1 (1865): 367.

Black Families in the City

In turning from the rural freedman, with his ideal of a self-sufficient farm family, to the urban black, one can see the same enduring optimism and aspiration for a stable family life functioning in a different setting. At first glance, the post-Emancipation chaos of Southern cities, where thousands of freedmen gathered, might not seem the best place to find future-oriented, family-minded efforts. Yet, as had the contrabands and many of the rural Negroes, urban black families fought bad physical conditions with level-headed dedication. A traveler described one black worker in Richmond as a "stalwart young black, twenty-one years old, married, and the father of two children." His salary was $1.50 a day. Asked if he could get along on that wage, the Negro answered, "It's right hard, these times. . . . I have to pay fifteen dollars a month rent and only two little rooms. But my wife takes in washing and goes out to work; and so we get along." Asked whether he were not better off under slavery, he answered, "Oh, no, sir! We're a heap better off now."[43] Other reports reaffirmed this image of the freedman in the city as a hard-working family man. Writing specifically of those contrabands who started life in the District of Columbia after the war, a Negro newspaperman observed that "aside from the very few imperfections in the physical and spiritual anatomy of the contraband, he was a model working man, a faithful and good citizen, and devoted husband and father—and owner of right smart horse sense." He saw them "ascend[ing] higher and higher in the scale of civilization and progress."[44]

Against the impressionism of such statements about the life and morals of urban freedmen, ex-slave Henry Pryor provides a well-documented insight into Negro resourcefulness in the city and its relationship to stabilization of the family. In 1869, Pryor organized a group of freedmen to purchase a piece of land in Richmond that became and still is known as Zion Town. Under his leadership, the blacks developed the land, repurchased it when the original deed proved to be bogus, and maintained a stable community life.[45] Zion Town maintained this stability of family and community even into the Depression of 1929. In 1935 some 65 percent of both men and women in the town were married and living together. Less than 5 percent of married men were living alone, mostly because of the death of their spouses; 9 percent of the women headed households, mostly because they had been widowed. Most interesting of all was that, with Negro migrations to the North occur-

---

[43] J. W. Trowbridge, *The South . . . Being a Description of the Present State of the Country* (Hartford, Conn.: L. Stebbins, 1867), p. 151.

[44] John E. Bruce, "Washington's Colored Society" (1877), Schomburg Collection, New York Public Library, New York, N.Y., pp. 6–8.

[45] Howard H. Harlan, *Zion Town—A Study in Human Ecology* (Charlottesville: University of Virginia Press, 1935), pp. 14–16.

ring from all over the South, over half those living in Zion Town in 1935 were descendants of founding families.[46]

Children, Education, and the Role of Women

While interest in families and their stability may be measured circumstantially through statistics, there is more personalized evidence that suggests the great stake Negroes put in their families in the first years after Emancipation. Above all, the blacks' attitudes toward their children reflected their hopes and great concern for the family. Against the discouraging memories of slavery, in which the parental role might be terminated at weaning, freedmen devoted much of their time to building a future for their children. "There was good massas and good missuses," explained one Negro woman, "but what was all dat if your chill'n could be sold away from you, and you got to keep quiet?" Freedom meant that children could not be sold away, and so the slave-born generation of freedmen cherished their offspring all the more.[47]

More specifically, children represented the extension of the family into the future. Providing material wealth and education thus became a passionate interest of parents and grandparents, as well as of the entire community. Booker T. Washington remembered, for instance, the interest the older people demonstrated when he left home for Hampton Institute, offering him whatever spare change they could afford for his trip. "They had spent most of their lives in slavery," Washington noted, "and hardly expected to live to see the time when they would see a member of their race leave home to attend a boarding-school."[48] Many black parents set as their goal the accumulation of some sort of property or capital they could leave for their children. One elderly couple, for example, built a house and paid almost all the debts on it. The man hoped that he had "strength enough in these old bones of mine to earn enough to pay it all, and have it to the chill'en free." With the house paid off, he then wouldn't "mind if de Master came and called me home to'morror."[49]

Most black parents, however, focused their zeal on education. With the help of missionaries and the Freedmen's Bureau, Negro parents sacrificed much time and money to provide for their children the literacy and education that they themselves had been denied in slavery. Even on the remotest plantations, some freedmen "asked the proprietors to reserve out of their wages

---

[46] Harlan, *Zion Town,* pp. 19–20.

[47] David MacRae, *Americans at Home; Pen and Ink Sketches of American Men, Manners, and Institutions,* 2 vols. (Edinburgh: Edmondston & Douglas, 1870), 1:236.

[48] Washington, *Up from Slavery,* p. 43.

[49] MacRae, *Americans at Home,* 1:234–35.

enough to hire a teacher for their children."[50] The children themselves responded excitedly to their new opportunity. Booker T. Washington recalled that as a little slave boy he "had the feeling that to get into a schoolhouse and study . . . would be about the same as getting into paradise."[51] J. W. Alvord, educational inspector for the Freedmen's Bureau, reported the sacrifices some young blacks made just to get to school: "At daylight in winter, many of the pupils in the sparsely populated country places leave their home breakfastless for the school-house, five, six, or seven miles away."[52]

Whatever its immediate benefits, schooling also posed some long-term problems for the family. It created a chasm of values and perceptions between a generation that grew up as illiterate slaves and one that was educated in freedom. For the slave, emancipation was the central goal and accomplishment of life. The freedmen's children, however, had been schooled in the competitive values of American society, and the closing opportunities of the post-Reconstruction South caused demoralization and physical migration. On another level, education and immediate economic advancement conflicted for the post-Emancipation family, since children otherwise able to do farm labor were sent to school. No long-range promises could cure the financial ills many families faced because they sent their children to school instead of to work. "My stepfather," wrote Booker T. Washington of his pre-Hampton days, "had discovered that I had a financial value, and so when the school opened, he decided that he could not spare me from my work." It was Washington's mother who finally saved her child from oblivion in the salt furnaces of the Kanawha Valley and let him go to school.[53]

Such a conflict between mother and father was not uncommon. That the mother often won reflected the self-reliance developed by black women under slavery. That the mother played a major role in the decision-making process also may be explained by the fact that black families frequently consisted of a mother and her children from slave days, with a husband who was stepfather to all or part of her offspring. But maternal strength did not have to mean domination. For example, black educator Robert Russa Moton, who grew up during Reconstruction, assigned equal importance to each of his parents and found his mother "a woman of very strong character in many ways, very much like my father."[54] Freedom, in a sense, balanced the old

---

[50] Whitelaw Reid, *After the War: A Tour of the Southern States, 1865–1866,* ed. C. Vann Woodward (reprint ed., New York: Harper, 1965), p. 511.

[51] Washington, *Up from Slavery,* p. 18.

[52] J. W. Alvord, *Seventh Semi-Annual Report on Schools for Freedmen, January 1, 1869* (Washington, D.C.: U.S. Bureau of Refugees, Freedmen and Abandoned Lands, 1869), p. 15.

[53] Washington, *Up from Slavery,* p. 34.

[54] Robert Russa Moton, *Finding a Way Out* (New York: Doubleday, 1920), pp. 13–14.

importance of the mother with the males' "right, just found, to have their own way in their families and rule their wives—that is an inestimable privilege!"[55]

In the immediate post-Emancipation era, there was less debate over the mother's role in decision making than over whether she should work or stay at home to do the chores. Many freedmen viewed the idea of women at work in the fields as a mark of slavery, and the general tendency was for the women to retire to the home. The *Loyal Georgian,* a Negro newspaper, cited "the development of a womanly nature" as one of the most important ways black women could help in "the elevating and refining of their race."[56] Husbands seeking to establish themselves as the providers for their families encouraged their wives in this direction. One freedman, when asked by his ex-master to allow his wife to work in the "big house," answered: "I tell you, Bishop, when I married my wife I married her to wait on me and she got all she can do right here for me and the children."[57] Yet economic conditions often intervened. "My husband never did like for me to work," remarked an old Negro lady about Reconstruction days. "He used to ask me how come I work when he was doing all he could to give me what I wanted."[58] Many husbands, however, just couldn't earn enough to support a family. The *Christian Recorder,* an organ of the African Methodist Episcopal Church, therefore urged black women to teach their daughters not to shun work, since "many of them [would] marry men that [would] not make on the average more than 75cts per day."[59]

Such demands were not too much for black men and women during Reconstruction as long as they felt that a secure future could be gained for themselves and their families. Family stability, after all, depended on both material and psychic factors. If black families were to struggle against all odds for a self-sufficient farm or for a decent job, they had to have some strong notion that the goal could eventually be accomplished. If black parents eagerly sent their children to school and exerted themselves for their offspring in other ways, it was because they had a faith in the success of future generations in finding a solid place in American life. The success of the freedmen's family efforts would depend on the success of Reconstruction in effecting a substantial change in economic, political, and social relations upon the South.

---

[55] Laura M. Towne, letter of 1 June 1867, in Rupert S. Holland, ed., *Letters and Diary of Laura M. Towne, written from the Sea Islands of South Carolina, 1862–1884* (Cambridge: Riverside Press, 1912), p. 184.

[56] *Augusta Loyal Georgian,* 3 February 1866.

[57] Fisk University, *God Struck Me Dead,* pp. 135–36.

[58] Fisk University, *Unwritten History of Slavery,* pp. 115–16.

[59] "To Mothers," *Christian Recorder,* 21 January 1863.

The Aftermath

The loss of hope in Reconstruction certainly began before 1877, but by that year the spark of optimism that was the essence of the black family's response to freedom had been all but snuffed out. By the 1880's land ownership, which at one time was the fondest dream of most freedmen, amounted to very little. Those who once "believed that their first duty would be possibly to secure lands and secure homes" often found themselves homeless and landless and without the satisfaction, "even when they acquire[d] homes, of knowing that they [would] be secure in the possession of them in every respect."[60] In the cities, overcrowding, bad housing, and the realization that social mobility meant a dead end for most blacks had their effects on the family. Illegitimacy rose sharply, migrations broke up families and communities, and the few fortunate ones isolated themselves in enclaves like Zion Town.

From one point of view, it may be of little importance that for perhaps a decade after the Emancipation Proclamation black family life seemed to be stabilizing and functioning positively in the South. After all, such success was soon obliterated and a malaise set in from which the black population has not yet fully recovered. Yet those numerically few years in which the family did have some success go a long way in refuting the analysis which holds that the slave experience insured tragedy for the post-Emancipation black family. First of all, the freedmen's display of energy in seeking out and reuniting kin defies the notion that slavery witnessed a general disintegration of the idea and actuality of family ties. Secondly, the freedmen's actions in regard to land, homes, and education show that slavery did not prevent the black man from sensing the requisites of life in freedom.

The Reconstruction years are also important to our understanding of the black family because they demonstrate the social and psychic ingredients necessary for familial success. Legalized family institutions respected by the rest of the community played an important role. So did the minimal economic and educational opportunities that were made available to the black man. More important than these factors, however, was a belief in the future, an energizing optimism that allowed blacks to persevere against what they hoped would be temporary setbacks. We may well be reminded of the words of O. S. B. Wall, a black man testifying before Congress, in trying to gauge the significance of the freedman's optimism:

> Just after the war our people were in good condition. From the wreck of matter and the crush of worlds that passed over us our people emerged

---

[60] *Report and Testimony of the Select Committee of the U.S. Senate to Investigate the Causes of the Removal of the Negroes from the Southern States to the Northern States, 1879–1880,* Senate Report 693, 3 vols. (Washington, D.C.: 40th Congress, 2nd Session, 1880), 1:218–19.

into a condition where there seemed to be a little sunlight, and into what was for a while a better state of things, and . . . our star seemed to be rising.[61]

Wall was speaking in 1880, looking back at those days from the final calamity of the Redemption governments, which killed the last vestiges of Radical Reconstruction. By then the black man had been thrust from political office, was being terrorized by vigilante groups, and found himself in many cases being forced back into a peonage in some respects not far different from slavery itself. Black families fell victim to these changes in their way of life and in the outlook for the future. Nonetheless, the early years of the postwar era stand as a monument to the transformation that can be effected when men believe they can guide their own destinies and secure a better life for their descendants.

---

[61] *Report and Testimony of the Select Committee,* 1:45.

1 SUGGESTIONS FOR FURTHER READING

Abbott, Martin, *The Freedmen's Bureau in South Carolina, 1865–1872*. Chapel Hill: University of North Carolina Press, 1967. ▪ One of the best studies of the Freedmen's Bureau in operation at the state level.

Botkin, B. A., ed., *Lay My Burden Down: A Folk History of Slavery**. Chicago: University of Chicago Press, 1945. ▪ A volume of insightful narratives by ex-slaves that was compiled as part of the 1930's Federal Writers' Project.

Cox, James, and Cox, LaWanda, *Politics, Principle and Prejudice, 1865–1866**. New York: Free Press, 1963. ▪ The civil rights issues of the mid-nineteenth century are diligently analyzed in this study.

Frazier, E. Franklin, *The Negro Family in the United States**. Chicago: University of Chicago Press, 1939. ▪ Despite some flaws, it remains the starting point for any study of the black family.

Johnson, Charles S., *Shadow of the Plantation**. Chicago: University of Chicago Press, 1934. ▪ A pioneering study in black rural life.

McFeely, William S., *Yankee Stepfather: General O. O. Howard and the Freedmen**. New Haven: Yale University Press, 1968. ▪ The most scholarly treatment of this controversial figure.

McKitrick, Eric L., *Andrew Johnson and Reconstruction**. Chicago: University of Chicago Press, 1960. ▪ A highly informative account of Andrew Johnson's political ineptitude as President and the effect on national policy.

McPherson, James M., *The Struggle for Equality: Abolitionists and the Negro in the Civil War and Reconstruction**. Princeton: Princeton University Press, 1964. ▪ A well-researched study demonstrating the intense post–Civil War interest in the freedmen on the part of the abolitionists.

---

* Available in paperback edition

Powdermaker, Hortense, *After Freedom: A Cultural Study in the Deep South**. New York: Viking Press, 1939. ▪ A description of black society in a small Mississippi town based on the tools of cultural anthropology.

Rose, Willie Lee, *Rehearsal for Reconstruction: The Port Royal Experiment**. Indianapolis: Bobbs-Merrill, 1964. ▪ A revealing account of the first large-scale experiment in freedom.

Singletary, Otis A., *Negro Militia and Reconstruction**. Austin: University of Texas Press, 1957. ▪ The only adequate study of a relatively unexplored aspect of Reconstruction history.

Stampp, Kenneth M., *The Peculiar Institution: Slavery in the Ante-Bellum South**. New York: Alfred A. Knopf, 1956. ▪ The most comprehensive and least romanticized survey of slavery.

Whitten, Norman E., and Szwed, John F., eds., *Afro-American Anthropology: Contemporary Perspectives**. New York: Free Press, 1970. ▪ A collection of articles that offer many insights into the complexities and variations of social contexts that bear on the family.

Williamson, Joel, *After Slavery: The Negro in South Carolina During Reconstruction, 1861–1877**. Chapel Hill: University of North Carolina Press, 1965. ▪ One of the best recent state studies, it addresses itself in part to the day-to-day life of blacks after Emancipation.

Wood, Forrest G., *Black Scare: The Racist Response to Emancipation and Reconstruction**. Berkeley: University of California Press, 1970. ▪ An excellent work that provides a lucid backdrop for the period.

2

Black
Workers
and
Jim Crow

Black Workers in the New South, 1865-1915

PAUL B. WORTHMAN and
JAMES R. GREEN

Paul Worthman, visiting lecturer of American labor history at the
Center for Social History, University of Warwick, in 1970–1971,
is assistant professor of history at the University of California,
Los Angeles. James R. Green is a member of the history department at Brandeis University. They are both at work on studies of
working-class history with an emphasis on race relations. In the
following essay, Mr. Worthman and Mr. Green describe the post-
Emancipation struggle of black workers—in alliance and in conflict with white workingmen—against economic manipulation.
Going beyond celebrated spokesmen and heralded events, the
essay examines the exploitative agricultural and industrial systems
that replaced slavery and the process by which blacks became
part of the South's industrial proletariat.

Between the end of the Civil War and the outbreak of World War I
black workers struggled to find a way to benefit from Southern industrialization and to free themselves from manipulation by their
former owners and new employers. While some blacks merely relied on the
benevolence of their employers, others recognized that such dependence would
not free them from the domination of whites. They insisted that overcoming
their status as a propertyless, subservient laboring class and substantially
improving their working and living conditions required working-class organization and cooperation. Because historians have focused on the institutional history of unions, the activities of these little-known black workers
have not generally been noted. Instead, historians too often have unquestion-
ingly assumed that better-known, more publicized black men like Booker T.
Washington or W. E. B. Du Bois had large followings among the black masses.
As a result historians have ignored the important roles of black labor leaders
like Isaac Myers (a Baltimore shipbuilder), Richard Davis (an Ohio miner and
member of the United Mine Workers of America's national executive board),
B. L. Greer (an Alabama miner and union organizer), Ben Fletcher (a revolu-

tionary who led the powerful Philadelphia longshoremen's union), and many others—most of them as yet unknown.

The success of working-class organization, of course, depended not merely on the class consciousness of blacks but also on the willingness of whites to accept blacks in their unions and to cooperate with black labor. Historians have properly focused attention on the exclusionary practices and racism of many unions. But emphasis on the racially restrictive policies of some trade unions at the end of the nineteenth century and beginning of the twentieth should not obscure efforts made by some white and black workers to build an interracial labor movement in the face of enormous obstacles. Even though the assaults of Southern employers and their allies defeated these efforts, by the outbreak of World War I black workers had gained from white employers some improvement in their living and working conditions, often as a result of class cooperation and organization, and they had made themselves an integral part of the industrial structure of the New South.

New Forms of Slavery

At the end of the Civil War the status of freedmen remained ambiguous. Victorious Northerners insisted that slavery was dead and that a system of free wage labor must replace it. Many of them agreed with the editor of the *New York Times,* however, who wrote that Emancipation merely meant that Southerners would have to learn the "art of managing Negroes as paid laborers without the lash."[1] Southern agricultural and industrial employers took advantage of this Northern attitude, and as soon as the war ended they took measures to keep former slaves in their traditional place.

Convinced that freedmen would not work unless coerced, Southern employers looked for ways to keep blacks in their place—as a permanent, subservient class of cheap laborers. Black Codes were enacted in 1865 and 1866 to control a supposedly free labor force. They required blacks to sign contracts with employers and established coercive vagrancy and licensing laws to force freedmen to work and thus guarantee their former masters a constant supply of cheap labor. "To put it bluntly," Kenneth Stampp concluded in *The Era of Reconstruction,* "the Black Codes placed the Negro in a kind of twilight zone between slavery and freedom."[2]

Although Reconstruction governments abolished the Black Codes after 1867, these laws nevertheless established an important precedent for controlling black labor in the following decades. Southern lawmakers kept strict vagrancy laws on the books and adopted other laws designed to keep black workers on the job and to prevent labor agents from "enticing" them

---

[1] *New York Times,* 12 May 1865.

[2] Kenneth Stampp, *The Era of Reconstruction, 1865–1877* (New York: Alfred A. Knopf, 1965), p. 80.

away from their employers with promises of higher wages and better working conditions.

The convict lease system was another means of providing a ready supply of cheap, tractable black labor, primarily for the South's extractive industries (mining, lumbering, turpentine). Thousands of blacks were given lengthy sentences for trivial offenses, sometimes for violating stringent vagrancy and debt laws, and then were forced to work for employers who contracted with state or county governments for their services. Southern railroad contractors, mine owners, and lumbermen made large profits by exploiting this reserve of inexpensive, forced labor. In 1889, for example, an Alabama legislative investigating committee computed that the Tennessee Coal, Iron, and Railroad Company—the largest mining company in the state and the largest lessee of convicts—had saved $200,000 in wages through the years by leasing convicts.[3]

The convict lease system, moreover, provided employers with a training program for rural and unskilled blacks. The *Birmingham Chronicle,* for example, commented in 1889 that "there is one good thing about the convict system, it is giving us a race of miners. A Negro is sent to the penitentiary for two or three years and when he gets out he goes to work in the mines."[4] More than 50 percent of the convicts sent to Alabama's mines allegedly remained there to work for wages after the expiration of their sentences.

Numerous investigations documented the degradation and brutality produced by the convict lease system. Convict laborers were "tasked" a certain amount of work each day and were flogged if they failed to complete it. Blacks in the Florida turpentine camps worked at a trot with "stride" or "waist" chains riveted on their bodies. In Mississippi a grand jury investigation in 1887 reported that convicts were "all bearing on their persons marks of the most inhuman and brutal treatment. Most of them have their backs cut in great wales, scars and blisters, some with skin peeling off in pieces as the result of severe beatings. . . . We actually saw live vermin crawling over their faces, and the little bedding and clothing they have is in tatters and stiff with filth."[5] The death rate among black convicts in Mississippi in the nineteenth century was almost 20 percent, while it approached or exceeded that figure in other states of the Deep South.

Such reports induced middle-class reformers to join with labor unions in efforts to abolish the leasing of convicts. Nevertheless, this barbaric relic of slavery still existed in every Southern state at the beginning of the twentieth century. Although extension of the system to other areas of the Southern

[3] *Report of the Special Committee of the Alabama General Assembly to Investigate the Convict Lease System* (Montgomery, Ala., 1889), p. 28.

[4] *Birmingham* [Ala.] *Sunday Chronicle,* 19 January 1889.

[5] *Jackson* [Miss.] *Clarion,* 13 July 1887, quoted in C. Vann Woodward, *Origins of the New South, 1877–1913* (Baton Rouge: Louisiana State University Press, 1951), p. 214.

economy failed, convict labor was instrumental in the development of the South's extractive industries, because it enabled many employers to avoid the use of free black labor.

Black Agricultural Laborers: The Rural Proletariat

Although few plantation owners used convicts in their fields, the abolition of slavery and the abrogation of the Black Codes did not mean that black agricultural workers had freed themselves from the planters' control. After slaves left the plantations at the end of the Civil War during what W. E. B. Du Bois called a "general strike," the Freedmen's Bureau cooperated with desperate Southern planters to urge freedmen to return to the land, often under clearly exploitative contractual arrangements. Post-bellum planters at first initiated a wage labor system with gangs of black laborers directed by drivers. Ultimately, only sugar and rice growers found this efficient. Black field hands found the gang labor system painfully reminiscent of slavery and resisted it with various slowdowns and unorganized strikes, causing most cotton planters to abandon it. In Louisiana's Sugar Bowl, where the wage system persisted, well-organized, militant black workers continued to strike for higher wages and better working conditions throughout the late nineteenth century. Deprived of the "forty acres and a mule" that the Freedmen's Bureau promised and unwilling to accept the gang labor system that Southern cotton planters demanded, freedmen settled for a sharecropping arrangement, which they hoped would allow them to live relatively free from the planters' surveillance on their own plots of land.

As a sharecropper, however, the freedman became more dependent on the planter than he had been as a wage laborer. The cropper escaped the wage system by farming a small plot of land for the planter, for which he paid rent with a share of his cotton crop (usually one-half). But from the start, black tenants relied on their landlords for tools, seed, and animals. The cropper, moreover, was under contract—usually an oral agreement which gave him no standing in court—to farm his land according to the commands of the planter. In the early years of sharecropping some black farmers attempted to escape from the control of planters by securing credit through a crop lien from rural merchants. After a few years of competition, however, planters and merchants consolidated and used their control over the rural credit system to keep black croppers in a virtual state of peonage. In the end, black sharecroppers found that they were not potential farm owners but rather wage laborers paid in kind and more subject than ever to the planters' manipulation.

When Southern farmers rebelled against oppressive credit and marketing systems in the late 1880's, some black farmers joined with their white counterparts to seek relief through collective action and cooperative marketing schemes. The Colored Farmers' Alliance and Cooperative Union, formed in Texas in 1886 by a white Baptist preacher, was the major spokesman for black tenants and farmers. At its peak it claimed over one million members, which probably made it the largest black organization in the United States before Marcus Garvey's Universal Negro Improvement Association. In 1891 the Colored Alliance promoted a cotton pickers' strike which failed when the white Southern Alliance, many of whose members employed black cotton pickers, opposed it. Shortly after the strike's failure, the Colored Farmers' Alliance also collapsed.

Despite disagreements between the white and black farmers' alliances, rebellious black farmers joined with whites in the Populist party in the early 1890's. In most Southern states the Populists openly espoused political rights for blacks and opposed lynching. The Populist movement in the South, however, was led by white landowning farmers who attacked specific problems like the crop lien system and the contraction of currency, while ignoring the special plight of tenants and sharecroppers, whites as well as blacks. By the turn of the century, many white Populists, disillusioned by their failure to use blacks to defeat the planters who controlled the Democratic party in the South, had become proponents of increased racial segregation and disfranchisement of blacks. Black agriculturalists thus derived little benefit from their short-lived coalition with white farmers. By 1900 only a few black farmers had managed to scratch their way up to farm ownership, while the majority of black men who produced the South's vast cotton crop remained in a state of semiserfdom. Unlike industrial laborers, the place of black agricultural laborers in the Southern economy remained almost the same at the outbreak of World War I as at the close of the Civil War.

From Agriculture to Industry

The miserable conditions on the plantations drove many black farm workers into the South's cities and towns. There, they hoped, industrial jobs would allow them to free themselves from the paternal despotism of their rural masters and to improve their condition. White employers, however, frequently expressed doubts about the freedmen's fitness and willingness to work as industrial laborers, even though free blacks and slaves had worked in skilled as well as unskilled industrial jobs before the Civil War. Consequently, some whites urged that black labor be replaced by white immigrants, who were supposedly more dependable and less disruptive than Southern blacks. More European immigrants were recruited into the Southern working class than historians have realized, but these replacements were generally concentrated in a limited number of skilled occupations in major Southern cities. White foreign-born craftsmen and mechanics worked as skilled ironworkers, railroad trainmen, coopers, blacksmiths, tailors, and building tradesmen. Although they successfully displaced many black artisans, Southern employers did not succeed in substituting immigrant whites for native blacks in agriculture and heavy industry. Not only were most immigrants reluctant to come to the South, but few industrialists actually intended to dispense with blacks as the base of the Southern labor force, despite their complaints about the ineptitude of free black labor.

While Southern industrialists and planters often grumbled about the "lazy, shiftless, ignorant black laborer," they contradicted themselves by expressing a clear preference for black workers. Most of the industrialists testifying before a congressional investigating committee that toured the South in 1883 agreed with one iron manufacturer who asserted: "We find the colored men . . . are fully as good as white men; they are as steady as workmen; they are as reliable in every way, and the product of their labor is fully as good as anything we have got from white labor. . . . I believe that the future labor of the South in all industrial departments must be colored."[6] Surveys of Southern manufacturers conducted by the *Chattanooga Tradesman* in 1891 and 1901 similarly concluded that "the general tenor of the replies indicated perfect satisfaction with Negro labor. . . . The Negro, as a free laborer, as a medium skilled and common worker, is by no means a 'failure'; he is really a remarkable success."[7] By the early twentieth century, in fact, it was clear that blacks played an essential role in the South's rapid industrial expansion.

Although most Southern blacks remained agricultural workers during the fifty years following Emancipation, an ever increasing number of them moved into industry. The formal end of Reconstruction in 1877 and the end of a severe depression in 1878 brought a massive infusion of Northern and English capital into the South. During the following decades Southern railroad mileage expanded dramatically, while corporate speculators carved huge domains out of the rich timberlands of the Gulf states and exploited thousands of acres of mineral lands in the Lower South. Iron foundries, tobacco factories, and cotton mills rapidly transformed agricultural regions and old port cities into booming industrial communities.

By 1910, 1,200,000 Afro-Americans worked in the manufacturing, mining, and transportation industries of the United States, most of them in Southern states. With the exception of the cotton textile industry, unskilled black workers played an important part in the development of all major Southern industries. By 1910 almost one-third of the railroad firemen and brakemen and well over half the trackmen in the South were black. In Alabama 55 percent of the coal miners and 80 percent of the iron ore miners were Afro-Americans. They also held a majority of the unskilled jobs in the Gulf Coast lumber industry and in the iron and steel industry of Alabama. Two-thirds of the Virginia shipbuilders, the New Orleans dock workers, and the North

---

[6] Senate Committee on Education and Labor, *Report of the Committee to Investigate the Relations Between Capital and Labor, 1883,* 3 vols. (Washington, D.C., 1885), 3:133.

[7] Quoted in W. E. B. Du Bois, *The Negro Artisan,* Atlanta University Publications no. 7 (Atlanta: Atlanta University, 1902), p. 180.

Carolina tobacco workers were Afro-Americans. Even the ranching and cattle industry of the Southwest, especially along the Texas Gulf Coast, depended on black labor; more than one-fourth of the 35,000 cowboys who drove cattle north from Texas between 1866 and 1895 were black. Black drivers predominated as teamsters and draymen in Southern cities. In Atlanta, Memphis, and Birmingham, for example, they held over 80 percent of those jobs. And black craftsmen played a significant role in the construction of Southern cities. By 1910, 15 percent of the carpenters, 35 percent of the brickmasons, and 38 percent of the plasterers were blacks.

The large proportion of blacks in Southern industries mocked the earlier fears of Southern industrialists that Afro-Americans were unfit for industrial employment. Indeed, more blacks than whites seemed willing to work. Low pay, irregular employment, and racial discrimination forced entire black families to enter the job market. As a result, by 1910, 71 percent of the black population over ten years of age was employed, compared to 60 percent of the foreign-born whites and 48 percent of the native whites. Many more black women were employed than white women (54 percent as compared with 17 percent), and they worked in a wide variety of jobs—as domestics, seamstresses, cotton pickers, and laborers in laundries and tobacco factories.[8]

That large numbers of black women and children were forced to work and that black men were relegated to the most difficult, dangerous, and degrading jobs should make clear that blacks were the ones who paid the human price for Southern economic development. Living in the primitive huts of upland company towns and segregated in the disease-infested "slave quarters" of Southern cities, black workers had good cause to wonder why they had left the farms. Wages were higher (if they were paid regularly and not "discounted") and hours were shorter than in the cotton patch, but the day-to-day conditions of life and labor seemed far worse.

Faced with the harshness of urban living conditions and the relentless new demands that industrial work made upon their minds and bodies, black workers tried to cushion the shock of industrialization by clinging to the traditions and habits of rural life. Although the church and other formal institutions were weakened in the transition to industrial and urban life, the black family became more important than ever. As Herbert Gutman has demonstrated, the assumption that the black home disintegrated is not substantiated by statistical evidence.[9] In fact, in some industrial areas black families remained more stable than comparable white working-class fam-

---

[8] Compiled from *U.S. Census, Thirteenth Census, 1910: Population* (Washington, D.C., 1911), and Sterling D. Spero and Abram L. Harris, *The Black Worker* (New York: Columbia University Press, 1931), pp. 159–61.

[9] Herbert G. Gutman, "Persistent Myths About the American Negro Family" (Paper read at the Fifty-fourth Annual Meeting of the Association of the Study of Negro Life and History, Birmingham, Ala., 10 October 1969).

ilies despite especially disruptive social and economic pressures. Black workers, moreover, continued to honor pre-industrial cultural traditions, like sacred and secular folk celebrations, even though they conflicted with the demands of industrialism. When laborers took off for traditional holidays, to celebrate "blue" Monday, or simply to trade at the company store, employers denounced blacks as lazy and undependable. Actually, the preservation of these pre-industrial work habits, common among European immigrants at the same time, was a conscious effort on the part of black workers to resist the mechanical discipline that an industrial society demanded.

Artisans and Craftsmen

Although unskilled workers and their families suffered most from the demands of industrialization, black artisans and craftsmen also felt its impact. Living and working conditions were better for skilled workers, but unlike unskilled industrial workers, they found that their proportion of jobs shrank after the Civil War. A study conducted by the federal government in 1865 indicated that 100,000 of the South's 120,000 skilled artisans were black.[10] Although these figures undoubtedly overstated the proportion, nevertheless by the end of the nineteenth century the percentage of black craftsmen in Southern states declined even though their numbers increased in some building trades.

There are many reasons for the decline of black artisans. For one thing, the expansion and development of Southern cities and industries after 1880 drew not only white Southerners to the cities but also white Northerners and Europeans. As noted earlier, many of these migrants were skilled craftsmen. Second, the ante-bellum black artisan had often been a "jack-of-all-trades," especially on the plantation. Able to shoe a horse, build a house, fix a cotton gin, or make barrel staves, he gave way after the war to the better-trained white specialist. The introduction of machinery and the technological innovations of the post-bellum period, moreover, extensively modified the nature of many trades, requiring the acquisition of new skills. Denied apprenticeship and lacking training, black artisans often failed to learn the new skills necessary for these trades. Third, the discrimination and hostility of whites and their unions often prevented young blacks from entering the trades and older blacks from obtaining employment. Fourth, since pay scales for semiskilled and unskilled blacks in railroad construction as well as in the mines, furnaces, and foundries exceeded the pay of agricultural workers, some black laborers merely accepted these jobs rather than meet the hostility of skilled whites. Finally, throughout the last quarter of the nineteenth century skilled blacks frequently left the South to seek employment and better living conditions in the North or the West.

---

[10] Charles H. Wesley, *Negro Labor in the United States* (New York: Vanguard Press, 1927), p. 142.

Despite the decline of artisanship, the status of black craftsmen did not seem completely bleak to all Afro-Americans. W. E. B. Du Bois, for example, in his outstanding study *The Negro Artisan,* published in 1902, granted that while there was much "to deplore and criticize . . . on the whole, the survey has been encouraging." A correspondent from Atlanta reported to Du Bois that "the opportunity for wage-earning for the Negro artisan is good." A special report on Tuskegee, Alabama, concluded that the "Negro artisan is gaining for the past six or eight years." In Pensacola, Florida, skilled work was about evenly divided between the races, and in the larger cities of Georgia—Atlanta, Savannah, Macon, and Augusta—black craftsmen were said to be "conspicuous." A report from Baton Rouge, Louisiana, concluded that the ante-bellum craftsmen were training "an exceptionally good community of Negro artisans" who seemed to be "gaining."[11]

Du Bois' survey also showed that at the beginning of the twentieth century black craftsmen worked on important construction projects and not merely on menial repairs. In Lynchburg, Virginia, for example, one respondent asserted that black bricklayers were seen "constructing churches and business houses on the principal streets of the city, requiring the best skilled labor necessary to do such work." And in New Orleans, contractors were said to "appreciate the Negro workmen"; "a majority of the most imposing structures in the city were built by colored men."[12]

To make these limited gains at the end of the nineteenth century and beginning of the twentieth, however, black artisans were forced to undercut white labor. Du Bois' 1902 study revealed that blacks received 25 percent to 100 percent less pay for the same work as white carpenters, masons, machinists, painters, and other skilled wage earners. In Atlanta, for example, white painters received $2.30 per day while blacks got $1.80; white carpenters earned $2.07 per day but blacks only $1.82; white electricians were paid $5.00 per day to blacks' $3.50. In Memphis, white carpenters received $3.50 to $4.00 per day but blacks were paid $2.50; white stationary engineers there got $3.00 to $4.50 per day while blacks were paid only $2.00 to $2.50.

Strikebreaking and the Labor Philosophy of Booker T. Washington

During the period of postdepression recovery at the turn of the century, white employers fought the growing union movement in the South by hiring black artisans at these lower wages. Thus, black artisans were in effect forced to help employers fight union activity in order to maintain their place in the crafts. In industries where exclusionary white unions were powerful enough to bar their nonwhite competitors, desperate black workers deliberately adopted strikebreaking as a means of gaining entrance into various jobs

---

[11] Du Bois, *The Negro Artisan,* pp. 102, 107, 112, 113–14.

[12] Ibid., pp. 149, 127.

and trades. In more cases, however, black strikebreakers probably were merely unaware that a strike was in progress. Deceived by company guards, the "scabs" or "blacklegs," who were almost always brought from distant areas, naturally interpreted the strikers' hostility simply as racial hatred. Many of these strikebreakers were recruited from cotton fields and urban ghettos and had only the vaguest notion of what union activity meant; these unemployed blacks could not understand why they should not take jobs that white men had seemingly abandoned. In the final analysis, however, although employers did turn to black workers to break strikes by their white and sometimes their black employees, the amount of strikebreaking by blacks has been exaggerated. As Sterling Spero and Abram Harris pointed out in their study *The Black Worker,* "The number of strikes broken by black labor have been few as compared with white labor. What is more, the Negro has seldom been the only or even the most important strike-breaking element."[13] Because special hostility was focused on the blacks who "scabbed," even in strikes where both races struck side by side, the introduction of black replacements stirred up racial antipathies, and black workers were stigmatized as strikebreakers.

Some black leaders, like Booker T. Washington, actually urged blacks to break strikes in order to gain access to industrial jobs and to demonstrate loyalty to employers. Washington found black labor losing ground in many crafts, excluded from unions, and threatened with increased competition from European immigrants, and he plotted what seemed to him the most practical strategy. Black workers should rely on the paternalism and good will of Southern employers. As one of Washington's disciples put it, every black worker "should strive to make friends with his employer . . . [and] take whatever wages the company offers."[14] In turn, Washington appealed to Southern employers by telling them that "you are in debt to the black man for furnishing you with labor that is almost a stranger to strikes." He denounced trade unionism as "that form of slavery which prevents a man from selling his labor to whom he pleases on account of his color."[15] A black worker, Washington insisted, "should be free to work when, where, and for whom he pleases." In the struggle with racially discriminatory labor unions, black strikebreakers would have the advantage, he felt, because they were "engaged in a struggle to maintain their right to labor as free men," a struggle employers would reward.[16]

---

[13] Spero and Harris, *The Black Worker,* p. 131.

[14] The Reverend William McGill, in *Birmingham* [Ala.] *Hot Shots,* 23 July 1908.

[15] Booker T. Washington, "Speech Before the Southern Industrial Convention, Chattanooga, Tennessee, 1899," in E. Davidson Washington, ed., *Selected Speeches of Booker T. Washington* (New York: Doubleday, 1932), pp. 81–82.

[16] Booker T. Washington, "The Negro and the Labor Unions," in *Atlantic Monthly* 111 (1913): 756. The best analysis of Washington's thought on labor unions is in August Meier,

This antagonism to unions and enthusiasm for employers was an integral part of Booker Washington's labor philosophy. By teaching craft skills at industrial schools like Tuskegee and Hampton and by promoting fealty to Southern industrialists, Washington hoped to recoup jobs black craftsmen lost after Emancipation. But, as C. Vann Woodward concluded, "Brickmaking, blacksmithing, wheelwrighting, harness making, basketry, tinsmithing — the type of crafts taught at Tuskegee — had more relevance to the South of Booker Washington's boyhood than to the South of United States Steel."[17] W. E. B. Du Bois estimated that only one-fourth of the students trained at industrial schools went on to practice their trade and that by 1900 fewer than 1,000 graduates had become craftsmen.[18] Despite Washington's reputed popularity, moreover, few black workers responded to the strategies of strikebreaking and industrial education he suggested; the former brought considerable danger but little security, and the latter failed to regain the lost status of the black artisan.

Washington's philosophy, though, did ultimately affect the place of the black worker in Southern industrial life. Attracted by Washington's opposition to unions and his willingness to train an efficient, tractable work force, corporation executives became major financial supporters of the industrial schools. Industrialists used black teachers trained by Washington and his disciples to implement a system of welfare paternalism in the twentieth century that improved some black workers' living and working conditions while keeping them poorly paid, nonunion laborers. The outstanding example of this policy occurred after 1908 when the United States Steel Corporation introduced an ambitious welfare and educational program for its black workers in Alabama's mines and steel mills to increase efficiency, reduce labor turnover, and eliminate the threat of unionism. Washington, and later the journal of Hampton Institute, praised the program lavishly because it "worked toward the same ends as those which Hampton and Tuskegee and the whole system of education they represent are striving for." Relatively few workers benefited from this and other such programs, but the colleges nevertheless rejoiced that "Hampton and Tuskegee graduates are having a large part in [directing] such work."[19]

Black workers thus adopted several strategies in confronting the new industrial order. A few blacks took advantage of industrial schools to develop skills that might enable them to continue to work in traditional crafts. Along with other blacks they sometimes managed to retain these artisans' jobs or gain access to other crafts and newer industries by working for lower

---

Negro Thought in America, 1880–1915 (Ann Arbor: University of Michigan Press, 1966), Chapter 7.

[17] Woodward, *Origins of the New South,* p. 365.

[18] Du Bois, *The Negro Artisan,* pp. 69–79.

[19] Quoted in Woodward, *Origins of the New South,* pp. 365–66.

wages than whites and in some cases by strikebreaking. If they followed the advice of Booker Washington they labored diligently and dependably, relying upon the good will of their employers for improvements and advancement. Most black workers, however, did not accept the degrading jobs and miserable living conditions assigned to them without a struggle. Some laborers simply mounted a rear-guard action against the ever increasing demands that employers made. They resisted by taking traditional rest spells and holidays which conflicted with the disciplined regularity of the industrial order. Other blacks migrated to the North. Although the "great exodus" did not occur until after 1915, throughout the late nineteenth and early twentieth centuries a steady stream of black migrants fled the South for Northern cities. But malingering and migration were not sufficient means for most Southern blacks to improve their lowly status during this period. What was needed, some recognized, was working-class organization.

Black Workers and the Labor Movement

Black workers responded enthusiastically to the post–Civil War American labor movement. In fact, Afro-Americans had displayed incipient interest in labor organizations before the war and had also formed some benevolent labor societies of their own. Immediately after the war, black skilled workers, hod carriers, longshoremen, and waiters in Northern cities and Southern border states formed their own organizations. In 1869, 160 delegates from these various organizations met in Washington, D.C., for the Colored National Labor Convention, the first national convention of black workers in the United States to discuss the relations of white and black labor. Led by Isaac Myers, a Baltimore ship caulker who had recently established a successful cooperative shipbuilding company owned entirely by blacks, the convention stressed the right of labor to organize. But, reflecting the attitude of the labor movement of the time, it also urged land reform and the establishment of cooperative enterprises and even insisted that there was no real conflict between labor and capital; indeed, it should be the aim of every black man to become a capitalist.

Although no decision was reached about affiliation with the newly formed white National Labor Union at this meeting, Isaac Myers and three other delegates from a Maryland convention of black labor organizations later attended the 1869 convention of the NLU to propose cooperation between the white organization and the recently established Negro Labor Congress. The temporizing of the NLU discouraged the delegates. Moreover, the leaders of the Negro Labor Congress, most of them closely connected with the Radical Republicans and not wage earners, disagreed vigorously with the white organization's efforts to establish an independent political party. At its final meeting in 1872, the Congress repudiated the NLU, declared unswerving loyalty to the GOP, and then passed into oblivion. "Had there been fewer politicians in these organizations," Spero and Harris observed, "they might have become the spearhead of Negro labor organization."[20]

As the antagonism between the National Labor Union and the Negro Labor Congress demonstrated, however, successful working-class cooperation depended not merely on the increased class consciousness of black wage earners but also on the willingness of whites to welcome blacks into the labor movement. Many trade unions remained "lily white." At the beginning of the twentieth century, W. E. B. Du Bois reported that of a total membership of 1,200,000 workers in major unions in the United States, only 40,000 were black. The railroad brotherhoods—engineers, conductors, firemen, and trainmen—and machinists, electrical workers, boilermakers, and stonecutters openly barred Afro-Americans. Another two dozen unions reported few black members, usually fewer than ten, and Du Bois ascribed their absence both to the paucity of black mechanics in these trades and to color discrimination within the unions. Moreover, in many cases where the national union admitted blacks, locals were able to bar them from membership or even to refuse to recognize a black union member's traveling card despite prohibitions against such practices by the national organization. There were numerous cases toward the end of the nineteenth century and the beginning of the twentieth century in which black union members were driven from unions when whites simply refused to work with them.

The exclusion of black craftsmen from various unions stemmed not only from racial discrimination but also from the craft unions' "job-conscious" ideology. Craft unions in the United States looked upon themselves as organizations that could establish and guard a monopoly over particular jobs. By relying on the employers' acceptance of the competence and dependability of skilled workers who were union members, they could exclude outsiders from practicing the trade, maintain control over their jobs, and lessen future competition. Racial exclusion was part of a larger program designed to protect them against competition from unskilled workers and to preserve the domination of skilled workers in the labor movement.

National labor organizations dominated by these craft unions condoned discrimination against black workers simply by refusing to interfere with the autonomy and independence of craft unions. The short-lived National Labor Union, founded in 1866, insisted that "the interests of labor are one" and urged a "vigorous campaign [that] will unite the whole laboring population, white and black, upon our platform."[21] Skilled craft unionists in

---

[20] Spero and Harris, *The Black Worker,* p. 32.

[21] *Address of the National Labor Congress to the Workingmen of the United States* (1867), in John R. Commons et al., *A Documentary History of American Industrial Society,* 2nd ed., 10 vols. (1909–11; reprint ed., New York: Russell & Russell, 1958), 9:157–60.

the organization who opposed admission of blacks forced the leadership to retreat from this position, however. Although welcoming the "proferred [*sic*] cooperation" of black workers, in 1869 they exhorted them to form separate organizations which would send delegates to national conventions.[22] Far from demonstrating the cooperative spirit of the labor movement, these racially separate unions united in national conventions reflected the racial discord which would mark much of the labor movement for the next hundred years.

Similarly, at the end of the nineteenth century, the American Federation of Labor retreated from its earlier stand opposing racial discrimination in the international unions that belonged to it. The AFL sanctioned separate black locals and even separate central organizations in cities where affiliated unions would not accept blacks, and by 1900 it was admitting unions with exclusionary provisions in their constitutions and initiation procedures. Samuel Gompers, then head of the AFL, sacrificed "both his principles and the Negro workingmen, as well as the broader interests of the whole labor movement, to the short-sighted and selfish demands of the aristocratic officialdom of the craft unions, whose spokesman he had agreed to be," one historian concluded.[23]

Despite white discrimination, black workers still sought organization by demanding unionization and admission into national trade unions. In many Southern cities black barbers, brickmasons, carpenters, and plasterers repeatedly appealed to unions covering their crafts for organization. At the beginning of the twentieth century the handful of black delegates at the national conventions of both these trade unions and the AFL demanded that the organizations extend their activities in the South, employ more black organizers, and make concerted efforts to bring blacks into the unions.

These black workers' demands were not always unsuccessful. Fearing that unorganized blacks would be used by Southern employers in ever increasing numbers to depress wages or to replace striking white craftsmen, some national labor leaders and Southern white union members argued that unions should take in blacks. Effectively organizing the South, they asserted, depended upon the inclusion of black workers in the labor movement.[24] Even Samuel Gompers, who at one point admitted that he doubted the black workers' ability to grasp the essentials of trade unionism, claimed at the beginning of the twentieth century that unless blacks were organized they

---

[22] *Chicago Workingman's Advocate,* 4 September 1869, in Commons et al., *Documentary History of American Industrial Society,* 9:239–40.

[23] Bernard Mandel, "Samuel Gompers and the Negro Workers, 1886–1914," *Journal of Negro History* 40, no. 1 (January 1955): 60.

[24] American Federation of Labor, Twentieth Annual Convention, *Proceedings, 1900* (Louisville, Ky., 1900), pp. 12–13.

would "be used against any effort made by us for our economic and social advancement."[25]

Some craft groups that employed a large proportion of Afro-Americans in the South—brickmasons, carpenters, plasterers, painters, and barbers—attempted to organize black workmen. In most of these crafts, however, blacks were organized into separate locals and then restricted to employment on inferior buildings in black neighborhoods. Although expected to support white strikes, blacks were generally left powerless to protect their own jobs and were denied support when involved in disputes with their employers. In practice, therefore, these craft locals in the South were primarily a means of preventing blacks from competing with whites and provided little opportunity for black craftsmen to better their condition through working-class cooperation.

Unskilled blacks as well as skilled black men sought organization. For a short period at the beginning of the twentieth century the American Federation of Labor tried to circumvent the refusal of most trade unions to organize unskilled blacks by bringing Southern black laborers into Federal Labor Union locals directly affiliated with the AFL. Little is known about the number of blacks who belonged to these unions. In Birmingham, Alabama, however, more than 2,000 unskilled iron and steel workers, iron ore miners, and common laborers joined sixteen FLU locals between 1899 and 1904. Engaging in militant, occasionally violent strikes to improve their working conditions and secure union recognition, these unskilled black laborers ignored the opposition of Booker Washington, local black ministers, and industrial employers in the region in order to unionize and seek the support of the white labor movement. But without a national union to bargain for them, without funds to sustain them when on strike, and faced with the hostility of established craft unions and skilled white workers, these Federal Labor Unions of black workers could not protect their members' interests and rapidly faded into obscurity.[26]

Black railroad labor unions further illustrate this pattern of unsuccessful organizing. Although controlling a significant proportion of jobs as railroad trainmen and sectionmen in the South, black railroad workers never compelled the all-white railroad brotherhoods to admit them into their unions. Instead, black railroadmen countered with their own unions. The first such organization, the Colored Locomotive Firemen's Association, was formed in Georgia in the early 1900's. Soon after, in Alabama, Tennessee, and Kentucky, black firemen and switchmen on the Louisville and Nashville Railroad unsuccess-

[25] Samuel Gompers to H. N. Randle [sic], 19 March 1903, Samuel Gompers Letterbooks, Library of Congress, Washington, D.C.

[26] Paul B. Worthman, "Black Workers and Labor Unions in Birmingham, Alabama, 1897–1904," *Labor History* 10, no. 3 (Summer 1969): 394–98.

fully attempted to gain recognition from the company for their organizations. Between 1913 and 1915 several Afro-American railwaymen's associations were formed for benevolent purposes and to "guard against attacks upon colored railway employees." Dependent upon the sufferance of white employers for their jobs, subject to constant harassment from white railroad workers, and unable to persuade whites to cooperate, these black organizations, unlike their counterparts on the docks and piers of the South, quickly collapsed.

Black Workers and Industrial Unions

Afro-American dock workers in Southern ports were among the earliest groups of black workingmen to form labor organizations. In 1867 Charleston's black dockers formed the Longshoremen's Protective Union Association. By 1875, after several militant strikes, they had almost nine hundred members. In Galveston, Texas, conflicts between whites and blacks led Afro-American dockers to form a longshoremen's organization in 1870. After whites unsuccessfully tried to bar blacks from longshoring jobs and from jobs on shipboard, black screwmen, responsible for packing cotton bales on board ships, organized their own union in 1883 and concluded a work-sharing agreement with the white screwmen's union. In Baltimore a union formed in 1871 succeeded in raising wages 25 percent. A year later in New Orleans, black dock workers, who had cooperated with whites in an interracial strike in 1865, incorporated a Protective Benevolent Mutual Aid Association, which remained one of the strongest black labor unions in the country for more than half a century. Newport News, Virginia, had a black longshoremen's organization which flourished in the 1890's. Mobile's black dock laborers formed an organization in 1894, and ten years later over 2,000 of them quit work in a demand for higher wages. In Virginia's seaports coal trimmers organized and struck in 1914 over the firing of a black union organizer. The strength of these organizations forced white longshoremen to recognize the black dock workers' demands for a better share of work in Southern ports.

By 1900 more than half of the dock workers along the Gulf and South Atlantic coasts were blacks. The International Longshoremen's Association, which consolidated a variety of white and black waterfront unions during the first two decades of the twentieth century, recognized the importance of the black dockers' place in the industry. It attempted to surmount both racial hostility and job distinctions by building an interracial industrial organization. Scores of black delegates attended national conventions, and several black vice-presidents sat on its executive board. In New Orleans, Mobile, Galveston, Charleston, and Newport News, for example, black and white organizations of dockers came to work-sharing agreements which enabled them to preserve a united front throughout the early twentieth century. Joint committees of black and white locals of the ILA handled matters of common concern and maintained a uniform wage scale. Nevertheless, race distinctions and racial discrimination were not swept away. Locals and work gangs almost always remained segregated; whites often clung to the best jobs in the ports; and, since black workers outnumbered whites, agreements to share work equally between the races benefited whites at the expense of some black workmen. But the extensive cooperation between blacks and whites in the ILA in Southern ports enabled black longshoremen to make significant gains in improving their working conditions and obtaining some job security.[27]

As the International Longshoremen's Association demonstrated, cooperation between black and white workers in the South was not impossible. In several cases, moreover, white organizations took the lead in attempting to bring blacks into the labor movement. Most successful organizing of black workers was done by industrial unions which viewed the labor movement as an instrument for the cooperation of all workers, skilled and unskilled, native and foreign, white and black. Since industrial unions minimized occupational distinctions and committed themselves to organizing all workers in a particular industry regardless of skill or level of employment, they were, of course, better adapted than craft unions for organizing the large numbers of unskilled blacks who labored in the South's heavy industries. Industrial unions, moreover, were often socialist or radical and reflected an ideology that minimized racial hostility by stressing the solidarity of all wage earners.

The earliest industrial organization to recruit blacks actively was the Knights of Labor. Established as a secret society in 1869, the Knights threw off secrecy in 1878 and for a decade became an aggressive national organization with a rapidly growing membership. Based upon the idea that "an injury to one is an injury to all," the Knights stressed geographical and industrial organization, not merely organization along craft lines. Although many trade unions belonged to the Knights, the organization rejected their commitment to skilled workmen and their emphasis on bargaining with employers, seeking instead to consolidate all workers in one union in an offensive against "unjust accumulation of wealth."

Organization of black workers was the official and accepted policy of the Knights. Although many all-black locals were established in the South, integrated locals and district assemblies also flourished. Black organizers traveled throughout the South in the 1880's, and black men like Frank Ferrell of District Assembly 49 in New York City played important roles in the leadership of the organization. At the general assembly of 1886 in Richmond, Virginia, when Ferrell was refused admission to a hotel where the entire New York City delegation had made a reservation, delegates from the district asked Terrence Powderly, head of the Knights, to assign Ferrell the task of introducing Governor Fitzhugh Lee of Virginia, who was to address the

---

[27] F. Ray Marshall, *Labor in the South* (Cambridge, Mass.: Harvard University Press, 1967), pp. 60–68. Spero and Harris, *The Black Worker,* pp. 182–205.

convention. Not wishing to offend the mores of the community, but wishing to "do something to encourage the black workmen," Powderly had Ferrell introduce him and then he introduced the governor. The incident received national publicity and encouraged black workers to look to the Knights for support in improving their submerged status in Southern society. "The color line had been broken," a prominent labor leader asserted in 1887, "and black and white were found working together in the same cause."[28]

Black workers responded eagerly to the Knights' organization. In 1880, the official organ of the Knights reported several black as well as integrated locals in the South. Five years later a labor journalist claimed that there were "hundreds of colored assemblies in the South."[29] By 1886 the Knights claimed 60,000 black members, a figure which may have increased as the Knights' membership rose in the South during the remainder of the decade. "The colored people of the South are flocking to us, being eager for organization and education, and when thoroughly imbued with our principles are answering in their fidelity," the secretary-treasurer of the organization reported in 1886.[30] In Alabama and Tennessee coal mining villages, on the docks of New Orleans and Newport News, in Mississippi turpentine camps, in Florida and Virginia tobacco factories, on Arkansas plantations, on Southwestern railroads, and in cities and towns throughout the South, large numbers of blacks participated in the Knights' strikes and activities. They played an important role in the Knights' greatest victory, the Great Southwest Strike against the railroads controlled by financier Jay Gould in 1885. In fact, the poor treatment of black and white sectionhands in Texas and Arkansas was one factor leading militant railroad workers to strike. Although the Knights declined in the North after 1886, their appeal to Southern blacks helped the organization flourish in the South until the depression of the 1890's decimated local assemblies.

The traditions of the Knights influenced industrial unions that emerged during the last decade of the nineteenth century and the first decade of the twentieth. The United Mine Workers of America, founded in 1890 partly from the remnants of Knights of Labor locals in coal mining villages, were committed to interracial organizing. By the end of the century approximately 25,000 black coal miners could be found in the South, and thousands more toiled in the mines of the Midwest. The UMW assiduously worked to organize these black miners, and perhaps more than any other union it overcame the racial prejudice of its white members as it drew black miners and mine laborers into the union. Richard L. Davis, a black miner from Ohio who attended the

---

[28] George E. McNeill, *The Labor Movement: The Problem of Today* (Boston: M. W. Hazen, 1887), p. 171.

[29] *John Swinton's Paper,* 12 April 1885.

[30] Knights of Labor, *Proceedings of the General Assembly of the Knights of Labor of America, 1886* (Richmond, Va., 1886), p. 44.

founding convention in 1890 as an officer of his district organization, served on the national executive board several times before his death in 1900. Other black miners served as organizers and as officers in all-black and integrated locals in Southern states. In Alabama, District 20 of the UMW successfully compelled coal mine operators to pay black and white miners equally and to assign work places in the mines without regard to race. When in 1901 some Birmingham merchants refused to allow an integrated union meeting to convene in a hall they owned, the white district president informed them that "the Negro could not be eliminated. He is a member of our organization and when we are told that we can not use the hall because of this fact then we are insulted as an organization." By threatening to boycott all the city's merchants, the 20,000 black and white members of the UMW's Alabama district compelled the merchants to apologize for their "oversight and misunderstanding."[31]

By 1900 more than 20,000 black miners, most of them in the South, belonged to the union. Black organizers and district officials throughout the South displayed a deep loyalty to the union, often in the face of violence committed by whites antagonistic to labor unions, and praised the UMW for resisting segregation and opposing the increasing racial discrimination in Southern states. The mine workers' union, one black miner maintained, "has done more to erase the word white from the Constitution than the Fourteenth Amendment."[32] In Alabama's mines, UMW organizers reported "great enthusiasm for union among the colored brethren."[33] Throughout the 1890's and into the early twentieth century black miners in the state steadfastly resisted the efforts of mine operators to split them from the integrated coal miners' union. In 1908, during a large and violent upheaval that paralyzed Alabama's coal industry, more than 10,000 black miners joined their white comrades in a strike for better wages and union recognition. Despite attacks on the union by some of Birmingham's "best" citizens, the black miners "were standing out better than the whites," one white miner commented. "They will not be bribed to return to work until the union is recognized."[34] The strike failed when the governor called in the state militia to destroy the interracial tent camp erected by the union for miners evicted from company housing, and total union membership in Alabama declined from 18,000 to 700 by the following year. National UMW black membership, however, did not decline precipitously, as the mine workers' organization continued to bring black miners into their union in the rest of the country.

Building consciously on the traditions of the Knights, the Brotherhood

---

[31] *Birmingham* [Ala.] *News,* 3 July 1901, quoted in Worthman, "Black Workers and Labor Unions in Birmingham," p. 401.

[32] O. H. Underwood to Editor, *United Mine Workers' Journal,* 20 July 1899.

[33] *Birmingham* [Ala.] *Labor Advocate,* 5 February 1898.

[34] *Birmingham* [Ala.] *Labor Advocate,* 10 September 1904.

of Timber Workers, an independent industrial union, organized thousands of black and white lumber workers in the Louisiana-Texas pine region beginning in 1910. The BTW energetically sought the support of black mill hands who held more than half the unskilled jobs in the region, but in response to Southern folkways, now institutionalized by statutes that outlawed interracial meetings, the union organized separate locals for blacks. In 1912, however, the BTW affiliated with the Industrial Workers of the World, a revolutionary, syndicalist union which advocated militant egalitarianism and industrial unionism. William "Big Bill" Haywood, national leader of the IWW, traveled to Louisiana in 1912 and joined with Southern radicals in urging white union men to meet jointly with the blacks in open violation of segregation laws. The BTW responded favorably to this appeal for interracial unionism, and its leaders assured black timber workers that "the B.T.W. . . . takes the Negro and protects him and his family along with the white wage worker and his family on an industrial basis." "No longer," they added, "will we allow the Southern oligarchy to divide us on lines of race, craft, religion, or nationality."[35] In the violent Louisiana "lumber war" which followed in 1912 and 1913, black workers, who constituted about half the Timber Workers' 20,000 members, struck in solidarity with their white fellow workers under the radical leadership of the "One Big Union." At Merryville, Louisiana, in 1913, the Brotherhood called a desperate strike to protest the firing of white union members indicted after a gun battle with company guards. Black timber workers showed their loyalty to the union by walking out with the white workers in the IWW's last Southern campaign to promote the solidarity of white and black labor.

As Sterling Spero and Abram Harris observed, had the AFL and its affiliated national craft unions been able to follow the strategy of the IWW and the UMW, "It is not illogical to assume . . . that at least the seeds of working class solidarity would have been sown among the masses of Negroes and whites before the Northern hegira [of World War I]."[36] Indeed, despite the growing segregation and discrimination in the South at the beginning of the twentieth century, organized black workers were not completely isolated from the rest of the labor movement in the region; some city central labor councils and state labor federations admitted black delegates in an effort to develop an interracial labor movement. A leading union expert wrote in 1886 that the formation of the Central Trades and Labor Federation in New Orleans did "more to break the color line than anything since emancipation."[37] In the 1880's what labor historians have regarded as one of the most inclusive sympathetic strikes in this country occurred when almost

---

[35] *Industrial Worker,* 26 September 1911. See also Covington Hall, "Negroes Against Whites," *International Socialist Review* 13 (1912): 349.

[36] Spero and Harris, *The Black Worker,* p. 325.

[37] McNeill, *The Labor Movement,* p. 168.

every craft union in New Orleans struck in protest against employers who refused to deal with a powerful black draymen's union. The Knights of Labor, building on waterfront unions, helped to maintain interracial unionism in New Orleans until the 1890's, when the general strike of 1892 paralyzed the life of the city for three days. Forty-two unions with more than 20,000 members struck in an unsuccessful effort to compel the city's businessmen to deal with both black and white unions. Although the alliance of black and white unions foundered during the depression of the 1890's, the city's long tradition of interracial unionism erupted in 1907 in yet another struggle in which black and white workers struck together.[38]

New Orleans was not an isolated example of interracial working-class cooperation. In some Florida cities at the beginning of the twentieth century black and white workers met in integrated central unions. The Georgia State Federation of Labor refused to join the 1898 "peace jubilee" parade because black workers could not march. In Birmingham, Alabama, black workers marched under their union banners in Labor Day parades the first half-dozen years of the new century, and black delegates belonged to the city's central labor council even after the AFL permitted the formation of separate white and black centrals in 1901. The Alabama State Federation of Labor, formed in 1900, not only included all-black and integrated locals from every area of the state but also had black men in leadership positions during the first five years of the twentieth century. Committed to the goal of organization for the state's black workers, the Alabama Federation appealed to the AFL to send them salaried organizers who would devote "their entire time and energy" to organizing black unskilled laborers. White as well as black delegates to the 1903 and 1904 conventions denounced skilled white steelworkers for refusing to support a strike of unskilled black laborers at their mill. The state's workingmen, insisted the white Federation secretary (himself a member of the Amalgamated Association of Iron, Steel, and Tin Workers), must "lay aside all malice and prejudice against color, creed or nationality, and as we are all wage-earners under the same banner of trades unionism, let us all work with one end in view."[39]

The Failure of Industrial Unionism

These efforts of Southern black and white wage earners to surmount racial hostility, instill class consciousness, and create an interracial labor movement collapsed by the second decade of the twentieth century. Industrial organizations like the United Mine Workers, the Brotherhood of Timber Workers, and the Industrial Workers of the World, moreover, did not survive

---

[38] Roger W. Shugg, "The New Orleans General Strike of 1892," *Louisiana Historical Quarterly* 21, no. 2 (April 1938): 547–59.

[39] *Birmingham* [Ala.] *Labor Advocate,* 9 May 1903.

the assaults of Southern employers. The industrial unions' militant and often radical challenges to the supremacy of Southern white industrialists and the unions' willingness to organize black and white workers along class lines subjected them to vigorous attacks from industrialists and their allies. Unable to withstand the hostility of their opponents, these organizations collapsed, either permanently or, in the case of the UMW in Southern states, until the Depression in the 1930's. Their disappearance removed the most important institutional bulwark in the South against racial hostility and meant that no important catalytic agent advocating class consciousness persisted to oppose the racial divisions fostered by industrialists.

The organized campaigns of discrimination and segregation ushered in with the Progressive era intensified the racial prejudices of white workers. By depriving black men of their right to vote, intensifying the residential and other forms of racial segregation that isolated urban blacks from white communities (except as domestic servants), and subjecting black Southerners to legal and physical harassment and intimidation in their daily lives, white Southern employers not only increased their control over the black proletariat but also made the possibility of political and economic cooperation between black and white workingmen almost impossible in the eyes of white workers. Craft unionism, moreover, was still the dominant philosophy within the American labor movement, and its exclusionary policies prevented cooperation between skilled whites and skilled and unskilled blacks. In addition, even though skilled white workingmen never completely excluded blacks from various jobs, skilled white workers nevertheless came to form an "aristocracy of labor" consisting of skilled and supervisory workers, most of whom enjoyed a high degree of privilege and joined with their employers in policing the exploitation of black wage earners.

Leading the social and political assaults on blacks, Southern employers still managed to retain the right to manipulate their black workers without submitting to the absolute employee barriers demanded by many white skilled workers. Shortly before and after World War I, Southern employers, aided by graduates and propagandists from several black industrial schools, successfully implemented an extensive program of "welfare capitalism" that upgraded some black laborers into semiskilled and even skilled industrial jobs and raised the living conditions of these black employees. To ensure that labor organizing did not interfere with their domination over black workers, employers militantly—and often violently—barred any union activity among their employees. Although working for higher wages and living in better circumstances than previously, the black workingmen were still seen as servants to white masters. Being servants implied that they were unfree. They could not have unions to negotiate on their behalf and they could not form organizations that might give them the chance to share in political power. Restrictions and harassment outside the factory gates prevented them from attaining the kind of bargaining power that comes from living in a stable, free community. Segregated and contained, their homes were fenced and policed; the company quarters and segregated sections of Southern cities became a kind of compound for black families. The unions' inability to interfere with these arrangements or to raise the status of black wage earners left black workers with little choice but to rely on employers for improvements in their working and living conditions, even though this kept them locked into a system of paternal despotism.

By 1915 the place of black labor in the industrial economy of the New South had generally improved after fifty years of hard work and bloody struggle. The paternalism of employers as well as the continued struggle of blacks had brought about this improvement. But blacks were still worse off than most white wage earners and lived in dire poverty under abominable conditions only slightly improved by the welfare of a few large corporations. Nevertheless, black workers had made themselves part of the region's industrial structure and had demonstrated their readiness to organize along class lines in order to challenge their assigned status as a permanent, propertyless, subservient labor force. In the decades ahead black workers would continue their struggle not only to improve their economic status and to weaken the control of new masters but to preserve the gains made after Emancipation.

The Economic and Racial Components of Jim Crow

OTEY M. SCRUGGS

Otey M. Scruggs, professor of history at Syracuse University, has written many articles on American history, including "Why Afro-American History," published in *7 On Black* (J. B. Lippincott, 1969). He is presently at work on a biographical study of Alexander Crummel, prominent nineteenth-century Afro-American. In the essay that follows, Mr. Scruggs analyzes the interplay of economics and racism that produced the Southern maze of discriminatory law and social practice known as Jim Crow. Focusing on the years between the Civil War and World War I, he examines the ways in which caste and class lines solidified in the South to effectively disfranchise Southern blacks.

Because of their skin color and their history as slaves, Negroes have been regarded as "the depth below the depth." Plantation slavery was *black* servitude. It lasted for over two hundred and fifty years— long enough to implant itself in the memory of all generations, black and white, in the century since slavery; long enough for caste to become a way of life, with a clearly defined ritual and etiquette that offer social and psychological rewards to the dominant caste, even when there is no offer of economic gain. The fact is that hatred of blacks has been so powerful as to exist virtually independent of all other considerations, to be used and abused as circumstances—economic and otherwise—decree. Without question, economic factors have been a powerful force. The black man has been poor because he is black and at the same time he has been kept in poverty because others have derived economic as well as social and psychological benefits from his powerlessness. He has been a victim of both caste and class pressures. The two have acted reciprocally to keep him down. Customarily, caste and class interests have existed in tension side by side. Sometimes they have intersected, resulting in further solidification of the color bar. It is in their coexistence and in their intersection that we must seek a historical understanding of Jim Crow.

The Ideology

When first used in connection with segregation on the basis of color, the term "Jim Crow" was applied to public transportation, first in the North before the Civil War, later in the South into the twentieth century. However, Jim Crow has come to mean the whole system of racial proscription, including disfranchisement, based on the belief in white supremacy. And it is in this larger context that the term is used in this essay. In rapid succession in the late 1880's, several Southern states passed Jim Crow laws segregating white and black passengers on railroads. In theory, facilities were to be equal in comfort and convenience. In practice, those for Negroes never equaled those made available to whites. Beginning in 1890, the ex-Confederate states, through constitutional revision or by statute, disfranchised all but a handful of black voters. Once drawn, the color line was extended to virtually every human activity from the cradle to the grave. By the time the United States entered World War I in 1917, the process of solidifying color caste in law was, for all intents, completed.

Color caste — segregation based on skin color (for, truthfully, it was more a color, or color mixture, than a race question) — existed in the South long before it was codified. And in major social areas, in the North as well as in the South, Jim Crow laws requiring separate schools and forbidding marriages between blacks and whites were on the books long before the late 1880's.

Color caste rested on belief in white supremacy, the deeply ingrained, satanic conviction, shared by all classes of whites, that the black man's natural place — social, economic, and political — was below that of the white man. The corollary of this idea was that white men, by right and for their own and the Negroes' protection, should control black men. Scriptures, science, and history were all ransacked and made to contribute to a full-blown ideology of white superiority, one that would be embellished but hardly altered in its fundamentals in the hundred years after 1850. In most cases its elements were merely thinly disguised intellectual formulations of the racist views of the untutored white masses. God, the theorists posited, had created the black man different from (that is to say, inferior to) the white man; had the Divinity intended equality, He would most certainly have created all men the same.

The "findings" of science confirmed such racist "truths." Experiments in comparative craniology found the Negro wanting in intellectual capacity. These results, together with deductions from the evolutionary speculations of geologists and biologists, like those of Darwin, were made to serve the spurious theory of separate creation—different species. Where pseudo science failed to justify white supremacy, the black man's degraded state in slavery was available as source material from which corroborative conclusions could be drawn. Supporters of slavery argued that Negroes were natural-born thieves and adulterers, happiest when at work under white super-vision, leaving the problems of freedom to the superior caste innately endowed to cope with them. Indeed, this reading of history led many whites to con-clude that there could be no black advance without white rule, the absence of which would leave blacks mired in their own backwardness. The intellec-tual and economic assault of whites drove blacks back upon themselves, upon human resources that enabled them to enjoy life despite its hardships.

As marshaled by the ideologies of white supremacy, the evidence led inexorably to the conclusion that the Negro was a species of inferior being, a "missing link" between man and the lower forms, at best a child doomed to eternal adolescence. This view and those similar to it account for whites' deep-rooted fear and horror of miscegenation, for sexual intermingling would have the disastrous consequence of polluting the master race. The crime of crimes was rape involving a black male and a white female. So visceral, so demonic, so loaded with blind unreasoning fury were the white man's fears of racial impurity that the killing of a black man merely suspected of rape seemed justified.

There is truth in the assertion that the key to the ideology and practice of white supremacy was the Southern planters' desire for cheap black labor. But like many such truths, it is an oversimplification. Blacks were first brought to America for their "arms and legs," and they did continue to be wanted merely for the dirty work they performed, which whites balked at doing, and for the economic and social benefits that their labor conferred. However, the attitudes and practices of whites were contradictory. Southern whites agreed that Negroes were fit to be little more than hewers of wood and drawers of water, a view reinforced by the generally servile and menial status of the blacks. But the knowledge that they were dependent for their own wealth and prestige upon this despised black labor force produced tensions within the members of the Southern ruling class. After Emancipation, they fre-quently voiced their dissatisfaction with their dependence on so "unreliable" a labor force, and they mounted half-hearted and unsuccessful campaigns to induce outside labor—white and therefore more "dependable"—to come to the South. But whenever Negroes voiced any intention of leaving, the cry of labor shortage was raised, and force and fraud were employed to anchor them to the soil.

Paradoxically, although convinced the black man was incapable of suc-ceeding economically and moving up in status, whites feared that the black man would succeed. And, when Negroes did indeed appear to be advancing too rapidly in the 1880's, the net of caste was ever more tightly drawn. How-ever, whites resented other things besides black advancement. Whites often perceived that they were standing still or that their economic and social position was actually deteriorating. But they directed their frustration and anger toward the Negro instead of toward the social and economic system. It has been established, for example, that in the fifty years after 1882, whenever cotton prices declined and hardship followed, the number of lynchings of Negroes in the South rose. Indeed, white poverty, as well as black desire for upward mobility and improved status, has created fears and anxieties among poor and aspiring whites and has heightened racism, especially in times of crisis and rapid social change. Whenever blacks have been moving up the status ladder while whites have been descending it, Negroes have been humiliated and degraded and reminded again of their "place" as the white man's arms and legs. Yet, could it be that blacks, through all this, were in some ironic way advantaged?

The Old Economic Order

Before the Civil War, power was in the hands of the large planters. Afterward they increasingly shared it with a middle class of merchant-bankers and owners and operators of railroads, mines, and factories. The power and prestige of the ante-bellum planter class rested on property in land and slaves. Slavery and the plantation provided the leverage for a small coterie to impose its world view on the entire South. In many ways feudal, this view centered on the local community, often the plantation, and was characterized by paternalism and a gentlemanly concern for honor, style, gracious living, and politics and statecraft. Fitting smoothly into this view, as part of the divinely inspired order of things, was the belief in white supremacy. So central were the planters and their values to the life of the South that they carried all before them for years afterward. In defense of these values, the poor bled profusely during the war for Southern independence. In the 1880's, the values themselves, if not their architects, were firmly enough entrenched to vie with the capitalist values of the New South. The masses of poor white laborers, only a little less hard-pressed than most Negroes, became increasingly dependent upon the landowning class. Nevertheless, with a few notable exceptions, black and white poor did not join hands in a common assault on the classes above them. Stratification among whites in the South did indeed exist, and unity of the masses of poor whites and blacks would seem to have been to their economic advantage. But recognition of common class interest was too often deflected by color prejudice.

In contrast to the South, a full-blown capitalism prevailed in the North even before the Civil War, and money getting became an end in itself. Since each man was in eager pursuit of his own economic gain and since Northern Negroes were not bound by slavery after the early nineteenth century, black workers tended to be viewed by white workingmen as direct competitors for jobs. However, because Negroes were seldom numerous in most Northern communities before World War I, white fears of black competition in the labor market were not as intense as they would otherwise have been. But they did exist, as shown by such periodic outbreaks of violence against black people as the draft riots in New York City in 1863. This wanton aggression against black life and property was the response of white workers to the passage of a draft law during the Civil War and to rumors of an impending influx of newly emancipated blacks to underbid whites for jobs. Significantly, the rumored influx did not materialize. Hatred of blacks, as well as fear of job competition, was very much a factor in the riots. The South had no monopoly on color caste.

The New Economic Order

Between the Civil War and World War I, the entire country was caught in the whirl of increasingly swift social change. New economic institutions, rapidly expanding systems of transportation and communication, and a cornucopia of technological developments transformed the United States from a nation of isolated communities into a nation of interconnected cities and farms. The South, where most of the freedmen lived, was affected by these changes at every turn. Indeed, the death of slavery in the Civil War had forced the South to confront change on a vast scale earlier than other sections. Emancipation altered, though it can scarcely be said to have destroyed, the Southern way of life based on the planter's world view. The sudden liberation of four million black men was viewed with alarm in the South.

The same fears existed in the North, for what was to prevent the newly freed black hordes from migrating North en masse, threatening the maintenance of racial purity and providing unwanted competition for jobs? Ironically, although Americans have always paid lip service to the notion that the black man is among America's earliest arrivals, at the level of objective social interaction, whites have always treated blacks as foreigners. Thus, Americans are startled by the reminder that the black man, being really white, black, and red, urban and rural, Southerner, Northerner, and Westerner, is par excellence, to borrow from Albert Murray, the omni-American.

However, the order of things had been upset in the North and in the large cities of the South before the Civil War. With the restrictions of slavery removed in the North and loosened in Southern cities by the relative ease of physical mobility in the city, ways other than those provided for in the slave codes had to be found to maintain white control. In North and South the white majority had imposed the color line. With the possible exception of some of the subtleties of race etiquette, virtually the whole system of segregation on the basis of color that emerged in the South in the post-bellum period existed in the North before the war. Black people were excluded from railroad cars and other public conveyances or were assigned to Jim Crow sections. They were permitted to sit only in designated parts of theaters, barred from entering hotels and restaurants, educated (when facilities existed at all) in segregated schools, punished in segregated prisons, nursed in segregated hospitals, and buried in segregated cemeteries. In Southern cities, where the problem of whites maintaining social distance from blacks within a limited physical space was especially acute, the situation was further complicated by the proximity of black freedmen and slaves. Whites feared that the system of social control so carefully nurtured by slavery would be undermined by such contact. This fear was reinforced by the greater freedom of movement in the city. Perhaps whites unconsciously realized that freedom of movement afforded the Negro, with his remarkable receptivity to change, an opportunity most conducive to the full flowering of his latent creative powers. In any event, since both freedmen and slaves were black, they were easily lumped together and segregated in the primary areas of life: housing, employment, worship, transportation, and recreation. The contour of the color line might vary with the community, but the line was always solid enough to be a constant reminder to Negroes of their inferior position.

Economic factors had been a cause of segregation in ante-bellum Southern cities. At issue was which race was going to be allowed to work in the city, a question increasingly answered in favor of white labor. But economic problems then were as nothing compared to those raised by Emancipation. Freedom meant to four million ex-slaves the power to move about, and they acted quickly to test it. They left the plantation (and perhaps returned) and moved from farm to farm, from cabin to town, and especially from country to city. This urban-directed movement posed a threat to whites in the cities. And, despite talk of importing foreign labor, it was clear to the planter class that it had immediate need of the black man to do the backbreaking labor of the South. Along with economic need existed fear of blacks among all classes of whites. Indeed, who could tell how, in his wandering, the Negro might try to upset the order of things? Would he not attempt reprisals for generations of suffering by rising up behind his holy men and falling on the master race in an orgy of murder and revenge? Whatever else he was seen to be in the mind of whites, the black man was in this regard given the attributes of man in all his fury. The planter class, therefore, hastily moved to reinstitute the bonds of authority that had been dissolved in the upheaval of war. The result was the Black Codes, an economic settlement along racial lines, which had as their intent the forced return of the black man to the plantation and his retention there in a new state of slavery. The Black Codes did not stand for long; they came too soon after Northern victory and flew too heavily in the face of Northern opinion. But achievement of the economic and racial purposes of the codes continued to be sought. In this the South received the help of the North.

Although Northern opinion had by 1866 forced abandonment of the Black Codes, whites North and South were by that time in firm agreement that there was to be no "forty acres and a mule" for the freedman. With a few, though increasing, number of exceptions, the black man would survive by continuing to work the soil for others.

Cotton pickers "weighing up" at the end of the work day. Courtesy of Culver Pictures.

But freedom was supposed to mean the opportunity to work free from the prying eye and imperious command of white bosses. And the planter preferred an arrangement other than the wage system, one that attached the laborer to the land for at least the crop season and forced him to share the risk of falling prices. So, facilitated by the federal Freedmen's Bureau, set up to aid the Negro in the transition from slavery to freedom, the interests of black laborer and white planter were brought together in the sharecropping system, in which the tenant or "cropper" received a percentage of the cotton crop in proportion to his investment in labor and equipment, the rest going to the landlord planter. Because of the steady decline of cotton prices in the last third of the nineteenth century, and because the illiterate cropper seldom brought more than his labor to the contract, the black tenant stood little chance of avoiding perpetual indebtedness to the country merchant (possibly the planter himself), who advanced supplies for the season in return for a lien on the crop. Except that the black man might escape its coils by leaving—an act fraught with peril—the new system was hardly more humane than its slave plantation predecessor. Croppers, both blacks and the growing number of whites who slipped into tenancy, made up the broad base of an agricultural system that was becoming increasingly capitalistic and that included planter, merchant-banker, and Northern capitalist.

As the planters became more enmeshed in the net of capitalism, the old prewar planter world view underwent subtle changes. Concern for a world of markets, railroads, and banks vied with concern for the local community. And though the old planter paternalism did not completely disappear, the planters of the New South were likely to be more concerned with Northern industrial values such as efficiency (which, they were convinced, the Negro cropper lacked) and with labor costs. The part of the old order that remained unchanged in the new, however, was the belief that blacks existed chiefly to serve whites.

The new economics reached its ultimate in harshness and violence in convict leasing and peonage. Originating in the turmoil of the war's aftermath, the leasing of prisoners, most of them Negroes convicted of petty theft, solved the problem of scarce jail facilities (doubtless made scarcer by segregation) and netted money-starved state and local governments profitable sums. Favored planters and railroad, mine, or forest operators were able to obtain the most defenseless of laborers and work them under conditions so brutal and inhumane that the death rate among prisoners in Arkansas, for example, was reported in 1881 to be 25 percent annually. Peonage laws, which took up where the discredited Black Codes left off, existed in all Southern states and required impoverished croppers to work off their debts. Convict leasing and peonage were conjoined when penurious blacks charged with misdemeanors were brought before unscrupulous judges who paid their fines in exchange for labor service and sold or leased their contracts. And since the hapless victims were likely thereafter to be pursued by a succession of trumped-up charges, a new form of involuntary servitude resulted. The depths of avarice had been plumbed. The black man was indeed in his economic "place."

In the face of Black Codes and Northern failure to carry through a policy of confiscation and redistribution of Southern land, blacks soon recognized their economic helplessness. They thought that perhaps through politics they could advance their interests, or at least protect themselves from the worst features of the new economic order. Black reconstruction promised such an opportunity.

The black cause had received support when Northern Republicans, led by a radical handful, realized that defeat in battle had not altered the opinion of Southern whites that blacks existed primarily to serve whites. The Radical Republicans knew that unless Southern blacks were enfranchised, continued Republican control of the federal government would be jeopardized. Bills were passed, and the Fourteenth and Fifteenth amendments, guaranteeing the black man his civil and political rights, were added to the Constitution. After a Republican administration withdrew the remaining troops in 1877, Republican coalitions—blacks, Southern whites, and Northern white immigrants—were kept in power in Southern states mainly by black votes. Realizing the value of office holding to the protection of their newly acquired rights, black men eagerly sought and frequently gained public office. Especially was this true at the local level, where, as aldermen, constables, tax assessors, justices of the peace, sheriffs, chancery and circuit clerks, and members of school boards and boards of supervisors, they were sometimes in a position to help protect the masses of poor black laborers. Unquestionably, they were hamstrung by the opposition of die-hard whites, whose control of economic resources remained complete. Doubtless, too, they were at times betrayed by their upbringing in a slave society and occasionally by their own incompetence. For all that, however, they were not without effect in preventing the grossest inequities. Consider the case of education.

Aside from making a living, education and civil rights remained the Negro's major concerns once it had become clear there was to be no substantial change in his relation to the land beyond emancipation from chattel slavery. Stress came to be laid on education as the path to a future free from economic dependence and inhuman physical toil. Private organizations, involving both blacks and whites, and the Freedmen's Bureau had worked hard during and after the war to dot the South with freedmen's schools. And Reconstruction governments, prodded by blacks and whites not blinded by bigotry, assumed responsibility for public education for all. Just as whites insisted on separate schools as the price for their support, so black political leaders strove, on the whole successfully, to prevent the inclusion in the new state constitutions of provisions sanctioning segregated schools. It was not that they were eager to have black children go to school with whites, for they shared to an extent the desire of their constituents to be free of white abuse and intimidation. However, they did fear that constitutional sanction of school segregation would result in shortchanging black schools of funds. In practice, so long as blacks exercised significant political power, the difference in financial support for black and white schools was minimal. But after blacks had been largely excluded from the ballot box and denied public office, the gulf became vast. For example, the per capita school expenditure for whites in North Carolina increased from $1.00 in 1876 to $1.91 in 1905, while that for blacks was $0.95 in both years. Without political power, what blacks ended up getting was an education intended by whites to keep them forever hewers of wood. But with all its deficiencies, the education they got encouraged a gifted few to go on, and some became black leaders wise in the ways of the whites.

New Codes for Separation

Although Reconstruction was a time when black people, supported by Northern will, achieved a limited measure of political power in the South, it was not a time when the walls of color caste came tumbling down. The building and maintenance of those walls had been a prime concern of whites of all classes from the moment of Emancipation, just as it had been in Southern cities before the war. As then, the problem during Reconstruction was to maintain as much physical and social separation as necessary to impress upon the black man his inferiority.

Despite disallowance of the Black Codes, which would have stabilized race relations as they had been under the slave codes, separation of the races went forward in all areas of life. Sometimes segregation was sanctioned by law; more often it was not, though it was no less effective on that account. By the end of Reconstruction, the new code had been pretty well worked out. As early as 1871, for example, Mississippi was called upon to face the question of what streets white and black children should use in their play. The existence of blacks in politics reinforced the determination of whites to strengthen the walls of color caste. Indeed, rather than transact public business with appropriate black officials, whites in many cases would deal only with white officials.

The desire for separation was not confined to whites. A Georgia Negro spoke for many black people when he stated in January 1865 that they preferred to live by themselves, because it would take years to eradicate the prejudice against them. They went to their own churches, sent their children to black schools, and preferred the isolation of the cropper's cabin to the supervision of the white boss. Even so, their leaders, unquestionably with their support, battled for civil as well as political equality in constitutional conventions, in legislatures, and in the streets. To the leadership as well as the followers, freedom meant equal and exact justice to all. As men and as men of affairs who paid taxes, they could not tolerate the stigma of caste or its inconveniences without at least attempting to push back the color line. Their attempts succeeded in incorporating civil rights provisions in the constitutions and statutes of the Southern states.

Backed by the law and emboldened by the federal presence, black leaders in urban communities with a sizable black middle class launched attacks to desegregate places of public accommodation. Beginning in 1867, for example, New Orleans Negroes, led by mulattoes who believed true equality and color caste to be incompatible, took to the streets and the courts in an assault on segregation in streetcars, restaurants and taverns, and the public schools. As much as anything, fears aroused by such actions—as indeed by black political activity generally—determined whites on violence and disfranchisement. The sight of black men acting like Americans in defense of their rights and interests was responsible for the brutality and violence that ended Reconstruction in the South.

Amid mounting violence in the South and continuing acts of discrimination in both the North and the South, the federal government, in its last significant effort at reconstruction, passed the Civil Rights Act of 1875, guaranteeing equal access to public places. Civil rights laws, together with the Negro's efforts to help himself, may have had some effect in slowing segregation. This appears to have been true, for example, in the case of streetcars, where black boycotts sometimes proved effective. The drift, however, was unfailingly toward ever tighter proscription.

Reconstruction ended when Northern opinion would no longer support it. In particular, Northern capital came to approve a policy of laissez faire toward the South. Many of the raw materials of the new industrialism— coal, iron, timber—were there, along with abundant sources of power. But most important, labor was plentiful and cheap. Reconstruction had proved this to Northern money men: blacks could be profitably employed as free labor. The dominant business wing of the Republican party was therefore more than willing in 1876 to give local government back to the Southern conservatives in return for the opportunity to exploit the resources of the South.

Social and Economic Upheaval

After the war, economic imperatives and hatred of blacks had operated in double harness to reinforce the inferior position of the Negro. But near the close of the century, despite the collapse of Reconstruction and the end of any semblance of Negro rule, the impact of new social and economic forces hastened change; class interest threatened to overcome color prejudice and possibly alter the position of the lowly black man.

The new social and economic forces stemmed from industrial capitalism and demography. The cotton kingdom of the New South identified much more with industrial values than had the Old South. Planter stress on efficiency and labor costs was largely a response to the depressed condition of the cotton market for much of the last quarter of the nineteenth century. Hoping to exercise greater control over the market, many planters supported the regional effort to bring textile mills to the cotton fields. The establishment of textile factories in the Carolinas and Georgia was part of a large pattern of economic diversification that included the expansion of railroads, the development of coal and iron mines and a lumber industry, and the establishment of cotton-seed oil, furniture, and paper manufacturing based on Southern resources. Agriculture continued to dominate the Southern economy, but the new industries had a significant impact on a growing number of local communities. They attracted some Northern capital, though much of it appears to have been local. One thing is certain: there was more than enough labor, black and white, to meet the demands of field and factory.

The labor surplus was a product of enormous population growth. In 1870 slightly less than 5,000,000 blacks lived in the South; by 1910 the number had reached 8,700,000. But the white increase was even greater. From

8,600,000 in 1870, their number soared to 20,500,000 in 1910, a feat accomplished without benefit of any substantial foreign immigration. This population explosion was one of the remarkable social forces of the age. Not only did it pose employment problems; it exacerbated black-white relations. The problem of space, which before the war had been a problem of the cities, became a problem of the entire South. People bumped into each other more often, and what was true of individuals was true of races.

Slowly at first, black youth began to leave black belt plantations, moving a few at a time into the cities and towns and finding employment in mines, turpentine camps, and tobacco factories, where the work was dirtiest and the pay lowest. At the same time, sons of white farmers engulfed by debt and falling prices began moving down from the hills and upland areas, sometimes sinking into tenancy, at other times finding work in the textile mills of the Piedmont, where they endured the hard lot of exploited labor as unprotestingly as any black man in the mines of northern Alabama. Moreover, led by a new breed of politician whose appeal combined the enthusiasm of the preacher with the racism of the untutored, whites in areas on the margins of the black belt and the uplands, where whites and blacks were elbowing each other for the first time under new and strange conditions, became rabid in their insistence on disfranchisement and legal segregation.

By the late 1880's, population pressures, declining farm prices, the evils of sharecropping, and the impact of industrial capitalism had combined to foster a spirit of protest and rebellion among Southern rural and urban laborers, both black and white. Hundreds of thousands of white farmers and tenants joined the Southern Farmers' Alliance movement to counter low prices and high transportation costs by the formation of cooperatives. Blacks, with white support, formed the Colored Farmers' Alliance and Cooperative Union, which claimed over one million members. While the alliance movement was spreading across the countryside, the Knights of Labor and, in the 1890's, the United Mine Workers made fleeting inroads among industrial workers, black and white. The American Railway Union confined its growing membership to whites, however.

When economic action was deemed insufficient in the early 1890's, dissidents among farmers and the new townsmen formed Populist, or People's, parties to wrest political rule from the conservative, business-oriented Democratic party, which had dominated Southern politics since the end of Reconstruction. Despite continued intimidation and violence, the black electorate remained a political factor in the South after 1877. White Populist leaders knew they must have the black vote or at least be able to neutralize it. They also hoped that recognition of a common economic interest would overcome antagonism toward color, and so they appealed for black-white political unity and moved to bring the black man into the party. Where this proved unfeasible, they endorsed "fusion" with the minority Republicans. In 1892 and again in

1894, Populists made substantial gains across the South, and where fusion triumphed, as in North Carolina, blacks were elected to office. At long last, it seemed, economic self-interest would prevail over hatred of color, and a new day in black-white relations was about to dawn.

Not since Reconstruction had the ruling party clique of politicians, land-owners, merchants, lawyers, and editors faced such a threat to their hegemony. Mixing concession, force, corruption, and strident appeals to racism, they proceeded to put it down. Always they stressed the threat to white supremacy: they dwelt on the danger of Negro rule; they depicted the "horrors" of Recon-struction; they ranted about the "evils" of miscegenation. They stuffed ballot boxes, herded compliant blacks to the polls, used their economic power to keep the noncomplying away from the polls.

Populists employed some of the same tactics, but they were no match for their opponents. Tarred with the brush of Negro rule, they remained on the defensive. In truth, they were soft on white supremacy. They believed that self-interest always controls, but they also believed that whites must lead and blacks follow. Though the white Southern Alliance wanted federal pro-tection against railroad abuses, it opposed the Lodge, or "Force," Bill of 1890, which sought to protect the voting rights of blacks in the South. The Populists continued to oppose federal regulation of voting procedures. The Colored Alliance supported adoption of the ill-fated bill.

In economics, too, the interests of the two alliances were dissimilar—more so than has commonly been assumed. Penniless croppers or farm labor-ers, most Colored Alliancemen could hardly have had the same enthusiasm as white Southern Alliancemen for currency reform. By the same token, South-ern Alliancemen, who tended to be farm owners, in 1891 opposed a Colored Alliance proposal for a general strike by cotton pickers for higher wages. Most blacks who voted free of intimidation undoubtedly continued to vote Republican. The Republicans won the Presidency in 1896, while the Dem-ocrats won most of the local elections in the South. Southern Populists never recovered from these defeats. In their anger they turned on the hapless Negro and joined in the growing movement toward disfranchisement and Jim Crow.

Southern Populism was largely undone by racism, of which Populists themselves were not free. Fear and hatred of blacks were simply too deeply embedded in white consciousness to yield to appeals for class solidarity. These feelings, which had been intensified in the years following Reconstruc-tion, were aggravated by conservative appeals to racism in the 1890's. The cause was the arrival, socially and economically, of the first black generation removed from slavery. Though the masses of blacks remained laborers and tenants, Negroes made modest gains in farm ownership. In Georgia, for ex-ample, the number of black landowners increased from 5,968 in 1888 to 16,716 in 1900, and the total black-owned acreage grew from 586,664 to 1,075,073 acres during these years. Cheated in the distribution of school funds after Reconstruction, Negroes still managed to reduce illiteracy drastically, send increasing numbers of their children to school to get the rudiments of an education, and provide the increasing number of teachers (28,560 in 1900) needed to instruct them. They continued to establish schools and colleges, many of which, like Tuskegee Institute, founded in 1881 by Booker T. Washington, were ostensibly devoted to industrial education. Along with those founded during Reconstruction, these colleges provided the nucleus of black teachers, who began organizing themselves professionally in the 1880's. In comparison with gains made by whites, these gains were pitifully small, and they were in no way commensurate with the problems facing the black population. But to many whites, confused and insecure in the swirl of change they were being caught up in, this much seemed clear: too many blacks were getting out of their place; they must be put back in it.

Nowhere was the black advance more dramatic than in Southern cities. Southerners did indeed remain overwhelmingly a country people; but, in addition to a few large cities, the region now contained countless small cities and towns, which, in the wake of industrial development, grew rapidly. All contained sizable black populations. In 1890, for example, Negroes were one-half of the population of the twelve major urban centers of North Carolina. They were one-third of Atlanta's 155,000 people in 1910. Thrust suddenly into the disorganized cities of the time, the new townsmen—black, mulatto, and white—rubbed together, and friction ensued. In 1906, amid augmented tales of criminal assaults by Negroes on white women and following a gubernatorial campaign filled with vilification of blacks, a race war broke out in Atlanta, and gangs of whites attacked and killed innocent blacks. A significant aspect of the riot was a white attack led by county police on the black middle-class suburb of Brownsville, ostensibly to disarm the Negroes, who were determined to defend themselves, but unquestionably to impress upon the "uppity" blacks and mulattoes the dangers of climbing out of their place. In addition to attractive and well-furnished homes, Brownsville included several black-owned stores, two black colleges, and a public school built with funds supplied by the residents themselves.

Indeed, over the years urban blacks had developed a thriving group life of their own. A few doctors, lawyers, and journalists, many of them graduates of black colleges, joined the other professionals—ministers and teachers—in the black middle class in the 1880's and 1890's. Black fraternal orders underwent an amazing growth in the 1880's, as black organizers traveled from town to town within the South. Out of these organizations emerged at the end of the century the first black insurance companies. Orphanages, homes for the aged, hospitals, and sanitariums were also established in many communities. Many of these humanitarian enterprises were the work of black women, who organized in 1895 as the National Association of Colored Women. Black group activity was designed to meet the life needs of black people in a Jim Crow world. It did not go unnoticed by whites, whose own position in a rapidly changing society was far from secure, and they determined that the black man's place must be clearly defined—by law if necessary.

Disfranchisement and Jim Crow

By the late 1880's, the crisis in Southern society had become acute. One response had been the farmers' alliances and Populist upsurge. A second response was disfranchisement and Jim Crow: the Negro was stripped of his remaining badges of citizenship. This time the process of humiliation was all-embracing; it included the new and fragile black middle class as well as the defenseless masses. Especially it included the aspiring blacks. To many whites the educated black man was the great menace to white supremacy, because he would not rest content to let the white man do his voting for him.

The two responses were not unrelated. In the eyes of many whites, both were attempts to purge Southern society of its economic and political ills. Moreover, the two occurred almost simultaneously. It was immediately after the farmers became an organized force in many Southern states in the 1880's that anti-Negro laws began to be enacted. In 1887, Florida and several other states passed Jim Crow laws requiring separation of the races on all passenger trains. Tennessee had already enacted such a law in 1881. Conservative Democrats in control in these states hoped that such measures would win the support of poor whites and help stem the tide of reform. They were a good beginning, but they were not enough for either conservatives or reformers. In Alabama in 1891, after reformers had begun to woo black voters along class lines, the conservatives proceeded to pass two more measures. One was the A. D. Sayre election law, which made it illegal to assist or instruct voters on procedural matters connected with state elections—a law estimated to have disfranchised 40,000 black voters. The second made railroad segregation lawful. The purpose was twofold: to strengthen the hold of the Democratic party on the white rank and file as the party of white supremacy and to warn the black man, particularly those of his leaders who were avowedly opposed to such legislation, that political activity could have negative consequences. The political debaucheries of succeeding years, as Democrats and Populists sought to nullify or manipulate the black vote for their own purposes, finally led both groups to seek purification of the political process by completely eliminating their innocent victims through constitutional revision.

Mississippi, not unusually, led the way in 1890. Recently migrated white farmers and townsmen—tired of conservative Democratic black belt domination of state politics through control over black voters—and conservative Democrats—facing the threat of federal regulation of elections in the Lodge Bill—joined forces to rewrite the state constitution to remove the Negro as a political factor. By imposing poll tax and literacy requirements, and even more by increasing the power of local registrars, the new constitution effectively got around the Fourteenth and Fifteenth amendments and disfranchised virtually *all* blacks, while continuing to permit ignorant whites to vote. Over the next two decades, state after state amended its constitution or enacted disfranchising statutes. Innovations such as white primaries and grandfather clauses (which enfranchised the sons and grandsons of those who had the right to vote on January 1, 1867) effectively barred the black man from voting and provided a loophole through which illiterate whites could enter the polling booth. With the vestiges of black political power removed, Jim Crow laws issued from Southern state capitals and city halls in great profusion.

From the turn of the century to America's entry into World War I, the Southern states, like the other states, battled corporate industrial influence, but they were just as busy warring against the black man. While Southern cities were concerned with municipal corruption, they were equally preoccupied with expanding the circle of segregation. The New South's dream of economic expansion was in the process of realization in this period, and this was reflected in the physical growth of cities and towns. Where before urban residential segregation had been more or less on a block-by-block basis, white civic leaders demanded larger segregated neighborhoods. Ordinances were passed barring blacks from purchasing homes in certain areas. A whole host of urban promoters and developers grew up with vested interests in segregation. Much of the voluminous body of Jim Crow legislation of the time of necessity dealt with the varied and complex problems of urban living. Whether in country or city, two societies, one black, the other white, existed in law as well as in custom.

The existence of two societies was also a fact of life in the North. Indeed, for the South to strip the Negro of the remnants of civil and political equality required Northern compliance. In case after case, beginning in the 1870's, the federal courts had gradually returned handling of race relations to the states, a process that culminated in 1896 in *Plessy v. Ferguson,* in which the Supreme Court approved separation of the races by state action provided accommodations were equal. In his Plessy opinion, Justice Henry B. Brown expressed well the North's view (which was the South's) of black-white relations when he said that the Fourteenth Amendment could not "enforce social, as distinguished from political equality, or a commingling of the two races upon terms unsatisfactory to either." Northern whites, to a greater extent than Southerners, viewed the black man as an economic competitor. The Negro did, after all, have an economic place in the South; he had none in Northern cities filling up with foreign ethnic groups. And labor unions, partly in reaction to his use as a strikebreaker but basically out of hatred of color and the desire to control entry into the job market, generally denied him access to the organized labor market.

Hatred of blacks and economic fears became more acute after 1900, when more blacks began arriving in Northern cities as part of the movement by the first postslavery generation out of the Southern fields. The growing antagonism in the North toward blacks did not, to be sure, take the form of disfranchisement and all-inclusive legal segregation, but it did express itself in race riots and more rigid neighborhood separation. And as in the South, Northern blacks turned increasingly to their own organized group life. The pattern of two societies was clearly discernible by 1917, when the first great migration of Negroes began. The North could pose no effective counterweight to Southern racism because it, too, was very much infected with that disease.

What Does It All Mean?

Incontestably, there has been economic exploitation by whites of blacks. Equally indisputable has been the existence of an arrogant, intellectualized belief in white racial superiority, which has decreed that a black is nonhuman. And the two over time have produced the separation of the races. But is this all that has come of it? Have not the components been compounded into something unforeseen by the separatists? For all their preoccupation with separation, have not blacks and whites profoundly affected each other? For whites, did not preoccupation with racial purity cause a great blindness to white Western inhumanity around the world? It was hardly coincidence that at the very time that black Americans were segregated legally and red Americans were being penned up in the arid wastes of the Western plains, the United States joined the other industrial nations of the world in taking up "the white man's burden." For all the talk of Christianizing and civilizing, the burden essentially involved a rapacious extension of technology and industrial values to the black and brown peoples of the world.

For blacks, paradoxically, did not white mistreatment enable them to retain their humanity? Denied access into the inner confines of technological society, they fell back on their own resources. Those resources were spiritual and aesthetic. They involved profound human elements: recognition of the absurd, tenuous nature of human existence, an appreciation of life's seasonal round, arrogant faith in the redemptive value of tragedy, and an inner resistance to oppression. These became the spiritual mainstays of a black life style that expresses itself in uninhibited joviality, in feasting and the art of cooking, in the freedom of black body movement, in the rhythms and improvisations of the blues, which more than anything else reflects the openness and remarkable adaptability of American Negroes.

American culture has been incontestably mulatto. There could have been no such thing as preserving white civilization, for in reality it did not exist. Nor has it been a simple case of whites doing the contributing and blacks the receiving. Whites as well as blacks took as well as gave. In Jim Crow, whites tried to run away from themselves and in the effort culturally deprived themselves of the reality of their heritage. Today, as technology threatens to overwhelm humanity, not only blacks but many whites have come to the realization that in the black response to dehumanization lie valuable lessons. In a physical sense Jim Crow was separatist. Inwardly, the results of commingling have been most enduring and profound. What does it all mean? Who, indeed, has been the master and who the slave?

2 SUGGESTIONS FOR FURTHER READING

Baker, Ray Stannard, *Following the Color Line**. New York: Doubleday, 1908.
■ A journalist's survey of race relations in America in the early 1900's.

Bond, Horace Mann, *Negro Education in Alabama: A Study in Cotton and Steel**.
Washington, D.C.: Associated Publishers, 1939. ■ A penetrating study of
the impact of social and economic interests on the education of black Americans.

Brotz, Howard, ed., *Negro Social and Political Thought, 1850–1920**. New
York: Basic Books, 1966. ■ The problems of black labor are a major theme
in this excellent collection of writings by black leaders.

Du Bois, W. E. B., *Black Reconstruction in America, 1860–1880**. New York:
Harcourt, 1935. ■ Mandatory reading for an understanding of the economics of the South, despite its rather Utopian visions of black and white proletarian
unity.

————, *Dusk of Dawn: An Essay Toward an Autobiography of a Race Concept**.
New York: Harcourt, 1940. ■ A discussion of the race problem as related to
the author's life.

Jacobson, Julius, ed., *The Negro and the American Labor Movement**. New York:
Doubleday, 1968. ■ Contains some excellent articles analyzing the interaction
of blacks with the labor movement in both the North and South during the late
nineteenth century.

Lewinson, Paul, *Race, Class and Party**. New York: Oxford University Press,
1932. ■ The racial and economic factors in the disfranchisement of the black
man are the primary concern of this fine work.

Litwack, Leon, *North of Slavery**. Chicago: University of Chicago Press, 1961.
■ An excellent study of pre–Civil War Jim Crow in the North.

---

* Available in paperback edition

Newby, I. A., *Jim Crow's Defense: Anti-Negro Thought in America, 1900–1930**. Baton Rouge: Louisiana State University Press, 1965. ▪ An analysis of the intellectual components of racism in the early twentieth century.

Nolen, Claude H., *The Negro's Image in the South: The Anatomy of White Supremacy**. Lexington: University of Kentucky Press, 1967. ▪ A lucid study of white attitudes toward the black man and their effect on white supremacy in the late nineteenth century.

Shugg, Roger, *Origins of Class Struggle in Louisiana**. Baton Rouge: Louisiana State University Press, 1939. ▪ A well-researched analysis of the many dimensions of black and white worker relationships before and after the Civil War.

Spero, Sterling D., and Harris, Abram L., *The Black Worker**. New York: Columbia University Press, 1931. ▪ A resourceful study that delineates a paradox of American labor thought: demand for black workers and simultaneous racial discrimination.

Wesley, Charles H., *Negro Labor in the United States, 1850–1925: A Study in American Economic History.* New York: Vanguard Press, 1927. ▪ A dated analysis, but highly useful for details on the early role of black labor in a changing economy.

Woodward, C. Vann, *Origins of the New South, 1877–1913.* Baton Rouge: Louisiana State University Press, 1951. ▪ A major study that examines the impact of post-Reconstruction economic forces on the South.

———, *The Strange Career of Jim Crow**. New York: Oxford University Press, 1966. ▪ A good description of the development of Jim Crow and its disfranchisement of most black Americans.

3

Resistance and Accommodation in Black Thought

The Gnawing Dilemma:
Separatism and Integration,
1865-1925

FRANCIS L. BRODERICK

Francis L. Broderick is chancellor and professor of history at the University of Massachusetts at Boston. He is author of *W. E. B. DuBois, Negro Leader in a Time of Crisis* (Stanford University Press, 1959) and numerous articles and short stories. In the essay that follows, Mr. Broderick shows that the Afro-American's quest for manhood, citizenship, and identity forced him to explore the roads of both separatism and integration. But while both paths failed black men as ultimate goals, the author maintains the time and the struggle have not been wasted. Mr. Broderick points out that by the end of the sixty years discussed in this essay, the Negro had come to what Du Bois described as a "manly self-assertion."

The North had triumphed; its victory in the Civil War meant that legal slavery had been buried beyond recall. In 1865 everyone understood that the elemental issue of personal physical freedom was settled. While white plantation owners counted their losses, the former slaves dreamed of the future: today freedom meant they could move to the next turn in the road, to the next county, to the next state. Tomorrow it might mean some acres of their own and a steady cash income large enough to provide wholesome food and direct shelter. The day after tomorrow it might even mean education, security, and the full human dignity of American citizenship. If the North's victory did not guarantee fulfillment of these hopes—and it did not—at least it made them the normal goals.

The journey to equality would be long, the route uncertain. The 400,000 free Negroes who had lived in both the North and the South before the Civil War could have told their newly freed brethren that technical freedom did not bring the vote, even in most Northern states. The testimony of a black man, when admitted at all in state courts, was likely to be discounted when weighed against a white man's. Many Northern schools refused to educate Negroes. For the most part, Negroes plodded through the dreary life of the poor primarily as servants, laborers, or marginal farmers, and more rarely as artisans, small businessmen, or professionals (such as ministers) serving the needs of the black community. Regardless of their position in life, they could expect routine slights in their daily contacts with whites.

Now, to a widely scattered free Negro population, the war suddenly added 3,500,000 new souls, mainly uneducated rural laborers in the newly impoverished Southern countryside. Frederick Douglass, the black abolitionist whose voice carried far in the pre–Civil War period, spoke for many in his race when, in May 1865, he warned the American Anti-Slavery Society that, Thirteenth Amendment or no Thirteenth Amendment, the society's work was not yet done: "Slavery is not abolished until the black man has the ballot. While the legislatures of the South retain the right to pass laws making any discrimination between black and white, slavery still lives there."[1]

Four million people faced that new form of living slavery. Their shared color and experience of oppression led Negroes to identify with their race at the expense of, or even to the exclusion of, all loyalties beyond race and family—a separatist position. At the same time, they desired the freedom that America promised to every individual; they looked to the day when black men would be fully recognized as American citizens, the color of their skin as irrelevant to their civic status as the color of their eyes—an integrationist position.

Together the two ideas led the Negro into paradoxes and contradictions. To gain his rights as an American citizen, to make his voice heard and his will felt, he associated himself with other Negroes. Ironically, in this process of association he set aside the goal of an America of freestanding individuals. On the other hand, if he stood aloof from other Negroes, saying that he had no more in common with them than with other Americans, he withheld his contribution to the united effort needed to secure his status as a freestanding American individual. With every decision, this dilemma gnawed at his peace of mind.

During this period between 1865 and 1925, while white Americans created the conditions of the struggle, black Americans, responding to the challenges of manhood and citizenship, ranged the gamut from integration to separation in quest of an identity that offered more than merely technical, physical freedom.

From Slavery to Caste

In the fall of 1895, Booker T. Washington, principal of the Tuskegee Institute in Alabama, assured a predominantly white audience at the Atlanta

---

[1] Frederick Douglass, "The Need for Continuing Anti-Slavery Work," in Philip S. Foner, ed., *The Life and Writings of Frederick Douglass,* 4 vols. (New York: International Press, 1955), 4:167.

Exposition that there need be no antipathy between the black and white races, for "in all things that are purely social we can be as separate as the five fingers, yet one as the hand in all things essential to mutual progress."[2] From that day Washington became a national figure, and from that speech Negro thought took on a new cast for most of a generation. If in many ways the speech was a triumph, it was also a sad capitulation to the thirty years of pressure that followed the Civil War.

Immediately after the war, Negro voices spoke joyously of a new birth of freedom. The bitterness of the war they hoped to put behind them, just as they hoped that their former masters and other fellow citizens would draw a screen over the days of slavery and that the two races would live a new life of equal partnership. They saw the issue of Negro suffrage as the true test of American democracy and, therefore, of America's capacity to lead the world in developing institutions blind to race and color.

The Republican Congress gave Negroes firm ground for hope. Acting from motives that ranged from desire for vengeance against the South, through lust for political gain, to the highest idealism about the rights of man, Radical Republicans forced the two major Reconstruction acts and the Fourteenth Amendment through Congress: former Confederates were barred from office and even from the polls until they had been pardoned. Having cut down the numbers of the enemy, the Radicals then sought out new friends to buttress the Republican majority in Congress. Their eye fell on the millions of newly liberated Negroes. Both civic virtue and political wisdom endorsed the Negro's right to vote. If the Negro was to become a full citizen, if the subordinate caste to which he had been confined for two hundred years was to disappear, if he was to function as a man in America, then he must have his rights as a citizen, most of all the right to vote, the guarantee of all other rights. So much for civic virtue. Political awareness led the Republican Congress to the same conclusion; they could never maintain a position of power in the South without black votes. The Fifteenth Amendment, though late in coming, seemed to tie up the tidy package of civic equality.

The mood of this legislation encouraged the notion of absorbing the Negro into American political life, a view that became increasingly associated with the name of Frederick Douglass. Douglass correctly saw that Appomattox had ended one struggle—the fight against slavery—only to begin another: the struggle for equality. His approval of Radical Reconstruction was tempered by an awareness of the gap between legislative promise in Washington and real achievement in the South. Yet he recognized that Negro political activity was growing, and he appreciated the Republicans' role in this process. "The Republican ship is the deck; all else is open sea,"[3] he proclaimed—a judg-

---

[2] Booker T. Washington, *Up From Slavery* (New York: Doubleday, 1902), pp. 221–22.

[3] Booker T. Washington, *Frederick Douglass* (New York: Haskell House, 1968), p. 286.

ment that thoughtless repetition soon made into a sterile slogan. The Republicans, even after they had forfeited their claim to this accolade, managed to hold Douglass' loyalty through a succession of minor political jobs. Until his death in 1895, Douglass continued to see politics as a means to Negro advancement, as a way to solve what he sometimes called "the white problem."

For many years after the Civil War, most articulate Negroes held the same view, even when they did not regard the Republican party as the ark of salvation. T. Thomas Fortune, for example, used his *New York Age,* perhaps the most prominent Negro newspaper of the era, to argue the virtues of political independence: dangle the Negro vote between the two major parties, to tempt the Democrats to make concessions and to warn Republicans not to take the Negro vote for granted. Both views, Douglass' defense of the Republicans and Fortune's wary nonpartisanship, looked anxiously toward the absorption of blacks into the customary political processes of White America.

Yet even Douglass and Fortune recognized that progress toward political integration required separate Negro organization. Fortune's pithy slogan for political success—"Race first; then party"—summarized in four words the political dilemma of black men who wanted to absorb and be absorbed by American culture, but who could not ignore their identity as a separate community. As Fortune urged his readers to use their political clout to extract a response to Negro needs—no support until street lights in Negro areas were fixed or until schools ceased to be racially segregated—he also confirmed in them a sense of separateness from their white neighbors. Some blacks, irritated by the call for united action, decried Negro gatherings and denied the existence of a Negro interest independent of any other citizen's interest. Douglass dismissed this view as "either baseness or imbecility." Perhaps he was the more indignant because he sensed the fundamental ambivalence of this political position; for how could Negroes decry the color line that they themselves preserved and extended by their separatist activities? Douglass thought he had the answer:

> We may yet congratulate ourselves upon the fact, that the laws and institutions of the country are sound, just and liberal. There is hope for a people when their laws are righteous, whether for the moment they conform to their requirements or not. But until this nation shall make its practice accord with its Constitution and its righteous laws, it will not do to reproach the colored people of this country with keeping up the color line—for that people would prove themselves scarcely worthy of even theoretical freedom, to say nothing of practical freedom, if they settled down in silent, servile and cowardly submissions to their wrongs, from fear of making their color visible. They are bound by every element of manhood to hold conventions, in their own name, and on their own behalf, to keep their grievances before the people and make every organized protest against the wrongs inflicted upon them within their

power. They should scorn the counsels of cowards, and hang their banner on the outer wall.[4]

Douglass never lost faith in his Republican sponsors, nor, thereby, in the political process. Indeed, as he grew older, he became more insistent on integration as the goal and on uninterrupted public protest as the route.

But Douglass' world was changing far more rapidly than his perception of it. The Republican party of the North lost interest in Negroes when it learned it could count on political allies in the West and Midwest to produce a national majority. At almost the same time the Northern industrialists, so influential in the Republican party, found that they could do business with the new entrepreneurial class emerging in the South. State by state the white South wrested control of the governmental machinery from coalitions of Negroes, dissident white Southerners, and transplanted Northerners and restored to power the traditional ruling class, now supplemented by a new generation of Southern entrepreneurs. The Compromise of 1877 completed the process: federal troops were removed from the last three Southern states, and the last Radical regimes collapsed. As late as 1890 a Northern senator spoke in favor of sending troops back into the South; but no one, possibly not even the senator himself, took seriously the possibility that the nation would try to compel by force of arms the postwar promise of political power for Southern Negroes.

Thus the Negro's political force eroded. White men did not unanimously conspire to restore Negroes to a subservient caste; but gradually, a white group in this state or that found reasons and ways to disfranchise its poor black citizens (and sometimes its poor white citizens as well). For example, Thomas E. Watson, the Populist leader of Georgia, began his career as a champion of Negro suffrage; he ended it as one of the most startlingly articulate racists in that highly competitive era. At first the white South used violence to prevent Negro voting: hooded riders with a fiery cross, whips, shotguns. Trickery served the same purpose more genteelly through stuffed ballot boxes and complicated voting practices. Finally, beginning with Mississippi in 1890, Southern states, ignoring protests of black legislators, adopted new constitutions that, with one transparent device or another, successfully ruled out Negro votes.

Even before this development, and certainly all the more after 1890, segregation in public facilities became the custom and then the law. The move came earliest in education—first the separation of the races, then the conveniently disparate allocation of public funds. W. E. B. Du Bois, as a student at Fisk University, received $30 a month for teaching in a public school in backcountry Tennessee during the summer of 1885. His sporadically attended

---

[4] *National Convention of Colored Men at Louisville, Kentucky, September 24, 1883* (Louisville, 1883), quoted in Herbert Aptheker, ed., *A Documentary History of the Negro People in the United States,* 2 vols. (New York: Citadel Press, 1966), 2:660–61.

classes were the only education his black pupils had for that year. From schools, legal segregation spread to other public facilities like tramways and libraries, and then to the private sector — to factories and shops. Negroes were accustomed to more or less voluntary segregation in fraternal organizations like the Odd Fellows, in burial associations and insurance cooperatives and in early ventures in banking, in the wide range of social activities that clustered around churches, where they found the related joy of associating with people with whom they were unguardedly comfortable. But the separate life that brought joy when sought voluntarily became a brand of bitter oppression when forced from the outside.

As the dark night of discrimination and segregation settled over the South, Frederick Douglass' dogged assertion of Negro rights became increasingly separated from the reality of his people's plight. Yet he never stopped insisting that Negroes accept nothing less than their full rights. Douglass could accept the separatism necessary to assert the Negro's demands. But he looked upon this unity only as a tool by which each individual Negro would one day become part of the greater unity that was America. Toward the end of his life, although disfranchisement and segregation were well on their way, Douglass' voice continued clearly and resolutely. But fewer people heard: White America had all but stopped listening, and Black America could not turn his passion into straw and bricks.

A Temporary Holding Action

Booker T. Washington, however, understood about straw and bricks. The product of one industrial school and the principal of another, he spoke at the Atlanta Exposition of 1895 in the rhetoric of uplift familiar to Negroes and at the same time so reassuring to whites. The Exposition, designed to celebrate the South's economic comeback after the war, had arranged for a display on Negro progress, and Washington appeared as "a representative of Negro enterprise and Negro civilization." A heavy, stolid, cautious man decked out in a dark suit and an accommodating manner, he urged the white South to turn to Negro labor as "the most patient, faithful, law-abiding, and unresentful people that the world has seen."[5] Of his own people he said:

> Ignorant and inexperienced, it is not strange that in the first years of our new life we began at the top instead of at the bottom; that a seat in Congress or the state legislature was more sought than real estate or industrial skill; that the political convention or stump speaking had more attractions than starting a dairy or truck garden. . . . Our greatest danger is that in the great leap from slavery to freedom we may overlook the fact that the masses of us are to live by the production of our hands, and fail to keep in mind that we shall prosper in proportion as we learn to dignify and glorify common labor and put brains and skill into the common occupations of life; shall

[5] Washington, *Up From Slavery*, pp. 218–19.

prosper in proportion as we learn to draw the line between the superficial and the substantial, the ornamental gewgaws of life and the useful. No race can prosper till it learns that there is as much dignity in tilling a field as in writing a poem. It is at the bottom of life we must begin, and not the top. Nor should we permit our grievances to overshadow our opportunities.[6]

The path up for the Negro, in other words, was the familiar route of nineteenth-century sermons—self-help through moral righteousness, thrift, and hard work. To these Washington added a fourth prescription: friendly relations with white neighbors. Blacks had heard these virtues touted as long as they had been listening to their own ministers or reading their own newspapers or tuning in on the surrounding white culture. During a period that Rayford W. Logan, the historian, has called the "nadir" of Negro history, Washington cheerfully urged his people to seek the benign interest of their white neighbors, who, he believed, could not fail to be impressed with good workers, good work, and good will. Washington's immense appeal to white men, North and South, lay in his reassurance that the day when the Negro would claim his rights was still remote:

> The wisest among my race understood that the agitation of questions of social equality is the extremest folly, and that progress in the enjoyment of all the privileges that will come to us must be the result of severe and constant struggle rather than of artificial forcing. . . . It is important and right that all privileges of the law be ours, but it is vastly more important that we be prepared for the exercises of these privileges. The opportunity to earn a dollar in a factory just now is worth infinitely more than the opportunity to spend a dollar in an opera-house.[7]

At Atlanta and over the next twenty years, Washington urged Negroes to follow a policy of integration. Washington maintained and his defenders ever since have insisted that he was no less diligent than Frederick Douglass in asserting that Negroes should enjoy all the "privileges" of America. But Washington used a different tactic and sought assimilation at a level quite different from Douglass'. He proposed that Negroes accommodate themselves to the dominant society on terms that whites found acceptable. Those terms did not face up to the cultural values of Negro society itself; they deferred to a distant future the enjoyment of full equality. For the present, they defined Negro aspiration exclusively in terms of the most menial manual labor and small enterprise; the dream of spending money in an opera house—Washington's own example—or equality before the law and in society was postponed to some future moment sufficiently remote to pose no threat to Southern whites. Moreover, Washington and his followers ignored cooperative black action as a distinctive political program.

---

[6] Ibid., p. 220.
[7] Ibid., pp. 223–24.

Washington put together a package that was attractive to the South's rulers. The region was turning to industry, and Washington offered the South a black labor force that was cheap and docile. The South feared an independent and self-conscious bloc of Negro votes, as the disfranchising constitution of Mississippi had already demonstrated. Washington consented to disfranchisement for the time being; elsewhere he piously said that the same provisions should apply equally to whites and blacks. In fact, no one expected equal treatment to occur. Washington put off agitation for social equality as "extremest folly," and his judgment was a self-fulfilling prophecy, since he would not even fight openly for the vote. Well might the governor of Georgia pump Washington's hand after the speech at the Atlanta Exposition. Well might President Cleveland say that the Exposition would have justified itself if it had done nothing more than provide the occasion for the speech.

The instant white acclaim and the burst of philanthropy that followed the Atlanta speech, together with Washington's indefatigable political skill, made him the leading Negro power broker until his death in 1915. Acclaim and power gave him standing among his own people, and his careful cultivation of the Negro press, of businessmen, and of local farm organizations gave him an ever ready audience.

Even as he spoke publicly of second-class citizenship, in practice he worked closely with such racially organized groups as the Afro-American Council, the National Negro Business League, and the Tuskegee-based Negro Farmers' Conferences. All these organizations assumed a cohesive Negro group that saw value, if not necessarily virtue, in racial self-help. At a moment when political progress had halted and respect for the Negro was at a new low, these organizations hoped that economic self-help could at least turn up a few coins.

Dissent came from a small band of Negro militants who felt that a few coins were not enough. What is personal humiliation compared to a chance to earn a living, W. E. B. Du Bois (then a professor of sociology at Atlanta University) asked sarcastically in 1904. "Earn a living; get rich, and all these things shall be added unto you. Moreover, conciliate your neighbors, because they are more powerful and wealthier, and the price you must pay to earn a living in America is that of humiliation and inferiority."[8] The following year, in response to an invitation from Du Bois, twenty-nine Negro business and professional men launched the Niagara Movement to challenge Washington's pervasive power. The men of Niagara scorned Washington's conciliatory prose and bluntly voiced the full range of black demands: manhood suffrage, equal treatment in public places, equal access to jobs (rather than "peonage and virtual slavery" in the rural South and exclusion from unions

---

[8] W. E. B. Du Bois, "The Negro Problem from the Negro Point of View," Part 5, "The Parting of the Ways," *World Today* 6 (April 1904): 522.

in the North), adequate educational resources at all levels, equal justice in courts, churches that did not "segregate black men to some outer sanctuary," and support for "persistent manly agitation" as the "way to liberty."[9] The thrust of the Niagara appeal was toward white society, demanding that White America open itself equally to all its citizens, black and white.

The Niagara Movement, unable to meet its organizational expenses, never really got moving. Its significance lies in its clear rejection of Washington's facile accommodation of white society and in its status as a precursor of the National Association for the Advancement of Colored People, formed in 1909. Quite a few Niagara men aligned themselves with the NAACP. Most prominent of these was Du Bois himself, who, in 1910, left Atlanta University to become director of research and publications for the NAACP and editor of the organization's monthly journal, the *Crisis.*

The NAACP, in its early years overwhelmingly black in membership and predominantly white in leadership, looked toward the full integration of black citizens. Through nationwide organization, formal lobbying, legal action in the courts, and an extensive propaganda campaign directed at White America, the NAACP hoped to topple the walls of prejudice in America.

Du Bois, sensitive and thoughtful as he was, viewed integration more subtly. A Northerner with one degree from Fisk and three from Harvard, he had lived for many years in Massachusetts and in Georgia. He had written history and sociology, not to mention poetry, short stories, essays, and speeches beyond count. He knew black culture and white, and he saw strengths and weaknesses in both. Thus he refrained from any simple choice between separatism and integration:

> One ever feels his two-ness,—an American, a Negro; two souls, two thoughts, two unreconciled strivings; two warring ideals in one dark body, whose dogged strength alone keeps it from being torn asunder. The history of the American Negro is the history of this strife,—this longing to attain self-conscious manhood, to merge his double self into a better and truer self. In this merging he wishes neither of the older selves to be lost. He would not Africanize America, for America has too much to teach the world and Africa. He would not bleach his Negro soul in a flood of white Americanism, for he knows that Negro blood has a message for the world. He simply wishes to make it possible for a man to be both a Negro and an American, without being cursed and spit upon by his fellows, without having the doors of opportunity closed roughly in his face.[10]

Du Bois worked with the NAACP, and his columns in the *Crisis* supported the integrationist views of the predominantly middle-class black membership and the black and white board of directors. At the same time

---

[9] *The Niagara Movement, Declaration of Principles, 1905,* Schomburg Collection, New York Public Library, New York, N.Y.

[10] Du Bois, *The Souls of Black Folk* (Chicago: McClurg, 1903), pp. 3–4.

he held on to certain ideas about Negro separatism that accorded ill with the professed integrationist stance of his organization. A people must work out its own destiny, he said: "Conscious self-realization and self-direction is the watchword of modern man, and the first article in the program of any group that will survive must be the great aim, equality and power among men."[11] Negroes had to create their own loan associations, cooperatives for production and distribution, and charitable organizations; they had to create their own poetry and painting; they even had to form their own political party. The NAACP itself had to be captured for Negro objects, Negro aims, Negro ideals.

The ambiguity of Du Bois' position as an employee and also a critic of the NAACP accurately reflected the dilemma facing advocates of Negro progress. A segregated institution might serve as a stimulus to Negro endeavor. Black schools and colleges, for example, provided work for Negro teachers who found white institutions closed to them and offered Negro students opportunities to learn that they would never have had otherwise. Yet the presence of separate black institutions for black students reduced the pressure on white schools and colleges to admit Negroes and postponed the day when institutions would be neither black nor white but simply available for all. At the same time, a reverse logic applied to jobs. Most jobs above the menial level were in modern industry, not in the handicraft trades taught at Tuskegee. A Negro breakthrough into the market of skilled jobs in heavy industry was vital; it would not only increase the earnings of the Negroes who obtained those jobs but, as they exercised their new purchasing power and the money passed from hand to hand, the impact would be felt throughout the black community. A step toward an integrated work force thus became identical with economic progress, progress unlikely to occur if Negroes had to form their own big business enterprises, their own United States Steel Corporation. Who, then, was to weigh the immediate gains from segregated institutions against the slower, more tortuous route of integration? The scales tipped back and forth, swayed by evidence, need, and ambition. Here was a dilemma, said Du Bois, calling for "thought and forebearance."

The New Search for Freedom

With the death of Washington in 1915, Du Bois used his prominent editorial position on the *Crisis* and the nationwide exposure of his annual speaking tours to become the Negro's most prominent spokesman. World War I gave him a dramatic chance to use the strategies of both integration and separatism. Without hesitation, he lobbied for segregated Negro officer training camps, for he was certain that Negro officers would be produced in no other way. Then he came to see in the idealism of the war an unprec-

---

[11] Du Bois, "The Immediate Program of the American Negro," *Crisis* 9 (April 1915): 310–12.

edented opportunity to advance the Negro's cause. As Negro troops were trained under Negro officers, as Woodrow Wilson spoke out against lynching, as segregation declined here and there, as employment and income rose, Du Bois rejoiced to see the new day when "the walls of prejudice crumble before the onslaught of common sense and racial progress."[12] Negroes forgot their grievances and fought for "our country" and "our war," he said; they closed ranks "gladly and willingly with . . . eyes lifted to the hills."[13] The crisis of war, Du Bois believed, had led America to outgrow racial discrimination, to get caught up in the idealism of the war for democracy, to prepare the way for a just society at home.

Du Bois miscalculated. The height of his wartime hope was the measure of his postwar despair. Far from outgrowing racial discrimination, the American Federation of Labor (AFL) bluntly labeled skilled black workers "scabs." Reflecting on the spent idealism of the war for democracy, a wrathful Du Bois found evidence of officially encouraged discrimination wherever American Negro troops had set foot in Europe. The just society at home somehow had to be squared with the two dozen race riots that occurred in American cities in the bloody summer and fall of 1919. Angry and humiliated at having been taken in, Du Bois openly spoke of Negro violence as a conscious weapon of defense.

Neither anger nor violence helped. Finally Du Bois voiced his despair: "Fools, yes that's it. Fools. All of us fools fought a long, cruel, bloody and unnecessary war and we not only killed our boys — we killed Faith and Hope."[14] Now Negroes knew that there was no "royal road" to emancipation. "It lies rather in grim, determined, everyday strife."[15]

The grimness of the strife, its daily fervor, its urgency, did not clarify its tactics. The NAACP, committed to integration as both possible and desirable, continued its persistent assault on white discrimination, using extensive research to mobilize public opinion against lynching and to petition Congress for an effective antilynching bill, fighting the spread of segregation in Northern schools, plying the courts with test cases to break down the disfranchising provisions of Southern constitutions, reaching out to the AFL for conversations about black jobs. Nationally, the Urban League sought employment and housing for Negroes, its efforts depending substantially on white favor, its results showing more in individual cases than in overall improvement of the status of the Negro in America. In the South, the Commission on Interracial Cooperation sought to join blacks and whites in projects that would reduce tensions and benefit the Negro. But these efforts were

---

[12] Du Bois, unsigned editorial in *Crisis* 15 (December 1917): 77.

[13] Du Bois, unsigned editorials in *Crisis* 16 (August 1918): 164, *Crisis* 16 (July 1918): 3.

[14] Du Bois, "The Judge," *Brownies' Book* 2 (February 1921): 41.

[15] Du Bois, unsigned editorial in *Crisis* 20 (February 1920): 213.

peripheral to the larger black needs, insignificant side skirmishes that left untouched the desperate poverty felt by Negro workers and farmers and their families. The daily gain was small, and even a year's efforts could yield no more than a few isolated achievements. Who could say with confidence that integration was any nearer at the end of the year? A thousand new jobs in the automobile industry would not even balance the normal growth in population, and a school prevented, at great cost, from becoming segregated left unchallenged thousands of schools where the battle for integration had not even begun. The old slogans of integration were threadbare, but, in the aftermath of World War I, integrationists came up with nothing new.

Those who favored separation had more dramatic ideas. Du Bois, ever the vibrant, restless seeker, reached beyond his entente with white American liberals to associate the Negro with black Africa. In 1919 a pan-African conference that he organized in Paris gained some attention from the peace delegations there, and throughout the decade Du Bois tried, with less and less success, to interest Black America in the rising tide of anticolonial sentiment elsewhere in the world and to promote a sense of community with nonwhite colonial rebels everywhere. Du Bois' pan-African ideas were brilliantly prophetic of the world after 1945; in the 1920's they were scarcely more than a reflection of his alienation from American life.

His disillusionment after the war turned Du Bois toward Negro separatism at home. At the same time that he looked to the world beyond America, he looked anew at the Negro community as a separate culture. To preserve that separate culture, colleges worthy of the race were necessary. When white philanthropy to Negro colleges fell off after the war, Du Bois welcomed the loss of support as an opportunity to throw off subservience to white donors and to establish Negro pride in Negro culture. He snarled at Fisk, Lincoln, and Howard universities for their timidity. When three-quarters of the students at Fisk, Du Bois' own university, walked out in protest against white discrimination, Du Bois reported exultantly that he was "uplifted by the student martyrs at Fisk." Here was "real radicalism of the young—radicalism that costs, that is not mere words and foam."[16] He felt confident that the Negro students had caught a glimpse of their own roles as leaders of a separate Negro culture.

Meanwhile, a substantial literary force known as the Harlem Renaissance, or the New Negro movement, was aiming at the same cultural separatism. Like Du Bois, other black writers and artists felt the immobilizing chill of white intransigency after the war. And there were enough of them, even in New York alone, to reply to white superiority with haughty disdain for everything except the black culture they sought to capture in line or in word. Ironically, the "New Negro" drew much of his support from white patrons. Indeed, it was white markets and white publishers that permitted the move-

---

[16] Du Bois, unsigned editorial in *Crisis* 29 (April 1925): 250.

ment to thrive outside racially oriented magazines like the *Crisis*. Nevertheless, the substance of the artistic resurgence came from Negro themes, Negro traditions, Negro life. Harlem's writers insisted on giving dignity to Negro culture as a separate entity. The picture was not always pretty: Claude McKay in *Home to Harlem* presented a lascivious view of black lower-class life, and in *Banjo* he satirized the black upper class. George Schuyler's *Black No More* hilariously lampooned Negro leaders. Still, all the writers of the Harlem Renaissance treated Negro culture seriously, not as a bizarre refraction of white society or a servile appendage to white life, not as a dark mystery shrouded in delicacy and reassurance, but as a culturally complete society — varied, lusty, joyous, and tragic. In the next decade, when Du Bois was to champion the idea of an internally self-sufficient Negro economic community, he would call upon Negro writers to serve as its heralds.

Du Bois' pan-Africanism and the New Negro movement touched only a handful of people — literate people who cared, affluent people who bought books, dedicated people who made the fight against racial inequality an important aspect of their lives. By contrast, Marcus Garvey reached many thousands with a movement that defiantly set black against white and spoke of moving the whole colored population out of the country. Garvey founded the Universal Negro Improvement Association (UNIA) in 1914 in his native Jamaica. During the war he organized a chapter in New York, and by 1919 his organization had more than thirty branches in the United States. Garvey's appeal reached the streets of America just as massive numbers of blacks were emigrating to the cities, especially Northern cities. After 1918, Garvey preached a new gospel to a population scarred by the war years and later by the horrors of the Red Summer of 1919: the beauty of black. If the message of the riots in East St. Louis and Chicago was that the Negro should stay in his place, Garvey had a new answer: the Negro should emigrate, bag and baggage, out of America and pour his strength into making Africa one mighty, redeemed nation.

Garvey was certainly a showman, and possibly a charlatan. He was also the greatest mass leader that the Negroes in America have known. They listened to Washington. They built on Du Bois. Garvey they thronged around. To a race drilled in its own inferiority, he offered racial pride in a remote past that included a black God and a black Christ. He aroused confident hope in a not too remote future when, as provisional president of the empire of Africa, he would lead his people to the promised land. He introduced drama into the lives of urban dwellers crammed pitilessly in slums. To people whose plodding steps toward integration never carried them into a home of their own, he gave an alternate philosophy of racial separatism that allowed them to scorn the whites and the "caste aristocracy" of Negro college graduates (Garvey had Du Bois very much in mind). For their diffuse bitterness, he supplied apt targets. For a sense of not belonging, he substituted a coherent community that included, under UNIA auspices, restaurants and grocery stores. After Garvey was jailed for fraud in his ill-fated Black Star Steamship Company, his grandiose schemes collapsed. Little remained— little, that is, except the stark fact that tens of thousands of black Americans, alienated by the oppression of white society, found more reality in his implausible promises of a separate black life than they had ever found in the promises of integration into American life.

The Enduring Dilemma

Sixty years after freedom was technically achieved, the goal of equality still eluded the black community. Even worse, no road led clearly to the goal; no leader had yet drawn a plausible map. Violence in response to violence gave a moment of release, but the long-range odds in a nation that was 90 percent white cast doubt on violence as a viable racial tactic. Emigration promised relief from the inequities of White America, but would black Africa welcome its brothers, and could anyone really come up with solutions to the immense logistical problems involved? Complete commitment to integration yielded dubious results slowly, and at no small cost to the culture of the black man. Full-fledged Negro separatism helped foster racial pride, but it mocked the promises of the America that belonged to blacks as well as to whites. No one, not even Du Bois, arrived at a satisfactory solution to the dilemma of integration and separatism; the advantages and the drawbacks always seemed to cancel one another out.

Yet in sixty years, the Negro had progressed: in numbers, in skills, in education, in wealth, in pride, in what Du Bois called "manly self-assertion," in acceptance as a citizen and as a person. In a triumph of pragmatism over ideology, an increasing number of black men had moved upward, frequently at an indecently high cost, and had reached new levels that were a source of pride to the white community as well as to themselves. The sixty years before 1925 formed a historical background, a memory, for the sixty years that were to follow. That memory suggests, perhaps, that neither separatism nor integration is a useful ultimate goal, but that devices springing from both can prove productive in moving the nation toward a goal that will not be clearly defined until it has been achieved.

The Flowering of Black Nationalism: Henry McNeal Turner and Marcus Garvey

EDWIN S. REDKEY

Edwin S. Redkey, associate professor of history at the State University of New York College at Purchase, is the author of *Black Exodus: Black Nationalist and Back-to-Africa Movements, 1890–1910* (Yale University Press, 1969) and the editor of *Respect Black! The Writings and Speeches of Henry McNeal Turner* (Arno Press, 1971). In the following essay, Mr. Redkey shows that the frustrations and failures of accommodation and protest—tactics of most Negro leadership following the Civil War—prompted the growth of Back to Africa movements among Afro-Americans. He examines the important but little-known movement led by Bishop Henry McNeal Turner and the more familiar crusade of Marcus Garvey and emphasizes the broad mass support of both leaders. Assessing their effectiveness, Mr. Redkey suggests that they helped inspire a sense of black nationalism that will continue to be a strong influence on Afro-Americans.

Afro-Americans have reacted in different ways to the problems they have faced in the United States. Quite understandably, many have tried to get along as best they can, eking out a living, trying to avoid trouble, never losing hope for a better day. Others have protested to whites, asking for fair treatment, civil rights, and integration into American life. And others have militantly called for separation from whites, unity and pride in the black community, and a new political arrangement in which they control their own destinies. This last approach, generally labeled "black nationalism," has taken a number of different forms through the years, but the basic elements of black separatism and solidarity, race pride and political independence, have always been recognizable.

Some black nationalists have called for all-black states, cities, or towns within the United States; others have wanted to carve a separate country out of American territory. Often black nationalists have proposed establishing ties with blacks in other parts of the New World and in Africa. Recently this has taken the form of a sophisticated cultural identification with black

Africa, whose peoples have inspired Afro-Americans by gaining political independence after a century of European domination. In earlier years, black nationalists urged that a significant number of Afro-Americans emigrate to their fatherland and establish there a powerful new nation. Twice between 1890 and 1925 this "Back to Africa" form of black nationalism generated widespread enthusiasm among black Americans. Although few blacks actually emigrated to Africa, the movement's stress on race pride and the rejection of White America was indelibly impressed in many minds and inspired a new generation of militant black nationalists.

Conditions in the South in 1890

Although the concept of emigration to Africa to establish a powerful new black nation had been formulated before the Civil War, most notably by Martin R. Delany, the idea was then limited to a few black intellectuals, mostly free blacks in the North. As a mass enthusiasm, black nationalism first flowered during the 1890's among the black peasants who farmed the cotton plantations of the South. It was clear to them that, even though it was twenty-five years after the end of the Civil War, most white Southerners intended to keep blacks as near slavery as possible. Having built up elaborate intellectual defenses for slavery during the early nineteenth century, the whites were not willing or able to change their concept of blacks as inferior, almost subhuman beings. Nor could they imagine for them any role in society other than that of the lowest class, possessing a minimum of rights, power, and status. When ex-slaves tried to assert their rights and privileges as citizens, whites used every possible means to keep them "in their place."

Violence had been a frequent tool of repression in the days of slavery, and it continued to be used during and after Reconstruction. Lynching was a particularly terrifying means of social control, for it deprived its victims of any chance to prove themselves innocent of whatever charges were made against them; frequently they were brutally tortured and humiliated before being hanged, shot, or burned to death. The rate of lynchings increased rapidly during the 1880's and reached a peak in 1892.

Whatever political power blacks had gained during Reconstruction, Southern whites now whittled away through violence, fraud, and deceit. By 1890 it had become evident that Northern whites, who had supported the blacks for political reasons, had grown tired of their efforts and were no longer going to interfere in Southern racial politics. White Southerners quickly took advantage of this development and began formally and legally to strip away what little political power remained to the blacks. Mississippi led the way in 1890 with the passage of a new state constitution that effectively stopped blacks from voting. During the next eighteen years most Southern states followed Mississippi's example. Though legally free, blacks could not use politics to protect their freedom.

The economic life of blacks was also restricted by whites, who, as they had before the Civil War, still owned the land and controlled the economy. Blacks worked the farms and paid a large share of their crop to the white landowners as rent. And the portion of the crop retained by the sharecropper was probably already mortgaged to the white storekeepers for food and supplies. Therefore, after the merchants and landowners were paid off, the farmer was left with little or no profit from the harvest and usually remained in debt. When cotton prices declined, as they did in the late 1880's, or when a general depression gripped the nation, as it did during most of the 1890's, the black farmer could see little improvement in his situation since slavery.

Reactions to this social, political, and economic oppression took several forms. Undoubtedly, most blacks, unsophisticated in business and politics and dominated by the landowner, the merchant, and the sheriff, simply endured the hardships and made the best of a bad deal, no matter what dreams of escape they may have had. The spokesman for this group was Booker T. Washington, who made "accommodation" an ideology. He urged his people to work hard, live clean, quiet lives, save money, and demonstrate their worthiness so that whites would someday recognize and honor their virtue and thrift. Others, mainly intellectuals and middle-class Northern blacks, protested and appealed to the conscience of the nation to grant them equality and integrate them into white American life. Frederick Douglass was the early spokesman for this viewpoint; others, including W. E. B. Du Bois, followed. But as conditions in the rural South worsened during the 1890's, a significant number of blacks began to despair of ever attaining the good life in the United States. Neither accommodation nor protest seemed to make life any better for the vast majority of black farmers and workers, who had little chance of earning enough or learning enough to reach the middle-class standard of living. For a time, in the late 1880's, some black farmers joined with their white counterparts in the Populist movement, which sought better economic conditions for all farmers. But racial prejudice soon split the Populists, and the blacks realized that the main reason for their hardships was their color, not their occupation. Many began to dream of establishing a nation of their own where they could be free of white oppression, own their own land, and control their political destiny. The black nation of their dreams would be a credit to the entire race and gain respect for blacks wherever they lived. The chief advocate of this brand of black nationalism during the years between the Civil War and World War I was Bishop Henry McNeal Turner.

Bishop Turner's Nationalist Vision

Turner was born a free man in South Carolina in 1834, but restrictions on his "freedom" irritated and challenged him. He sought advancement through the church, becoming a preacher first in the Methodist Episcopal Church and then, after moving North, in the all-black African Methodist Episcopal (AME) Church. A vocal and militant advocate of black emancipation and equality, he was appointed a chaplain in the Union army during the Civil War. When the war ended, his church assigned him to work in Georgia, where he had tremendous success in winning blacks away from their old, white-controlled churches to the AME Church. At the same time he actively organized blacks for the Republican party. He served in Georgia's Reconstruction constitutional convention (1868) and was elected to the legislature that same year. His hopes for black equality and participation in American life reached their highest point with that election. They were dashed soon afterwards when the white members of the legislature expelled Turner and all other blacks and reasserted white political control. Turner became embittered and denounced both Democrats and Republicans for betraying the freed slaves.

Bishop Turner had long been interested in Africa as a potential home for Afro-Americans, whom he wanted to evangelize and civilize their fatherland. He had known of the American Colonization Society (ACS) and its offspring in Africa, the Republic of Liberia, before the Civil War. Now with his increasing disillusionment with whites, the idea of building a powerful black nation in Africa took hold of him. In 1870 he began to advocate emigration by a select group of blacks skilled and resourceful enough to build a powerful modern nation. Their example would lend strength to black men everywhere by showing conclusively that blacks were not inferior to whites in ability, virtue, or power.

Turner never deviated from this black nationalist posture throughout the rest of his long life. With colorful rhetoric and persistent attacks on all who disagreed with him, he condemned white American racism and urged blacks to emigrate. Of the United States he wrote, "We were born here, raised here, fought, bled and died here, and have a thousand times more right here than hundreds of thousands of those who help to snub, proscribe and persecute us, and that is one of the reasons I almost despise the land of my birth."[1] When the response of his fellow blacks was less than enthusiastic, he blasted the "scullion coons" who would neither fight nor run from oppression. And middle-class blacks, most of whom opposed both Turner and his ideas, he accused of wanting to be white: they did "nothing day and night but cry: Glory, honor, dominion, and greatness to White."[2] Turner stressed race pride and even proclaimed that "God is a Negro: Even the heathen in Africa believed that they were 'created in God's image.' But American Africans believed that they resemble the devil and hence the contempt they have for themselves and for each other!" All the more reason, wrote the Bishop, for a "Negro nationality where black men can be taught to respect themselves."[3]

---

[1] Henry McNeal Turner, letter to the editor, *Christian Recorder,* 22 February 1883.

[2] Henry McNeal Turner, *A.M.E. Church Review* 1 (January 1885): 246.

[3] Henry McNeal Turner, *Voice of Missions,* November 1895.

Before 1890 most Afro-Americans responded negatively to Turner's emigration propaganda. The articulate middle-class blacks had clearly progressed since the time of slavery, so despite their handicaps they had reason to believe in the American dream. The great masses of blacks, however, were still tied to the cotton plantations and clinging to what little security they had. Even though Turner spoke and wrote widely about his African dream, most blacks were reluctant to leave home and head for a still unfamiliar and uninviting "dark continent." Occasional bursts of "African fever" led to the departure of small groups for Africa, usually with the help of the old and impoverished ACS, which annually sent about a hundred settlers to Liberia. Although most blacks had long opposed the ACS, fearing that it wanted to deport them forcibly, Bishop Turner, an honorary vice-president of the society, urged his followers to write to the ACS for free passage to Africa. As the economic condition of blacks grew increasingly worse, and as political oppression and lynching increased in 1890 and 1891, the society received more and more letters. The idea of escaping to Africa was flourishing among Southern black peasants whose circumstances made the American dream seem a cruel hoax.

Bishop Turner, sensing both the increase in oppression and the rising interest in emigration, decided to seize this moment to promote his brand of black nationalism. Late in 1891 he visited West Africa for the first time. Although other Afro-American travelers and settlers had described Liberia as a death trap of malaria and poverty, Turner focused on the bright side. "One thing the black man has here," he wrote, "and that is manhood, freedom, and the fullest liberty." He wrote back glowing accounts of the prospects for building a great nation in Africa, accounts that received wide circulation in the black press. He advocated settlement by Afro-Americans both for their own salvation and as a way of saving Africa from the domination of the European powers who were then dividing the continent into colonies. "I get mad and sick," Turner wrote, "when I look at the possibilities God has placed within our reach, and to think that we are such block heads we cannot see and use them."[4]

The quick response among Southern blacks overwhelmed the ACS. Thousands applied for passage aboard a small ship scheduled to depart for Liberia in March 1892. All but 50 were informed that there was no room for them. Yet so eager were they to flee to a place where they could have land of their own and find economic and political independence that over 300 blacks, mostly from Arkansas and Oklahoma, arrived in New York expecting transportation to Africa. Most were penniless, ragged, and uneducated—typical of Southern black farmers—but like many others, they believed that life could only get worse in the United States.

---

[4] Turner's letters from Africa were collected in the *A.M.E. Church Review* 8 (April 1892): 446–98.

The ACS, already faced with internal problems and lack of money, was unable to help these people, who were left stranded in New York. After 1892, reacting to adverse publicity and to attacks from both whites and blacks, the society stopped sending settlers to Liberia. However, the ACS remained in existence for another twenty years, hoping that someday it could aid a black exodus from the United States.

After the effective collapse of the ACS, Bishop Turner launched an intensive campaign to secure other means for black emigration. First, he tried to get the federal government to pay reparations to blacks for their years in slavery; he asserted that whites owed blacks some forty billion dollars, "estimating one hundred dollars a year for two million of us for two hundred years."[5] The money, according to Turner, should be used to finance emigration to Africa. He and his followers sent such petitions to the government for many years, and emigration bills occasionally came before Congress, but all to no avail. Next, Turner urged businessmen, both white and black, to take part in the growing trade with Africa, a trade that was bringing new wealth to European nations. He maintained that every ship bound from America to Africa would be crowded with Afro-Americans seeking new homes. But that scheme also failed, for American shippers and merchants had more profitable interests in Latin America and the Orient.

Finally, Turner urged black people themselves to band together to finance their own migration. That was a difficult task, however, for black farmers seldom saw much cash. In addition, they suffered with the rest of the nation the effects of the economic depression during most of the 1890's. Further complicating the picture was the fact that a number of fraudulent ticket-to-Africa-for-a-dollar schemes had duped many blacks eager to leave the United States. There were numerous reports of groups who had sold or given away their possessions and camped by the railroad tracks waiting for trains to take them to nonexistent ships bound for Africa.

Despite these obstacles, in 1892 the Afro-American Steamship Company was started with Turner's support. Stock was to be sold at a dollar a month to "ship club" members throughout the country; the ships thus financed would earn profits by taking cargo and passengers to Africa. There was plenty of interest in the plan, and ship clubs sprang up in many places. But depression dollars were scarce and members could not affort to keep up the payments. By mid-1893 the company and its clubs collapsed, having purchased no ships and transported no emigrants.

Turner, though disappointed, once more pressed on with his efforts to create a powerful black nation led by Afro-Americans. Early in 1893 he started a monthly newspaper, the *Voice of Missions,* which advocated both evangelism and nationalism. Its wide circulation among preachers meant that the Bishop's propaganda reached into the entire South and everywhere

---

[5] Turner, letter to the editor, *Christian Recorder,* 22 February 1883.

else that black people lived. Turner made a second visit to West Africa in the summer of 1893. Again his many letters and reports painted a glowing picture of Africa and the progress being made by Liberia. These reports excited the interest of many a black peasant who longed for some land of his own, a chance to control his life, and independence from whites.

But peasants were not the kind of settlers needed by Liberia, nor could they finance either emigration or nation building. So Turner tried to persuade middle-class blacks to support his schemes. Late in 1893 he assembled a national convention at Cincinnati, Ohio, where he tried to convince the educated, middle-class delegates that the only practical response to the oppression facing them in the United States was emigration. Although the black laborers and farmers in the galleries cheered the Bishop's eloquent attacks on American racism, the delegates refused to endorse black nationalism or to support emigration to Africa, Mexico, Canada, or anywhere else. One black newspaper observed that "all the radical propositions bearing upon the future welfare of the race were talked to death. . . . The Afro-American went to down the would-be African, and so far as the convention is concerned, he succeeded. But he did nothing else. [The convention] was passive when it should have been radical. It was cowardly when it should have been heroic."[6]

Despite the failure of the convention, Turner was still convinced that if only transportation could be arranged, hundreds of thousands of lower-class blacks would leave the United States. Since the ACS no longer sent settlers to Liberia, and since the black elite refused to finance the movement, the Bishop turned to whites for help. As a result, a group of Birmingham, Alabama, businessmen organized the International Migration Society (IMS) early in 1894 to recruit emigrants, sell them passage at moderate prices, transport them to Liberia, and help them get established there. The backers of the IMS planned to make a profit by doing a large volume of business with the thousands of blacks who Turner had said were ready to go. The IMS also profited from defaults on the monthly payments on the passage contracts, but its operations were basically honest.

Cheering the new organization, Bishop Turner publicized its operations in the *Voice of Missions*. Black local representatives of the IMS signed up would-be emigrants throughout the South. Although the depression still made dollars scarce, hundreds of black farmers nevertheless started paying on the $42 contracts. But by November only thirteen people had paid the full sum. The society sent them to Africa by way of Europe, hoping thereby to generate enough new excitement and payments to warrant chartering a ship to sail directly to Liberia.

The publicity, aided by Turner's steady barrage of propaganda, succeeded. Early in March 1895 a train carrying some 200 blacks from Arkansas, Mississippi, Alabama, Tennessee, and Texas pulled into Savannah. After a few

---

[6] Editorial, *Denver Statesman,* 9 December 1893.

days' delay they sailed for new homes in Africa. Despite some mismanagement by the IMS both in the United States and in Africa, Bishop Turner, then on his third visit to West Africa, reported the new settlers comfortably settled and at work clearing their land and building new homes.

Again the successful departure of emigrants generated new enthusiasm among rural Southern blacks. Dollars were still scarce, so it took another year to generate a third IMS "colony." But in March 1896 another ship carrying 321 emigrants left Savannah for Monrovia. The fate of this group, however, was not so fortunate. When the ship arrived in Liberia the officials of the IMS did not provide the food and care they had promised, and before many weeks had passed a number of the newcomers died of malaria and other diseases. Most others wanted to return to the United States, claiming they had been misled by false descriptions of easy wealth in Africa.

The adverse publicity hurt the recruiting operations of the IMS in the South. Furthermore, the American economy began to improve in 1897. Although the legal and social oppression of blacks continued, their economic condition improved somewhat as the price of cotton rose. At the same time, the threat of war with Spain began to generate a new patriotic enthusiasm among both whites and blacks. Bishop Turner sensed this threat to his nationalist dream and condemned the United States for planning to help Cuban rebels against Spain. He warned that once they realized that most of the Cuban rebels were black, white Americans would lose their zeal for "liberty from Spain." "We hope no Negro in this country will allow himself to be beguiled with [patriotic] sophistry," he wrote. "If the United States gets into war with Spain we shall stump the country against the black man taking up a gun."[7]

But the coming of the war and the increased prosperity of the economy proved too great a challenge to Turner's plans. Furthermore, in 1895, Booker T. Washington began increasingly to overshadow Bishop Turner and other black leaders as a result of his "Atlanta Compromise" address. Payments to the IMS fell off and few people went to Africa. The first mass flowering of black nationalism had come to an end. It is impossible to tell how many people had endorsed Turner's ideas, but signs of emigrationism had appeared in all the states of the Deep South and the Southwest, where over 90 percent of Afro-Americans lived. Thousands were directly caught up in one or more of the emigration schemes that sprang up during this period. Although only about a thousand people actually went to Africa, many other blacks seem to have shared Turner's pessimism about the United States.

Although mass enthusiasm for emigration collapsed after 1897, the idea of going to Africa to build a new nation was by no means at an end. The nationalist dream of a modern black state that would generate pride and independence among blacks everywhere continued to stir a few Afro-Amer-

---

[7] Henry McNeal Turner, *Voice of Missions,* April 1896.

icans. Bishop Turner, in particular, predicted that the black man must "emigrate or perish." During the years before World War I he encouraged a number of small, again unsuccessful Back to Africa organizations. The most significant of these was the Colored National Emigration Association, organized in 1901 by Turner himself. For five years the association struggled in vain to raise money for a ship, while the Bishop continued to publicize Africa and condemn the United States. He drew national attention in 1906 when he reportedly proclaimed that "to the Negro in this country the American flag is a dirty and contemptible rag. Not a star in it can the colored man claim, for it is no longer the symbol of our manhood rights and liberty."[8] Turner kept up his attacks until his death in 1915, but he was never able to launch a successful emigration plan, even though individuals and small groups occasionally migrated to Africa. Nevertheless, his efforts kept alive the dream of a strong African nation as a goal for Afro-Americans.

In 1913 an isolated African emigration was launched in Oklahoma by Chief Alfred C. Sam, reportedly of the Gold Coast, West Africa. Drawing on the residue of interest created by Turner and the despair caused by political oppression and another drop in cotton prices, Chief Sam managed to collect enough money from disillusioned black farmers to purchase a ship. With about sixty emigrants and a black crew, he and his ship sailed for the Gold Coast from Galveston, Texas, in August 1914, leaving behind hundreds more who planned to sail on the next trip. But diplomatic, political, and financial troubles cost Chief Sam his ship, and most of the emigrants eventually returned to the United States. Like the others before it, Chief Sam's effort did little more than demonstrate that many Afro-Americans, particularly farmers and laborers, were sufficiently unhappy with American conditions to want to flee the country.

Black nationalism had flowered during the 1890's, but it had not borne much fruit. Nevertheless, it proved to be a hardy plant that could wait another generation before flowering again, when disillusionment with the United States, and another vigorous nationalist spokesman led masses of blacks to work for African nationhood. Those conditions came with the end of World War I and the arrival in New York of Marcus Garvey.

Urban Blacks and Marcus Garvey

During the war years 1914–1918, the general situation of hundreds of thousands of blacks changed radically. Ever since the days of slavery blacks had looked upon the North as a kind of promised land of political and social freedom. But after Emancipation the economics of cotton farming had kept 90 percent of them in the South. Bishop Turner, among others, realized and publicized the fact that there was much prejudice and racism in the North,

[8] Henry McNeal Turner, *Atlantic Constitution,* 24 February 1906.

especially among recent immigrants from Europe who were competing with blacks for jobs. Nevertheless, a small but steady stream of blacks, mostly from Virginia and Kentucky, migrated to the industrial cities of the North and founded communities there.

With the coming of World War I, however, the labor situation in the North changed dramatically. Immigration from Europe was drastically reduced, while the demand for manufactured goods expanded. Industrialists in Chicago, Detroit, Cleveland, New York, Philadelphia, and other cities were crying for unskilled labor and began sending agents into the South to recruit blacks. Afro-American newspapers also summoned Southern blacks to the new bonanza, while letters home from early arrivals lured still others away from their cotton farms. In 1915 and 1916 those cotton farms were having hard times anyway, as the boll weevil marched across the South, destroying crops and making life even more difficult than usual for blacks.

The result of these forces was a sudden, dramatic spurt in the migration of blacks from the Deep South to the cities of the North. Almost overnight major cities gained large black populations. Attracted by jobs that paid in dollars instead of credit at the local store, by the growing all-black communities inside the cities, and by the relative political and social freedom in the North, nearly half a million black migrants had moved into the Northern cities by 1920, and the tide was to continue for several decades to come.

But the North was hardly a paradise for blacks. Friction over jobs, housing, and life styles quickly arose. And when the war ended, returning soldiers and new European immigrants displaced many of the black workers. Furthermore, the infamous Ku Klux Klan, with all its virulent racism, was revived and began to reach into the North as well as the South. The expanding black settlements spread from block to block in the major cities, displacing whites, changing neighborhoods, and altering political patterns. To these friction-generating changes were further added 400,000 black soldiers who had been away helping to "make the world safe for democracy," but who came home from Europe to find the same old racial oppression in the United States.

The result was a long series of race riots, many in Northern cities, in which blacks invariably suffered the most. During the economic recession that followed the war, urban blacks, who had been "last hired," found themselves "first fired" and frequently out of work. Although the North still offered more opportunities than the South, and despite the fact that blacks continued to pour into the cities, it became clear that even in the "promised land" black people were oppressed. Uprooted from familiar surroundings, crowded into small quarters in expanding ghettos, shunned by whites and restricted to the lowest levels of society, some blacks began to recall Bishop Turner's African dream of a free and powerful black nation outside the United States. Into this urban scene of black newcomers with new homes, new jobs, and new problems stepped Marcus Moziah Garvey, the man who was to mobilize them in the second mass flowering of black nationalism.

Garvey was born in the West Indian island of Jamaica in 1887; there he grew to manhood and learned the trade of printing. He tried his hand at labor organizing and newspaper publishing, first in Jamaica and then in various other Caribbean countries where black Jamaicans worked on sugar and banana plantations. Dismayed at the miserable living conditions of the workers and their exploitation by white or mulatto overseers, Garvey tried in vain to persuade Jamaican officials to intervene. In 1912 he went to London to carry his appeals to the British people and to learn about conditions of black people in other parts of the world. While in London he met Duse Mohammed, a black Egyptian who was promoting the defeat of European colonialism everywhere. He worked on Mohammed's magazine, *African Times and Orient Review,* met Africans, studied about Africa, and caught Mohammed's zeal for African nationalism.

Garvey also read Booker T. Washington's autobiography, *Up From Slavery,* and suddenly perceived that his own life work was to be a leader of the black race. Returning to Jamaica in 1914, he set about building an organization that would "unite the 400,000,000 Negroes of the world for the purpose of building a civilization of their own."[9] He called the organization the Universal Negro Improvement Association and African Communities League (UNIA) and began work among the black peasants of his home island. Among his goals was the creation of industrial schools to teach trades and skills—schools patterned after Booker T. Washington's Tuskegee Institute.

Garvey moved to New York in 1916 and took up residence in Harlem, then a fast-growing black ghetto. He began recruiting members for the UNIA, but his success was small in the booming war years. Not only were the newly arrived Southerners doing well, but Garvey's West Indian accent and style were foreign to them. However, with the end of the war, the collapse of the boom, and the beginning of the race riots in 1919, the message of the UNIA suddenly made sense. By the end of 1919, aided by his newspaper, the *Negro World,* and by his sometimes sensational publicity in the general press, Garvey reported that he had two million members in thirty chapters scattered across the United States and the West Indies. The second mass flowering of black nationalism was under way.

Central to Garvey's philosophy was the need to unite all black people and to give them a racial self-confidence that would enable them to throw off white oppression. Like Bishop Turner a generation earlier, Garvey hoped to stimulate race pride both by direct propaganda and by the establishment of a powerful black nation in Africa. Whenever he spoke, he urged Afro-Americans to shed the old thinking that "white was right" and that blacks were powerless. "Up you mighty Race! You can accomplish what you will!" was one of his mottoes. To the thousands of blacks who were caught in the

---

[9] Amy Jacques Garvey, ed., *The Philosophy and Opinions of Marcus Garvey,* 2 vols. (New York: Universal Publishing House, 1923, 1925), 2:95.

anonymity of the big cities and who felt as helpless under the grinding wheels of Northern society as they had under the oppression of white Southerners, those words held out new hope.

To help stimulate pride and independence, Garvey demanded racial purity. He was himself of unmixed African descent, and, reflecting the three-way split in West Indian society, he despised mulattoes. Such distinctions between brown and black, however, were not as important in the United States. But Garvey's stress on the glories of the African heritage helped many Afro-Americans, both brown and black, to find new confidence in themselves and in one another. Garvey advised them not to be too concerned with political rights and social equality in the United States, but rather to become as independent as possible in the white man's country. He organized his followers into marching units of uniformed African Legions and Black Cross Nurses whose colorful parades inspired thousands of Harlem residents.

Economic independence was another factor in the UNIA plan. Garvey urged his followers to "buy black"—to patronize their own businessmen. Following Booker T. Washington's stress on self-sufficiency, the UNIA opened several business projects, including the Negro Factories Corporation, to assist black businesses. More important, Garvey founded the Black Star Steamship Line to serve as a commercial and spiritual tie among blacks wherever its ships traveled. Like Bishop Turner's shipping attempts, the Black Star Line was intended to carry freight as well as passengers. But contrary to popular belief, carrying emigrants to Africa was not one of the original motives of Garvey's enterprise. Black Star Line stocks were sold to blacks only, and Garvey promised stock buyers that they would not only be helping their race but might also make a handsome profit. To the surprise of his critics, Garvey collected enough money between 1919 and 1925 to buy four second-hand ships and to begin trade with the Caribbean.

For Garvey, the major path to black pride and economic independence was the redemption of "Africa for the Africans." "The only wise thing for us ambitious Negroes to do," he wrote, "is to organize the world over and build up for the race a mighty nation of our own in Africa."[10] It would be "strong enough to lend protection to the members of the race scattered all over the world, and to compel the respect of the nations and races of the earth."[11] He believed that "power is the only argument that satisfies man," and that "it is advisable for the Negro to get power of every kind . . . that will stand out signally, so that other races and nations can see, and if they will not see, then FEEL."[12]

The Garvey movement reached a peak in August 1920 at a month-long

---

[10] Garvey, *Philosophy of Marcus Garvey,* 1:58.

[11] Ibid., 1:52.

[12] Ibid., 1:21, 22.

convention held in New York City. At least 25,000 people attended the many meetings, at which Garvey used all of his oratorical power to proclaim black nationalism. The emphasis was on the redemption of Africa. "The other races have countries of their own and it is time for the 400,000,000 Negroes to claim Africa for themselves," he announced, "and we mean to retake every square inch of the 12,000,000 square miles of African territory belonging to us by right divine."[13] Garvey was designated "Provisional President of the African Republic"; other officials of the UNIA were given similar titles. The convention adopted a long "Declaration of the Rights of the Negro Peoples of the World," which embodied most of Garvey's philosophy. A truly impressive affair in its magnitude and splendor, the convention brought Garvey to the attention of the world. He had managed to do what Bishop Turner and many other black leaders had failed to do: he had mobilized the black masses. Thousands of urban blacks were drawn to the red, black, and green flag of black nationalism. Many more read the *Negro World* and responded eagerly to the agents of the Black Star Line who circulated among them selling stock.

Garvey was aware that many difficulties stood in the way of the redemption of Africa. European imperialists controlled most of Africa by military force. Furthermore, the Africans themselves would need help in learning to cope with the powers and problems of the twentieth century. Garvey therefore proposed sending a limited number of Afro-Americans with skills, professions, and capital (twenty or thirty thousand families to begin with) to settle in Liberia. Liberia was at that time the only independent West African nation, and it was governed by an elite group of descendants of earlier Afro-American settlers who ruled the indigenous Africans. After 1920 several teams of Garvey's representatives visited Liberia to lay the groundwork for the newcomers. But the UNIA seemed a threat to these Americo-Liberian rulers, especially after they discovered Garvey's secret plan to take over the country. With the approval of the European colonial powers, which also felt threatened by Garvey's "Africa for the Africans" policy, Liberia broke off negotiations and refused to allow any UNIA members to settle there.

Thus ended Garvey's only real attempt to repatriate the descendants of Africa. The enormous appeal he had for Afro-Americans, however, was not based solely on the Back to Africa idea. Although he maintained that "the future of the Negro . . . outside of Africa, spells ruin and disaster," he did not actually call for mass emigration of American blacks. But mass emigration to escape oppression in the United States was an appealing concept to many of Garvey's working-class followers, and he did little to discourage that popular misinterpretation of his plans.

It was not only the Liberian government and the European colonial powers

---

[13] Ibid.

that were alarmed at Garvey's promises to redeem Africa through his African Legion and Black Flying Eagles; many Afro-Americans also opposed the UNIA leader. The black elite of businessmen and intellectuals resented Garvey just as they had resented Bishop Turner. Labor leader A. Philip Randolph, of the socialist journal *Messenger,* thought Garvey's Africa would be a reactionary dictatorship, not a democracy. Robert Abbott, of the influential *Chicago Defender,* arranged to have Garvey harassed for selling stock in Illinois without a license. Black churchmen resented Garvey's establishment of an African Orthodox Church, which threatened to win the allegiance of black Christians to a black God. W. E. B. Du Bois, editor of the NAACP magazine the *Crisis,* accused Garvey of being the worst enemy of the black race. Du Bois was then involved in a series of pan-African conferences which tried to bring together intellectual and upper-class blacks in an organization aimed at pressing for independence for colonial Africa. Although the Pan-African movement shared some basic goals with the UNIA, its style was quite different and its membership much smaller than that of the UNIA; Garvey despised Du Bois. The black elite, or "talented tenth," as Du Bois called them, not only opposed Garvey's black nationalism but also criticized the man himself for being uneducated, a foreigner, and a "demagogue." Many whites, including federal government officials, also viewed the UNIA as a dangerous "anti-American" movement.

At first, such opposition did little to dim Garvey's popularity with the black masses, but the Jamaican also had to take his "friends" into account. Although the UNIA was far-flung, its organization rested chiefly on Garvey himself rather than on strong local leaders. Nevertheless, the UNIA attracted a number of men who saw in it an opportunity to gain personal power or profit. At first Garvey was too trusting of his associates and allowed them to make decisions that later hurt the movement, especially their financial decisions for the Black Star Line. Despite the fact that millions of dollars had apparently been collected from UNIA members, most of it was never accounted for. And, although the organization eventually bought four ships, they either turned out to be unseaworthy or were lost because of debt. The other financial affairs of the movement were also apparently mismanaged, so much so that Garvey's opponents, including some defectors from the UNIA and some disgruntled stock owners, alerted the United States government and charged that the Black Star Line was making false claims about its finances.

In February 1922 Garvey and three of his lieutenants were indicted by the federal government for using the United States mails to sell fraudulent stocks. Garvey insisted that he had left his financial affairs to subordinates who had betrayed him. His opponents rejoiced at his impending downfall, but the masses of the UNIA rallied behind their leader and the trial was delayed until May 1923. Now distrustful of most of his friends, Garvey dismissed his attorney and tried in vain to defend himself. The court record attests to the shabby financial procedures of the Black Star Line, although it seems clear that Garvey himself had no intention of defrauding his supporters. In spite of such evidence, his three subordinates were found not guilty. The fact that Garvey himself was found guilty suggests that the jury may have been more alarmed by his black nationalism than by his business practices. He was sentenced to five years in prison; but after serving two years, he was released in 1927 and deported as an "undesirable alien."

Garvey's opponents were delighted, of course, and they published the details of how the UNIA members and Black Star Line investors had lost their money. They expected the movement to quickly collapse. During Garvey's two years in prison there was indeed a decline in the activities of the UNIA, for it had been held together primarily by the personality of Garvey himself. Nevertheless, some local chapters continued to function, waiting for the day when their leader would again rally them to the cause of black nationalism. But when Garvey was released from prison and tried to rekindle the old enthusiasm from a distance in Jamaica, he had little success. Even though there was a temporary rally, particularly in the West Indies, the damage had been done. Vestiges of the UNIA lingered on in the United States, but it was torn by factionalism, dissension, and bankruptcy. By 1930 it had ceased to be a major organization in Afro-American life. Garvey died in London in 1940, still clinging to the dream of a powerful African nation that would unite the descendants of Africa scattered around the world. But this second flowering of mass black nationalism in the United States had withered. Yet another generation would pass before such ideas again stirred American blacks.

Turner and Garvey in Perspective

Garvey's UNIA, of course, received much more public recognition than had Bishop Turner's movement. The reasons lie in the differences between their followers. Turner lived and worked in the South, where most blacks were farmers and where white oppression was much more personal and pervasive. Garvey, on the other hand, worked primarily in the large cities, where communications were better, leisure time more plentiful, white oppression less personal, and mass meetings more feasible. Furthermore, Turner's followers rarely saw much cash, whereas the urban blacks, though underpaid and underemployed, were paid cash wages. This made it easier for Garvey to raise money for his operations. In addition, many UNIA members, having recently moved to the North, found it easy to think of moving to yet another "promised land." These factors partially explain why Garvey, rather than Turner, succeeded in creating a large, visible nationalist organization.

However, Garvey and Turner shared not only a dream of African redemption and black pride but also certain personal qualities that influenced their activities. Although neither was superhuman and each had his glaring weaknesses, both possessed an overwhelming desire to see the black race achieve honor and equality with whites. They shared a vision of African power. Both were impressive speakers with a flair for the dramatic and a willingness to speak bluntly about white racism, and to speak it in the language of the masses. But, although Garvey and Turner were competent organizers on a surface level, neither possessed the shrewdness or ability to mobilize his followers efficiently and fend off attacks both by whites and by other blacks.

In contrast, Booker T. Washington, the dominant black leader in the years between Turner's and Garvey's heydays, was able to use people, publicity, politics, and personality to maintain his own power for almost twenty years. Of course, Washington paid a price for that power—namely, the humiliation of Southern blacks in their own eyes and in the eyes of whites in return for telling white businessmen what they wanted to hear about "happy, docile blacks." And although Washington's power gained him the respect of many blacks, he commanded little enthusiasm among the black lower class because he had no great, militant vision of the future of Afro-Americans. But he was a shrewd and capable organizer and manipulator of ideas and men. In the final analysis he was the most powerful black man in American history.

Had either Bishop Turner or Marcus Garvey combined Washington's organizational ability with their black nationalist understanding of what had to be done, the outcome might have been different. Although Turner fought for African redemption and Afro-American emigration throughout most of his long life, he had other interests, particularly church affairs, and so did not give his wholehearted attention to black nationalist agitation. Garvey had only one consuming passion, but his fatal weakness was his failure to select competent and loyal assistants.

There were other reasons why neither Turner nor Garvey was able to achieve ultimate success. Each had active opponents and, in the end, was overwhelmed by them. For, just as Turner's propaganda was taking effect in the mid-1890's, Booker T. Washington gained national attention and soon dominated black leadership. Garvey was overwhelmed, not by a new leader with new ideas, but by a concerted attack from his opponents, who succeeded in physically removing him from the scene. Both Turner and Garvey failed to get substantial support from the black upper class—the small but influential elite who had skilled jobs, professions, or college educations and who yearned for stability and integration more than race pride. Although Garvey was much more successful in getting money and ships, in the end neither he nor Turner was able to arrange a strong settlement of Afro-Americans in Africa or otherwise create a powerful black nation. Each man was so aware of the pervasive reality of white oppression and the powerlessness of blacks around the world that he ignored the necessary details of organization and nation building.

It was the concept of black nationalism rather than its organization that fired the imaginations of Turner's oppressed Southern followers and Garvey's Northern urban admirers. To be sure, there was a major element of escapism in the popular interpretation of black nationalism. That escapism forced both leaders to include mass emigration in their thinking, even though both maintained that a full exodus was both impractical and unnecessary for the establishment of a free black nation in Africa. But blacks seemed to want a nation of their own that would command the respect of the world, an idea they clearly adopted from whites; both the 1890's and 1920's were times of intense nationalism in both Europe and the United States. Southern and Northern whites proclaimed that this was a "white man's country." The ideas and arguments employed by Turner and Garvey were learned from these whites.

Central to the concept of black nationalism was the unity of all blacks in all parts of the world. Unity meant more than strength in numbers; the international approach reinforced the nationalists' awareness that the root of their problems lay not in racial inferiority, personal traits, or bad luck, but in white oppression. This was true not only in the United States and the Caribbean but in Africa as well. Bishop Turner watched in alarm as the European powers established their imperial control over the homeland during his lifetime. Both he and Garvey were early contributors to the small but growing movement for African nationalism among the Africans themselves, a movement that eventually led to their independence.

For Turner, Garvey, and their followers, Africa became a symbol more powerful than reality. As the home of their ancestors, it had a strong appeal to Afro-Americans, whose knowledge of Africa was clouded by generations of separation and years of brainwashing. New World blacks easily romanticized Africa and ignored its difficult problems—first of European control, second of economic growth in societies that had not yet begun to industrialize, and third of nation building on a continent containing hundreds of different ethnic groups. Both Turner and Garvey tried to learn about Africa, however, and their visions of an independent, powerful African nation were more than empty dreams.

The primary impact of both Turner and Garvey, of course, was on American blacks. Black nationalism gave Afro-Americans a feeling of independence and power in the face of suffocating, ever present white oppression. It also gave them a sense of working toward the day when black men would indeed have their own nations and be respected in the councils of the world. This sense of purpose drew together a people who had been lost in an American society supposedly very individualistic but actually very group-oriented, especially where race was involved. It got some of them—for a time, at least—to work together, to dream, to build, and brought a self-pride that mere rhetoric could never have produced.

The flowerings of black nationalism under Bishop Turner and Marcus

Garvey left seeds that are still growing. First, the promise of African freedom inspired Africans to work for independence from Europe. Second, the stress on black accomplishments built a new pride in the Afro-American lower class that would one day blossom into a new black power and independence.

The Concept of the New Negro
and the Realities of Black Culture

LAWRENCE W. LEVINE

Lawrence W. Levine is professor of history at the University of
California, Berkeley. He has edited several collections of essays
on American history and is the author of *Defender of the Faith:
William Jennings Bryan, the Last Decade, 1915–1925* (Oxford
University Press, 1965). Mr. Levine's recent studies have been
in the field of Afro-American folk culture, and his special concern,
the problems of adapting folk materials to history, is explored
in "Slave Songs and Slave Consciousness," published in *Anonymous Americans* (Prentice-Hall, 1971). In the following essay, Mr.
Levine urges extensive study of traditional Negro culture. Sharply
critical of the tendency to define a "New Negro" every generation, he demonstrates that a thoughtful exploration of their
unique historical record reveals the continuity in the values and
self-concept of Afro-Americans.

The Ubiquitous New Negro

Americans in general and American scholars in particular have not yet
really come to terms with a challenge posed by Ralph Ellison a number of
years ago: "Everybody wants to tell us what a Negro is. . . . But if you would
tell me who I am, at least take the trouble to discover what I have been."[1]
Most scholars have failed to penetrate with sufficient energy and imagination the rich and varied cultural sources of the black masses. I want to consider not the reasons for but the effects of this failure. It has left scholars
as vulnerable as other Americans to the mood that prevailed in the decades
following World War II, which, in terms of race relations, might well be
called the period of the rediscovery of the Negro in American life.

White Americans, to be sure, have always been preoccupied with Negroes,
but rarely since the years immediately preceding and following the Civil
War have black people occupied so important a place in the national con-

---

[1] Ralph Ellison, *Shadow and Act* (New York: Random House, 1964), p. 115.

sciousness as they have in the past several decades. The standard mechanisms by which whites were able to repress their recognition of the Negro's plight were rendered increasingly ineffective by the middle of the twentieth century. The belief that Negroes, being inferior, could not really object to an inferior status, that they were in fact quite content with the caste-ridden life they were thrust into after the Civil War, and that if there was any problem, it centered around a handful of white and black radicals, agitators, and neurotic malcontents was undermined as black Americans became more and more able to articulate and act upon their dissatisfactions and their aspirations. The fantasy, indulged in by so many whites at the turn of the century, that what they liked to call the "Negro problem" was at best temporary, since Negroes, unable to stand the rigors of either the Northern climate or of free competition, were in the process of extinction as a people, was belied by the increasing presence of blacks in all parts of the country. Not even the comfortable conviction that, since the United States was an open society, those Negroes on the bottom of the socioeconomic ladder had no one to blame but themselves (though it is a conviction that retains potency to this day) could be totally persuasive to a people who had just experienced the irrationality and injustice of the Great Depression.

That Negroes came to occupy an increasingly prominent place in the national consciousness has been one of the healthier aspects of the postwar era. Nevertheless, it is important to recognize that this rediscovery has taken place in a historical vacuum. Knowledge of the historical Negro is still obscured by the myths and stereotypes of the past. Whites have construed their dawning awareness of the feelings of blacks as a change in Negroes rather than as a change in themselves. This has given rise to the tendency to think in cataclysmic terms such as the "New Negro" when characterizing black people in contemporary America.

In one sense the concept of the New Negro is undeniably valid. The twentieth century has witnessed striking changes in the status and situation of black Americans. While at the beginning of the century 90 percent of the Negroes in the United States lived in the South and 75 percent were rural, by the middle of the century more than 50 percent lived in the North and 73 percent were urban. These demographic changes have had important social, economic, and political implications. As Negroes moved from rural to urban areas their economic position and occupational opportunities increased markedly. As they moved from the South to the North their political position improved greatly. And both shifts enhanced their opportunities for an improved education. Thus by mid-century Negroes were in a better position to make their demands felt than ever before in American history. But this has been a gradual and cumulative change; it has not been cataclysmic and its effects have been manifest throughout the twentieth century. If black people were more and more able to confront the white man directly and to articulate their feelings, this was not necessarily an indication that the feelings were new.

The problem with the concept of the New Negro is that it has not centered upon these crucial external developments but has taken more important internal changes for granted. It is predicated on the assumption that Negroes before World War II had internalized the white man's image of themselves so that they believed they were somehow inferior and deserving of their fate and consequently did not protest in any effective way. Blacks, to borrow Norbert Wiener's telling phrase, have been seen as reaching up to kiss the whip that lashed them. This image has been enhanced by much of the scholarship of the past few decades. One study, which has had enormous influence in spite of the fact that it totally ignored almost every aspect of slave culture from religion to music to folklore, concluded that Negroes were infantilized by the system of slavery, that they were virtually reduced to a state of perpetual childhood in which their sense of self was derived from the master class upon whom they depended and who constituted their only "significant others."[2] Other studies, paying equally little attention to black culture, have projected this picture into the era of freedom. Confusing group consciousness and a firm sense of self with political consciousness and organization, manhood with armed rebellion, and resistance with the building of a revolutionary tradition, these scholars have been able to find little more than dependence, servility, and apathy in the black masses until relatively recently.[3]

The tendency to see Negroes primarily as reactors to white society rather than as actors in their own right has been intensified by contemporary social scientists who have been unable to perceive a distinctive set of black folkways or institutions at least potentially capable of sustaining Negroes against the worst ravages of the system they live in. "The key to much in the Negro world," two sociologists maintained in their study of ethnic groups in New York City, is that "the Negro is only an American, and nothing else. He has no values and culture to guard and protect."[4] A 1965 government report on the Negro family found that "it was by destroying the Negro family under slavery that white America broke the will of the Negro people. *Although*

---

[2] Stanley Elkins, *Slavery* (Chicago: University of Chicago Press, 1959), Chapter 3.

[3] See, for example, Eugene D. Genovese, "The Legacy of Slavery and the Roots of Black Nationalism," *Studies on the Left* 6 (November–December 1966): 3-26. Ironically, Genovese has been one of the most perceptive and effective critics of the Elkins thesis for the period of slavery. See his article "Rebelliousness and Docility in the Negro Slave: A Critique of the Elkins Thesis," *Civil War History* 13 (December 1967): 293–314, in which he criticizes "Elkins' inability to see the slaves as active forces capable of tempering the authority of the master."

[4] Nathan Glazer and Daniel Moynihan, *Beyond the Melting Pot* (Cambridge, Mass.: M.I.T. Press, 1963), p. 53.

that will has reasserted itself in our time, it is a resurgence doomed to frustration unless the viability of the Negro family is restored."[5] "Being a Negro in America," a psychologist asserted in 1964, "is less of a racial identity than a necessity to adopt a subordinate social role."[6] Nor has this line of argument been confined to white scholars. The sociologist E. Franklin Frazier summed up much of his research by concluding in 1957 that "unlike any other racial or cultural minority, the Negro is not distinguished by culture from the dominant group. Having completely lost his ancestral culture, he speaks the same language, practices the same religion, and accepts the same values and political ideals as the dominant group."[7]

The thrust of these studies has been to see black history in the United States as an almost straight line from slavery to the recent past and to envision the distinctive features of that history not as cultural forms but as disorganization or pathology. Thus a scholarly foundation for the concept of the New Negro has been constructed. That it is a foundation without much substance is due not to the necessary invalidity of its central arguments but to the narrow and culture-bound research that has gone into the construction of these arguments. The easy assumption that black history has merely been a pathological version of white history and that the Negro has been little more than "an exaggerated American," as Gunnar Myrdal put it, has worked to inhibit the open and painstaking study of all areas of Negro life and history, without which a complete understanding of the validity of the concept of the New Negro is impossible.

In fact, of course, Negro protest is not new. Indeed, as August Meier has shown, the term "New Negro" itself has been a ubiquitous one. It was used at least as early as 1895 by the *Cleveland Gazette* to describe a group of Negroes who had just secured a New York civil rights law. Booker T. Washington spoke of a New Negro who was emerging as a result of his policies of self-help and economic betterment. The journalist Ray Stannard Baker wrote in 1908 that while "the old-fashioned Negro preferred to go to the white man for everything . . . the New Negro . . . urges his friends to patronize Negro doctors and dentists, and to trade with Negro storekeepers." In 1916 Dean William Pickens of Morgan College wrote a series of essays entitled *The New Negro,* in which he saw the Negro on the threshold of a renaissance of civilization and culture. For W. E. B. Du Bois, the New Negro was embodied

---

[5] [Daniel Moynihan], *The Negro Family: The Case for National Action* (Washington, D.C.: Office of Policy Planning and Research, Department of Labor, March 1965), p. 30. Italics added.

[6] Thomas F. Pettigrew, *A Profile of the Negro American* (Princeton, N.J.: D. Van Nostrand, 1964), p. 25.

[7] E. Franklin Frazier, *The Negro in the United States,* revised ed. (New York: Macmillan, 1957), pp. 680–81.

in the group of businessmen who were developing a group economy.[8] The term was used most frequently in the decade after World War I to describe the young artists and poets who were engaged in what was hopefully called a Negro Renaissance. Alain Locke, in his 1925 anthology of Negro writing, *The New Negro,* was virtually alive with the possibilities of the golden day that was dawning:

> There is ample evidence of a New Negro in the latest phases of social change and progress, but still more in the internal world of the Negro mind and spirit. . . . We are witnessing the resurgence of a people. . . . Negro life is not only establishing new contacts and founding new centers, it is finding a new soul. . . . There is a renewed race-spirit that consciously and proudly sets itself apart. . . . The day of "aunties," "uncles" and "mammies" is equally gone. Uncle Tom and Sambo have passed on, . . . the Negro is becoming transformed. . . . The American mind must reckon with a fundamentally changed Negro.[9]

Statements like these stemmed not only from the demographic changes already referred to but also from the ferment that was taking place among Negroes throughout the nation. Although this ferment was not often marked by direct mass action, there was nonetheless more action than has been recognized. August Meier and Elliott Rudwick have demonstrated that the bus boycotts in Montgomery, Alabama, and other Southern cities during the mid-1950's were by no means a radical break with the past. Negroes had adopted similar tactics in the late nineteenth and early twentieth centuries to oppose segregation in Southern transportation and Northern education. As early as Reconstruction, Negroes in Richmond, New Orleans, Charleston, and Louisville conducted successful boycotts against the introduction of segregated horsecars. During the 1890's, Negroes in Atlanta, Augusta, and Savannah successfully boycotted attempts to segregate local transportation facilities. Between 1900 and 1906, similar protest movements occurred in more than twenty-five cities in every state of the former Confederacy. For periods ranging from several weeks to several years, Negroes in these cities refused to ride on newly segregated streetcars. Negro hackmen and draymen developed informal transit systems to accommodate the protesters, and in Portsmouth, Norfolk, Chattanooga, and Nashville all-black transportation lines were created. Similarly, in Alton, Illinois, in 1897 and in East Orange, New Jersey, in 1899, Negro residents refused to send their children to schools in which they were being segregated. Identical movements took place in

---

[8] August Meier, *Negro Thought in America, 1880–1915* (Ann Arbor: University of Michigan Press, 1963), Chapter 14.

[9] See the foreword and "The New Negro," in Alain Locke, *The New Negro* (New York: Albert & Charles Boni, 1925), pp. xv, xvii, 5, 6, 8.

Springfield and Dayton, Ohio, in the 1920's. All these movements were ultimately suppressed, as they had to be, with no aid or encouragement from the courts or the government. But, considering the power relationships existing at the time, the important thing about them, as Meier and Rudwick have concluded, is not that they failed "but that they happened in so many places and lasted as long as they often did."[10]

In all this protest there was so great a diversity of means and ends, so frequent a blurring of tactical differences, that it is hard to categorize it without oversimplifying. Bearing this in mind and recalling also that throughout the twentieth century there has always been an important strain of militant action—from the boycotts at the turn of the century, to the campaigns during the Depression to force stores in black neighborhoods to employ Negroes, to the 1941 March on Washington movement to bring about the hiring of Negroes in defense industries, to the accelerating activities of the postwar years—it is possible to isolate several major streams of action that predominated at different times. The political abandonment of the freedmen by the Republican party in the 1870's and 1880's abruptly ended the dream that Negro rights could be secured through conventional political behavior and gave rise to the line of thought epitomized by Booker T. Washington's emphasis upon self-help and economic activity. Operating in an age imbued with the belief that man could progress according to the Horatio Alger model and confronted with the blocking of political channels by federal indifference and Southern disfranchisement, Negro leadership preached the possibilities of advancement through moral and economic development: Negroes must band together and further their own cause through mutual aid and self-help; Negroes must show themselves the equal of white men by developing their own capabilities. Although this philosophy of Negro progress persists with some interesting variations on the theme, World War I dealt it a blow from which it never fully recovered.

With few exceptions, Negroes flocked into the American army during the war and served with enthusiasm and hope. When 200 Negro college graduates were asked to volunteer for officer training, 1,500 responded almost immediately. Here was a situation made to order for the Alger philosophy, whose heroes had always proved their worth through inspired acts of heroism and devotion. "We believe that our second emancipation will be the outcome of this war," the Texas Grand Master of the Negro Masons announced in 1918.[11] This loyalty and hope was rewarded by a hardening of the lines

[10] August Meier and Elliott Rudwick, "The Boycott Movement Against Jim Crow Streetcars in the South, 1900–1906," *Journal of American History* 55 (March 1969): 756–75; "Negro Boycotts of Jim Crow Streetcars in Tennessee," *American Quarterly* 21 (Winter 1969): 755–63; and "Negro Boycotts of Jim Crow Schools in the North, 1897–1925," *Integrated Education* 5 (August-September 1967): 1–12.

[11] William Muraskin, "Black Masons: The Role of Fraternal Orders in the Creation of a

of discrimination, by increased humiliation, and by the bloody Red Summer of 1919, which saw major race riots in city after city. Blacks had played the game by the rules and had discovered definitively that the rules simply did not apply to them. The anxiety that accompanied this discovery was marked by the dramatic rise of Marcus Garvey and his Back to Africa movement and by the Negro Renaissance, whose poets and writers flirted with the dream of Africa and a separate Negro people. In organizational terms it was marked by the emergence of the NAACP, with its emphasis upon legalism as the dominant form of protest. If black leaders in the Reconstruction era put their faith in the political process, and those of Booker T. Washington's time stressed the American dream of self-help and success, the new postwar spokesmen turned to the American system of justice. There were endless appeals to the courts to force the application of the rules of the game to Negroes as well as everyone else.

Ironically, it was the very success of this movement that brought about its demise. In the wake of its greatest legal victory, the *Brown v. Board of Education of Topeka* school desegregation decision of 1954, the NAACP found itself beleaguered by the challenges of new organizations and new tactics. It was not long before it began to appear as though the school victory had only symbolic importance. More than ten years after the court spoke, only 8 percent of the Negro youths in the South attended integrated schools. New organizations—CORE, SNCC, SCLC—abandoned legalism for direct action, the courts for the streets. Their appeal was directly to the American conscience; their tactic was the graphic demonstration of the injustices and brutalities of the system, along with added economic pressure from boycotts and picket lines. Their results were in many ways impressive, and yet in the more than ten years in which they dominated the Civil Rights movement the relative economic position of the Negro masses declined and the stubborn problems of the urban ghettos became even more intense. As a result of these developments there is the crisis of our own day, in which we are witnessing the rise of new leadership and the use of new methods lumped under the rubric "Black Power."

The variegated and shifting spectrum of Negro protest thought and action has provided still another fertile seedbed for the concept of the New Negro. It has been in periods of transition from the dominance of one set of leaders and tactics to that of another that we have most frequently heard the assertion that a New Negro was arising in the land. The failure to see the Negro rights movements as a totality has made it easy to confuse the rise of new organizations and the adoption of new methods with the birth of a New Negro. But there has been an even greater error. In attempting to understand the reaction of Negroes to the society in which they lived, there has

Middle-Class Black Community" (Ph.D. diss., University of California, Berkeley, 1970), p. 186.

been far too great a concentration on organized movements and on the articulate middle-class and upper-class Negroes upon whom the title of "Negro leaders" has been bestowed. The larger masses of lower-class and lower-middle-class Negroes, who are anything but inarticulate in their own lives, have thus been rendered silent, and this silence in turn has been interpreted as acquiescence or apathy. Failure to understand the reaction of the Negro masses has stemmed directly from failure to look seriously at their lives and their culture. It is precisely at this point that the concept of the New Negro is weakest.

The long-standing notion that blacks have understood whites far better than whites have understood blacks can be overdone, but there is much to substantiate its essential validity. It has been true not simply because of white indifference to Negro feelings but because Negroes have taken pains — have had to take pains — not to let whites understand them too well. W. E. B. Du Bois spoke of a "veil" that prevented whites from seeing the inner world of blacks.[12] Paul Laurence Dunbar spoke of a mask:

> Why should the world be overwise,
> In counting all our tears and sighs?
> Nay, let them only see us, while
>   We wear the mask.[13]

This has been a constant message in Negro letters from the late nineteenth century to the present. Ralph Ellison wrote in 1964:

> I found the greatest difficulty for a Negro writer was the problem of revealing what he truly felt, rather than serving up what Negroes were supposed to feel, and were encouraged to feel. And linked to this was the difficulty, based upon our long habit of deception and evasion, of depicting what really happened within our areas of American life, and putting down with honesty and without bowing to ideological expediencies the attitudes and values which give Negro American life its sense of wholeness and which render it bearable and human and, when measured by our own terms, desirable.[14]

The pervasiveness of this phenomenon has been amply demonstrated by the radically different results that research pollsters and social scientists have gotten when using black rather than white investigators. During World War II, Memphis Negroes were asked, "Would Negroes be treated better or worse if the Japanese conquered the U.S.A.?" While 45 percent answered "worse" when the interviewer was white, only 25 percent did so when the interviewer was black. North Carolina Negroes in the early 1960's demon-

---

[12] W. E. B. Du Bois, *The Souls of Black Folk* (1903; reprint ed., New York: Fawcett, 1961).

[13] Paul Laurence Dunbar, *The Complete Poems of Paul Laurence Dunbar* (New York: Dodd, Mead, 1922), p. 71.

[14] Ellison, *Shadow and Act,* p. xxi.

strated higher educational aspirations, agreed more readily that there had to be changes "in the way our country is run," and were more prone to support student sit-ins when they were questioned by black interviewers. Of the Boston Negroes questioned during the same period, 87 percent were willing to agree that "the trouble with most white people is that they think they are better than other people" when questioned by other Negroes; only 66 percent admitted this to whites. Studies made of black youths from two-year-olds to college students have confirmed these results.[15] All this bears out the truth of a song sung by generations of blacks:

> Got one mind for white folks to see,
> 'Nother for what I know is me;
> He don't know, he don't know my mind.

Unfortunately, this truth has not yet sufficiently penetrated the methodologies and perceptions of scholars who have too facilely summed up the attitudes and reactions of blacks. In *The Peculiar Institution,* the most important and perceptive history of United States slavery yet written, Kenneth Stampp anticipated recent theories about the process of "infantilization" by which white masters attempted to produce a childlike race, but he did not commit the mistake of confusing the planters' ideal with reality. His study contains a wealth of suggestions about the private and *sub rosa* tactics used by slaves to resist the white man's design, maintain a sense of individual integrity and self-respect, and manifest a spirit of communal consciousness and solidarity with their fellow blacks.[16] Surprisingly few scholars have attempted this kind of analysis for the postslavery era.

For millions of Negroes in the decades after Emancipation, the normal outlets for protest were closed. They were denied the right of political expression and active demonstration. To understand their reaction to the system under which they lived it is necessary to broaden our definition of protest and resistance, to make it less restrictive and more realistic. This is particularly important because so much of the recent discussion has been concerned with the effects of American racial patterns upon Negro psychic and emotional development. Scholars have written about the psychic effects of the role that many blacks have had to assume among whites without having a full understanding of the roles Negroes have been able to play in black society. The assumption has been that the crucial roles for blacks have been the ones they have played before whites, but this must remain an untested hypothesis until the racial veil has been penetrated and the functions of such institutions as Negro churches and fraternal organizations have been

---

[15] The results of these tests and interviews are conveniently summarized in Pettigrew, *A Profile of the Negro American,* pp. 50–51.

[16] Kenneth M. Stampp, *The Peculiar Institution* (New York: Alfred A. Knopf, 1955), Chapters 3, 8.

understood. In these institutional enclaves blacks were able to assume many of the social, economic, and political roles denied them in the outside society. What effects these surrogates have had upon black psychic development and concepts of self cannot be understood until scholars drop their assumption that the white stage has been the central one for the development of Negro personality and study in a more open and detailed way the alternatives blacks have been able to construct for themselves.

Similarly, scholars have spoken too easily of Negro apathy and acquiescence without looking in any systematic way at the role spatial mobility has played for blacks. Precisely what has been the meaning of the migrations that have sent millions of Negroes from the South to the North and from rural to urban centers? How have Negroes perceived these demographic shifts? What effects have they had upon black social and psychic life? There have been equally superficial and incomplete discussions of the available peer group models upon which Negro youth could pattern their lives and aspirations. On the whole, such discussions have ignored the evidence of black folklore, black music, and black humor with their array of such heroes and models as tricksters, bad men, and signifiers, and the evidence of lower-class black culture in which entertainers, preachers, and underworld hustlers often occupy central positions.[17]

One can easily extend this list of omissions, but it should be evident that, for all their contributions, too many studies of black history and society have been written in a cultural vacuum, have ignored whole areas of black life and culture, and have emphasized one stratum of Negro society to the exclusion of the masses of blacks. Surely, this is too frail a framework upon which to base hypotheses about the internal life of Negroes in the United States. The remainder of this essay will use the example of early twentieth century black music to indicate the kind of evidence scholars must consult before indulging in generalizations about Negroes—old or New.

Black Songs and Black Consciousness

In exasperation with a reporter who was questioning him about the nature of the music he played, Big Bill Broonzy once remarked: "All music's gotta be 'folk' music. I ain't never heard no horse sing a song." While his interpretation of folk music may have been too all-inclusive, Broonzy was reflecting the fact that for Negroes, probably more than for any other group in the United States, music has been historically (and for large numbers has remained) a *participant* activity rather than primarily a performer-audience

---

[17] There have been a number of recent studies which have focused upon the central elements of black culture. Among the most notable are Charles Keil, *Urban Blues* (Chicago: University of Chicago Press, 1966); LeRoi Jones, *Blues People* (New York: William Morrow, 1963); Roger D. Abrahams, *Positively Black* (Englewood Cliffs, N.J.: Prentice-Hall, 1970); and Bruce A. Rosenberg, *The Art of the American Folk Preacher* (New York: Oxford University Press, 1970).

phenomenon. It is precisely this folk quality of Negro music that makes it such a good medium for getting at the thought, spirit, and history of the very segment of the Negro community that historians have rendered inarticulate through their neglect. This is evident in Muddy Waters' recollections of his boyhood in Clarksdale, Mississippi, during the 1920's:

> I was just a boy and they put me to workin' right along side the men. I handled the plough, chopped cotton, did all of them things. Every man would be hollerin' but you don't pay that no mind. Yeah, course I'd holler too. You might call them blues but they was just made-up things. Like a feller be workin' or most likely some gal be workin' near and you want to say somethin' to 'em. So you holler it. Sing it. Or maybe to your mule or something or it's gettin' late and you wanna go home. I can't remember much of what I was singin' now 'ceptin' I do remember I was always singin', "I cain't be satisfied, I be all troubled in mind." Seems to me like I was always singin' that, because I was always singin' jest the way I felt, and maybe I didn't exactly *know* it, but I jest didn't like the way things were down there—in Mississippi.

This participant role was true not only of those who "hollered" in the fields, sang in the churches, or picked a guitar at home, but also of those who went out to listen and respond to professional entertainers. Norman Mason, a

Negro Boy, painting by Eastman Johnson. Courtesy of the National Academy of Design, New York City.

The Banjo Player, painting by
William Sidney Mount. Courtesy
of the Melville Collection,
Suffolk Museum and Carriage
House, Stony Brook, N.Y.

trumpet player who backed up such classic blues singers as Ida Cox, Mamie
Smith, and Ma Rainey, has testified that he liked the blues

> because it do express the feelings of people and when we used to play around
> through Mississippi in those cotton sections of the country we had the people
> *with* us! They hadn't much outlet for their enjoyment and they get together
> in those honkytonks and you should hear them. That's where they let out
> their suppressed desires, and the more suppressed they are the better the
> blues they put out, seems to me.[18]

What emerges from these statements—and they could be multiplied many
times—is the important role music played in the lives of lower-class Negroes, both urban and rural.

Black songs were rarely completely formalized—handed down from generation to generation with no changes—or wholly spontaneous. Most often
they were products of that folk process which has been called "communal
re-creation," through which old songs are constantly reworked into essentially new entities.[19] The white sociologist and song collector Howard Odum,
hearing the singing of a Negro road gang working in front of his Georgia

---

[18] Paul Oliver, *Conversation with the Blues* (New York: Horizon Press, 1965), pp. 29–30,
121–23.

[19] Bruno Nettl, *Folk and Traditional Music of the Western Continents* (Englewood Cliffs,
N.J.: Prentice-Hall, 1965), pp. 4–5.

home, promptly sat on a rock wall nearby in an effort to record the lyrics of their songs. When he finally made out the words, they were:

> White man settin' on wall,
> White man settin' on wall,
> White man settin' on wall all day long,
> Wastin' his time, wastin' his time.[20]

Utilizing a familiar structure and probably also a familiar tune, these black workers left themselves ample scope to improvise new words that fit their surroundings and their mood. An even better example of this process has been provided by the blues and jazz pianist Sam Price in relating an incident from his Texas boyhood:

> I'll never forget the first song I ever heard to remember. A man had been lynched near my home in a town called Robinson, Texas. And at that time we were living in Waco, Texas—my mother, brother and myself. And they made a parody of this song and the words were something like this:
>
>> I never have, and I never will
>> Pick no more cotton in Robinsonville,
>> Tell me how long will I have to wait,
>> Can I get you now or must I hesitate?[21]

The importance of this communal spontaneity is evident: the songs sung at work and at play constitute a record of events, impressions, and reactions which is rarely available through other sources.

To comprehend the importance of this record does not ensure that it will be read correctly. Despite their precocity in recognizing the centrality of music in black culture and their unremitting zeal in collecting that music, some of the most important students of early twentieth-century Negro folk music proved to be too deeply rooted in their own cultural milieu to comprehend the implications of much of what they had gathered. John Lomax, for instance, argued in a 1917 article that the prevailing mood of black songs "is one of introspection—self-pity is the theme that, perhaps above all others, dominates his singing," and printed lyrics like these:

> White folks go to college, niggers to de fiel';
> White folks learn to read an' write, niggers learn to steal.
> Well, it make no diff'ence how you make out yo' time,
> White man sho' to bring a nigger out behin'.
>
>> Ain't it hard, ain't it hard,
>> Ain't it hard to be a nigger, nigger, nigger?
>> Ain't it hard, ain't it hard,
>> Caze you can't git yo' money when it's due?

[20] Howard W. Odum and Guy B. Johnson, *The Negro and His Songs* (1925; reprint ed., Hatboro, Pa.: Folklore Associates, 1964), pp. 2–3.

[21] Oliver, *Conversation with the Blues*, pp. 34–35.

Or:

> Ought for ought an' figger for figger,
> All for white man an' nothin' for nigger.
> Nigger an' white man playin' seben-up, O my hon,
> Nigger win de money but 'fraid to pick it up, O my hon.

Yet, in spite of these songs and of his own perception of the introspective nature of Negro song, Lomax found the stereotypes of the past too much to overcome. Why blacks should sing songs of discontent, he concluded, "is difficult to say. There surely exists no merrier-hearted race than the negro, especially in his natural home, the warm climate of the South. The negro's loud laugh may sometimes speak the empty mind, but at the same time it reveals a nature upon which trouble and want sit but lightly."[22]

In their 1926 collection, *Negro Workaday Songs,* Howard Odum and Guy Johnson entitled one of their chapters "Just Songs to Help With Work" and characterized the songs presented as "songs for song's sake, expression for expression's sake, and 'hollerin' jes' to he'p me wid my work.'" Yet this chapter contains lyrics like these:

> I'm gonna buy me,
> Buy me a winchester rifle,
> Box o' balls,
> Lawd, Lawd, box o' balls.
>
> I'm gonna back my,
> Back myself in the mountains
> To play bad,
> Lawd, Lawd, to play bad.

Or this pick-and-shovel song for which the authors can find no "historical base" and in which they see little "sense":

> Well I can stan',
> Lookin' 'way over in Georgia,
> O-eh-he, Lawd, Lawd,
> She's burnin' down,
> Lawd, she's burnin' down.[23]

Perhaps the best example of this selective myopia can be found in one of the most valuable and scholarly collections of early twentieth-century black music, *American Negro Folk-Songs.* Its compiler, Newman I. White, concluded:

> In his songs I find him [the Negro] as I have found him elsewhere, a most naive and unanalytical-minded person, with a sensuous joy in his religion;

---

[22] John A. Lomax, "Self-Pity in Negro Folk-Songs," *Nation* 105 (9 August 1917): 141–45.

[23] Howard W. Odum and Guy B. Johnson, *Negro Workaday Songs* (Chapel Hill: University of North Carolina Press, 1926), pp. 120–21.

thoughtless, careless, unidealistic, rather fond of boasting, predominantly cheerful, but able to derive considerable pleasure from a grouch; occasionally suspicious, charitably inclined toward the white man, and capable of a gorgeously humorous view of anything, particularly himself.

Professor White's view of Negroes was hardly original. What was new is that it was accompanied by a good number of songs like these:

> Some o' these mornings, and 'twon't be long,
> Capt'n gwine ter call me and I be gone.   (1915–1916)

> The times are hard and money is sca'ce;
> Soon as I sell my cotton and corn
> I am bound to leave this place.   (1915–1916)

> If a white man kills a negro, they hardly carry it to court,
> If a negro kills a white man, they hang him like a goat.   (1915–1916)

> The old bee makes de honey-comb,
> The young bee makes de honey;
> Colored folks plant de cotton and corn,
> And de white folks gits de money.   (1919)

> White man in the parlor reading latest news,
> Negro in the kitchen blacking Roosevelt's shoes. (1915–1916)

> But God loves yo', yo' little black baby,
> Jes' de same as if yo' wuz white,
> God made yo', yo' little black baby,
> So I jes' says yo's all right.   (1915–1916)

White was scholarly enough to print these songs and others like them and thoughtful enough to feel the need to explain them, since they failed to fit his conclusions about black people. First, he discounted them quantitatively, arguing that "the very small number of such songs in my whole collection of nearly a thousand . . . is a matter of really primary significance." The impressive thing, of course, was not the small number of such songs (which were more numerous than White ever admitted) but the fact that in the repressive climate of the early twentieth century Negroes in the Deep South were willing to sing any of these songs openly. White himself must have realized this, for he constructed a more elaborate explanation in his theory of the "transcending of verbal meaning" in black songs. "It is very easy, in fact," he wrote, "to over-interpret all Negro folk-songs through forgetting that to the folk Negro the music, and not the words, is the important matter."[24] This is a particularly fascinating argument, coming as it did from a man who

---

[24] Newman I. White, *American Negro Folk Songs* (1928; reprint ed., Hatboro Pa.: Folklore Associates, 1965), pp. 30, 258, 286, 382, 384, 377, 27.

spent some ten years collecting the lyrics—not the music—of black songs and who, in the five hundred pages of his text, devoted only one seven-page appendix to "Specimens of Tunes." Newman White understood fully the importance of Negro folk lyrics; he resorted to the tortured logic and wishful thinking of arguments like verbal transcendence only when those lyrics threatened an image he needed to preserve.

Indeed, it is extremely doubtful that someone as familiar with black songs as Newman White could have failed to perceive that their most important element was the words, not the music. As Harold Courlander has argued for the blues—and his argument applies to the other basic forms of Negro song as well—"It is easy to overlook the reality that genuine blues in its natural setting is not primarily conceived as 'music' but as a verbalization of deeply felt personal meanings. It is a convention that this verbalization is sung." One finds this theme in the testimony of one Negro blues singer after another. As one of them put it:

> When you make a new blues and it says exactly what you got on your mind, you feel like it's pay day. Some blues, now, they get *towards* it, but if they don't quite get to what you got on your mind, you just got to keep on trying. There have been times when I sang till my throat was hoarse without really putting my difficulties in the song the way I felt them. Other times, it comes out just right on the first try.[25]

The concentration on content underlines the functional nature of most black music. This functionality stemmed from the fact that for black Americans, as for their African forebears, music was not primarily an art form but an integral part of life. One of the most important functions of black songs was the verbalization of personal and group feelings which had few, if any, other outlets. This too has been documented by many black singers. Lil Son Jackson recalled the massive burden of economic and social injustice his sharecropper father labored under:

> That was the onliest way he could get relief from it, by singin' them blues. Just like me or anybody. I can get vexed up or somethin' or I have a sad feelin'; seems like to me that if I can sing, I feel better. But my father, he only just played at home and around. More or less at home is all I did know him to play. . . . They all played music, my father and mother too. . . . I never did take music to be a thing that I could make a livin' of; . . . I never did take interest enough in it to go to school and try to learn somethin' from the book, I more or less played what I felt.

[25] Harold Courlander, *Negro Folk Music, U.S.A.* (New York: Columbia University Press, 1963), p. 145. For similar arguments, see James Weldon Johnson's preface to *The Second Book of Negro Spirituals* (New York: Viking Press, 1926) and Jones, *Blues People*, p. 28. Jones goes even further and argues: "Even the purely instrumental music of the American Negro contains constant reference to vocal music. Blues-playing is the closest imitation of the human voice of any music I've heard; the vocal effects that jazz musicians have delighted in from Bunk Johnson to Ornette Coleman are evidence of this."

"I tell you," Henry Townsend agreed,

> In most cases the way I feel, the song will come to you when you are really depressed you know. I mean, words'll come to you and you feel them and you decide you'll do something about it, so the thing that you do about it is more or less to put it in rhymes and words and make them come out. It gives you relief—it kinda helps somehow. I don't know—it kinda helps.[26]

If our understanding of the meaning of Negro folk songs has been hampered frequently by the predispositions of the pioneer analysts and collectors, it has been impeded as well by the nature of the songs themselves, which are often indirect and ambiguous. From the time Negroes first arrived in America, conditions have made it imperative for them to disguise their feelings from the white man and perhaps at times from themselves as well. As I have argued elsewhere, music has always provided one of the primary means for transcending the restrictions imposed by external, and even internal, censors. Through the use of innuendo, metaphor, and circumlocution, Negroes could utilize their songs as outlets for individual and communal release.[27]

The existence of double meaning in Negro folk songs has long been recognized. Howard Odum, for example, reflected upon the "paradoxes and contradictions" contained in the songs he collected, admitted that "the negro is very secretive," and spoke of "the resourcefulness and adaptability of the negro" and of "his hypocrisy and two-faced survival mechanisms."[28] The only instance in which this phenomenon was studied in any detail by the early twentieth-century collectors, however, focused upon sexual relations. In 1927 Guy Johnson pointed out that when black songs depict men stealing, cheating, and dying for a piece of their woman's jelly roll, angel food cake, or shortening bread, it is difficult to believe that these terms are meant to refer to food:

> Dupree was a bandit,
> He was brave an' bol',
> He stole that diamon' ring
> For some of Betty's jelly roll.
>
> Two little niggers layin' in bed,
> One turned over to the other an' said,
> "My baby loves short'nin', short'nin' bread,
> My baby loves short'nin' bread."

---

[26] Oliver, *Conversation with the Blues,* pp. 24, 33–34.

[27] Lawrence W. Levine, "Slave Songs and Slave Consciousness," in Tamara Hareven, ed., *Anonymous Americans* (Englewood Cliffs, N.J.: Prentice-Hall, 1971).

[28] Howard W. Odum, "Religious Folk-Songs of the Southern Negroes," *American Journal of Religious Psychology and Education* 3 (July 1909): 269. Odum and Johnson, *The Negro and His Songs,* pp. xvii, 9.

Johnson found that words like "cabbage," "keyhole," "cookie," and "cake" were frequently used as symbols for the female sexual organs, and it would be possible to add many similar metaphors to his list. Johnson never claimed that all double meanings in Negro music were of a sexual nature, and in a footnote he indicated: "There are, for example, many hidden references to the white man in the Negro's songs. This is an interesting field of research in which little has been done."[29] But it was doubtless easier for him and many of his colleagues to admit the existence of double meaning in sexual relations, since it merely confirmed their image of the low moral state of the Negro. They were much less ready to analyze double meaning that reflected lack of contentment or anything less than total adjustment. Once the door is opened, however, it is difficult to close again. Once the existence of *double-entendre* and veiled meaning is admitted in one area, it is hard to rule it out in others.

What precisely have Negroes meant in their twentieth-century religious music when they complained continuously, "Why doan de debbil let-a me be?" or asked, "What makes ole Satan hate me so?" and answered, "Cause he got me once an' let me go," or boasted, "Ole Satan thought he had me fast, / Broke his chain an' I'm free at last," or observed:

> Just let me tell you how this world is fixed:
> Satan has got it so full of tricks,
> You can go from place to place,
> Everybody's runnin' down the colored race.

In freedom, as in slavery, the Devil—over whom Negroes generally triumphed in their songs—often looked suspiciously like a surrogate for the white man. Similarly, while Negroes had long sung of "letters from the Lord" and "trains to glory," and while there can be no doubt that these phrases were frequently meant literally, during the early twentieth-century migration of blacks from the South to the North—which many Southern states desperately tried to stop—it is difficult to imagine that these metaphors did not assume contemporary connotations.

> Well, my mother got a letter, oh, yes;
> Well, she could not read it, oh, yes.
> What you reckon that letter said?
> That she didn't have long to stay here.
>
> Yes, I 'bleeged to leave this world,
> Yes, I 'bleeged to leave this world,
> Sister, I's 'bleeged to leave this world,
> For it's a hell to me.[30]

---

[29] Guy B. Johnson, "Double Meaning in the Popular Negro Blues," *Journal of Abnormal Psychology* 22 (April–June 1927): 12–20.

[30] Odum and Johnson, *The Negro and His Songs,* pp. 41, 42, 124, 131, 120, 116. For many similar songs, see Chapters 2–4.

Nonreligious work songs and blues are a bit less of a dilemma, since they tend to be more direct and open, but this is by no means invariable. Even in as relatively formalized and popular a Negro work song as "John Henry," the meaning is by no means clear cut:

> This old hammer killed John Henry,
> But it can't kill me.
> Take this hammer, take it to the Captain,
> Tell him I'm gone, babe, tell him I'm gone.[31]

The possible meanings of the following lyrics are also intriguing:

> Niggers gettin' mo' like white fo'ks,
> Mo' like white fo'ks eve'y day.
> Niggers learnin' Greek an' Latin,
> Niggers wearin' silk an' satin,
> Niggers gettin' mo' like white fo'ks eve'y day.[32]

In 1917 John Lomax interpreted those lines as presenting "the cheerful side of improving social conditions." But they could as easily, and perhaps more meaningfully, be seen as an example of lower-class black satire and anger directed at those Negroes who were trying to become culturally "white." An even greater interpretive challenge is presented by these lyrics sung by a black Georgia worker:

> Ever see bear cat
> Turn to lion,
> Lawd, Lawd,
> Down in Georgia?
>
> My ol' bear cat,
> My ol' bear cat
> Turn to lion,
> Lawd, Lawd, Lawd.
>
> 'Fo' long, Lawd,
> Yes, 'fo' long, Lawd,
> I'll be back here,
> I'll be back here.[33]

The number of songs containing ambiguous metaphors and intriguing but obscure symbolism could be extended indefinitely. Still, as many of the lyrics quoted indicate, there are hollers, work songs, field songs, and blues whose meaning is really not subject to a great deal of interpretation. There

---

[31] For many examples of "John Henry" songs, see Guy B. Johnson, *John Henry: Tracking Down a Negro Legend* (Chapel Hill: University of North Carolina Press, 1929).

[32] Lomax, *Nation* 105 (9 August 1917): 144.

[33] Odum and Johnson, *Negro Workaday Songs,* pp. 121–22.

are hundreds of songs from the first two decades of this century that make it unmistakably clear that Negro music has been a crucial, and perhaps central, vehicle for the expression of protest and discontent. There were constant complaints about the white "captain," about working conditions, about the unfairness of the sharecropping system. Sometimes these were expressed satirically:

> Reason I love my captain so,
> 'Cause I ast him for a dollah,
> Lawd, he give me fo'.

But often they were presented openly and baldly:

> Niggers plant the cotton,
> Niggers pick it out,
> White man pockets money,
> Niggers does without.[34]

During these years, blacks were still singing the words of a song first reported by Frederick Douglass during slavery:

> She sift de meal, she gimme de dust,
> She bake de bread, she gimme de crust,
> She eat de meat, she gimme de skin,
> An' dat's de way she tuck me in.[35]

There was often, one song admitted, "Plenty to eat, / Place to sleep," but "nothin' fer a feller, / Lawd, nothin' fer / A feller to keep."[36]

This sense of injustice, which certainly embodied no illusions about the American racial situation or the black man's place in it, was often accompanied by a great deal of anger, aggression, and self-pride:

> Well, if I had my weight in lime,
> I'd whip my captain till I went stone-blind.

> Well, you can't do me like you do po' Shine,
> You take Shine's money, but you can't take mine.[37]

Lines like "I wish my captain would go blind," "I didn't come here to be nobody's dog," "Ain't let nobody treat me dis way," "Ain't gonna be bossed aroun' no mo'," "Ain't gwine let you humbug me," "You call me dog, I don' ker," "I ain't gonna let nobody, / Nobody make a fool out o' me," were ubiquitous:

[34] Ibid., pp. 112, 115.

[35] Dorothy Scarborough, *On the Trail of Negro Folk-Songs* (1925; reprint ed., Hatboro, Pa.: Folklore Associates, 1963), p. 99. White, *American Negro Folk Songs.*, p. 161.

[36] Odum and Johnson, *Negro Workaday Songs,* pp. 115–16.

[37] Odum and Johnson, *The Negro and His Songs,* p. 253.

If you don't like the way I work, jus' pay me off.
I want to speak one luvin' word before I go:
I know you think I'm pow'ful easy, but I ain't so sof';
I can git another job an' be my boss.[38]

Often this anger took the form not of aggression so much as of refusing to play the game by the white man's rules: "Cap'n says, hurry, I say take my time," "Dere ain't no use in my workin' so hard," "When you think I'm workin', I ain't doin' a thing."[39]

    If you work all the week,
        An' work all the time,
    White man sho to bring
        Nigger out behin'.[40]

These lyrics are important because they are an assertion of a break with the idealized Puritan values and mores of white society. The "Bad Man" songs like "Stagolee" and "Dupree" ("I'm de bad nigger, / If you wants to know; . . . Shoot, nigger, / Shoot to kill") and the blues, especially in their depiction of sexual conduct, are similarly filled with assertions of independence from the cold, mocking world of bourgeois values and dicta that seemed so hypocritical.[41]

The same independence from the values of the larger society can be seen with regard to color. Certainly, Negro songs were often marked by the color preferences of white American society. What is more important, given the stereotype that most blacks during this period longed to be white, is that at least as often they were characterized by color pride. Negro troops in France during World War I were often heard singing: "It takes a long, tall, slim, black man to make a German lay his rifle down."[42] Again and again, black-skinned and brown-skinned women and men were held up as objects of desire and admiration:

    Some says yellow
    While others say brown,
    But for me I'll take the blackest in town.[43]

---

[38] Ibid., pp. 171, 257. Odum and Johnson, *Negro Workaday Songs,* pp. 76, 128. White, *American Negro Folk Songs,* pp. 255, 258. Scarborough, *On the Trail of Negro Folk-Songs,* p. 190.

[39] White, *American Negro Folk Songs,* pp. 255, 302. Scarborough, *On the Trail of Negro Folk-Songs,* p. 235. Odum and Johnson, *The Negro and His Songs,* p. 163.

[40] Odum and Johnson, *The Negro and His Songs,* p. 255.

[41] For example, see Odum and Johnson, *Negro Workaday Songs,* Chapter 4, and Paul Oliver, *Blues Fell This Morning* (New York: Horizon Press, 1960).

[42] White, *American Negro Folk Songs,* p. 355.

[43] Ibid., p. 316.

> A yellow girl I do despise,
> But a jut-black girl I can't denies.[44]

> Ain't crazy 'bout no high yellows, worried about no brown,
> Come to picking my choice, gimme
> The blackest man in town.[45]

> Some say, give me a high yaller,
> I say give me a teasin' brown,
> For it takes a teasin' brown,
> To satisfy my soul.[46]

Black songs of the early twentieth century could be accompanied by a deadening sense of fatalism and despair: "I didn't bring nuthin' in dis bright worl'; / Nuthin' I'll carry away," or "Trouble, trouble, / Been had it all my day; Believe to my soul / Trouble gonna kill me dead."[47] This mood, however, was often modified by the strong sense of change, freedom of movement, and mobility that pervaded these songs: "I jest come here to stay a little while," "Gwine whar' I never been befo'," "Oh, goin' down dat lonesome road, / An' I won't be treated this-a way," "I'm gonna row here few days longer, / Then, Lawd, I'm goin' on."[48] Frequently there seemed to be a new self-consciousness about movement and a need to distinguish it from mere running away. Thus in "John Henry" and similar work songs the request to "Take my hammer . . . to my captain, / Tell him I'm gone," was accompanied by this admonition:

> If he asks you was I running,
> Tell him no,
> Tell him no.
> Tell him I was going across the Blue Ridge Mountains
> Walking slow, yes, walking slow.[49]

Occasionally there was even a sense of the possibility of turning the tables on the whites:

> Well, I'm goin' to buy me a little railroad of my own,
> Ain't goin' to let nobody ride but de chocolate to de bone.

---

[44] Odum and Johnson, *The Negro and His Songs*, p. 193.

[45] White, *American Negro Folk Songs*, p. 326.

[46] Odum and Johnson, *Negro Workaday Songs*, p. 146.

[47] Odum and Johnson, *The Negro and His Songs*, p. 162. Odum and Johnson, *Negro Workaday Songs*, p. 40.

[48] Odum and Johnson, *The Negro and His Songs*, pp. 171, 176. Odum and Johnson, *Negro Workaday Songs*, pp. 46, 112–13.

[49] White, *American Negro Folk Songs*, p. 259.

Well, I'm goin' to buy me a hotel of my own,
Ain't goin' to let nobody eat but de chocolate to de bone.[50]

Conclusion

The purpose of this essay is not to argue that Negro music has functioned primarily as a medium of protest. To state this would distort black music and black culture. Negroes have not spent all their time reacting to whites, and their songs are filled with comments on all aspects of life. But it would be an even greater distortion to assume that a people occupying the position that Negroes have in this society could produce a music as rich and varied as they have with few allusions to their situation or only slight indications of their reactions to the treatment they were accorded. While black music is not dominated by such reactions, it is a rich repository of them and offers a new window onto the lives and into the minds of a large segment of the black community that has been ignored because its members have not left behind the kind of sources that historians are used to working with.

To argue that music constituted a form of black protest does not mean that it necessarily led to any tangible and specific actions, but rather that it served as a mechanism by which Negroes could be relatively candid in a society that rarely accorded them that privilege, could communicate with other Negroes whom they would in no other way be able to reach, and could assert their own individuality, aspirations, and sense of being. Certainly, if nothing else, black music makes it difficult to believe that early twentieth-century Negroes internalized their situation so completely, accepted the values of the larger society so totally, or manifested so pervasive an apathy as we have been led to believe.

As it has been applied both implicitly and explicitly, then, the concept of the New Negro requires serious modification. As a historical phenomenon, of course, it retains great importance. For almost every generation of blacks since Emancipation, the idea of the New Negro, in all its varying forms, has been a crucial rallying cry and a source of great optimism and ego gratification. But its very ubiquity should make scholars wary of taking it too literally. It has had unquestionable utility as a vehicle for action, but as a means of historical understanding it has tended to obscure as much as it has revealed. And it will continue to do so until it is made to encompass not merely select groups of historically articulate Negroes but the entire spectrum of black society and all the realities of black culture.

---

[50] Lomax, *Nation* 105 (9 August 1917): 144.

3 SUGGESTIONS FOR FURTHER READING

Abraham, Roger D., *Positively Black**. Englewood Cliffs, N.J.: Prentice-Hall, 1970.
- A study of black street culture in Philadelphia.

Bracey, John H., Jr., Meier, August, and Rudwick, Elliott M., eds., *Black Nationalism in America**. Indianapolis: Bobbs-Merrill, 1970. ▪ An excellent collection of documents that recounts the many varieties of black nationalism to be found in American history.

Broderick, Francis L., *W. E. B. DuBois: Negro Leader in a Time of Crisis**. Stanford, Calif.: Stanford University Press, 1959. ▪ A respectful, analytic view of this great Negro leader of the early twentieth century.

Cronon, Edmund David, *Black Moses: The Story of Marcus Garvey and the Universal Negro Improvement Association**. Madison: University of Wisconsin Press, 1955. ▪ The first scholarly study of Marcus Garvey, it remains the most knowledgeable account of his organization.

Du Bois, W. E. B., *The Souls of Black Folk**. Chicago: McClurg, 1903. ▪ A classic set of essays especially noted for the author's criticism of Booker T. Washington's policy of accommodation.

Ellison, Ralph, *Shadow and Act**. New York: Random House, 1966. ▪ The writer's viewpoint on various aspects of Negro art and Negro identity.

Garvey, Amy Jacques, *Garvey and Garveyism**. Kingston, Jamaica: A. Jacques Garvey, 1963. ▪ A reflective account of the Garvey movement by the leader's wife.

Garvey, Marcus, *The Philosophy and Opinions of Marcus Garvey**, 2 vols., ed. Amy Jacques Garvey. New York: Universal Publishing House, 1923, 1925.
- A collection of his writings and speeches, and some documents from his trial.

---

* Available in paperback edition.

148

Johnson, James W., and Johnson, J. Rosamond, *The Second Book of Negro Spirituals.* New York: Viking Press, 1926. ▪ The best compilation of black spirituals presently available.

Jones, LeRoi, *Blues People: Negro Music in White America**. New York: William Morrow, 1963. ▪ An excellent series of essays that places black music in a broad social context.

Kellogg, Charles Flint, *NAACP, A History of the National Association for the Advancement of Colored People,* vol. 1, *1909–1920.* Baltimore: Johns Hopkins Press, 1967. ▪ A painstaking, thorough probe of the NAACP archives and related manuscript collections.

Locke, Alain, "The New Negro," in *The New Negro**, ed. Alain Locke. New York: Albert & Charles Boni, 1925. ▪ A prerequisite for an understanding of the Harlem Renaissance.

Logan, Rayford W., *The Negro in American Life and Thought: The Nadir, 1877–1901.* New York: Dial Press, 1954. ▪ A rich study that relies heavily on periodicals in describing the post-Reconstruction denial of Negro rights.

Meier, August, *Negro Thought in America, 1880–1915: Racial Ideologies in the Age of Booker T. Washington**. Ann Arbor: University of Michigan Press, 1963. ▪ An authoritative analysis of the integration-separation polarity associated with Booker T. Washington and W. E. B. Du Bois.

Quarles, Benjamin, ed., *Frederick Douglass**. Englewood Cliffs, N.J.: Prentice-Hall, 1968. ▪ A unique collection of articles on the life and work of Frederick Douglass that surpasses even Quarles's biography of the same title (Washington, D.C.: Associated Publishers, 1948).

Redkey, Edwin S., *Black Exodus: Black Nationalism and Back-to-Africa Movements, 1890–1910**. New Haven, Conn.: Yale University Press, 1969. ▪ A scholarly account of the ideas and events surrounding Bishop Henry McNeal Turner's nationalist campaigns.

Rosenberg, Bruce A., *The Art of the American Folk Preacher.* New York: Oxford University Press, 1970. ▪ An excellent study of the oratorical tradition among black preachers.

Spencer, Samuel R., Jr., *Booker T. Washington and the Negro's Place in American Life**. Boston: Atlantic-Little, Brown, 1955. ▪ A skillful biography of Booker T. Washington, but, like all others to date, it fails to make exhaustive use of Washington's papers preserved in the Library of Congress.

Turner, Henry McNeal, *Respect Black! The Writings and Speeches of Henry McNeal Turner,* ed. Edwin S. Redkey. New York: Arno Press, 1970. ▪ A collection of documents that summarizes the philosophy of Bishop Turner and the goals of his nationalist movement.

White, Newman I., *American Negro Folk Songs.* Hatboro, Pa.: Folklore Associates, 1965. Originally published in 1928. ▪ An invaluable collection of Afro-American songs, despite its faulty interpretations.

4
The Urban Setting

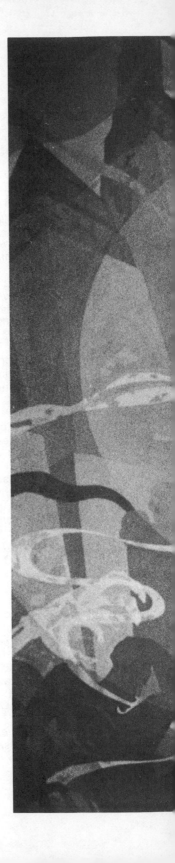

The Origins of the Urban Ghetto, 1870-1915

ALLAN SPEAR

Allan Spear is associate professor of history at the University of Minnesota. His published works in the field of urban history include *Black Chicago: The Making of a Negro Ghetto, 1890-1920* (University of Chicago Press, 1967). In the following essay, Mr. Spear discusses the roles white racism and the black self-help ideology have played in the ghettoization of Afro-Americans. Appraising scholarly investigation of black history, he states that historians have generally focused exclusively on the role of elites and suggests that greater attention be given to the lives of the black urban masses.

The Historian and the Urban Ghetto

Perhaps no subject in Afro-American history—with the exception of slavery—has received as much attention in recent years as the development of the urban ghetto. The contemporary crisis in our cities has impelled historians to search for the roots of the ghetto and to explore the forces that relegated black people to a separate and subordinate status in urban life. Before the 1960's, there had been no important historical studies of the ghetto. There had, of course, been many perceptive treatments of ghetto life —by St. Clair Drake and Horace Cayton, Robert Weaver, James Weldon Johnson, Claude McKay, W. E. B. Du Bois, E. Franklin Frazier, Roi Ottley, and others[1]—but these writers rarely attempted to place their analyses in historical context. In the period 1965-1970, however, there were two full-length works on the development of the black community in New York, one

---

[1] See St. Clair Drake and Horace Cayton, *Black Metropolis* (New York: Harcourt, 1945); Robert Weaver, *The Negro Ghetto* (New York: Harcourt, 1948); James Weldon Johnson, *Black Manhattan* (New York: Alfred A. Knopf, 1930); Claude McKay, *Harlem: Negro Metropolis* (New York: E. P. Dutton, 1940); W. E. B. Du Bois, *The Philadelphia Negro* (Philadelphia: University of Pennsylvania Press, 1899); E. Franklin Frazier, *The Negro Family in Chicago* (Chicago: University of Chicago Press, 1932); and Roi Ottley, *New World A-Coming* (Boston: Houghton Mifflin, 1943).

on Chicago, and one on Washington.[2] Other studies, in progress in 1970, examine the origins of the black ghettos of Philadelphia, Detroit, Cleveland, and Baltimore. Moreover, historians have begun to explore in depth some of the major racial conflicts that developed in the North and some of the organizations and institutions that have grown out of black urban life.[3]

Although recent studies of the ghetto have varied in emphasis and approach, certain broad patterns clearly emerge from them. Robert Weaver's assertion that the Northern ghetto was a product of the migration of blacks from the South during World War I has been seriously questioned.[4] In New York, Chicago, and Washington, black enclaves have existed since early in the nineteenth century, and by 1900, well-developed ghettos, with separate institutions and a distinctive life style, had begun to emerge. The migrations during World War I, the 1920's, and World War II accelerated the formation of ghettos and exacerbated urban problems, but the ghetto itself was the product of pre–World War I years.

Recent historians of ghetto life have viewed white hostility as the major force behind the racial polarization of urban society. Restrictions in housing and employment forced black people into separate communities where they had little choice but to provide for themselves the facilities and services that the larger community denied them. This does not mean that Afro-Americans were merely passive figures. They worked actively and positively to create a viable social and cultural life of their own. The physical ghetto was the product of white racism, but the institutional ghetto was the creation of black civic leaders and entrepreneurs determined to make the black community a decent place to live. Yet this development can only be understood within the context of the racial proscriptions that continually circumscribed their activities.

New historical literature on urban black life demonstrates clearly that the black ghetto differed in significant ways from the European immigrant enclaves of our major cities. It calls into serious question the thesis advanced by historian Oscar Handlin and by sociologist Philip Hauser that the experience of black migrants in the cities parallels that of European immigrant groups. Handlin has maintained that Afro-Americans in the urban North,

---

[2] See Gilbert Osofsky, *Harlem: The Making of a Ghetto* (New York: Harper, 1966); Seth Scheiner, *Negro Mecca* (New York: New York University Press, 1965); Allan Spear, *Black Chicago: The Making of a Negro Ghetto* (Chicago: University of Chicago Press, 1967); and Constance M. Green, *The Secret City* (Princeton, N.J.: Princeton University Press, 1967).

[3] See Arthur I. Waskow, *From Race Riot to Sit-In* (New York: Doubleday, 1966); Elliott Rudwick, *Race Riot at East St. Louis* (Carbondale: Southern Illinois University Press, 1964); Arvarh E. Strickland, *History of the Chicago Urban League* (Urbana: University of Illinois Press, 1966); and Flint Kellogg, *NAACP* (Baltimore: Johns Hopkins University Press, 1967).

[4] Weaver, *The Negro Ghetto*, p. 16.

like the Irish, Germans, Italians, and Yankees, "chose . . . to live in communities of their own because they could thus best satisfy their social and cultural needs."[5] In assessing the contemporary situation, he has concluded that "the Negroes and Puerto Ricans have followed the general outline of the experience of earlier immigrants. . . . Their adjustment, difficult as it is, is but the most recent of a long series. These newest arrivals have thus but assumed the role formerly played by European immigrants."[6] Similarly, Hauser has argued that "it is a serious mistake to assume that the 'color stigma' is different in kind or even in degree from the stigma which accompanied many of our foreign-white immigrant groups. . . . Color difference can be bridged even as religious and other cultural differences have been bridged, through social interaction and consequent acculturation."[7]

Handlin and Hauser overlook basic differences between the white immigrant and the black migrant experiences. Immigrants settled in closely knit enclaves because of their cultural distinctiveness and because poverty prevented them from acquiring better housing elsewhere. Discrimination was only a secondary cause of their isolation. Indeed, once the immigrants were Americanized and reached a certain degree of affluence, they were usually able to move into the general white community with little difficulty. Cultural distinctiveness and poverty played significant roles in the development of the black ghetto too, of course. Black migrants from the South, like European immigrants, frequently desired homes close to people of similar background and convenient to the institutions and services that catered to their needs. Moreover, poverty limited them, too, to certain sections of a city. Yet, beyond this, similarities cease.

First, the avenues of mobility that were open to European immigrants and their children were usually closed to black urbanites. The son of the immigrant could—and frequently did—rise to a supervisory or managerial position and move with relative ease into the general white American community. The black, on the other hand, was confined before 1915 to service and domestic jobs, and even after the World War I labor shortage opened industry to him he could rarely advance beyond the most menial types of employment. The rare black man who, despite the odds, did acquire a good job and make money still found it difficult to escape the ghetto. A systematic pattern of housing discrimination confined him to the black section of the city even when he could afford property elsewhere. For instance, Sophonisba Breckinridge of Hull House noted that in Chicago in the early twentieth century the problem of the black family was "quite different from the white man and

---

[5] Oscar Handlin, *Firebell in the Night* (Boston: Atlantic-Little, Brown, 1964), p. 97.

[6] Oscar Handlin, *The Newcomers* (Cambridge, Mass.: M.I.T. Press, 1959), p. 118.

[7] Philip Hauser, "Demographic Factors in the Integration of the Negro," *Daedalus* 94 (Fall 1965): 874. For a critique of this argument, see Charles Silberman, *Crisis in Black and White* (New York: Random House, 1964), pp. 36–67.

even that of the immigrant. With the Negro, the housing dilemma was found to be an acute problem, not only among the poor, as in the case of the Polish, Jewish or Italian immigrants, but also among the well-to-do."[8]

Second, blacks have not adapted to the dominant American culture in the same way as European immigrants. The concepts of acculturation and assimilation have frequently been troublesome ones for social scientists; there is no general agreement as to how these processes have operated in American society. Yet a few observations may be in order. While the first-generation European immigrant frequently clung tenaciously to his Old World culture and life style, his children and grandchildren became increasingly "Americanized." They learned English, in many cases modified their traditional religious beliefs and practices, and adopted the values and life goals of middle-class Anglo-Americans. Acculturation was not always completed, and ethnic distinctiveness does persist in many aspects of American life today, but, by and large, even those white ethnic groups that maintain a degree of structural cohesiveness generally conform to Anglo-American cultural values.[9] Black Americans, on the other hand, have not gone through a similar process of transition from Old World to New World culture. The degree to which African culture has survived in the New World remains a matter of sharp dispute.[10] But whether or not Africanisms have persisted, black Americans have developed a culture rooted in their special historical experience in the United States. This culture has manifested itself in a distinctive dialect, a unique musical tradition, and some special attitudes toward work, family, sexual relationships, and community. Many social scientists have argued that the language, arts, and world view of Black America represent less a distinctive culture than a pathological version of white American values. According to Elliot Liebow, for instance, the behavior of the street corner black man "appears not so much as a way of realizing the distinctive goals and values of his own subculture . . . but rather as his way of trying to achieve many of the goals and values of the larger society, of failing to do this, and of concealing his failure from others and from himself as best he can."[11] And Oscar Lewis has argued that what passes for black culture is just one manifestation

---

[8] Sophonisba P. Breckinridge, "The Color Line in the Housing Problem," *Survey* 40 (1 February 1913): 575–76.

[9] The most lucid discussion of the concepts of assimilation and acculturation is Milton Gordon, *Assimilation in American Life* (New York: Oxford University Press, 1964). For a view that differs from both Gordon's and the one presented here, see Nathan Glazer and Daniel P. Moynihan, *Beyond the Melting Pot* (Cambridge, Mass.: M.I.T. Press, 1963).

[10] The classic argument for African survivals is Melville J. Herskovits, *The Myth of the Negro Past* (New York: Harper, 1941). The Herskovits thesis has been challenged by E. Franklin Frazier, *The Negro Family in the United States,* revised ed. (New York: Citadel Press, 1948), pp. 3–16.

[11] Elliot Liebow, *Tally's Corner* (Boston: Atlantic-Little, Brown, 1967), p. 222.

of a "culture of poverty" shared by the less affluent throughout the world.[12] But in recent years a growing number of students of Black America have rejected what Robert Blauner has called the "dogma of liberal social science . . . that Negroes lack any characteristic of a distinctive nationality."[13] Charles Keil has maintained:

> Negroes are the only substantial minority group in America who really have a culture to guard and protect. The small but crucial retentions of African tradition, the slavery experience, the post-slavery history of oppression, the re-emergence of the non-white world, and America's refusal until recently to allow integration—all have combined, for better or for worse, to give the Negro a different reality, a unique perspective by incongruity on American society that may be this nation's outstanding and redeeming virtue.[14]

Keil may go too far in seeing Afro-American culture as existing apart from dominant American cultural patterns, for many blacks have at least partially accepted white values and standards of behavior. Yet he is convincing in his argument that blacks, unlike white ethnic minorities, have developed a distinctive perspective on the world and a unique set of folkways—in both the rural South and the urban North—that are not merely carry-overs from the Old World past but a means of survival in a hostile American present.

White Racism and the Rise of the Ghetto

The Afro-American, unlike white ethnic minorities, lived constantly in the shadow of racial discrimination. Regardless of his economic status, regardless of his cultural preferences, he was isolated from whites in the Northern city. To understand Harlem or the South Side of Chicago, to fully comprehend the distinctive culture that developed there, it is necessary to examine the context of prejudice and discrimination within which the ghettos developed. And because the period 1870–1915 is crucial in the development of the ghetto—as every recent historian of the subject agrees—it is important to understand the racial attitudes of Northern whites during these formative years.

There is a strong temptation to portray the history of white racism in the United States as a continuum without change or variation. And indeed the continuity in white racial attitudes from the eighteenth century to the present is remarkable. Racial stereotypes still current today had their origins

---

[12] Lewis' most recent formulation of his concept of the culture of poverty appears in *La Vida* (New York: Random House, 1965), pp. xlii–lii.

[13] Robert Blauner, "Black Culture: Myth or Reality?" in Norman E. Whitten, Jr., and John F. Szwed, eds., *Afro-American Anthropology* (New York: Free Press, 1970), p. 348.

[14] Charles Keil, *Urban Blues* (Chicago: University of Chicago Press, 1966), p. 191. Other arguments for the existence of a distinctive Afro-American culture appear in Whitten and Szwed, *Afro-American Anthropology*.

in the colonial and precolonial experience.[15] A systematic pattern of discrimination in housing, employment, municipal services, and police practices has characterized race relations in American cities for the past century and a half. Gilbert Osofsky, in a provocative essay entitled, significantly, "The Enduring Ghetto," has argued regarding the period from the early nineteenth century to the mid-twentieth:

> Little has been accomplished that permanently improved the fundamental conditions of life of most Negroes in New York, nor has any ideology or program radically bettered the tone of race relations in the North, if the largest city is a suitable model. What has in our time been called the social pathology of the ghetto is evident throughout our history; the wounds of centuries have not been healed because they have rarely been treated.[16]

Yet, despite the pervasiveness of white racial hostility, there have been changes over the years in the manifestations of racism, particularly during the period between Reconstruction and World War I, when race relations in the Northern cities were far from static. Evidence suggests that white attitudes and practices were far more rigid after 1890 than before. Just as Southern race relations became crystallized and systematized between 1890 and 1910, so too race relations in the North hardened during these years. Northern whites did not institute a system of disfranchisement and segregation, but they did develop patterns of housing and employment discrimination that led directly to the growth of ghettos. New York, for instance, witnessed "the creation of a Negro community within one large and solid geographical area [that] was unique in city history."[17] And in Washington, even "cultivated Negroes . . . discovered that each passing year made it harder for them to purchase or rent comfortable houses without paying exorbitant prices. . . . By 1900 the barriers of caste, seemingly collapsing in the late 1860's, had become stronger than ever."[18]

Earlier, in the 1870's and 1880's, the old ante-bellum pattern of formalized Jim Crow had broken down for a short while. School systems were integrated throughout the North, blacks were enfranchised, and public accommodations were legally opened to all on a nondiscriminatory basis. Massachusetts passed a civil rights law as early as 1865; New York and Kansas followed in 1874; and within two years after the 1883 Supreme Court deci-

---

[15] The best study of the early development of American racial attitudes is Winthrop Jordan, *White Over Black* (Chapel Hill: University of North Carolina Press, 1968).

[16] Gilbert Osofsky, "The Enduring Ghetto," *Journal of American History* 40 (September 1968): 255.

[17] Osofsky, *Harlem: The Making of a Ghetto*, p. 127.

[18] Constance M. Green, *Washington: Capital City* (Princeton, N.J.: Princeton University Press, 1963), pp. 106–07.

sion overturning the federal Civil Rights Act of 1875, eleven other Northern states barred discrimination in public places.[19]

Racially mixed residential areas were not uncommon during these two decades. In Chicago, for instance, there were few solidly black blocks before the turn of the century, and a significant number of Afro-Americans lived interspersed in white neighborhoods.[20] The color line in employment persisted, but exceptional black people did succeed in business and the professions—frequently drawing on a white clientele—and they were commonly hailed by whites and blacks alike as indications of the "progress of the race." The North between 1870 and 1890 was hardly a paradise of interracial amity, but there was probably more contact between the races during these years than at any time before or since.

After 1890, the situation throughout the North underwent significant changes. Residential patterns hardened as blacks were driven out of white districts by neighborhood improvement associations, economic boycotts, frequent acts of violence, and, later, restrictive covenants. The civil rights laws were effectively nullified by lack of enforcement and nonconvicting juries. The black upper class, which had business and social contacts with whites, declined and was replaced by a new middle class with economic and social ties in the ghetto. Blacks continued to vote, and with residential concentration their potential political power increased. However, the possibility of a predominantly white constituency electing a black candidate—which had occurred in the 1870's and 1880's—diminished sharply after 1900. In Chicago, for instance, blacks had been elected to the state legislature and to the county board of commissioners by predominantly white constituencies in the 1880's and the early 1890's. In 1906, however, when a black attorney ran for the municipal court, he aroused vigorous white opposition and was the only Republican candidate to lose in what was otherwise a Republican sweep.[21]

It should be noted that the change that occurred in the 1890's and early 1900's was not an unalloyed step backward for the black people. Some historians have referred to the period of the late nineteenth and early twentieth centuries as the nadir in Afro-American history. The unspoken assumption in such a characterization is that black progress must be judged in terms of acceptance by white people. The post-Reconstruction period was no nadir. It was a time of great ferment in Afro-American thought, of burgeoning protest organizations, and of independent institutional growth. Increasingly

---

[19] Leslie H. Fishel, Jr., "The Genesis of the First Wisconsin Civil Rights Act," *Wisconsin Magazine of History* 49 (Summer 1966): 326.

[20] Spear, *Black Chicago,* pp. 11–15.

[21] Harold Gosnell, *Negro Politicians* (Chicago: University of Chicago Press, 1935), pp. 65–67, 81–83, 85. Spear, *Black Chicago,* pp. 118–20.

forced to rely on their own resources, black people began to build self-sufficient communities and to develop strong, independent leadership.[22] The point, then, is not that the quality of Afro-American life declined, but that race relations changed, that the attitudes and policies of whites toward blacks became more repressive and contact between the races more distant.

What caused these changes? Recent literature suggests several possibilities. First, ideological racism increased throughout the country. The doctrine of racial inequality, long an implicit assumption of most white Americans, became an explicit and positive credo. The works of such early anti-egalitarians as Josiah Nott, Samuel George Morton, and the Frenchman Count Arthur de Gobineau had enjoyed only select and rather specialized audiences in ante-bellum America. By the early twentieth century, however, theorists of racial inequality were widely read and respected, and racist ideas permeated popular culture. Social Darwinism and imperialism had assured racist ideologies of a receptive audience. Many Americans had come to regard nonwhites as representatives of an earlier evolutionary stage, people inherently unable to compete in the struggle for survival. At the same time the United States' acquisition of the Philippines and Puerto Rico was accompanied by the notion that it was the "white man's burden" to control the affairs of inferior peoples who were essentially incapable of governing themselves. Reflecting these views, the novels of Thomas Dixon, the pseudoscientific writings of Madison Grant and Lothrop Stoddard, and countless religious tracts that cited biblical justification for racial inequality found avid readers in the North as well as in the South.[23] The familiar stereotype of the lazy, shuffling, irresponsible "darky" was a staple of the vaudeville stage, and D. W. Griffith's *The Birth of a Nation,* with its hostile caricature of black aspirations in the Reconstruction period, was the most successful motion picture of its time.[24] As I. A. Newby points out, Southern racial

---

[22] Rayford W. Logan, who bases his study primarily on the attitudes of white magazines and newspapers, characterizes this period as "the nadir" (*The Negro in American Life and Thought: The Nadir, 1877–1901* [New York: Dial Press, 1954]; published in paperback under the title *The Betrayal of the Negro*). Conversely, August Meier, who examines the internal history of the black community, sees it as a period of ferment and vitality (*Negro Thought in America, 1880–1915* [Ann Arbor: University of Michigan Press, 1963]).

[23] "Scientific" attitudes toward race in the ante-bellum period are discussed in William Stanton, *The Leopard's Spots* (Chicago: University of Chicago Press, 1960). On the rise of racist thought in the late nineteenth and early twentieth centuries, see Thomas Gossett, *Race: The History of an Idea in America* (Dallas: Southern Methodist University Press, 1963). On antiblack thought in particular, the best account is I. A. Newby, *Jim Crow's Defense* (Baton Rouge: Louisiana State University Press, 1965).

[24] Osofsky analyzes the prevailing theatrical stereotype of the black man at the turn of the century in *Harlem: The Making of a Ghetto,* pp. 37–40. See also James Weldon Johnson's *Black Manhattan.* On *The Birth of a Nation,* see Everett Carter, "Cultural History Written with Lightning: The Significance of *The Birth of a Nation,*" *American Quarterly* 12 (Fall 1960): 347–57.

orthodoxy "was the core of ideas to which non-Southerners also generally subscribed."[25] The Southern belief was the American belief.

It is difficult to assess the influence of racist literature on Northern racial attitudes and practices. The question of cause and effect in the interplay of ideas and action is always a perplexing one, and it is of little use to ask whether Northerners became racists because they read Thomas Dixon or whether they read Dixon because they were already racists. The point is that both the racist literature of the day and the policy of racial repression came out of a general mood of racial animosity and reinforced one another. More than white-black relations were involved here, for this was also the age of imperial expansion and of the move toward immigration restriction. Nearly all the trends of the day pointed toward an increasingly intense feeling of white superiority.

To assess the change in racial attitudes after 1890 it is necessary to proceed beyond a discussion of general mood and to examine the situation in Northern cities. John Higham, in his perceptive analysis of nativism in this period, has shown that hostility to immigrants was significantly influenced by the nature of social conflict in the late nineteenth and early twentieth centuries. Ideological racism was only one facet of the overall picture. Nativism, Higham argues, rose and fell in proportion to the intensity of economic and social anxieties felt by white Americans.[26] C. Vann Woodward posits a similar analysis in discussing the rising tide of racial repression in the South in the period after 1890:

> It is one of the paradoxes of Southern history that political democracy for the white man and racial discrimination for the black were often products of the same dynamics. . . . As the two races were brought into rivalry for subsistence wages in the cotton fields, mines and wharves, the lower-class white man's demand for Jim Crow laws became more insistent. . . . The barriers of racial discrimination mounted in direct ratio with the tide of political democracy among whites.[27]

A similar dynamic helped shape white-black relations in Northern cities between 1890 and 1910. Although the black population of the North grew slowly during this period—from 1.7 percent to 1.9 percent of the total population—growth in specific cities was significant, if not spectacular. In Chicago, the black population increased from 1.3 percent to 2.0 percent, in New York from 1.4 percent to 2.0 percent, in Philadelphia from 3.8 percent to

[25] Newby, *Jim Crow's Defense,* p. 4.

[26] John Higham, *Strangers in the Land* (New Brunswick, N.J.: Rutgers University Press, 1955).

[27] C. Vann Woodward, *The Origins of the New South* (Baton Rouge: Louisiana State University Press, 1951), p. 211.

5.5 percent, and in Pittsburgh from 3.3 percent to 4.8 percent.[28] More important than population growth was the increasing social visibility of black people in the North. Black organizations such as the Afro-American Council, the Niagara Movement, and, after 1909, the National Association for the Advancement of Colored People pressed for equal rights, sometimes with the support of white progressives. Although barred from many jobs, a significant minority of Afro-Americans achieved middle-class status. As a black attorney in Chicago noted, the growth of the Afro-American community "brought [blacks] into contact with whites who hardly knew that there were a thousand Colored people in Chicago." Moreover, "Colored children have appeared in numbers in many of our schools," and "Colored men have pushed their way into many employments. All these things have a tendency to cause whites to resort to jim crow tactics."[29]

Many observers at the turn of the century noted that racial hostility was most conspicuous among working-class whites, particularly among immigrants and the sons of immigrants — the same group that has been characterized in current journalistic jargon as "backlashers," "hard hats," and "the silent majority." Black spokesmen made frequent references to this. A group of black leaders in Milwaukee charged that discrimination came chiefly from "the lower classes of ill-bred and poorly-educated people,"[30] while the *New York Age* noted "how easily . . . foreigners catch on to the notion . . . to treat Afro-Americans disdainfully and contemptuously."[31] It is not surprising that hostility should have been greatest among whites who felt insecure. Woodward, commenting on the South, has observed that "it took a lot of ritual and Jim Crow to bolster the creed of white supremacy in the bosom of a white man working for a black man's wages."[32] Much the same was true in the North. Black neighborhoods usually were adjacent to immigrant enclaves, and population growth led to housing competition. Although black workers had not yet entered industry in large numbers, they competed with poor whites for jobs on the docks and in construction.

It is important to understand that tension between white and black workers was not always spontaneous; frequently it was fomented and carefully nurtured by a white power structure eager to see the working class divided along racial lines. Most conspicuous was the use of black strikebreakers by major Northern employers to destroy the predominantly white labor union movement. In Chicago in the stockyards strike of 1904 and the teamsters strike

---

[28] *Negro Population in the United States, 1790–1915* (Washington, D.C.: U.S. Bureau of the Census, 1918).

[29] *Chicago Broad Ax,* 31 December 1910.

[30] Fishel, "Genesis of the First Wisconsin Civil Rights Act," p. 329.

[31] Quoted in Osofsky, *Harlem: The Making of a Ghetto,* pp. 45–46.

[32] Woodward, *Origins of the New South,* p. 211.

of 1905, and nationally in the steel strike of 1919, thousands of blacks were brought in from the South to work as "scabs." In these situations, employers consciously played upon racial fears in order to deflect the white workers' hostility from themselves to the black strikebreakers. "Remember," said South Carolina's rabidly racist Senator Ben Tillman to an audience of white stockyard workers in Chicago in 1904, "it was the niggers that whipped you in line. They were the club with which your brains were beaten out."[33]

What Tillman did not emphasize, of course, was who was wielding those clubs. Often both black and white workers were but pawns in the efforts of the economic and political elite to weaken any threat to its own hegemony. Employers, real estate dealers, politicians, and newspaper editors fanned the flames of racial tension for their own gain. Lillian Smith, in her perceptive parable of Mr. Rich White and Mr. Poor White, tells how the Southern white upper class kept the poor whites occupied with racial repression while it raked in the profits.[34] Her analysis is equally applicable to the North. Those who would attempt to forge an alliance between white and black workers had to face not only the prejudices of white workers but the racial demagoguery of the white elite. Nearly every overt racial clash in the North in the early twentieth century involved conflict between blacks and working-class whites. In many instances, labor disputes led directly to attacks on black workers by white strikers and their sympathizers.[35] Housing competition also produced violent conflict, and white youth gangs, often Irish, led forays into black neighborhoods. The police force—always a bastion of working-class white sentiment—usually displayed open sympathy with whites in racial situations.[36] The Populist dream of a united front of white and black labor never seemed more distant.

Black Self-Help and the Institutional Ghetto

The growing racial tension of the late nineteenth and early twentieth centuries created the physical ghetto in the Northern city; it isolated Afro-Americans from the white community and forced them into a well-delineated black quarter. But the ghetto was more than an area of black concentration; it became increasingly in the early twentieth century a city within a city, containing within its borders facilities and services closed to black people

---

[33] Senator Ben Tillman, quoted in *Chicago Broad Ax,* 15 October 1904.

[34] Lillian Smith, *Killers of the Dream,* revised ed. (New York: Doubleday, 1963), pp. 154–57.

[35] Chicago's worst racial clash before World War I grew directly out of the 1905 teamsters strike. See my *Black Chicago,* pp. 40, 47.

[36] For detailed analyses of the competitive factors that led to the race riots of the World War I period, see the works by Waskow and Rudwick already cited.

elsewhere. The physical ghetto was the direct result of white racism. The institutional ghetto grew out of the activities of middle-class black leaders who attempted to build a viable and inhabitable black metropolis.

Just as the interracial aspects of the formation of the ghetto must be understood within the context of increased tensions in American society at large, so the intraracial aspects of ghettoization must be understood as a function of ideological and class developments within the black community. The black response to white racism in America has fluctuated between advocacy of integration and support of several varieties of nationalism and separatism. As August Meier has noted,[37] integrationist thought has generally prevailed in periods of relative hopefulness, when the prospects of creating a truly interracial society seem feasible. During the Reconstruction era and in the 1950's and early 1960's, for instance, black leaders emphasized the desirability of integration. When white hostility has seemed an insurmountable barrier, when the American caste system has seemed permanent, blacks have been inclined to turn to the emigrationist thought of a Martin R. Delany, the black Zionism of a Marcus Garvey, or the black power philosophy of a Stokely Carmichael. Black ideology has not, of course, been simply an automatic response to white attitudes; events within the black community and on the international scene have been important determinants. Still, black ideological development cannot be understood apart from the general context of the American racial system.

The mounting racism of the late nineteenth century gave Afro-Americans little reason to maintain hope in the good faith of white Americans. Particularly in the South, many poor black farmers and workers, seeing the dreams of Reconstruction shattered and faced with economic and political peonage, listened receptively to the nationalist message of Bishop Henry Turner and seriously considered emigration to Africa.[38] The Northern black bourgeoisie saw salvation in a kind of black capitalism, a determined effort to build up their own communities and develop independent and self-sufficient black institutions. Convinced that integration could not be achieved in the foreseeable future, they sought a peculiarly American solution to their problem. They tried, in classic Horatio Alger terms, to pull themselves up by their own bootstraps through a concerted program of self-help and racial solidarity. Nationally, Booker T. Washington was the leading exponent of this philosophy.[39] But black Northerners did not need a message from Tus-

---

[37] August Meier, *Negro Thought in America*, pp. 13–14.

[38] For a recent thorough account of Bishop Turner's remarkable career and of the emigrationist movement in the late nineteenth century, see Edwin S. Redkey, *Black Exodus* (New Haven, Conn.: Yale University Press, 1969).

[39] Booker T. Washington, whose historical reputation was at low ebb during the era of militant integrationism in the early 1960's, has received more sympathetic treatment of late by historians who view him as an early advocate of black power. See, for example,

kegee. Their reliance on self-help solutions grew out of the logic of their situation—out of the increasing futility of attempts to bring about an integrated society.

The growing acceptance of the self-help approach at the turn of the century mirrored a change in the class structure of the Afro-American community. Before 1890, the leaders of black society in New York, Chicago, Philadelphia, Washington, D.C., and Baltimore had been members of a proud and exclusive elite—men and women who traced their ancestry to ante-bellum free blacks and who frequently had close economic and social ties with the white community. Many of these leaders had roots in the abolitionist tradition and retained a commitment to a direct onslaught against every form of discrimination and prejudice in American life. To them, integration seemed the best solution to America's racial problems. Before 1895, their unquestioned leader was the great old abolitionist warrior Frederick Douglass, and after the turn of the century many of them drifted into the camp of the militant young intellectual W. E. B. Du Bois. But by this time, a new leadership was displacing the old elite within the black communities of the North. The new leaders were self-made men, blunter, more aggressive than the old integrationists. They were businessmen and politicians, ministers and journalists who lacked the ties with the white community that their predecessors had nurtured. Their primary economic and social loyalties were within the Afro-American community, and they worked to create a cohesive and self-sufficient black metropolis. They were the architects of the institutional ghetto.[40]

The self-help advocates of the early twentieth century attempted to transform a necessary evil into a positive good. Barred from white society, they announced their independence, declared their refusal to beg for scraps from the white man's table, and attempted to create a society of their own. But their dream of a black metropolis was doomed. Black businessmen and civic leaders lacked the resources to build viable institutions. Denied credit by white banks, black businesses were undercapitalized and usually short-lived. Deprived of access to the real centers of power, black politicians could offer little more than token patronage and small political favors. Unable to afford

---

Eugene D. Genovese, "The Legacy of Slavery and the Roots of Black Nationalism," *Studies on the Left* 6 (November-December 1966): 14–16. Certainly there are parallels between Washington's philosophy and the more conservative versions of the black power ideology, such as that advanced by Stokely Carmichael and Charles Hamilton in *Black Power* (New York: Random House, 1967). But the contemporary movement toward black power and black nationalism involves far more than black capitalism, and it is well not to overemphasize the early-twentieth-century self-help movement as the forerunner of current trends.

[40] The interrelationship between black ideology and class structure in this period was first suggested by August Meier, "Negro Class Structure and Ideology in the Age of Booker T. Washington," *Phylon* 23 (Fall 1963): 258–66. For a detailed application of this thesis, see my *Black Chicago,* Chapters 3, 4.

professional staffs and adequate facilities, black social agencies could barely begin to respond to the pressing problems of ghetto life. The dream of a black-controlled community, growing out of the frustrations of turn-of-the-century race relations and nurtured by the population growth of the World War I era and the 1920's, collapsed with the Depression—to be revived, in different form of course, in the 1960's.

Prospects in Black Urban History

This essay is, in a sense, an interim report, based on the significant (though still preliminary) work in black urban history that has appeared since 1965. Work in progress on the emergence of the ghetto will expand our knowledge of the dynamics of race relations in a number of Northern cities and allow us to make more meaningful generalizations. Several forthcoming studies will make extensive use of quantitative material, especially manuscript census data—that is, the original forms as completed by the census-takers. Quantitative analysis may provide an important key to solving one of the major problems in writing black history—the difficulty of finding data on the lives of ordinary, formally inarticulate people. Nearly all black history—and black urban history has been no exception—has suffered from an over-emphasis on the ideas and activities of an articulate leadership group; perhaps through the use of quantitative material we can begin to understand something of the family life, the economic problems, the occupational and geographical mobility of the masses of black urbanites. And yet the range of questions that census data can answer is limited. There is still a pressing need for sensitive, qualitative studies of the culture and life style of black people in Northern cities. And we need to know much more than we do now about relations between poor whites, particularly immigrant groups, and urban blacks; historians have often avoided attempting such studies because of the language skills required.

Nonetheless, studies made in recent years have left us with significant insights into the dynamics that shaped the Northern ghetto. Between 1890 and 1915, a relatively fluid pattern of race relations gave way to a rigid one. As in the South, this was in part the result of ideological racism. But it was also the result of profound class tensions within American society. It was within this context that black urban ghettos emerged. Barred from white institutions and facilities, black Northerners fell back upon their own resources and attempted to create a community structure of their own. Thus the interplay between white racism and the black ideology of self-help provides a major key to understanding the formation of the ghetto.

Political Change in the Negro Ghetto, 1900-1940's

MARTIN KILSON

Martin Kilson is professor of government at Harvard University. His many books and articles on African and Afro-American affairs include *Political Change in a West African State* (Harvard University Press, 1966) and *Politics in Black America: Crisis and Change in the Negro Ghetto* (to be published by St. Martin's Press in 1973). In the essay that follows, Mr. Kilson describes the political life of the black ghetto during the first half of the twentieth century. Critical of the continuing ethnicity of American politics, he analyzes the forces that promote or retard political change in black urban communities and presents a new conceptual framework for interpreting the political development of ghettos.

The Modernization of Negro Americans

The term "political change" or "development" has many meanings, depending upon the context of one's usage; but when referring to the kinds of political adjustments characteristic of modernizing social systems, it means what S. N. Eisenstadt has called the spread or dispersal of power—that is, the easing of ordinary people's access to the institutions of authority, decision making, command, and administration in a social system.[1] After the spread of power from the few to the many, political change takes on additional features: it becomes a matter of the growth of political structures like interest groups, parties, and movements which in turn are used to politicize hitherto politically inert strata and relationships.

Thus conceived, political change is modern in at least three senses: it is associated most frequently with the industrial, urban civilization which evolved out of the nineteenth century; the individual is assumed to be a subject of the political process; and a person's achieved status rather than his

---

[1] S. N. Eisenstadt, "Modernization and Conditions of Sustained Growth," *World Politics* (July 1964): 576–94.

socially ascribed or inherited status increasingly determines his relationship to authority and power.[2]

In the past century, the pattern of political modernization has varied greatly among nations and between groups, classes, and regions within nations. For black Americans, political modernization since the 1870's has been characterized by marked variation and disparity between blacks and whites in the acquisition of effective political attributes. With the end of Reconstruction, which was coincident with the rise of urban America, the Negro, resident mostly in the South, was coercively (albeit through laws) and violently deprived of formal political rights.[3] This loss of political rights contributed to the massive migration of blacks out of the South that began in the first decade of the twentieth century, though in itself the loss of political rights was not always enough to induce migration.

The important consequence of this migration was the endowment of thousands of Negroes with the political rights they were forcibly denied in the post-Reconstruction South. Had migration not been feasible for Negroes in this period, doubtless the acquisition of basic political rights and thus the primary stages of political modernization would have been delayed for another half-century. The white leadership of the South had the political will to effect such a delay, and, alas, the connivance of the North was hardly unthinkable. The Supreme Court upheld the segregation of schools in the South (and outside it) in 1893, Congress refused to use its legislative powers to protect and extend the Negro's civil rights either in the South or outside it, and city and state governments outside the South seldom used their authority and power either to cultivate the Negro's rights or to extend them.

In addition to the acquisition of formal political rights, migration afforded blacks their first intensive experience of urbanization. The significance of urbanization to the political modernization of Negroes cannot be overemphasized: it afforded them the quality of social organization and institutional differentiation or specialization without which effective political development is impossible. As W. E. B. Du Bois, one of the first systematic observers of the urban Negro, recognized, there is a strong correlation between the social and institutional differentiation available to Negroes in cities and their political modernization.[4]

The initial urban experience of rural or peasant blacks was disorienting because of their pervasive social disorganization. Yet, as the late E. Franklin

---

[2] For the application of this concept of political change, see Martin Kilson, *Political Change in a West African State* (Cambridge, Mass.: Harvard University Press, 1966).

[3] Cf. Paul Lewison, *Race, Class and Party: A History of Negro Suffrage and White Politics in the South* (New York: Grosset & Dunlap, 1932), and C. Vann Woodward, *The Strange Career of Jim Crow,* revised ed. (New York: Oxford University Press, 1966).

[4] W. E. B. Du Bois, *The Philadelphia Negro: A Social Study* (Philadelphia: University of Pennsylvania Press, 1899), pp. 233–34.

Frazier was the first to perceive, such disorganization was the price urban Negroes had to pay for a more effective social system.[5] Only through urbanization could a black working class skilled in and adapted to modern industry emerge. Only in cities, despite their special stress and strain, was a differentiated Negro elite available, capable of coping with a range of leadership functions more demanding than those typical of the Negro elite in the South.[6] Political modernization is, after all, a matter of highly differentiated strata and institutions sustaining political articulation and order beyond parochial settings (ethnic, religious, regional) in order to provide public services.

The urbanization of the Negro from 1900 onward was not, of course, simply any urbanization. It was a particular form of city dwelling; it occurred in a historically specific place and time. Of all the variables governing Negro city dwelling outside the South, preeminent were those associated with white racism. No other major American immigrant community—Irish, Jews, Italians—faced such systematic and hateful restrictions upon its urban adaptation as did the Negro.[7] W. Lloyd Warner, the distinguished sociologist of mainstream America, discovered this in Yankee City: "The caste barrier or color line, rigid and unrelenting, has cut off this small group [blacks—0.48 percent of the population] from the general life of the community."[8] The Lynds discovered a comparable situation in their study of a typical American community, the city of Muncie, Indiana (35,000 population in 1920):

> The sense of racial separation appears in widely diverse groups. At a meeting of school principals held at the Y.M.C.A. to arrange for interschool basketball games, one of the Y.M.C.A. secretaries said that any school having a Negro on its team could not play in the Y.M.C.A. building, but would have to play in the high school. . . . The secretary of the Trades Council has tried to persuade the Molders' Union to take in Negro molders, but they have consistently refused. One is struck by the absence of Negroes at a place like the large tabernacle built for a community revival. They appear to keep very much to themselves, and Klan agitation has emphasized this tendency.[9]

---

[5] Cf. E. Franklin Frazier, *The Negro Family in Chicago* (Chicago: University of Chicago Press, 1932).

[6] On the Negro elite strata and their leadership roles in the South, see Hortense Powdermaker, *After Freedom: A Cultural Study in the Deep South* (New York: Viking Press, 1939) and Allison Davis et al., *Deep South* (Chicago: University of Chicago Press, 1941).

[7] See Robert Weaver's classic account of barriers to Negro urban adaptation, *The Negro Ghetto* (New York: Harcourt, 1948). For a viewpoint that differentiates little, if at all, between the adjustment barriers of blacks and white ethnics, see Oscar Handlin, *The Newcomers* (Cambridge, Mass.: Harvard University Press, 1959).

[8] W. Lloyd Warner and Paul S. Lunt, *The Social Life of a Modern Community* (New Haven, Conn.: Yale University Press, 1941), p. 217.

[9] Robert S. and Helen M. Lynd, *Middletown: A Study in Modern American Culture* (New York: Harcourt, 1929), p. 479. Cf. Frank U. Quillin, *The Color Line in Ohio: A History of Race Prejudice in a Typical Northern State* (Ann Arbor, Mich.: George Wahr, 1913), pp. 125–65.

What W. Lloyd Warner called the separation of blacks "from the general life of the community" is central to grasping the dynamics of Negro political modernization in the years 1900–1940. Whatever the general life of a modern community is, surely politics is a salient feature, for politics is the process through which services and benefits are allocated among competing sectors of society. Thus restrictions by whites on the Negroes' social adaptation to cities jeopardized the political capacity of the group; it made city blacks victims of the whims and caprice of white politicians, political machines, and bureaucracies, few of which were notable for exemplary political behavior.[10]

In the reaction of white city politicians and officeholders lay the key to Afro-American political modernization. Where white politicians surmounted, relatively speaking, the normal tendency of whites to restrict Negro access to the general life of a city, the Afro-American urban community proved nearly as capable as its white ethnic counterparts at acquiring the attributes and habits conducive to political modernization. This situation, however, obtained only in rare instances—most markedly in Chicago from 1915 onward.[11] The usual situation for black city dwellers outside the South was one where white politicians, consciously or not, followed restrictive and coercive patterns toward blacks. Herbert Gans, placing this situation in historical context, remarks that white ethnic immigrants "came into a society in which the Negro was already discriminated against":

> In fact, had it not been for discrimination, the North might well have recruited Southern Negroes after the Civil War. . . . [But] once the immigrants came they were able to take jobs away from Negroes, even pushing them out of the few urban occupations they had dominated, for example, catering and barbering. . . . The immigrants and their descendants who controlled the [political] machines were anti-Negro and gerrymandered ghetto neighborhoods so that they would not have to share their power with Negroes.[12]

Moreover, the coercive and regulatory agencies of cities—especially police—facilitated the exclusion of blacks from effective social and political participation. As Myrdal remarked some thirty years ago:

---

[10] See the classic account of the ways of political machines by Harold F. Gosnell, *Machine Politics: Chicago Model* (Chicago: University of Chicago Press, 1937). See also Harold Zink, *City Bosses in the United States: A Study of Twenty Municipal Bosses* (Durham, N.C.: Duke University Press, 1930).

   On the notion of victimization as the outcome of white barriers to Negro urban adaptation, see St. Clair Drake, "The Social and Economic Status of the Negro in the United States," *Daedalus* 95 (Fall 1965): 771–73.

[11] See Ralph J. Bunche, "The Negro in Chicago Politics," *National Municipal Review* 17 (May 1928): 261–64.

[12] Herbert J. Gans, "The Ghetto Rebellions and Urban Class Conflict," in Robert Connery, ed., *Urban Riots: Violence and Social Change* (New York: Random House, 1969), pp. 52–53.

In most Northern communities Negroes are more likely than whites to be arrested under any suspicious circumstances. They are more likely to be accorded discourteous or brutal treatment at the hands of the police than are whites. The rate of killing of Negroes by the police is high in many Northern cities. . . . The attitudes of the police will sometimes be found among the most important items considered in local Negro politics in the North. [13]

Confronted, then, with pervasive and mean restrictions upon their access to the social system of American cities outside the South, the Negroes' adaptation to the political structure of cities necessarily took unique form during the period 1900–1940. Inevitably, the patterns of Negro political adaptation to cities were not nearly as conducive to the long-run political modernization of blacks as were the modes of adaptation available to white immigrant groups like the Irish, Poles, Jews, and Italians.

Clientage Politics

One of the patterns of Negro political adaptation to cities in the formative years 1900–1940 may be described as clientage politics, or patron-client politics. [14] This rather primary pattern of Negro politics, widespread in the years of Negro urbanization (1900–1920), entailed a small group of blacks who fashioned personalized links with influential whites, becoming clients of the whites for a variety of sociopolitical purposes. Some students of this period of Negro history see clientage politics as conterminous with Negro politics in general. [15] In fact, it was nothing of the sort: it was almost exclusively the political method of the Negro middle class—a bourgeois affair. The black bourgeoisie ideologically portrayed clientage politics as "race politics," presumably beneficial to all blacks, though in reality it was of benefit more to the elites than to the urban Negro masses. [16]

---

[13] Gunnar Myrdal, *An American Dilemma* (New York: Harper, 1944), p. 527. On the role of police in facilitating violent acts (especially riots) of the white lower and working classes against Negroes in cities outside the South, see Robert Fogelson, "Violence as Protest," in Connery, *Urban Riots,* pp. 28–30. See also Gilbert Osofsky, "Race Riot 1900: A Study of Ethnic Violence," *Journal of Negro Education* 32 (Winter 1963): 16–24.

[14] On the nature of clientage political ties as a form of political linkage, see M. G. Smith, *The Economy of Hausa Communities of Zaria* (London: Colonial Social Science Research Council, 1955).

[15] See, for example, Leslie H. Fishel, Jr., "The Negro in Northern Politics, 1870–1900," *Mississippi Valley Historical Review* 42 (December 1955): 466–89.

[16] Cf. August Meier, "Negro Class Structure and Ideology in the Age of Booker T. Washington," *Phylon* (Fall 1963): 258–66.

Professor Meier's work on ideologies of Negro elites at the turn of the twentieth century is seminal, and his larger study should be consulted: *Negro Thought in America, 1880–1915* (Ann Arbor, Mich.: University of Michigan Press, 1963). For an analysis of the ideas of Negro elites in the 1920's and 1930's, Ralph Bunche's studies are the best. See Ralph J. Bunche, "The Programs of Organizations Devoted to the Improvement of the Status of the American Negro," *Journal of Negro Education* 9 (July 1939): 539–50.

The prestige available to the elites within the urban Negro ghetto enabled them to enter clientage relations with influential whites. Though within the Negro subsystem the prestige of elites (clergymen, doctors, teachers, clerks, foremen, gamblers) was circumscribed by a variety of cleavages (class, color-caste, sectional), this prestige had enough credibility to be converted into political influence. Clientage politics was the first means for realizing this influence in both Northern and Southern cities, and in the late nineteenth century both Negro clients and white patrons seized it.[17]

Politically, white support lent substance to the bid for leadership by the prestigious elements in the Negro ghetto in the formative period of black urbanization. It enabled the Negro client leadership to obtain positions in community and government institutions reasonably commensurate with their leadership-claimant status. It permitted the Negro client leadership to control or at least influence some part of the political process that allocated services to the Negro urban subsystem, especially welfare and settlement services. In a word, white support of Negro claimants for leadership of urban blacks in the period 1900–1920 helped legitimate this black leadership: it enabled it to appear in the eyes of the lower-class Negroes as the agent of the political "payoff," or benefits, that accrued to the Negro subsystem. Thus in Minneapolis in the late 1920's (Negro population 6,000 out of 400,000) the clientage political pattern provided much of the welfare and community settlement services available to the Negro lower classes.[18]

On the client's side of the typical white-black clientage relationship there is often much more leeway in the client's mode of reciprocation than is usually recognized. The political forms of client reciprocation often occur outside the presence of specified white patrons. In these situations the reciprocating behavior of black client elites becomes part of a discrete leadership pattern: the black client elites structure their leadership role in a manner presumed to be acceptable to white patrons.

Data illustrating this type of leadership among urban Negroes were reported by Frank U. Quillin in his invaluable study of Negro political adaptation in Ohio cities before World War I. One situation described by Quillin involved a collective effort by urban Negro client leaders to alleviate discord between blacks and whites:

> A colored photographer, a man far above the average of his race, said that there was no question but that the ordinary negroes in Columbus merit the ill opinion of all decent people for the manner in which they live. They are

---

[17] On clientage politics among Negroes in the urban South, see the excellent material on Atlanta, Georgia, in Floyd Hunter, *Community Power Structure* (Chapel Hill: University of North Carolina Press, 1953).

[18] Ethel R. Williams, "Minneapolis Builds a Social Settlement," *Opportunity: Journal of Negro Life* 8 (August 1930): 236–37.

generally to be found living in miserable hovels, or in big "rat-and-fire-trap tenements," where every Sunday, especially, they get intoxicated, hold dog, cat, and chicken fights, play the banjo, dance cakewalks, and in other ways make the day hideous for their neighbors. . . . My informant said that, while this is true for the average negroes of the city, it applies especially to the new negroes that have lately come up from the South. A dozen colored women of the better class went to these negroes a short time ago and tried to do a little missionary work among them. They were received with insults on all sides, and were called "the white folks' niggers." A pastor of the leading colored church of the city and one of the best known colored preachers of Ohio, confirmed the above statements . . . and told me that these negroes were going about the streets dirty and half-clothed, with but an undergarment for a shirt, and that often open in front. They were used to doing this in the South, and they never thought of being tidy, and did not realize that they were making themselves and their race offensive to the white people. He said that he, and other ministers, had of late appealed to them to better these conditions.[19]

The second situation reported by Quillin illustrates how an individual Negro client, quite without direct inducement from a white patron, performs a client leadership function:

One other great complaint made by the white people against the negroes, aside from their shiftlessness and stealing, was that they had a strong desire to antagonize the whites in all possible ways, especially in public places. Their actions on street cars were condemned by all whites, and by the better class of blacks. . . . The following incident told by the colored photographer already referred to will illustrate this matter quite fully. He was on a street-car one evening when a negro, fresh from his work in the steel mill, with his filthy working clothes on, boarded the car and, although there was no room, crowded into a seat by the side of a white woman, elegantly dressed. When the colored photographer remonstrated with him for his action, he turned and said, "I'm no d — d white man's nigger like you. I have a right here, and I am going to take it." The conductor came along and put him off the car, the colored photographer giving the conductor his name as a witness if needed.[20]

In other cities there prevailed a form of clientage politics which entailed a political arrangement that made appointive political and civic posts the main means of exchange from white patrons to black clients. This pattern of urban white-black clientage politics was particularly developed in the first two

---

[19] Quillin, *The Color Line in Ohio,* pp. 150–51.
[20] Ibid., p. 152.

decades of the twentieth century in New Haven,[21] Philadelphia,[22] Cincinnati,[23] Baltimore,[24] and New York.[25] The appointive posts exchanged by white patrons in return for political mediation of black-white interactions by Negro clients were occasionally of little specific political import but of high social value — for example, appointment to the board of a YMCA or some other community agency financed largely by influential whites, like the Charity Organization Society in Baltimore in the early 1900's.[26] But other appointive posts were of very much political relevance. These included appointment to school boards, tax boards, police posts, post office positions, and teaching posts.

By World War I this particular form of clientage politics was well developed in the larger cities. Moreover, it became a stimulus to a qualitative transformation of clientage politics, which took the form of the political institutionalization of cliques and interest groups within the Negro subsystem. The reasons for this superseding of typical clientage politics by a more politically articulate pattern of Negro political adaptation to cities were many. One reason, central to the nature of black-white clientage politics, was the wellnigh universal failure of clientage politics to guarantee the furtherance of Negro group interests when issues or policies germane to those interests were under political consideration.[27]

Interest Group Articulation: The Context

In addition to clientage politics, another pattern of Negro political adaptation to cities in the years 1900–1940 was the institutionalization of cliques and interest groups, otherwise called interest group articulation. This was essentially a matter of groups like doctors, lawyers, grocers, gamblers, and long-standing clusters of influential persons (cliques) advancing their own needs and, by extension, presumably those of Negroes generally through specialized political organization. The effort to institutionalize cliques and

---

[21] Robert Austin Warner, *New Haven Negroes: A Social History* (New Haven, Conn.: Yale University Press, 1940), Chapter 9.

[22] Du Bois, *The Philadelphia Negro.*

[23] Wendell P. Dabney, *Cincinnati's Colored Citizens: Historical, Sociological and Biographical* (Cincinnati: Dabney Publishing, 1926), pp. 116–29.

[24] Henry Bain, "Five Kinds of Politics: A Historical and Comparative Study of the Making of Legislators in Five Maryland Constituencies," vol. 2 (Ph.D. diss., Harvard University, 1970).

[25] Gilbert Osofsky, *Harlem: The Making of a Ghetto* (New York: Harper, 1963), Chapters 4, 11.

[26] See Helen B. Pendleton, "Negro Dependence in Baltimore," *Charities* 15, no. 1 (October 1905): 50–58.

[27] See Aaron Wildavsky's study of Oberlin, Ohio, *Leadership in a Small Town* (Totawa, N.J.: Bedminster Press, 1964), pp. 41–47.

interest groups necessarily encroached upon and transformed typical clientage politics. For one thing, the failure of clientage politics to facilitate the political modernization of the Negro community *as a subsystem* stimulated the growth of interest group articulation. Second, and most important, from 1915 onward the sheer growth in number, scale, and range of socioeconomic differentiation of the Negro urban community rendered clientage politics short-lived, or at least insufficient.

The period 1915–1930 witnessed unprecedented demographic change in Negro urbanization. As shown in Tables 1 and 2, the population movement was northerly (including the Midwest) and westerly, toward the cities and away from the farms. The force of the pull of the cities on Negro population

TABLE 1
Negro Urban and Rural Populations by Region, 1900–1930

Region	1900	1910	1920	1930
South				
Urban	1,365,000	1,854,000	2,251,000	2,966,000
Rural	6,558,000	6,661,000	6,661,000	6,395,000
North and West				
Urban	637,600	830,000	1,309,000	2,228,000
Rural	274,000	248,000	242,000	302,000
Total				
Urban	2,002,000	2,684,000	3,560,000	5,194,000
Rural	6,832,000	6,909,000	6,903,000	6,697,000

SOURCE: From T. J. Woofter, "The Status of Racial and Ethnic Groups," p. 567, in *Recent Social Trends in the United States* by Wesley Mitchell et al. Copyright 1933. Used with permission of McGraw-Hill Book Company.

TABLE 2
Increase in Negro and White Populations in Selected Northern Cities, 1910–1920

City	Negro Population, 1910–1920		Increase in Negro Population 1910–1920	Percentage of Increase in Negro Population, 1910–1920	Percentage of Increase in White Population, 1910–1920
Detroit	5,741	40,838	35,097	611.3	107.0
Cleveland	8,448	34,451	26,003	307.8	38.1
Chicago	44,103	109,458	65,355	148.2	21.0
New York	91,709	152,467	60,758	66.3	16.9
Indianapolis	21,816	34,678	12,862	59.0	31.9
Philadelphia	84,459	134,229	49,770	58.9	15.4
St. Louis	43,960	69,854	25,894	58.9	9.4
Cincinnati	19,639	30,079	10,440	53.2	7.9
Pittsburgh	25,623	37,725	12,102	47.2	8.3

SOURCE: *Negroes in the United States, 1920–1932* (Washington, D.C.: Bureau of the Census, 1935), p. 55, Table 10.

TABLE 3
Occupations Among Negroes, 1890–1930

Occupation	1890		1900		1910		1920		1930	
Agriculture	1,757,403	57.2%	2,143,176	53.7%	2,893,674	55.7%	2,178,888	44.4%	2,150,000	43.9%
Domestic Service	963,080	31.3	1,324,160	33.2	1,099,715	21.2	1,064,590	22.7	1,000,000	20.4
Commerce and Transportation	145,717	4.7	209,154	5.2	425,043	8.2	540,451	11.2	575,000	11.8
Industry	172,970	5.6	275,149	6.9	692,506	13.6	960,039	19.9	1,060,039	21.7
Professions	34,184	1.1	47,491	1.0	68,898	1.3	80,183	1.7	107,833	2.2

SOURCE: Monroe N. Work, *Negro Year Book: An Annual Encyclopedia of the Negro, 1931–1932* (Tuskegee, Ala.: Tuskegee Institute Press, 1932), p. 347.

in the North is seen in the fact that in 1920, of the 198,483 Negroes in New York State, 75 percent lived in New York City; three cities in Ohio (Cleveland, Columbus, and Cincinnati) accounted for 46 percent of all blacks in Ohio, though these cities claimed only 22 percent of Ohio's population; and Philadelphia had 47 percent of all Negroes in Pennsylvania and, combined with Pittsburgh, claimed 60 percent of all Negroes in the state, though these two cities accounted for only 28 percent of Pennsylvania's population.

The sociological differentiation of the Negro in the years 1910–1930 was no less notable than the population change. The period saw a sharp transition of Negroes out of agriculture and into manufacturing, industry, commerce, and transportation. As shown in Table 3, marked growth of the Negro middle class and professional strata also occurred in the years 1900–1930, expanding the supply and differentiating the types of leadership.

These social and economic changes qualitatively altered the range and depth of the modern social system of the Negro ghetto outside the South in the years between the two world wars. World War I was central to these changes: it elaborated the complexity of urban life in the Negro ghetto and multiplied the interactions between the Negro urban subsystem and the dominant white social system. Moreover, the latter change spawned profound political by-products, for, alas, the war's multiplication of black-white interactions occurred before new political methods or agencies for mediating black-white relations were available. Thus discord and conflict frequently characterized black-white (particularly lower-class and working-class white) interactions during and immediately following World War I and often resulted in veritable warfare in the form of white-initiated riots.[28]

---

[28] See the Chicago Commission on Race Relations' incisive analysis of the impact of World War I on the Negro ghetto and expanding black-white interaction in Chicago, *The Negro in Chicago: A Study of Race Relations and a Race Riot* (Chicago: University of Chicago Press, 1922). This study was written largely by Charles S. Johnson, then head of the research division of the Urban League.

Interest Group Articulation: Some Cases

In the war-related context of increased black-white urban interaction, clientage politics, the dominant pattern of Negro political adaptation to cities in the period 1900–1920, began to give way to, or at least to coexist with, another pattern of Negro political adaptation which I call the institutionalization of cliques and interest groups. As a type of Negro political adaptation to cities, interest group articulation had one feature in common with clientage politics: both required influential white patrons as a major political resource enabling the Negro community, or rather special interests thereof, to derive benefits from the political process. Furthermore, the previous experience of clientage politics—lasting usually fifteen or twenty years, and nearly thirty years in some cities, such as Oberlin, Ohio—imprinted itself on the urban Negro leadership style, often irrespective of ideological cleavages within the Negro leadership, like radical-conservative or nationalist-integrationist.[29] This suggests a tendency among black leadership groups to depend excessively or uncreatively upon white allies or patrons, thereby short-circuiting the process of political modernization within the Negro urban subsystem.[30]

In initiating Negro interest group articulation in the years 1915–1930 the politically assertive individuals among the organized white-collar and professional Negroes proceeded along a variety of political paths. In some instances an established profession, whose members had usually been involved in clientage politics, moved to institutionalize its political potential, first through professional organization and then through national and local articulation as a political interest or pressure group. Thus in 1924 about 2,000 Negro lawyers formed the National Bar Association. Under the leadership of

---

[29] On the sway of the patron-client ethos among early black nationalists, see Edmund Cronon, *Black Moses: The Story of Marcus Garvey and the Universal Negro Improvement Association* (Madison: University of Wisconsin Press, 1962), especially Chapters 4 and 5, dealing with the Garvey movement's economic ties with whites. For the patron-client element in the relations of radical and race-conscious Negro intellectuals with whites in the 1920's and 1930's, see Langston Hughes, *The Big Sea: An Autobiography* (New York: Alfred A. Knopf, 1940), especially Parts 2 and 3. See also Harold Cruse, *The Crisis of the Negro Intellectual* (New York: Random House, 1967). For current black militants' ties to white allies or patrons, including the most politically aggressive groups, like the Black Panther Party, see Martin Kilson, "The New Black Intellectuals," *Dissent* 16, no. 4 (July-August 1969): 309–10, and "Political Sociology of Black Militancy," in Seymour Martin Lipset and S. M. Miller, eds., *Poverty, Stratification and Politics* (forthcoming). It may be noted, *en passant*, that much of the current outward show of bitterness by middle-class Negro militants toward whites—especially liberal whites—is no doubt a function of the inability of Negro political and interest groups, whatever their ideological proclivity, to dispense with white allies and thus to discard the context of the patron-client ethos.

[30] I intend to develop this thesis more fully in a forthcoming book, *Politics in Black America: Crisis and Change in the Negro Ghetto* (New York: St. Martin's Press, forthcoming).

politically assertive personalities like Raymond Pace Alexander, a Philadelphia lawyer who became a major political figure in that city, the association
quickly institutionalized Negro lawyers as an interest group. Addressing the
National Bar Association in 1931, Alexander exhorted the black lawyers:
"The political future of our race should intimately concern the Negro lawyer,
if he hopes to meet the problems . . . which retard the development of his people and his own development."[31] Alexander proceeded to make clear that the
new political cohesion of Negro lawyers meant the demise of clientage politics.
"We are forced by circumstances," he declared, "to adopt the position that we
shall cast our ballot, not by virtue of traditional allegiance, not because the
Republican Party was the party of Lincoln, but shall vote for the man—for the
party that offers opportunities to the men and women of color to participate
in the affairs of government by appointing to public positions of responsibility
and credit and by endorsing and supporting Negro men and women to high
elective or appointive offices."[32]

The foregoing mode of interest group formation was pursued by other
elements of the Negro professional strata. The large number of Negro social
welfare workers, including a small group of professional sociologists, who
formed the National Urban League in 1916 were part of the institutionalization of interest groups, as were the intellectuals—writers, teachers, orators,
journalists, critics—who had founded the National Association for the Advancement of Colored People (NAACP) six years earlier in 1910. The Negro
social workers who rallied around the Urban League and the intellectuals
who raised the banner of the NAACP had, like Negro lawyers prior to the
establishment of the National Bar Association, experienced mostly clientage
politics.[33]

In time the last two interest groups politically outdistanced others like
the National Bar Association. For example, the NAACP and the Urban League,
utilizing clientage relations with powerful whites for their finances and for
access to powerful national figures, forged national structures underpinned
by local urban chapters, which afforded them a range of pressure politics at
the federal and state levels unavailable to Negro groups with little national

---

[31] Raymond Pace Alexander, "The Negro Lawyer," *Opportunity: Journal of Negro Life* 9
(September 1931): 271.

[32] Alexander, "The Negro Lawyer," p. 271. For a more radical contemporary view of the need
to politicize Negro professional groups, see Loren Miller, "The Flight of the Negro Professional Man," *Opportunity: Journal of Negro Life* 9 (August 1931): 239–41.

[33] Du Bois' autobiography is informative on the clientage politics experienced by the Negro
intellectuals who helped found the NAACP. See W. E. B. Du Bois, *Dusk of Dawn: An
Essay Toward an Autobiography of a Race Concept* (New York: Harcourt, 1940). No
better source exists on the clientage political ties of Negro social workers and community organizers than the National Urban League's now defunct monthly organ, *Opportunity: Journal of Negro Life,* which was published between 1923 and 1948.

organization, like the National Bar Association. In fact, the NAACP and the Urban League specialized in national pressure politics, one crucial consequence of which was the integration into the national political arena of Negro urban voluntary associations (churches, mutual benefit societies, economic cooperatives) upon which branches of the NAACP and the Urban League rested.[34]

Still other modes of interest group articulation prevailed in the years 1915–1930. Of particular interest is the political movement based on the aggregation of voluntary associations. In this situation, a skillful and often charismatic leader first maximizes the politicization of his own voluntary association and then, having secured this initial base, branches out, penetrating first ideologically and then organizationally other nonpoliticized voluntary associations. The penetration or aggregation process was pursued by a highly politicized voluntary agency of the leader, and invariably ideology (usually racialist or black nationalist) proved the most important political resource.

Thus in the late 1930's the Reverend Adam Clayton Powell, Jr., formed precisely this type of political instrument, the Greater New York Coordinating Committee, with which he politicized a segment of the Harlem ghetto, especially the newly emerging middle class and the upwardly mobile skilled workers (usually a part of the lower middle class among Negroes).[35] Basing the Coordinating Committee initially on his own church, the Abyssinian Baptist Church in Harlem, Powell elaborated it to include a broad spectrum of Harlem's middle-class and lower-middle-class voluntary associations, aligning them often in sharp opposition to the established black bourgeoisie, who relied heavily upon and benefited from clientage politics. Powell's Coordinating Committee made explicit use of a black racialist or black nationalist ideology, often attacking the black bourgeoisie as an enemy of Negro advancement.

Along with similar organizations in other urban ghettos outside the South, the Coordinating Committee pioneered militant actions, like boycotts and picketing for jobs for middle-class and skilled working-class blacks. Of even more important long-run political significance, Powell transformed the Greater New York Coordinating Committee into a veritable political machine. In this new guise, often the terminal development of the process of aggregating interest groups, Adam Clayton Powell's political machine, exploiting the disarray of Tammany Hall's organization in Harlem and aided

---

[34] There is yet no good study of the role of the NAACP and the Urban League in politicizing the infrastructure of voluntary associations in the Negro ghetto from World War I onward. But see Ralph J. Bunche's writings on the political role of the NAACP and the Urban League, referred to by Myrdal in *An American Dilemma,* pp. 819–42.

[35] This account is based on Adam Clayton Powell, Jr., *Marching Blacks: An Interpretive History of the Rise of the Black Common Man* (New York: Dial Press, 1945), pp. 95–103.

by redistricting, successfully elected Powell in 1944 to the House of Representatives.[36] This made Powell the first Negro from the East to be elected to Congress.

Numerous other instances of interest group articulation occurred, of course, during the 1920's and 1930's, and in most of these the result was increased quality and scale in Negro political adaptation to cities. It should be noted, however, that one type of interest group articulation in this period contributed less to the quality of political institutional adaptation than to the ideological techniques underlying such adaptation. This was particularly true of the interest group politics of the Universal Negro Improvement Association, otherwise known as the Garvey movement, which reached maturity in the mid-1920's and continued into relatively inactive old age in the 1930's.

The Garvey movement pursued far less political activity through established political processes, like machine politics, city, state, and congressional elections, than the other interest groups that gained political articulation in the 1920's and 1930's. It seldom utilized its organization for the political growth of the Negro urban subsystem. Rather, the Garvey movement, largely dominated by the petty bourgeoisie and for this reason perhaps wary of political overextension, was obsessed with economic policies like the "Buy Black" movement and considered politics secondary.[37] Only occasionally did a branch of the Garvey movement assist Negro candidates for elective office or otherwise enter normal urban politics, and in such instances it did so without the support of the Garvey movement as a whole.[38]

The nearest Garvey himself came to formulating a practical view of politics for his movement was at their 1923 annual convention. He declared to his followers at the convention that "it is toward things political that the Universal Negro Improvement Association is now to turn its attention." But, alas, Garvey's notion of the uses of politics was bizarre. Rather than use political pressure to accomplish the possible, Garvey exhorted his followers to seek the impossible—mass migration to Africa. It was reported of the 1923 convention that Garvey "urged his followers to register and vote, claiming that in such a position they could demand a place in Africa, and the 7,000 enthusiasts cheered their leader's words."[39]

Yet the Garvey movement radicalized the style of Negro political adap-

---

[36] See James Q. Wilson, *Negro Politics: The Search for Leadership* (Glencoe, Ill.: Free Press, 1960), pp. 35–36. See also Wilson's incisive analysis of Powell in "Two Negro Politicians: An Interpretation," *Midwest Journal of Political Science* 4, no. 1 (1960).

[37] Cf. Cronon, *Black Moses.*

[38] See Harold Gosnell, *Negro Politicians: The Rise of Negro Politics in Chicago* (Chicago: University of Chicago Press, 1935), p. 113. The Chicago branch of the movement aided the primary campaign of a Negro candidate in the first ward, largely Negro, in 1924, and the candidate considered the support of some value.

[39] *Opportunity: Journal of Negro Life* 1 (November 1923): 348.

tation to cities in the interwar era: it pioneered the ideological manipulation of the historical experience of Negroes as material for sharpening the Negro's perception of his status in white society, and it proposed solutions, after a fashion, exclusive of white society. Accordingly, at the fourth annual convention of the Universal Negro Improvement Association in New York in 1924, Garvey laid down a formulation of the ideological politicization of urban blacks that has yet to spend itself: "We've got to teach the American Negro blackness," he remarked. "Give them black ideals, black industry, black United States of Africa and black religion."[40]

Thus was born modern urban black nationalism or ideological militancy, the primary function of which has been, since the 1920's, twofold: first, to politicize *and* radicalize apathetic lower-class Negroes, turning thousands into predictable nationalist followers; second, to create black nationalist leadership out of the lower-middle-class or newly emergent middle-class Negroes.[41] What rendered the lower-middle-class black artisans, paraprofessionals, petty businessmen (tailors, shoemakers, grocers, semi-educated, or "jack-leg," clergymen[42]) especially prone to politicization through black nationalist ideology was their special marginal status. They experienced not merely white caste dominance but the added rub of the peculiar status dominance within the Negro social system, controlled by a black bourgeoisie highly acculturated to white patterns.[43]

It should be reiterated that the growth of interest group articulation in the urban ghetto in the years between the world wars occurred not in place of but along with and supplementary to clientage politics. However, politically institutionalized interest groups, whether limited to cities (as most were) or operating on a national or federal level (as did the NAACP), constituted a more inclusive political process for the urban ghetto. This growth involved a greater variety of political groups and needs and a more demanding or spe-

[40] Quoted in *Opportunity: Journal of Negro Life* 2 (September 1924): 284.

[41] The special role of black nationalism in the politicization of the Negro lower middle class or emergent middle class awaits serious study. E. Franklin Frazier was one of the first to perceive this relationship. See his article "The Garvey Movement," *Opportunity: Journal of Negro Life* 4 (November 1926): 346–48. Furthermore, the Garvey movement still awaits serious and sophisticated political analysis. The political role of the Garvey movement is shrouded in black nationalist wishful thinking and mythology (e.g., membership figures of one to two million are surely mythological, the figure 85,000 preferred by Du Bois in the 1920's being nearer the mark), and purportedly serious accounts of the Garvey movement have not avoided the myths. A step toward demythologizing the study of black nationalism and a method of historical analysis are provided in Theodore Draper, *The Rediscovery of Black Nationalism* (New York: Viking Press, 1970).

[42] For one of the few studies of one group among this politically important segment of the Negro lower middle class, see Ira De Augustine Reid, "Let Us Prey!" *Opportunity: Journal of Negro Life* 4 (September 1926): 274–76. This petty middle class and the infinite variety of charlatans it spawned need serious study.

[43] Cf. E. Franklin Frazier, *Black Bourgeoisie* (Glencoe, Ill.: Free Press, 1956).

cialized political organization than clientage politics. It therefore served wider segments of the urban ghetto. In this sense, then, the growth of interest group articulation in the 1920's and 1930's did indeed supersede clientage politics as the dominant mode of Negro political adaptation. Yet clientage politics persisted within the emergent interest group system of urban Negro politics and remains relevant to it today. It also persisted within the third major mode of Negro political adaptation to cities in the years 1900–1940, namely, machine politics.

Machine Politics: The Rise of Modern Negro Political Behavior

The political adaptation of Negroes to cities by way of machine politics encompassed both formative and mature stages. Save where political machines interacted formally with the Negro urban subsystem, the formative stage for black urban communities was decidedly different and longer lasting than the formative stage for white immigrant communities. The mature stage seldom was experienced by Negro urban communities in the years 1900–1940, for maturity means the systematic inclusion of a given ethnic area or community into the dominant pattern of machine or boss rule in a given city. Such inclusion of the black urban area was extremely rare in those years, the notable exception being Chicago from 1915 onward.

The formative stage of the relationship between urban Negroes and machine politics differed from that of the relationship of white immigrants and the machine primarily in regard to the goals sought by city machines. For white immigrants the city machines sought, with few exceptions, to include the disparate ethnic turfs.[44] But for the Negro the machine lacked precisely this purpose or goal. Rather, in the years 1900–1940 the goal of white-dominated city machines toward Negroes was to neutralize and thus minimize the political clout of the Negro urban community and not infrequently even to distort that community's social and political modernization.

The goals of neutralization and distortion of the political position of the Negro urban community emanated largely from the racist perspective of the American social system. These goals appeared only occasionally in the relationship of city machines to white immigrant groups[45] but frequently in city machines' interaction with Negroes. Thus the patterns or ideology of white racism explain the extent and intensity of city machines' policy of neutralizing and distorting the political capability of the Negro urban subsystem in the years 1900–1940.

---

[44] Cf., for example, Oscar Handlin, *The Uprooted* (Boston: Atlantic-Little, Brown, 1951). See also Lawrence H. Fuchs, ed., *American Ethnic Politics* (New York: Harper, 1968).

[45] See, for example, Dayton David McKean, *The Boss: The Hague Machine in Action* (Boston: Houghton Mifflin, 1940).

Usually an influential Negro—a professional, businessman, small bureau-crat, gambler, or underworld figure—was singled out by city machines and cast as agent of the application of what can be called neoclientage politics to the Negro urban community in the years 1900-1940. Thus in East St. Louis, Illinois, from around 1910 onward, Dr. Le Roy Bundy, a Negro dentist, functioned as the agent of a neoclientage political linkage between the Negro community and East St. Louis Republican machine politics.[46] A similar relationship was forged between the Negro subsystem and the Republican machine in New York City from 1908 onward. In this case a professional Negro politician of the small bureaucrat variety, Charles W. Anderson, effected neoclientage control of the Negro voters in New York City by the Republican party. Anderson held a succession of typical jobs provided by the Republican machine—largely appointments in federal agencies located in New York, like the Internal Revenue Service—and thus was beholden to the machine for his existence.[47]

From 1910 to 1940 the function of Negro neoclientage machine politicians like Anderson was to guarantee the Negro vote for Republicans and when necessary discourage Negro voting altogether rather than allow Negro voting power to grow and diversify, as did the Italian vote in New Haven,[48] the Irish vote in Philadelphia,[49] and the Jewish vote in New York,[50] among others. However, Anderson's counterparts in other cities were less reputable figures than he. They were prone to play their neoclientage role in machine politics in ways starkly dysfunctional to Negro political modernization.

In Baltimore, Philadelphia, Buffalo, and elsewhere many of the Negro leaders in neoclientage machine politics were gamblers, successful hustlers, flophouse keepers, and occupants of other antisocial roles. From the 1900's

---

[46] The best account of Bundy's neoclientage role in East St. Louis is in Elliott M. Rudwick, *Race Riot at East St. Louis, July 2, 1917* (Carbondale: Southern Illinois University Press, 1964), pp. 174-96.

[47] The best account of Charles Anderson's neoclientage role in New York City politics in the first two decades of the twentieth century is Osofsky, *Harlem,* pp. 161-78.

[48] Raymond E. Wolfinger, "The Development and Persistence of Ethnic Voting," *American Political Science Review* 59 (December 1965). See also Robert Dahl, *Who Governs? Democracy and Power in an American City* (New Haven, Conn.: Yale University Press, 1961).

[49] J. T. Salter, *Boss Rule: Portraits in City Politics* (New York: Whittlesey House, 1935), pp. 73-207.

[50] David Burner, *The Politics of Provincialism: The Democratic Party in Transition, 1918-1932* (New York: Alfred A. Knopf, 1968), pp. 239 ff. Burner provides excellent data illustrative of diversity in the voting of Jews, Italians, and other white groups in New York and other cities as compared to the uniformity of the Negro vote for the Republican party. For evidence of a greater political clout and larger payoff due to diversification of an ethnic group's voting, see Theodore Lowi, *At the Pleasure of the Mayor: Patronage and Power in New York City, 1898-1958* (Glencoe, Ill.: Free Press, 1964), pp. 29-46.

to the 1920's one of the worst uses of such Negro leaders in the neoclientage linkage of Negroes to machine politics was to be found in Philadelphia, though a politically functional linkage of blacks to white machine politics later evolved. Du Bois, who had a keen sociological eye for politically dysfunctional relationships in the Negro urban community, observed in Philadelphia at the turn of the twentieth century the consequences of using Negroes of questionable occupation as leaders in machine politics:

> Next to this direct purchase of votes, one of the chief and most pernicious forms of bribery among the lowest classes is through the establishment of political clubs, which abound in the Fourth, Fifth, Seventh and Eighth Wards, and are not uncommon elsewhere. A political club is a band of eight or twelve men who rent a club house with money furnished them by the boss, and support themselves partially in the same way. The club is often named after some politician—one of the most notorious gambling halls of the Seventh Ward is named after a United States Senator—and the business of the club is to see that its precinct is carried for the proper candidate, to get "jobs" for some of its "boys," to keep others from arrest and to secure bail and discharge for those arrested. Such clubs become the centre of gambling, drunkenness, prostitution and crime. Every night there are no less than fifteen of these clubs in the Seventh Ward where open gambling goes on, to which almost any one can gain admittance if properly introduced; nearly every day some redhanded criminal finds refuge here from the law. Prostitutes are in easy reach of these places and sometimes enter them. Liquor is furnished to "members" at all times and the restrictions on membership are slight. The leader of each club is boss of his district; he knows the people, knows the ward boss, knows the police; so long as the loafers and gamblers under him do not arouse the public too much he sees that they are not molested. If they are arrested, it does not mean much save in grave cases. Men openly boast on the street that they can get bail for any amount. And certainly they appear to have powerful friends at the Public Buildings.[51]

What disturbed Du Bois about this political pattern was that machine politics, utilizing neoclientage ties, was articulated into the fiercely pathological social structure characteristic of lower-class Negro urban life throughout the twentieth century. He knew, or believed he knew, that effective institutional development, both social and political, for lower-class Negroes was impossible under this type of relationship to city political machines. He was correct in this belief, for perhaps no other factor has so marred and distorted Negro political adaptation to cities in this century as the way in which machine politics, by means of neoclientage ties, reinforced the structural pathologies of lower-class urban Negro life.[52]

---

[51] Du Bois, *The Philadelphia Negro,* pp. 378–79.

[52] There is precious little material on this important subject, and serious study of it is wanting; but see St. Clair Drake and Horace R. Cayton, *Black Metropolis: A Study of Negro Life in a Northern City* (New York: Harcourt, 1945), pp. 576 ff.

No doubt on balance neoclientage machine politics was a better relationship for the Negro urban community to the wider city politic than the alternatives of typical clientage politics and interest group politics or no relationship at all. For all its limitations and its distorting implications for Negro sociopolitical modernization, the neoclientage linkage of Negroes to machine politics from early in the 1900's to the 1930's provided several new political opportunities to blacks. Above all, it established, after a fashion, the principle of institutionalized interaction between the Negro urban community and the formal white power structure—a principle that white immigrant groups took virtually for granted.[53] The establishment of this principle was, after all, basic to the transformation of the Negro urban community into a viable subsystem of the wider urban polity.

A Negro Machine in Chicago, 1915–1940's

No detailed study of the special case of Chicago in the Negro's relationship to machine politics will be offered here, but the salient features of that relationship must be grasped if one wants an adequate understanding of the Negro experience with machine politics.[54] Perhaps basic to the Negro's success at having his ethnic turf in Chicago included fully in the city-wide machine organization was the keen competition between the Democratic and Republican parties for city office, as well as the internal divisions between city and state factions within the Republican party.[55] Unlike Philadelphia, Baltimore, and New York, where Republicans (Philadelphia) or Democrats (Baltimore and New York) had a veritable built-in majority, no such situation prevailed in Chicago. Both parties had to work hard for victory in Chicago, and when victory came the margin was small. A number of ethnic communities provided the margin of victory, and among them was the Negro community, 4 percent of Chicago's population in 1920 and nearly 7 percent in 1930.

For Negroes to help supply the margin of victory in keenly contested elections like those that occurred in Chicago between the two world wars required certain facilitating situations. One was the presence of white politicians—in fact just one major white politician was all that was needed—

---

[53] For a case study of the almost natural accession of white immigrants to machine politics and an equally natural succession in time to executive control of the machine, see Elmer E. Cornwall, "Party Absorption of Ethnic Groups," *Social Forces* 38 (March 1960): 205–10.

[54] Fortunately, there are both limited and detailed studies of Negro politics in Chicago, the best being the classic account by Harold Gosnell, *Negro Politicians* (1935), and the more recent study by Wilson, *Negro Politics* (1960). One should also consult Allan H. Spear, *Black Chicago: The Making of a Negro Ghetto, 1890–1920* (New York: New York University Press, 1967), and Drake and Cayton, *Black Metropolis* (1945).

[55] Cf. Gosnell, *Negro Politicians,* Chapters 3, 4.

reasonably indifferent to matters of race regarding supporters. Another was a group of Negro politicians who would not rest satisfied with limited co-optation as the defining feature of their relationship to machine politics, but rather sought within the Negro area the full-fledged control of the machine that their Irish, Jewish, Italian, and other ethnic political counterparts possessed within the boundaries of their areas.[56]

Both these situations prevailed in Chicago in the years between the two world wars. William Hale ("Big Bill") Thompson was the white politician who exhibited relative color blindness in his dealings with the Chicago Negro, particularly after his first bid (1915) to become the mayoral candidate of the faction-ridden Republican party was markedly enhanced, if not clinched, by Negro support in the largely Negro second ward. Thus the results of the city-wide Republican primary for mayor in 1915 were 87,333 for Thompson, 84,825 for Olson, and 4,283 for Hey. The Republican vote in the second ward was 8,633 for Thompson, 1,870 for Olson, and 47 for Hey.[57] This pattern prevailed in the four primaries in which Thompson was a candidate for mayor; Negroes in the second ward gave him over 80 percent of their votes. And, as Harold Gosnell has pointed out, the same held for elections:

> Upon a number of occasions the pluralities received in the districts inhabited largely by Negroes have been decisive. Without these pluralities Thompson could not have defeated his Democratic opponents in the mayority elections of 1919 and 1927. In the latter year, when Thompson ran against Mayor Dever, he received 91.2 per cent of the vote cast in the Second Ward.[58]

Thompson's mode of organizing Negroes in Chicago in order to guarantee their support was even more important to the eventual inclusion of blacks in Chicago machine politics than the voting pattern. Negro votes in the interwar years had been crucial in elections in Philadelphia, St. Louis, and Cleveland but had never resulted in Negro inclusion in the political machines. Unlike those in any other major city in this period, the Republican leaders in Chicago cultivated the independent-minded Negro middle-class leaders rather than those Negro political leaders inclined to neoclientage linkages with white power structures. Equally important, the Negro leaders who organized Big Bill Thompson's Negro support insisted upon something other than neoclientage ties to the Chicago machine.[59] In fact, Chicago seems to have had a larger group of Negro middle-class politicians of this persuasion

---

[56] On ethnic control of subdivisions of city machines, see Gosnell, *Machine Politics.*

[57] Gosnell, *Negro Politicians,* p. 41.

[58] Ibid., p. 47.

[59] See Ralph J. Bunche, "The Thompson-Negro Alliance," *Opportunity: Journal of Negro Life* 7 (March 1929): 78–80.

than other cities and in general probably had a more professionally and socially differentiated Negro elite than any other major city, including New York.[60]

Furthermore, the highly differentiated elite possessed a number of men who were very political-minded and perceived the many uses of politics. The two men most important in integrating the Negro community of Chicago into Thompson's machine were of this persuasion—namely, Edward Wright and Oscar De Priest. They were also, unlike their predecessors in Chicago's Negro leadership, self-made men, and politics was basic to their rise to professional status. Edward Wright worked in the late nineteenth and early twentieth centuries as a porter, clerk, and bookkeeper, among other jobs, and he had a preference for government jobs; he studied law in his spare time and qualified for the bar in 1892. In the same year he was elected Cook County Commissioner, his first public office in Illinois; he was the third Negro from Chicago to hold the post. Early in his political career, Wright displayed the qualities that determined the choice he made in relationship to the Thompson machine—qualities Harold Gosnell has vividly described:

> Commissioner Wright's activities on the county board showed him to be shrewd, forceful, and highly race conscious. Shortly after his election he deliberately held up the appropriation for the office of State's Attorney Charles S. Deneen in order to secure the appointment of a colored man as assistant state's attorney. When Deneen was informed as to why his appropriation was delayed, he is alleged to have said: "I want you to understand, Mr. Wright, that I am all powerful in this office." To this Wright replied: "Yes, and I am county commissioner." A few days later Ferdinand L. Barnett became the first colored assistant state's attorney for Cook County and Deneen's appropriation was passed.[61]

De Priest, like Wright, was self-made. He began as a house painter and interior decorator in the late nineteenth century and in 1904 gained election to the Cook County Board. In 1907 he entered real estate, utilizing his political relationships, and soon amassed a sizable fortune. His bid for major office came in 1915 when he stood as Republican candidate for city council in the second ward, following a brilliantly executed grass-roots campaign for the nomination.[62]

The special type of leadership offered by Wright and De Priest and the men who became their intimates and coworkers, in combination with Big Bill Thompson's particular attributes, produced the first machine-type po-

---

[60] Cf. Spear, *Black Chicago,* Chapters 3, 4.
[61] Gosnell, *Negro Politicians,* pp. 154–55.
[62] Ibid., pp. 170–71.

litical adaptation of a major Negro urban community. The details of the Negro subdivision of the Chicago machine from the 1920's to the 1940's will not detain us.[63] But the qualitative features of the Negro submachine, so to speak, must be mentioned. The available evidence indicates that the Negro subdivision of the Chicago machine from the 1920's to the 1940's was like subdivisions in other cities. By the late 1920's, the ward, district, and precinct heads were Negro, unlike the case in Philadelphia. The Negro submachine had one leader—Wright—appointed by Big Bill Thompson to a $100-a-day post as lawyer to the State Traction Commission in 1919; in 1923 the governor appointed him to the Illinois Commerce Commission, a $7,000-a-year post. Oscar De Priest was nominated and elected to Congress in 1926, being the first Negro to achieve that distinction in this century, and another Negro, Democrat Arthur Mitchell, succeeded De Priest. A variety of responsible and key posts went to members of the Negro elite who backed the Wright–De Priest machine. Concerning these officeholders, Ralph Bunche, one of the keenest observers of Negro urban politics in the interwar era, remarked:

> These men are all entrusted with responsible positions. In illustration, in the office of the corporation counsel, a Negro, as assistant corporation counsel and trial lawyer in property damage litigation, represents the city in suits mounting to millions of dollars yearly. There are approximately twenty Negro investigators in the various legal departments. Additional appointments in the many city departments, as teachers, clerks, police, etc., run into the hundreds.[64]

Other data support Bunche's observations: Negroes in Chicago, 6.9 percent of the population, held 25 percent of some 11,888 postal service jobs in 1930 and 6.4 percent of city civil service jobs in 1932. Moreover, these data show reasonable Negro representation in the white-collar and professional ranks of both city civil service and postal service jobs.[65]

The Chicago pattern persisted, moreover, through World War II and the postwar era.[66] Yet when profound crisis, characterized by widespread black nationalist militancy and lower-class aggression on white institutions through riots, engulfed the Negro urban subsystem in the early 1960's, the relatively successful Chicago pattern of adaptation of Negroes to cities through machine politics proved nearly as fragile as the neoclientage patterns that persisted in

---

[63] Ibid.

[64] Bunche, "The Thompson-Negro Alliance," p. 79. See also Bunche, "The Negro in Chicago Politics," pp. 263–64.

[65] For comparative data on Philadelphia, showing a much weaker pattern of payoff from participation in city politics, see John H. Strange, "The Negro in Philadelphia Politics, 1963–1965" (Ph.D. diss., Princeton University, 1966), Chapter 3.

[66] See Wilson, *Negro Politics.*

Philadelphia and elsewhere. This was due largely to the fact that the demands upon government and politics emanating from the postwar urban Negro were simply beyond any solution available to cities, Chicago or any other.[67]

Political Change and Differentiation Among Negroes

This study has described the political status of the Negro in the first half of the twentieth century in terms of the modes of political adaptation available to blacks in white-dominated cities. The delineated modes of adaptation were not merely a function of white power; they were also an outgrowth of the evolution of the Negro urban community as a subsystem and of variations within that system, which differ from city to city. Moreover, as a given urban Negro community progresses from one mode of adaptation to another there are a number of measures of the impact of such change: election behavior, patterns of racial discord, rates of violence, Negro occupational mobility as affected by politics. Election behavior as a measure of the impact of modes of Negro adaptation to cities has a utility the other measures lack: it conveys cleavages among the members of a community that derive from the community's particular mode of adaptation.

Electoral data from 1900 to the early 1930's reveal little differentiation within the Negro community as a result of the patterns of political adaptation then evolving. Neither the mode of typical clientage political adaptation nor that of interest group articulation produced a major change in Negro electoral behavior. The attachment to the Republican party persisted throughout the evolution of these patterns of Negro adaptation to cities.

It was not until some variant of machine politics characterized the adaptation of Negroes to cities that a sizable degree of differentiation in Negro voting became apparent. For the most part, city machines did not significantly affect wide segments of blacks in cities until the mid-1920's, and some voting data suggest that it was in this period that the Negro vote began to discard the deep-seated attachment to the Republican party. Thus data in Table 4 on the following page show that Negroes were more decidedly Republican than any other ethnic group in Chicago in 1924 but by 1928 exhibited a disaffection with Republicans which continued into 1932, the start of the New Deal.

Only in New York City does the evidence show a majority of Negroes breaking with the Republican party in 1932 in order to support Franklin D. Roosevelt's Democratic candidacy for President.[68] In the other industrial cities, a small movement of Negroes toward the Democratic party was recorded: for example, in Detroit, where 19.5 percent of the Negro vote

---

[67] Cf. Edward C. Banfield, *The Unheavenly City: The Nature and Future of Our Urban Crisis* (Boston: Atlantic-Little, Brown, 1970).

[68] See Burner, *The Politics of Provincialism,* p. 237.

TABLE 4
Presidential Voting of Ethnic Groups in Chicago, 1924–1932

Year		Democratic Vote	Republican Vote	Third Party Vote
1924	German	18%	52%	30%
	Jewish	37	43	20
	Polish	51	37	12
	Negro	5	91	4
1928	German	45	55	
	Jewish	78	22	
	Polish	83	17	
	Negro	29	71	
1932	German	59	41	
	Jewish	85	15	
	Polish	85	15	
	Negro	30	70	

SOURCE: From *The Politics of Provincialism: The Democratic Party in Transition, 1918–1932,* by David Burner. Copyright © 1965, 1968 by David Burner. Reprinted by permission of Alfred A. Knopf, Inc.

had been Democratic in 1930, 36.7 percent was Democratic in 1932.[69] But on the whole, in large industrial cities the Negro vote in 1932 remained overwhelmingly Republican. For example, in the four largely Negro wards of Cleveland where the Democrats had received 30 percent of the vote in 1928, only 24 percent was theirs in 1932 (although in other industrial cities the Democrats advanced on the previous vote of 1928).[70] Only in 1936 did the Democrats outstrip the Republicans in the Negro wards of industrial cities like Detroit and Cincinnati. The Democrats gained 63.5 percent of the Negro vote in the former and 65.1 percent in the latter. In Gary, Indiana, another industrial city, the predominantly Negro fifth ward voted Democratic by a margin of 2 to 1, whereas in 1932 the Negro vote was 85 percent Republican.[71]

In most cities from 1932 onward the impact of the Depression greatly influenced the voting of the lower class among both Negroes and whites.[72]

---

[69] Edward H. Litchfield, "A Case Study of Negro Political Behavior in Detroit," *Public Opinion Quarterly* 5 (June 1941): 271.

[70] Henry Lee Moon, *Balance of Power: The Negro Vote* (New York: Doubleday, 1948), p. 18.

[71] See Richard J. Meister, "The Black Man in the City: Gary, Indiana, 1906–1940" (Paper delivered at the Annual Conference of the Association for the Study of Negro Life and History, 1969).

[72] See Harold Gosnell, *Grass Roots Politics: National Voting Behavior of Typical States* (Washington, D.C.: American Council on Public Affairs, 1942).

One gauge of this may be seen in the fact that in many cities lower-class Negroes moved more sharply toward the Democrats than did middle-class Negroes. But still it would seem that city machines also influenced the Negro shift toward the Democrats which commenced somewhat tentatively in 1932 but was distinctly apparent by 1936.

For example, in both Detroit and Cincinnati the Republicans had negatively utilized neoclientage links with the Negro community.[73] The Democrats, on the other hand, cultivated the independent tendencies among the Negro elites of Detroit and Cincinnati in the 1920's, thereby providing the Negro subsystem more effective relations to the political machines. This policy of accommodating new changes in the urban ghetto won the Democrats in those cities no small political notice among blacks; and when combined with the relief and welfare policies of the Democratic administration from 1934 onward,[74] the Negro shift to the Democratic party in most major cities was hardly surprising. Moreover, this shift has persisted for over thirty years, and today the Negro is more strongly Democratic than any other ethnic group—a voting pattern the reverse of Negro political behavior at the dawn of Negro political modernization in the early 1900's.

It should be noted, finally, that in the post–World War II era there has been a drastic diminution of the efficacy of political machines for the upwardly mobile white ethnic groups. But there is no reason to expect this development to apply equally to urban blacks. Barring any substitute arrangement for performing the political functions heretofore performed by political machines for groups lacking effective political modernity, there is no reason whatever to expect a major decline in the efficacy of political machines to the urban Negro.[75] Just as the Negro was late in commencing the process of political modernization compared to white ethnic groups, it can be expected that blacks will be late in realizing this process and that thus they will require the services of political machines (with sizable Negro leadership) for at least a generation beyond the period machine politics lose their efficacy for white ethnic groups.

I say this, moreover, despite the fact that I am critical of the historical role of ethnicity (the political manipulation of ethnic variables) in modern American institutions. A number of notable American scholars have virtually

---

[73] See Dabney, *Cincinnati's Colored Citizens,* pp. 122–23.

[74] For comparative data on the incidence of relief among Negroes in several cities, see E. Franklin Frazier, "Some Effects of the Depression on the Negro in Northern Cities," *Science and Society: A Marxian Quarterly* 2, no. 4 (Fall 1938): 491–94. See also Robert Weaver, "The New Deal and the Negro," *Opportunity: Journal of Negro Life* 8 (July 1935): 200–02.

[75] I develop this issue more adequately in *Politics in Black America.*

—and most unfortunately—deified the ethnic factor in American history.[76] But no critical observer of the key problems of power and participation in American society can ignore the dysfunctional, as well as morally or intellectually indecent, attributes of ethnicity.

Surely, in the form of white racism toward blacks since the end of Reconstruction, ethnicity can be evaluated as nothing other than a deadly force: an albatross, or worse, around the neck of American society. Today ethnicity, in the hands of a new set of Negro leaders—bent like their Irish, Polish, Jewish, Italian historical counterparts on the ethnic redress of differentials between subordinate and superordinate groups—might well lead to profound political crisis at many levels of the American political system. If this should come to pass, the apologists, both black and white, for the historical pattern of ethnic manipulation—which too often resembles ethnic madness—must share a major responsibility.

---

[76] For a recent example of this kind of scholarship, see Andrew N. Greeley, "Turning Off 'The People': The War and White Ethnic Groups," *New Republic* 163 (27 June 1970), pp. 14-16.

Blacks and Ethnic Groups:
The Difference, and the
Political Difference It Makes

NATHAN GLAZER

Nathan Glazer is professor of education and social structure at Harvard University. He has published many articles on minority groups and urban problems and, with Daniel P. Moynihan, is the coauthor of *Beyond the Melting Pot* (M.I.T. Press, 1963). In the following essay, Mr. Glazer compares the black American's experience of America to the New World experience of the white immigrant. Arguing that race and ethnicity are part of a family of social identities, he finds a significant degree of continuity between the socioeconomic development of Northern Negroes and that of white ethnic groups.

Do Negroes in this country suffer from a unique prejudice and discrimination that we can sum up under the general heading "racism"? Or does the prejudice and discrimination they suffer form part of a common pattern that has also affected white ethnic groups—a general ethnocentrism? Or does it form part of a quite different complex, a general racism directed toward all nonwhite races but not toward white immigrant and ethnic groups? Or does it form part of yet another pattern that includes not *all* other nonwhite races but only groups that have or had the status of peoples colonized by Americans: American Indians, Mexicans, Puerto Ricans, Filipinos, Samoans, perhaps, and others?

When we consider black deprivation in this country, we are presented with a variety of models from which to interpret and understand it. I have suggested four. There undoubtedly are others. The issue is not one for interpretation and understanding alone, for it is clear that the interpretation one selects will affect one's political stance and one's involvement in practical measures. There is a range of possibilities, which can be placed along one critical continuum. At one extreme, we can see black experience as unique, shaped by the historical experience of African slaves and free men in this country. At the other extreme, we can see Negroes as one of a number of groups that have suffered from the prejudice and discrimination which has affected in some measure every distinct ethnic and racial group in this country.

Other interpretations are in the middle of the continuum: there are those link-ing the fate of Negroes in this country to that of other racial groups; and there are those linking it to that of other groups, whether of different races or not, that have had a colonial relationship to America.

On the reasons for black deprivation scholarly opinion is divided, and popular opinion, white and black, is also divided. Members of white ethnic groups say, "We worked hard and suffered from discrimination, and we made it. Why don't they?" And blacks retort, "You came after us and were never-theless favored above us and given all the breaks, both when we were in slavery and since." It is a question that cannot be asked without arousing emotions so strong that one wonders just how far scholarship will be allowed to go on this issue. In this essay I would like first to discuss some of the implications for policy and politics of the different views one can take on this issue and second to address the issue directly.

Political Implications

The political significance of black deprivation can be quite easily and simply set forth. There has been a process of what is variously called "assim-ilation" or "integration" of ethnic groups into this country. Without trying to elaborate definitions of these slippery terms, we may say that both suggest that a group once considered in some measure *outside* the polity, economy, and society is now considered *inside* the polity, economy, and society. For some time, most Negro leaders saw Negroes as outside and worked to get them inside. This formerly fairly uniform position of most prominent Negro orga-nizations and spokesmen has been transformed since about 1965. Now, it is argued, to get inside, the way white ethnic groups have done, is either in-conceivable, because of white opposition, or undesirable, because of black internal development. But if the path of assimilation or integration is rejected, difficult questions arise: What will be the *character* of the resulting separa-tism? What will be its legal status? What will be its relationship to land? What will be its relationship to those who do not want to take on the status? How will it affect relationships with the white majority? Separatism can mean anything from a separate state to various kinds of minority status or ethnic status. Thus the crucial nature of the argument.

It is an argument of peculiar complexity, because relevant to it is not only the history and social status of black Americans; equally relevant is the his-tory and status of white Americans of different groups. We are speaking of degrees of similarity and difference, and thus at least two terms are involved, both of which offer more than the usual difficulties for scholarly determination. Thus, whether we believe that Negroes share in some measure a position sim-ilar to that of white Americans or whether we believe they do not, we must have in mind some conception of what the status of white ethnic groups has been, is now, and will be in our society. We cannot carry through a compari-

son in which one term is left murky. I believe some of the difficulty in dealing
with black and white ethnic group comparisons is that we are not clear about
ethnic status in this country. There are a number of points on which opinion
diverges sharply. I will emphasize four that are particularly important for
this discussion: (1) What is the *time scale* in which we view ethnic status?
Is it temporary or enduring? If enduring, how long does it endure? (2) What
are the differences between white ethnic groups in political power, in economic
power, in social characteristics? Are these differences important or minor?
(3) If ethnic groups endure, in some manifestation, with substantial differences
in political and economic power and in social characteristics, do they endure
and maintain these differences because of prejudice and discrimination, because of social, economic, and cultural characteristics which precede entry
upon the American scene, or because of characteristics which have in some
degree emerged on the American scene and which must be reckoned, in some
measure, as owing to choice? (4) What is the role of race in this discussion?
Does race change all the terms of the discussion so that an ethnic group of
a nonwhite race faces, for that reason alone, a completely different situation
and history?

One can settle these matters neither by fiat nor by reference to authoritative studies and settled positions. Let me simply summarize my own position.[1] Ethnic status may be enduring—more enduring than expected and more
enduring for some groups than for others. The status of English-speaking
Canadians will merge rapidly into that of white Americans of English origin;
that of Italians will last longer; that of Jews, if history is any guide, will last
as long as any social identity. Ethnic groups differ in political power, in
economic power, in social characteristics. There is no common history for
white ethnic groups, no common status, though there are processes that in
some degree may be found in many groups. These differences are not simply
the result of differences in prejudice and discrimination alone, though these
play a role. They are the result, too, of cultural differences created in other
settings and of new differences that arise in this country because of the complex interaction between the pre-existing cultural characteristics, various
degrees of prejudice and discrimination, the economic and political skills
characteristic of each group, the political and economic situation of the country
and relevant parts of the country at the time of arrival, and other elements.
The line between white ethnic groups and ethnic groups of other races does
not determine their fate. Racial identities can change their meaning. Italians

[1] Presented more fully in Nathan Glazer, "Ethnic Groups in America: From National Culture to Ideology," in Morroe Berger et al., eds., *Freedom and Control in Modern Society*
(Princeton, N.J.: D. Van Nostrand, 1954), pp. 158–73; Nathan Glazer, "The Integration
of American Immigrants," *Law and Contemporary Problems* 21 (1956): 256–59; Nathan
Glazer, "The Immigrant Groups and American Culture," *Yale Review* 68, no. 3 (Spring
1959): 382–97; and Nathan Glazer and Daniel P. Moynihan, *Beyond the Melting Pot,*
2nd ed. (Cambridge, Mass.: M.I.T. Press, 1970).

and Jews, considered "racially" different by Americans at the turn of the century, are not so considered today. Southern Italians, who were considered "racially" different from Northern Italians fifty years ago, are not so considered today.[2] Neither in America nor elsewhere are race and ethnicity categories so different that the processes that affect the assimilation and integration of ethnic groups change completely when groups of a different race are involved. Brazilians of African origin seem less black as they rise in the social scale, and whites seem darker as they go down the social scale. Groups physically undifferentiable from the larger population may, on the other hand, be singled out for all the obloquy that has descended on members of the African race in the United States. Thus, in Hitler's Germany, Germans with one Jewish grandparent became subject to the status of Jews—including, eventually, extermination—and in Japan, the descendants of the old lower caste, the *eta* (now called the *burakumin*), are subject to ostracism and severe social penalties if their descent is discovered.[3] Thus one possible position on ethnicity and race, and the one I hold, is that they form part of a single family of social identities—a family which, in addition to races and ethnic groups, includes religions (in Holland) and language groups (in Belgium). All these categories can be included in the most general term "ethnic groups," groups sharing a common history and experience and defined by descent, real or mythical.

At the other end of the spectrum from the position which sees similarities between the status of Negroes and other groups are those positions which emphasize the differences. There, two approaches are possible. One is to emphasize the racial differences between blacks and whites, and perhaps between blacks and all other races. The other is to emphasize the significance of the colonized status, the status of slaves (in the case of Africans) or of derivation from subordinate colonized areas, in the case of some other groups. The latter approach has become increasingly popular in the last few years and encourages a perception of common interest (based on common status) among black Americans, Mexican-Americans, Puerto Ricans, and American Indians.

The debate has grown. A key point in the history of the debate was the Kerner Commission's report, which devoted a chapter specifically to the question of why the situation of Negroes is different from that of white ethnic groups.[4] And since the publication of the Kerner Commission's report, the question has moved further into the arena of public debate and common

---

[2] Leonard Covello, *The Social Background of the Italo-American School Child* (Leiden, Netherlands: E. J. Brill, 1967). Glazer, "The Immigrant Groups and American Culture."

[3] See George De Vos and Hiroshi Wagatsuma, *Japan's Invisible Race* (Berkeley: University of California Press, 1966).

[4] See Chapter 9, "Comparing the Negro and Immigrant Experience," in *Report of the National Advisory Commission on Civil Disorders* (New York: E. P. Dutton, 1968).

consciousness. The recent flood of articles and discussions of what are variously called the "white ethnic groups," the "working class and lower-middle class," "the forgotten Americans," and — in a recent issue of *New Generation* — "the other other America" indicates clearly that the comparison of experience, status, power, poverty, and affluence between different groups in American society is no longer a matter only for sociologists and persons with theoretical and scholarly concerns. It is a matter on which millions of Americans, drawing on their own experience — even if that experience is unrepresentative or distorted and misinterpreted in their minds — are coming to their own conclusions, conclusions sufficiently strongly felt that they affect elections and public policies. In 1968 I wrote, "We must consider the present crisis of the ghetto in the light of the experience of the groups that have gone before because the power to respond to Negro demands, to the problem of the ghetto, is in large measure in the hands of groups who themselves have had and can recall ghetto and slum experience."[5] After the municipal elections of 1969, this point became more important than ever.

The Social Scientist's Dilemma

The debate proceeds on a scholarly and popular level, among sociologists and other social scientists and among all of us, white and black, engaged simply in living in America, and there are subtle and complex relationships between the two levels. Scholars are people, and people are in some measure scholars trying to find guidance in understanding their lives, their places in society, their groups, and their groups' places in American society, from discussions, newspapers, magazine articles, books. As a result, the political consequences of the debate are important and have already deeply affected the way the debate is conducted among scholars. None of us, I hope, is so much a purist as to believe that scholarly work must be carried on in complete disregard of political consequences; in any case, I do not. The study of race and ethnic relations is perhaps the first field where a sober and judicious sense of what can be said and how it should be said must restrain scholars.

Let me bring to the fore the implications of this debate for political action. The most common position is this: if it is generally believed there has been a radical break between white immigrant experience and black experience, people will be impelled to adopt new and unprecedented measures to achieve for blacks the measure of status that white immigrant groups reached without them. If people are convinced that because Negroes have been subjected to the varied consequences of three hundred years of American racism, there is indeed no connection between white immigrant experience and Negro experience, and that all those who have benefited in some measure from Amer-

---

[5] Nathan Glazer, "Slums and Ethnicity," in Thomas D. Sherrard, ed., *Social Welfare and Urban Problems* (New York: Columbia University Press, 1968), p. 91.

ican society, as immigrants have, must bear some responsibility for its crimes and derelictions, then we might expect a greater measure of support for radical policies designed to change the position of the Negro. It is also possible that if the two experiences are seen as totally disparate, one response might be to conclude that American society cannot adopt measures necessary to achieve a reasonably satisfactory position for Negroes and thus revolution is necessary. On the other hand, if people believe there is a substantial degree of similarity in the experience of white ethnic groups and the black experience, arguments for unique and extreme measures to end black deprivation will be undermined. If the last-mentioned point of view is true, the social scientist who believes that there is considerable continuity in the experience and position of blacks and other ethnic groups but who also believes that strong and well-directed state action is necessary in many areas to improve the position of black and other minority groups is in a dilemma indeed and must consider whether it would be better for him to stay his research and hold his tongue.

However, I do not believe that we can draw the political consequences of the two positions in only one way. Political consequences quite different from those suggested might flow from seeing continuity or discontinuity between the experience of white ethnic groups and American Negroes. If one sees continuity, then one may take an optimistic view of the American Negro position: not only "If we made it, why don't they?" but "If we made it, so will they." This is the position that Irving Kristol argued in his article "The Negro Today Is Like the Immigrant of Yesterday."[6] And on the other side, one consequence of seeing radical discontinuity may be a pessimistic outlook: whatever it is the white ethnic groups have achieved, one may decide, the Negroes cannot achieve it, because the society is now different, they are different, or the society is different for them. Thus emphasis on the differences may not lead to a great effort to institute new kinds of political, social, and economic action or, even further, to the demand for revolution; it may simply lead to despair and to the feeling that nothing can be done.

Actually, it is rather too simple to assume that the scholars in this field are affected only by the political consequences of their scientific work. As a matter of fact, the relationships run the other way too; their scientific work is affected by their initial political considerations. (I do not exclude myself from this general observation.)

If one initially takes a pessimistic view of American society, one will tend to discount the possibilities of a satisfactory position for Negroes without drastic and revolutionary social change and will emphasize the uniqueness of the black position. If one initially takes an optimistic view of American society, one will tend to emphasize improvements in the Negro position, the ways in which the relatively successful integration of white ethnic groups is being duplicated for nonwhite groups. And these views will have further

---

[6] *New York Times Magazine,* 11 September 1966.

dynamic consequences, altering the views of other parts of the American social structure. For example, those who are pessimistic about the Negro sometimes argue not so much that *his* situation is unlike that of the immigrant ethnic groups but that the immigrant groups are *also* badly off. Thus, whereas until a short time ago most observers thought that there had been a rapid decline in the discrimination toward Chinese and Japanese and a rapid rise in their economic and social position, some supporters of Third World ideology now argue that they are badly off too, that they too suffer from racism. And if one were to suggest that Poles are not that well off either, as a way of moderating the view of the Negro position as unique, Third World supporters would answer, "Quite true. Poles too should join the revolution." The point is that the commitment may be to revolution, whatever the facts.

One hopes that whatever the political commitment, scholars will act as scholars. They will search out the facts, suppress none, give greater attention to those that dispute their political preconceptions than to those that support them, argue with other scholars on the basis of data and reasoned argument. Just as we must be aware that scholarly positions have political consequences, so we must be aware that political positions affect the way one views the data.

Thus scholarly investigation has consequences for policies, but what those consequences will be is not immediately and simply predictable. The human mind operates in strange ways, and along with scholarly investigation there is the reality of social change, which has great influence on public opinion. The very unpredictability of the impact of scholarly views on public opinion operates to give the scholar a certain degree of freedom—though not absolute freedom. He pursues his investigation and analysis, and while he may judge that certain findings will tend to strengthen certain political views, he also knows that many other things affect political views and that human reasoning travels surprising paths. Consider the political effect of rioting in the ghettos. It was widely believed—and certainly social scientists shared the belief— that riots would lead to backlash and repression. There has been a good deal of both, but we have seen a good number of cases now in which the backlash, instead of effecting the election of law-and-order men, has supported black and liberal candidates, on the reasoning that blacks and liberals have credibility with the black population and are able to prevent riots.

Not only are the political conclusions people draw from their beliefs unpredictable; in addition, and also helping to give the social scientist some measure of freedom, popular opinion on matters on which people feel they can come to their own conclusions is in large measure independent of the outcome of research. It can draw upon memory, even if distorted, and partial experience, even if limited; and it will certainly be influenced by people's present position and interests. Members of white ethnic groups may forget how much they suffered and how angry they were at even moderate discrimination, and their desire to maintain whatever position and property and power they possess will encourage them to believe that there is nothing special in the Negro situation. And Negroes may refuse to recognize elements of similarity between their position and the position of white ethnic groups—the presence of discrimination and prejudice, the effects of language and dialect in restricting opportunity, the effects of poor education and different cultural attitudes, the reality of real increases in political and economic power over time, and the diminution over time of discrimination and prejudice.

To sum up: Scholarly opinion does not dictate what people believe, but it will have consequences for what they believe. Scholarly opinion is not completely free of popular opinion. Scholars are affected by the outlook, experiences, and prejudices of their groups, whether ethnic, social, or scholarly. When one examines a question such as the relationship between immigrant and black experience, one should exercise great care in the discussion and in the presentation of data and position (as one should in all scientific discussion), but one must be true to one's role as a scientist.

The Argument for Internal Colonialism

The most influential scholarly statement to date of the position that there is a radical discontinuity between white immigrant and black experience in America is that by Robert Blauner, and I would like to examine, and set against the evidence, his argument that blacks, as against white ethnics, are internally colonized:

> Of course many ethnic groups in America have lived in ghettoes. What makes the black ghettoes an expression of colonized status are three special features. First, the ethnic ghettoes arose more from voluntary choice, both in the sense of the choice to immigrate to America and the decision to live among one's fellow ethnics. Second, the immigrant ghettoes tended to be a one and two generation phenomenon; they were actually way-stations in the process of acculturation and assimilation. Where they continue to persist, as in the case of San Francisco's Chinatown, it is because they are big business for the ethnics themselves and there is a new stream of immigrants. The Black Ghetto on the other hand has been a more permanent phenomenon, although some individuals do escape it. But most relevant is the third point. European ethnic groups like Poles, Italians, and Jews generally only experienced a brief period, often less than a generation, during which their residential buildings, commercial stores, and other enterprises were owned by outsiders. . . . Afro-Americans are distinct in the extent to which their segregated communities have remained controlled economically, politically and administratively from the outside. . . . The educators, policemen, social workers, politicians and others who administer the affairs of ghetto residents are typically whites who live outside the Black Community.[7]

---

[7] Robert Blauner, "Internal Colonialism and Ghetto Revolt," *Social Problems* 16, no. 4 (Spring 1969): 397.

All three elements of difference can be supported. But the differences are smaller and the similarities greater than this passage suggests.

First, there is the question of the voluntary character of the ghetto. Blauner argues that the Negro ghettos are involuntary, the ethnic ghettos more voluntary. The voluntary character has two sources: one the voluntary character of the migration itself, the other the voluntary choice to live among fellow ethnics. The nature of their migration is by far the most substantial difference between Negroes and ethnic groups, but it is not an absolute difference. A significant number of the blacks in New York City, for example, are immigrants from the West Indies who came by choice. (Their original migration to the West Indies was as slaves, but their arrival in this country constituted an act of choice not very different from that of white immigrants motivated principally by the pressure of economic deprivation.) In 1930, Ira De Augustine Reid pointed out, 17 percent of black New Yorkers were foreign-born.[8] In addition, the migration of Negroes from the South to the North and West has much of the quality of the migration of European and Asian immigrants from Europe and Asia to America. It meant moving into a very different social world, as memoirists and novelists make clear. It was a move from a situation of dire deprivation and persecution to one of some opportunity and a much more moderate degree of discrimination and prejudice.

Nor, if we consider the second element that distinguishes black from white ethnic ghettos in Professor Blauner's account—the more voluntary decision to live among one's fellows—will we find the distinction as sharp as he suggests. First, there is the simple economic limitation set by low income, a limitation that characterizes black and white immigrant groups alike.[9] Second, there are the positive attractions of a community of people of common descent and culture, one that plays probably as strong a role among Negroes as among white ethnic groups. Most Negroes do not want to live only among Negroes. Recent surveys make this clear. Nor do most want to live only among whites. This is not very different from immigrant ethnic patterns.

The degree to which residential concentration of Negro and immigrant ethnic groups occurs and the degree to which it can be ascribed to economic

---

[8] Ira De Augustine Reid, *The Negro Immigrant* (New York: Columbia University Press, 1949), pp. 235, 237.

[9] How large this limitation is is not simple to determine. There are varying positions: Karl E. Taeuber, in "The Effect of Income Redistribution on Racial Residential Segregation" (*Urban Affairs Quarterly* 4 [September 1968]: 5–14), presents data to show that it is quite small and that Negro residence is affected overwhelmingly by discrimination and much less by economic factors. Anthony H. Pascal, using a different model in *The Economics of Housing Discrimination* (Santa Monica, Calif.: Rand Corporation, 1967), concludes that economic factors explain 50 percent of the variance in percentage of Negroes in Chicago and Detroit neighborhoods. For a discussion and an effort at reconciliation, see Karl E. Taeuber, *Patterns of Negro-White Residential Segregation* (Santa Monica, Calif.: Rand Corporation, 1970).

factors or to other factors (which must include both discrimination and positive attachment to a community of one's fellows, two factors that cannot be easily sectioned out) have recently been subject to empirical research. What the research suggests is that the degree of segregation between white ethnic groups is still extensive and not rapidly declining. Nathan Kantrowitz has analyzed the degree of segregation between white ethnic groups and concludes the decline has been quite small:

> The segregation index between Norwegians and Swedes [in New York City], 45.4 [immigrants and their children only], indicates a separation between two Protestant Scandinavian populations which have partially intermarried and even have at least one community in common. . . . If Swedes and Norwegians are not highly integrated with each other, it is likely they are even less integrated with other ethnic populations. The index of segregation between various white ethnic groups that are more distant from each other than Norwegians and Swedes runs much higher—thus, the index of segregation between Swedes and natives of the U.S.S.R. and their children (primarily Jews) is 70.7. That is not very far from the higher indexes of segregation that characterize Negroes.[10]

These indexes are about 80. The segregation indexes for Puerto Ricans are the same. Thus the degree of segregation of Negroes in New York City, while high, seems to be at one end of a continuum, one shared by Puerto Ricans, rather than radically different from white ethnic segregation. Kantrowitz also demonstrates that New York City is not unique in this respect.

Kantrowitz's detailed analysis suggests that the assertion that white ethnic groups' segregation is voluntary and nonwhite segregation is involuntary must be re-examined. The segregations of the two kinds of groups have many features in common, and while the evidence I have referred to leaves inconclusive the degree to which a segregation is voluntary or forced, or, if forced, whether it is based on economic or discriminatory factors, our other knowledge of these communities suggests that voluntary motives play a large part, even if different in their importance for the two kinds of communities.

Blauner's second point is that the immigrant ghettos are a one-generation and two-generation phenomenon, while the black ghetto is more permanent. Once again, we can exaggerate this difference. Erich Rosenthal has documented the move of Jews in Chicago from Lawndale to the northern suburbs and their reconcentration there.[11] These are second-generation and third-generation Jews. The concentration of Jews in some communities that are by now largely of the second and third generation, and similiar concentrations of Italians and other ethnic groups, suggest that the ghetto, or something

---

[10] Nathan Kantrowitz, "Segregation in New York City, 1960," *American Journal of Sociology* 74, no. 6 (May 1969): 685–95.

[11] Erich Rosenthal, "Acculturation Without Assimilation?" *American Journal of Sociology* 66 (1960): 275–78.

like the ghetto, has a relatively long life for some groups, even though it may change its physical location. Negro ghettos have also moved; the original Lower West Side ghetto of Negroes in New York City is no more. The population of Harlem is already in decline; and were it not for the placement of permanent low-income housing projects in Negro ghettos, we would see some of them disintegrate more rapidly before the pressure of other uses. We already see the rise of middle-class, second- and third-generation (if measured by generations in the North) Negro areas in the major Northern cities. These are not so different from the concentrations established by white ethnic groups. Thus, against Blauner's second point I would argue that it underestimates the longevity of white ghettos and the mobility of Negro ghettos.

The ghettos of the "older immigrants" (Irish and German) have indeed largely disappeared, but their history began with heavy immigration one hundred and thirty years ago. We do not know what the state of Negro ghettos in Northern cities will be after such an expanse of time. While it is true there have been Negroes in Northern cities from their founding, the rise of *large* Negro populations in the North came *after* the major immigration of the Eastern European and Southern European ethnic groups — Italians, Jews, Poles. Indeed, one of the weaknesses in various comparisons of blacks and white ethnic groups is the choice of time spans used for comparison. From the national point of view, blacks are among the oldest components of the American population, and a very large component. But in the Northern and Western cities, as a mass element, they are relative late-comers. Thus, for example, in New York City in 1900, Negroes formed only 2 percent of the population — a minor group indeed, statistically — while the Germans and Irish and their children formed 20 percent each, Russians and their children (an index to the Jewish group, though it understates the size), 7 percent, and Italians and their children, 6 percent. Twenty years later, Russians and their children formed 18 percent of the population, Italians and their children, 14 percent, and Negroes formed only 3 percent. Not until 1940 did Negroes form as large a part of the population of New York City as the Italians and their children had formed in 1900.[12] Using a national measure, Negroes are first-comers and unquestionably deprived in light of their three-hundred-year history in the United States. In the Northern urban perspective, they are late-comers, and this perspective makes a good deal of sense to many people in the Northern city.

Economic and Political Power

Blauner's final point is that while European ethnic groups rapidly gained economic and political control over their ghettos, Negroes did not. This is perhaps the key point in his argument in support of the thesis of internal

---

[12] See Glazer and Moynihan, *Beyond the Melting Pot,* p. 318, Table 2.

colonialism. And yet it is remarkably difficult to support with empirical evidence on the ghettos of the Northern and Western cities that are Blauner's main concern in his article. Any responsible discussion of this problem must begin with some consideration of the problem of relevant time spans for comparison. If the issue is "rate" of acquisition of economic and political power in a new setting, then this rate must relate to a period of time. If the period of time is the three-hundred-year span of black experience in this country, compared with approximately two hundred years of German history, one hundred and fifty years of Irish history, and one hundred years of Italian history, then Blauner is right. But if we stay within the context of Northern cities, then blacks—who settled in the North in large numbers at a time when white Protestants exercised major economic power, Germans were already a solidly established middle class, the Irish exercised political power, and Jews and Italians were prominent in small business—are latecomers.

From the national point of view and the point of view of national responsibility for the black condition—a responsibility in which all share, even immigrants who came here long after the end of slavery—blacks are far behind. If we look at the Northern and Western cities and consider the history of groups within them in terms of generations spent in those urban areas (as did, for example, W. Lloyd Warner and Leo Srole in their pioneering work, *The Social Systems of American Ethnic Groups*), then the situation is quite different.[13] Blacks are still behind, but not as far behind.

There is a second point to be made about the problem of "rate." If we use as our model "white immigrant experience," not further differentiated, then blacks are far behind. But if we look at the experience of individual ethnic groups, the matter is quite different. The Irish have shown remarkable political success, the Jews remarkable organizational and economic success, and the Japanese remarkable educational success; but Poles and Italians, for example, are not distinguished in these areas. There was a *range* of experience. Within this range, my judgment on the basis of scanty data is that blacks fall near the bottom, but not on all scales, not uniformly, and not so radically that we must set up a new model called "internal colonialism" to explain their position in the Northern and Western city.

Unfortunately, neatly arranged data that proves this point is simply not available. We do not, for example, have good studies of the economic and educational status of Polish-Americans and other Slavic groups by generation and length of residence. If we did, I would think that there would be similarity in many respects between such immigrants and blacks; one would find that, at comparable times, these immigrant groups also exhibited a rising and substantial degree of home ownership, a substantial body of unskilled and

---

[13] W. Lloyd Warner and Leo Srole, *The Social Systems of American Ethnic Groups* (New Haven, Conn.: Yale University Press, 1945).

semiskilled workers, and considerable social disorganization and family break-up because of cultural change and economic distress. One would not find any economic power wielded by such groups outside the ghetto, except perhaps labor power.

The European immigrants' major economic differences from blacks seem twofold. First, they opened more retail stores. Was this owing to "internal colonialism"? Eugene Foley has made, as far as I know, the only detailed examination of black small business and other small business, and he finds no major difference in, for example, access to credit from banks between them.[14] The weakness of business among blacks is owing, first, to a tradition in which business and its practices are not widely dispersed and well known (and this may well be traced to slavery); second, to inadequacy of patronage by the black group itself because of factors such as the fact that, since blacks used English, language did not serve as a protective barrier for the black ghetto businessman. Interestingly enough, the Irish, another group that spoke English, also did poorly in establishing small retail businesses. The argument that racism destroyed black business in pre-immigrant American cities and prevented the rise of new black businesses has a good deal of merit but cannot be an exclusive explanation. Chinese and Japanese also met vicious racism; Jews faced a more moderate prejudice. A variety of factors were relevant.[15]

There was struggle, of course, over jobs and political power. In this struggle, racism—prejudice and discrimination—played a major role. These same weapons were used against other groups. In their struggle the small settled black communities of Northern cities lost, badly. But was this a matter of "internal colonialism" or did the fight go against the blacks for many reasons?[16]

The same issue is relevant for the second major difference—though I have no good statistics and know of no systematic comparison—between black and immigrant ethnic communities, and this is the view that there is a higher

---

[14] Eugene P. Foley, "The Negro Businessman in Search of a Tradition," *Daedalus* 95, no. 1 (Winter 1966): 107–44.

[15] For a particularly impressive analysis of Negro backwardness in business, which ascribes major weight to factors of internal organization and cohesion, formal and informal, familial and extrafamilial, see Ivan Hubert Light, "Sociological Aspects of Self-Employment and Social Welfare Among Chinese, Japanese and Negroes in Northern Urban Areas of the United States, 1900–1940" (Ph.D. diss., University of California, Berkeley, 1969).

[16] For the best account of this struggle, see W. E. B. Du Bois' *The Philadelphia Negro: A Social Study* (Philadelphia: University of Pennsylvania Press, 1899). See, too, Herman Bloch, *The Circle of Discrimination* (New York: New York University Press, 1969). Various people are doing work on the early history of Northern black urban communities, and in a short while we will have a more substantial basis for judgment on the serious question of the rate of achievement of economic and political power by blacks and other groups.

degree of unemployment and social disorganization among the blacks. I am not referring to comparisons made at this point in time. Today blacks do show much more unemployment and social disorganization than is true of other groups; but do they show more than, let us say, Poles showed in the 1920's and 1930's in the Northern city? And are these problems matters of formal or informal racial disqualification—colonialism—or the result of many factors: level of skill, cultural change, conflict with better organized groups?[17] The history of every ethnic group reveals how little was simply given, how much was achieved by conflict. Consider the history of the labor movement, which is largely a history of immigrant ethnic groups. And the history of the labor movement seems to me a record of almost uniform defeat for the immigrant groups throughout their first hundred years in this country.

We have better evidence for the rate of acquisition of political power, and it is hard to see any major difference between the black experience and the white immigrant experience except for the phenomenal political success of the Irish. White ethnic areas generally managed to elect members of their own group to represent them when they had a majority. So did black areas. This was not done without struggle—often very fierce struggle.[18] The same was true for black sections in Chicago, in New York City, and in other cities. Blacks are now being elected mayors, councilmen, state legislators, and congressmen, largely on the basis of statistical predominance, but not always. (Note the election in 1970 of three black congressmen from areas with black minorities.)

But just as in the case of economic power, a slow rate of acquisition of political power is not proof of "internal colonialism." Other factors prevent blacks in Northern cities from gaining political power proportionate to their numbers.

Arthur Klebanoff[19] has made a close analysis of Negro political power in Brooklyn, measured by the number of black assemblymen and senators in the state legislature. He shows that the increase in their numbers has not matched the increase in the Negro population. He also demonstrates that this is owing to two features: ingenious redistricting influenced by powerful Jewish and Italian state legislators in order to maintain their seats in the face

---

[17] For the disorganization that may afflict an immigrant ethnic group, see, for example, W. I. Thomas and F. Znaniecki, *The Polish Peasant in Europe and America* (New York: Dover Publications, 1958); W. I. Thomas, *The Unadjusted Girl* (Boston: Atlantic-Little, Brown, 1923); and Oscar Handlin, *Boston's Immigrants* (Cambridge, Mass.: Harvard University Press, 1941).

[18] For an account of a ferocious battle to gain representation for Italians, see Humbert S. Nelli's *The Italians in Chicago, 1880–1930: A Study in Ethnic Mobility* (New York: Oxford University Press, 1970). The Italians lost, which simply goes to make my point that groups other than blacks do lose.

[19] Arthur Klebanoff, "The Demographics of Politics: Legislative Constituencies in the Borough of Brooklyn" (Senior honors thesis, Yale University, 1969).

of increasing Negro and Puerto Rican population and a low rate of registration among Negroes and Puerto Ricans. I do not see any support for the colonial analogy here. Gerrymandering against new groups was not invented to keep Negroes unrepresented; rates of registration, just like rates of taking out citizenship and of voting, have varied for a long time between groups for various and complex reasons. The enormous difference between immigrant groups with regard to their interest in taking out citizenship and their participation in formal electoral politics was documented in the first decade of this century by the Immigration Commission. Only 4 percent of immigrant Greeks became citizens, as against 58 percent of the Armenians![20] And this was documented again in the 1920's.[21] Studies have been made of the voting rates of ethnic groups in New York City. One survey shows that Puerto Ricans vote least (32.5 percent); Negroes next (43.4 percent); foreign-born Italians and their children do somewhat better (56.2 percent); white Protestants are next (64 percent); the Irish and their children show a much higher rate of voting (73.9 percent); and native-born Jews show the highest (78.9 percent). Clearly rates of voting play a role in ethnic political representation. Yet how can internal colonialism explain this difference in rates between groups, today as sixty years ago?[22]

Blauner says, and many agree with him, that "the educators, policemen, social workers, politicians and others who administer the affairs of ghetto residents are typically whites who live outside the Black Community."[23] I have suggested that blacks have more power than Blauner's third point asserts; I would also argue that white ethnic groups had less power than he implies. They too did not staff—certainly not for the first generation—the schools, police forces, social work agencies, and political positions. The evidence on this is clear. Humbert Nelli records for the Italians of Chicago their small numbers in the police force and the school system.[24] Almost every ethnic group was initially educated, policed, and administered by persons of other ethnic groups, earlier arrivals. We are talking about rates. In some areas the rates of change have been slowed down by civil service laws. But it can hardly be argued that these reforms were instituted to maintain colonialism or with any thought that they would eventually serve to reduce the rates at which blacks took over government jobs in areas that affected them.

My point is *not* that there are no major differences between the large

---

[20] See *Abstracts of Reports of the Immigration Commission,* Senate Document 747, vol. 1 (Washington, D.C., 1911), pp. 485–87.

[21] John P. Gavit, *Americans by Choice* (New York: Harper, 1922).

[22] Jack Elinson, Paul W. Haberman, and Cyrille Gell, "Ethnic and Educational Data on Adults in New York City, 1963–1964," mimeographed (School of Public Health and Administrative Medicine, Columbia University, 1967), p. 155.

[23] Blauner, "Internal Colonialism and Ghetto Revolt," p. 397.

[24] Nelli, *The Italians in Chicago,* pp. 75–77.

immigrant ethnic groups and Negroes. Rather, in question is the character and scale of the differences, and whether they justify considering the experience of immigrant ethnic groups as one that leads to some degree of acculturation and assimilation, while considering the experience of Negroes (and perhaps some other groups) to be colonial or quasi-colonial and of the sort that does not lead to integration—or more precisely to that measure of integration that is characteristic of immigrant ethnic groups—but rather to separation and, if we push the colonial analogy far enough, to "independence."

North and South

Chapter 9 of the Kerner Commission's report gives another and to my mind a more balanced view of the differences between the experience of immigrant ethnic groups and the American Negro. There the differences are grouped into five categories. The first is the change in the economy between the time of major European ethnic migration and of major Negro migration to Northern cities—in particular, the decline of opportunities for unskilled labor. Second, the high visibility of race itself—racial discrimination is far more pervasive and severe than the moderate discrimination that some white ethnic groups faced. Third is the change in the political system and in particular the decline of ward-based politics and the rise of civil service. Fourth are the differing cultural orientations of white ethnic groups and Negro migrants—the first, the report asserts, were ready to accept poorly paid and low-status labor, had stronger families more able to pool resources and sponsor members' mobility, and had needs which required distinctive stores and services. Obviously this is a mixed bag, but an important one. And fifth, Chapter 9 refers to the "vital element of time." There, in a manner similar to my critique of Blauner, the report argues that ethnic groups did take a long time to reach whatever degree of economic affluence and political power they now possess and that Negroes are moving faster than many believe.

I would disagree with only one of the commission's points—that the economic situation Negroes face in Northern cities is harsher than that faced by white ethnic migrants. Admittedly there is less unskilled labor available now than in the periods of peak European migration. But this cannot be translated into the conclusion that there are fewer *jobs* available. For while the number of unskilled jobs has declined, the number of those who are capable of filling only unskilled jobs has also declined. Negro migrants have a higher level of education than European immigrants of the beginning of the century and are consequently not as restricted in the kinds of jobs they can fill. The fact that many jobs for the unskilled are not filled shows that there has not been a substantial decline in the ratio of jobs to applicants. Two other things have happened, however. There are now more alternatives to unskilled work. There are social programs, and consequently fewer people are driven to unpleasant and low-paying jobs by the need to feed their families. Secondly, there is a change in attitudes toward unskilled and low-paying work. It is less commonly seen as a suitable or acceptable lifelong activity for men. Expectations have changed, and fewer blacks or whites today will accept a life at menial labor with no hope for advancement, as their fathers and older brothers did and as European immigrants did.

One reason the Kerner Commission's report could emphasize as much as it did the degree of continuity between the immigrant and the Negro experience is that the commission concentrated on the Northern urban experience. If it had taken a national view (more than half of all black Americans still live in the South; perhaps three-quarters were raised in the South and almost all have been in some way shaped by the searing experience of Southern racism), it would not have found many elements of continuity—there are almost none between the experience of the Negro slave in the South and the free immigrant worker in the North. But if one concentrates, as the commission did, on the Northern Negro and on the cities in the North, there is a substantial degree of continuity between the experience of immigrant workers and Negro migrants.

If one takes the national view, the view that includes Negro enslavement, the legally inferior position of Negroes set forth in the Constitution and in state and local law for centuries, the disfranchisement of Negroes after the Civil War, and the heroic and not yet completed struggle to achieve full legal equality in the South, then it is indeed enraging to be answered with the ethnic comparison. The conservative and optimistic bias of this comparison underestimates what has been and still is necessary to achieve full equality for the Negroes.

But if one concentrates on the Northern urban experience, then the elements of continuity are important. There the Negro arrives as a migrant. There he arrives in a position in which, despite severe discrimination and prejudice, civil equality is protected in law. He is worst-off of the groups —but worst-off because he faces the most severe prejudice and discrimination on a scale of discrimination applied to almost every immigrant (one probably on which Chinese and Japanese fared as badly), because he comes with the poorest job and community skills, and because he is also the latest of the arrivals. As in the case of the other groups, this is not an unchanging situation: prejudice and discrimination decline (in part because of the struggles of the group itself and its growing power), skills improve, and time passes.

The Northern view emphasizes continuity because it is aware that there is a great range in the experience of the ethnic groups. They vary in time of arrival, skills at time of arrival, character of the cities into which they came, character of their cultural attributes, and degree of discrimination and prejudice they faced; thus they have a wide range of different experiences. In this range, the gap between the experience of the worst-off of the ethnic groups and the Negroes is one of degree rather than kind. Indeed, in some respects the Negro is better off than some other groups. He has more political power than Puerto Ricans in New York City, a somewhat higher income, a substantially higher proportion of professionals and experienced persons able to take leadership positions. If one takes all the ethnic groups and lumps them together, the Negro is at the bottom. If one views them in a more realistic manner—as groups—then the Negroes are worse off than most yet in some respects perhaps better off than some. They probably have more college graduates than Polish-Americans, more political muscle than Mexican-Americans, more clout in the mass media than Italian-Americans. It is the comparison of "blacks" against "whites" which shows such a radical distinction between black and white (and this is made even sharper in national figures by putting together North and South), but this is not so if we compare Negroes against the whole range of individual ethnic groups.

There is another point to be made about the consequences of taking the Northern view. From the point of view of the North, the differences in power and wealth of the varied groups that make up the Northern city are somewhat understandable. There is a sequence of arrival. There is a sequence of prestige. Some groups are considered superior, some for a time inferior. This inferiority is resented and fought. It was fought by the Irish, the Jews, the Italians. But it does not become a basic cause for divorce from society. The reason it does not is because there is an underground and grudging acknowledgment that those who were here first, who "started" the country, understandably and with some justice in the North have greater wealth and power. In the South, no such acknowledgment can be made. The Negroes were brought as slaves, and at the same time, they also built the country; they should have full and equal position, and the subtle and half-grudgingly accepted order of precedence of the ethnic groups in the North plays no part in their experience in the South.

Perhaps the tragedy of this country is that it did not become two nations, because the two sections have developed such a radically different orientation to the facts of ethnic diversity. I believe the main reason the argument that there is a radical discontinuity between ethnic experience and Negro experience is so powerful is the South—because there it is true, and because Southern attitudes have not been limited to the South. They have been brought North, physically, by blacks and whites; they have become an integral part of this country's history through the often disproportionate power of the white South as reflected in national policy; and models have been available —through the history of colonialism—that made it possible for intellectuals, social scientists, blacks, and others to apply the Southern model to the whole country.

How one views society is never a consequence simply of social reality (assuming that it is accessible); it is also a matter of how one wills to see society. I believe it is possible to see the position of Negroes in Northern cities in ethnic terms, that is, to see them as the last of the major groups, presently badly off, but due to rise in time to larger shares of wealth and power and influence. This is a possibility in harmony with as many facts as any other. However, there are credible alternatives. It is also possible — and equally true — to see the Negro's present plight as the consequence of the special crime and burden of American society. In this view, Negroes will not become part of American society without radical, almost superhuman efforts in every area of life. Without these efforts only separation is possible — hard as it is to imagine. These are alternatives both in social reality — where there is evidence for both — and in political reality. One can choose either, and one's actions can make one or the other dominant.

The ethnic analogy is losing among black youth. Some alternative — pluralism? separatism? a separate nation? — is winning out. It can take the relatively mild form of ethnic pluralism, in which case it is quite conformable to the experience of other ethnic groups, white and nonwhite. Or it can take — and among many of the youth it does take — a more radical form, one that cannot be realized within the present political structure of American society. If it takes the mild form, then we can see it as a stage in a process to fuller integration and a larger measure of power and wealth in American society. Such a stage — withdrawal in order to gather strength — is not a new pattern. But if it takes the more radical form of a demand for political restructuring to formally acknowledge the position of blacks as a permanently separate group, then we will have certainly entered a new and hazardous period in national development. For such a demand must have repercussions on other groups — Mexican-Americans, Puerto Ricans, American Indians. It will affect even the relatively prosperous Oriental communities. And it may begin to affect the white ethnic groups, to lead them to reflect on their experiences and position in American society and perhaps to decide that they too are subject to insupportable deprivation and that the American ethnic system has failed. The political consequence of the position that there is no relationship between black and white immigrant ethnic group experience might well be to divide the country, to the disadvantage of all groups. And if this is one potential political possibility, should it not be taken into account in the debate?

Black Americans and the
Politics of Poverty, 1900-1970

DANIEL M. FOX

Daniel M. Fox is assistant professor of history and public administration at Harvard University and a principal of the Organization for Social and Technical Innovation. Among his published works in the field of American history and social policy is *The Discovery of Abundance* (Cornell University Press, 1967). In the essay that follows, Mr. Fox discusses the claims of the black poor on the attention and resources of the nation. Maintaining that the recognized poor are never those at the very bottom of society, he traces the political emphasis on black poverty and outlines the changes in antipoverty constituencies and strategies thus far in the twentieth century.

Poverty persists in the United States despite three-quarters of a century of argument and action on the premise that the existence of poverty in the midst of plenty is contradictory, paradoxical, intolerable, or immoral. During this century there has been a vast increase in the share of national attention and wealth allocated to end human suffering. But general well-being and social harmony have not been achieved. Against the familiar image of social and economic progress and improvement of the standard of living must be set a counterimage: hungry children; overcrowded, deteriorating housing; violence and counterviolence by both those who are suffering and the forces of law and order; human obsolescence caused by technological changes in agriculture, manufacturing, and mining; the inadequately mitigated ravages of infections and chronic diseases; the loneliness and dependency of the elderly; confusion, shame, and intragroup conflict as successive generations of youth—white, black, brown, yellow, and red—are taught that their parents' languages, customs, beliefs, and loyalties are impediments to success.

The historical reality is that the concept of poverty in the midst of plenty is a polemical challenge, not a description of past or present conditions. Poverty and plenty, scarcity and abundance, have always been relative—matters of perception. Increasing national wealth and a constantly rising standard of living have raised, not reduced, citizens' expectations, hopes, and

frustrations. As long as some people have more goods, services, opportunities, and power than others, poverty—consciousness of relative deprivation—will continue.

Over the past century, life at the bottom of society has become less hazardous and has been shared by fewer people. But the problems of poverty
remain, for the poor as well as for those who would either ameliorate or
ignore their condition. These problems, different in detail but similar in
significance for each generation, are, at root, the distance between society's
promise and its performance; between citizens' aspirations and their achievement. Public and private agencies have been designing minimum subsistence
budgets as a basis for awarding subsidies to the poor since the turn of the
century. The amount and kind of goods and services deemed necessary for
subsistence or for comfort have progressively increased. It is, however, no
comfort to either those below the present "poverty line" or those who make
social policy to know that in 1928 half the American people would have been
eligible for the current Family Assistance Plan.

There have been "new poor" in every generation: people who, by their
condition, action, or potential effect on others, become the primary concern
of the policy and politics that we now label antipoverty. Those who would
help the poor have always had to operate within a scarcity of time, money,
and public attention. These resources have been scarcest when their application promised to disturb cherished values and institutional arrangements.
They tend to flow most readily for purposes which are perceived as reducing
or removing threats to the maintenance of the social order. The new or, more
accurately, the dominant poor in each generation of this century have never
been those at the very bottom of society. Rather, they have been the groups
whose political, social, and economic mobility posed the greatest challenge
to more affluent citizens.

It is in this context that the emphasis of social policy during the past
decade on the black poor must be understood. Attention to the needs of low-
income blacks is a result of the black challenge of the present, not white
atonement for the sins of the past. This emphasis on black poverty at a time
when only 30 percent of Americans below the official poverty line are black
is a result of the increasing potency of black votes, black consumer power,
organized pressure for better education and housing, black concentration
in potentially valuable urban real estate, and the threat and reality of violence.

Antipoverty Constituencies and Strategies, 1900-1930

At the turn of the century, as caste lines were strengthened in both the
North and the South, the black poor had little more than a moral claim on antipoverty resources. Black poverty was grinding, but to Americans concerned
with helping less fortunate citizens, recent immigrants from Europe were more

threatening. As long as labor unions refused to admit blacks or assisted in trapping them in low-status jobs, blacks, unlike immigrant workers, were not likely to combine in restraint of profits and authoritarian management practices. As long as most blacks lived in the South and were effectively disfranchised, they were not potential recruits for the new immigrant-oriented political machines. Blacks could be ignored, but the Americanization of European immigrants was considered both virtue and necessity by philanthropists and public officials: virtue because of the supposed superiority of the American way of life and the moral rewards to the stewards of wealth who aided the deserving poor; necessity because, among the immigrants' un-American traits were, it was alleged, a willingness to engage in class warfare and blind obedience to ethnic leaders.

Much of the agitation for social reform during the first two decades of this century can be interpreted as an effort to avoid polarization and social conflict by providing protection and opportunities for the most visible and potentially threatening of the poor. Most reformers occupied a middle ground between conservative defenders of the status quo and an increasing number of radicals advocating massive redistribution of power and wealth. Tenement house and factory safety laws, the workmen's compensation movement, support for the "responsible" unionism of the American Federation of Labor, and the substitution of professional casework for amateur philanthropy are outstanding examples of the desire to improve conditions and relieve frustrations among the most upwardly mobile of the lower classes.

Reformers' efforts to prohibit child labor and their advocacy of immigration restriction can be explained in this context. Child labor, whatever its inhumanity, was not viewed primarily as exploitation by the truly poorest Americans. Working children provided badly needed additional income in most low-income families. Without minimum wages or income supplements, prohibition of child labor impeded mobility for those on the very bottom. Similarly, immigration restriction was a hardship only to the most recent immigrants, those from southern and eastern Europe, whose families were often not yet in America. But prohibiting child labor and restricting immigration were favored by many of the more affluent members of the working class, those whose mobility had made them more concerned with reducing competition for jobs and protecting their children's futures than with basic family survival.

It is oversimple to explain the focus of social policy during the Progressive era as cynical political calculation. This focus on the most visible and volatile of the poor was a response to genuine social and political pressures: the reality of violence against and by organized labor; the first demonstrations of the voting power in urban politics of first- and second-generation Americans. To the turn-of-the-century poverty warriors, violence was abhorrent, and the immigrants' choice of political leadership lamentable. Moreover, as each generation of activists against poverty has discovered, it is easier to work with those of the unfortunate whose attitudes and behavior most closely resemble one's own.

For the first third of the century, the black urban poor, like many immigrants from southern and eastern Europe, were not major claimants for the attention, subsidies, and services directed at the lower classes. Both groups had to rely more on ethnic self-help and religious organizations to soften the harshest effects of city life than on the burgeoning public and private philanthropic bureaucracies. Black hospitals and service institutions, for example, were usually excluded from Community Chest campaigns, the major innovation in charitable fund raising and allocation in the second and third decades of the century. Considerable investigation and indignation were focused on industrial violence to the comparative exclusion of the common and virulent interracial violence — which was often a result of the cynical use of black workers as strikebreakers by white industrialists.

Moreover, during the first half of the twentieth century, the majority of the black poor were rural poor, affected both by their distance from the major constituencies for social and philanthropic reform and by the general decline of agrarian democracy. The failure of Populism, and the way many Populists first courted and then rejected blacks, is a familiar story. Less well known are the ways in which agribusiness, superbly organized at the county and state levels and dominating federal agencies, maintained a cheap, docile labor supply. Farm Bureaus and state universities, often operating through the quasi-federal Cooperative Extension Service, persuaded most urban Americans that they were dealing with rural problems, including the problems of poverty, through education and the diffusion of innovation. But local rural elites used various means of coercion to maintain a supply of labor at costs that met the needs of agribusiness. Rural workers — the landless, tenants, and small-holders — could not get a higher return for their services without migrating. And migration was inhibited by a lack of capital and of education — results of the organization of rural society — and often by a lack of opportunity in cities.

Ironically, disturbed by the anonymity and chaos of cities, many reformers and philanthropists idealized rural life. For many of them, born and raised in the rural and small-town middle classes, the healthy "primary bonds" of rural areas were superior to the fragmentation and disorganization of cities — especially urban neighborhoods occupied by newcomers to the nation or to city life. Many social caseworkers, settlement house residents, and city planners, for instance, were committed to asserting allegedly rural values in city neighborhoods.

Despite their compassion for human suffering, their personal frame of reference made it difficult for most urban reformers to identify with the meanness and harshness of life at the bottom of the rural caste and class structure. Philanthropic allocations to rural areas sought either the control of debilitating diseases like rickets or a more vicious control: education of rural youth to accept the social and economic structure they were born into. Whether the funds went to schools and colleges for blacks, Indians, or white Appalachians, they carried the same message: improve yourself by learning skills that will earn you modest economic security in return for your loyalty to the status quo.

A New Deal for Whom?

It is a current cliché of revisionist historiography that the programs of the New Deal, like those sponsored by the Progressives, ignored the poorest, most exploited Americans—particularly those with darker skins. An "invisible scar" appears to many to be the New Deal legacy.

The principal beneficiaries of New Deal "relief, recovery, and reform" policy were the temporary poor, those who had fallen in status as a result of economic forces beyond their control. However, it is distortion to ignore the ways in which New Deal innovations assisted other groups. Criticism of public social policy from 1933 to 1940 for expediency and pragmatism must be tempered by recognition that the New Deal contributed to the process by which new groups would express their postwar claims on national wealth.

New Deal programs, like most antipoverty efforts in this century, were addressed primarily to those whose frustrations and aspirations made them the greatest threat to national stability. The possibility of violent action by unemployed craftsmen and industrial workers was not a fantasy in the early thirties; nor was the possibility that they, along with clerical and professional workers, the elderly, and middling farmers, might be susceptible to political panaceas analogous to those that threatened democracy in Europe. Moreover, by 1933 the traditional sources of help for the poor—state and local government and philanthropies—were bankrupt of both money and ideas.

The New Deal's most important legacy for dealing with poverty was the assumption by the federal government of primary responsibility for funding and directing the relief of suffering. Federal responsibility meant that, in time, every group with a claim on the public interest would be heard, despite the necessity of compromise with power holders in state and local government. The national arena would provide the opportunity for groups repressed in smaller political units—because of limited numbers, unfavorable economic relationships, or inequitable social conventions—to pool their strength and coalesce with other groups.

But in the years between 1933 and 1940, the benefits of federal assumption of responsibility were more evident to those who had fallen from relative affluence than to those at the bottom of society. Federal work relief administrators, after a few heroic struggles to pay decent rather than prevailing wages, yielded to the pressure of businessmen and politicians who viewed federal intervention as a threat to the wage exploitation of those at the bottom of society. The Tennessee Valley Authority gloried in a policy of "grass-roots democracy" through which the Extension Service and the Farm Bureaus

—creations of agribusiness—decided which citizens would have a voice in planning and administration. The local committees that were elected to supervise crop control and soil conservation programs were quickly dominated by county political establishments. Social security and unemployment compensation legislation left considerable discretionary power to the states. The limited scope of legislation regulating wages and working hours effectively excluded the poorest citizens. The regulations governing federal housing subsidies frankly encouraged the creation and maintenance of neighborhoods that were racially and economically segregated.

Yet New Deal policy, both by design and default, also provided unprecedented benefits for the poorest Americans—and for blacks in particular. Many who in the past had been defined as ineligible for or undeserving of public or private charity now received federal relief. Black politicians benefited from the patronage opportunities in the management of public relief. Loans and grants from the Resettlement (later Farm Security) Administration provided thousands of decent homes and challenged the exploitative land tenure arrangements that existed in many rural areas, especially in the South. Indeed, there is a high correlation between the location of extensive FSA operations in the 1930's and the rapidity of political modernization in black communities in the South in the 1960's. Federal neutrality and tacit encouragement in the struggle to create industrial unions enabled more blacks to enjoy the benefits of collective bargaining than at any time in the past. In general, the new CIO unions were far less discriminatory than the American Federation of Labor. Some New Deal programs, finally, went beyond immediate relief for victims of the Depression and provided benefits for the least favored Americans; old-age and unemployment insurance, aid to mothers with dependent children and to the disabled and the blind, and public housing began to create a "floor" beneath which Americans' standard of living would not be allowed to fall.

World War II and After: The Growing Challenge

By the beginning of World War II, some of the preconditions were established for pressing the claims of the black poor for better housing, education, social services, for increased economic opportunity, more choice and voice in the distribution of wealth and services. Black voters were an important constituency for the national Democratic party. Also significant in the Democratic coalition, industrial unions, and, increasingly, craft unions as well, were enrolling and increasing the wages and job security of an ever larger number of blacks. The legislation that signified the belated coming of the welfare state to the United States, for all its limitations of coverage and susceptibility to state and local manipulation and discrimination, provided a last resort for the poor that was, usually, far superior to private charity in funds, fairness, and dignity.

Yet these preconditions did not guarantee that the black (and Spanish-speaking, Indian, and white rural) poor would receive special attention in the ways that the newly discovered poor of previous generations had. Challenge had to precede response, as it did in the instances of the upwardly mobile immigrant poor at the beginning of the century and the temporary poor of the Depression.

World War II made possible the contemporary black challenge. It can be argued that in this century wars have provided more benefits for the American poor, of all ethnic groups, than all the deliberate antipoverty strategies combined. The great demand for factory labor in World War I was a major force for black mobility: geographical movement out of rural areas and out of the South, and economic movement into more desirable jobs. The greater demand for labor over a longer period in World War II created even more mobility for blacks. The March on Washington movement of 1941, the sit-ins against discrimination organized by the Congress of Racial Equality in 1942, and the Detroit riot of 1943 were signs of a growing black challenge. This challenge reflected rising expectations and greater impatience with the economic and social distance between blacks and other citizens. New expectations were a result of more than increasing opportunity and affluence; the emergency conditions and shortages of wartime created unprecedented interracial housing, working, and educational situations. That these unprecedented situations also laid the basis for future interracial tensions is a related, but different, point.

What war-related social changes had begun was continued by exceptional postwar prosperity, successful court challenges to legalized racism, and the mechanization of Southern agriculture. Unlike the years after World War I, the late 1940's were a period of increasing national income, low unemployment, and exuberant consumer demand. Blacks as a group were still at the bottom of the economic ladder, although more of them could be found higher on it than at any time in the past. A Supreme Court responsive to liberal values and reflecting in its membership the new coalition of the Democratic party provided the legal basis for ending both enforced inequality in education and housing and, perhaps more important, white domination of electoral politics in the South. The increasing mechanization of Southern agriculture, a response to both market forces and the bitter recognition that black docility could no longer be taken for granted, spurred black migration from rural areas to towns and cities.

These facts should not be read as an argument that, given time and patience, blacks, like other Americans, inevitably move from poverty to affluence. Black affluence and aspiration increased markedly in the 1940's and 1950's. But income and opportunity were not increasing as rapidly for black (or Spanish-speaking, white Appalachian, Indian, or Eskimo) citizens as they were for the majority of Americans. Data about improvement in the condition of black citizens from 1940 to the early 1960's merely indicate that, as had happened in the past, the stage was being set for a confrontation between an increasingly aggressive minority and those citizens who counseled patience because they had more to be patient about.

From the Truman to the Kennedy administrations, no group of the poor was able to press a sustained claim on public funds and attention. Despite increasing evidence that many Americans could not afford decent health care, national health insurance was a cause that could not find a constituency. Although much housing was substandard or deteriorating, the eloquent promises of the Housing Act of 1949 were destroyed by conservative members of Congress responding to the fears of the banking, building, and real estate industries and the referenda votes of citizens who did not want the poor, especially the black poor, as neighbors.

The federal government had assumed responsibility for the poor. But for fifteen years the only noticeable federal initiatives were modest improvements in benefits and coverage under social security, categorical welfare programs, inadequate, poorly designed public housing units, and, of great importance for black economic opportunity, the desegregation of the armed forces. The argument, mistakenly attributed to John Maynard Keynes, that the manipulation of aggregate demand through national fiscal policy provided the best means to continue economic growth, maintain relative affluence, and eventually eradicate most poverty seemed to have become an article of faith to most Americans of the liberal, compassionate persuasion. Advocates of special remedies for the grievances of the poorest Americans had few allies.

Yet by 1964 the federal government had declared war on poverty. The comfortable belief that economic growth meant the inevitable end of poverty had been stated by *Fortune* magazine as an obvious truth in its 1960 end-of-the-decade summary; but four years later, that view had few vocal supporters.

Even though the metaphor of war externalized what were clearly internal flaws in American society, more deliberate social change was legislated or planned under this heading than at any time since the New Deal. Federal funds were allocated to areas whose economic development had stagnated as a result of technological change and the migration of industry in search of better markets and cheaper labor. For the first time, subsidies were available for training victims of structural unemployment—those out of work because of automation or lack of skills rather than as a result of weak consumer demand. Plans to provide medical care for the aged and the "medically indigent" were gathering increasing support; and subsidies to train health professionals marked at least token recognition that more services were required to meet increased demand. Legislation was planned for aid to schools that established programs aimed at poor children. Voting rights legislation, though not explicitly part of the antipoverty package, was a challenge to the political, industrial, and agricultural exploiters of the black poor in the South. A task force, headed by Sargent Shriver, was developing a comprehensive Economic Opportunity Act, the cornerstone of which was Community Action: a new means to plan, evaluate, and administer services to the poor based on recent federal experience with juvenile delinquency prevention and on a Ford Foundation program to stimulate coordinated planning and administration in cities.

Most of the legislation planned in 1963 and 1964 was enacted. Moreover, new measures increased the funds available for: manpower training and incentives to industry to employ trainees; innovations in the delivery of health services to the poor; subsidized business development among members of minority groups; incentives for developing housing for low-income citizens; and a Model Cities program to coordinate and concentrate services in neighborhoods in one hundred and fifty cities.

In its first two years, the Nixon administration not only continued most of these programs but proposed the Family Assistance Plan—which would, for the first time, set a national minimum income below which poor individuals or families could not fall. The facts that the proposed minimum is too low and that too much discretion is left to state administrators may prove to be minor objections if the nation accepts the concept that enough cash and services to survive and aspire to better things is a matter of right rather than of charity.

The Second Reconstruction: Antipoverty Strategies of the 1960's

The relative importance of various causes of the antipoverty activity of the 1960's is still vigorously disputed. But it is clear that a number of forces converged to create, for a time, a climate of opinion in which advocates of social reform on behalf of the poor claimed national attention.

In the early 1960's, a handful of scholars and journalists documented and publicized the fact that approximately 20 percent of the American people had incomes below the federal government's poverty line of about $3,600 a year for a family of four. These statistics disturbed many people, particularly in the office of the President. To them, aggressive action against poverty seemed to fit the style of an activist, compassionate administration. Because of later perceptions that the antipoverty programs were a response to black poverty, it is significant to note that President Kennedy's decision to sponsor antipoverty legislation was triggered, in October 1963, by a *New York Times Magazine* article on the white poor of eastern Kentucky.

Moreover, since the 1950's, there had been a growing realization among many people with access to public policy makers that social services for the poor were inadequate. Many services were fragmented, dealing with parts of families or segments of individuals: with psyches, budgets, stomachs, and misdemeanors rather than with people and their environment. Services were too often humiliating and degrading. Many citizens avoided the service agencies; others became "apathetic" or "bad clients" in reaction to the insensitivity of many professional helpers. In the absence of effective coordination among service agencies, people were, in a phrase used by reformers, "falling between the cracks."

Other administrators and observers of American government argued that the increasing fragmentation and powerlessness of local units of government contributed to the harshness and intractability of poverty. Such problems as declining regional economies, inadequate or nonexistent services, insufficient housing, and irrational transportation systems could not be solved as long as Americans continued to live in overlapping, anachronistic political units. Problems were particularly acute in the largest cities; mayors were blamed for their failure to affect the policies of agencies they did not control: elected school boards, state-regulated welfare departments, housing and renewal authorities appointed by officials at other levels of government. In addition, as more people moved to the suburbs and the inner cities became places where the affluent worked and the poor lived, city governments had to face growing problems with decreasing resources.

A major factor in the creation of an antipoverty constituency was the growing influence of social scientists' analyses of and remedies for poverty. For the first time since the 1890's, when the correlation of poverty and immorality was first challenged by systematic research, decision making in public and private agencies was dominated by those who regarded poverty as a disease rather than as a result of deficient character. Social scientists and their allies agreed that the root causes of poverty were environmental: that the "cycle" or "culture" of poverty and the disorganization of family life were primarily results of economic exploitation, discrimination, racism, and social neglect. There was general agreement that it was not the laziness or improvidence of the poor but the questionable values and structural flaws in the affluent society—racism, social exclusion, and economic exploitation— that produced most malnutrition, overcrowded housing, broken families, and unmarketable education.

But the concept of poverty as disease, as a pathological state, cut two ways when applied to the design of social policy: toward focus on individual or on social, institutional change. The central issue was whether it was politically possible to treat the causes rather than the effects of the disease called poverty. One influential group, which included many public officials, labor union spokesmen, and leaders of the oldest civil rights organizations, urged a focus on effects. Translated into public policy, this meant focusing on the problems of individuals and families, either through transfer payments (welfare reform, children's allowances) or through new and better services (educational reform, a national housing policy, job training, new health services, sensitive counseling to lift the psychological burdens of poverty).

Opposed to this approach, though agreeing that more transfer payments and better services were desirable, were advocates of social, institutional change. This group, composed of a small number of public officials and social scientists and the emerging "militant" leaders of minority groups, wanted to focus public policy on the causes of poverty. Translated into policy, this meant increasing opportunities for the poor by changing the distribution of power, particularly in state and local affairs. Public and private agencies, particularly those responsible for police, schools, housing, health, and welfare, would be made more responsive to their clients. Employers and labor unions would be forced to end practices that excluded the poorest citizens—for instance, discrimination in hiring and promoting members of particular groups and licensing requirements that operated as barriers to the employment of the poor rather than to ensure quality performance. Local governments would be forced to rectify through reapportionment the vicious gerrymanders by which the poorest citizens lost voice in decisions about their lives and neighborhoods.

Throughout the century this point of view had been part of the platform of the unsuccessful American Left. Now, largely as a result of the activist wing of the Civil Rights movement, it became part of the national debate about policies and priorities and influenced the allocation of millions of dollars. By the mid-1960's those concerned with the anomaly of suffering in the midst of surplus—with inadequate social services, fragmented government, economically depressed areas, and the debilitating pathology of the poor—had become a coalition strong enough to affect public policy. Moreover, the national mourning after John Kennedy's assassination created a temporary sense of shared idealism. That some social legislation would be enacted was guaranteed: it was conceived in the Kennedy image, supported by his most visible associates, and endorsed by the then overwhelmingly popular and powerful Lyndon Johnson.

The activist wing of the Civil Rights movement brought the structural flaws of society into sharp focus. The Montgomery bus boycott of 1955, the sit-ins, freedom rides, marches, school and consumer boycotts, voter registration drives, and demonstrations against the urban renewal bulldozer created widespread public consciousness in the late 1950's and the early 1960's that increasing numbers of black citizens were dissatisfied, frustrated, and prepared to make sacrifices and to disrupt other people's comfort in their quest for change. The growing number and sophistication of black voters were increasingly impressive to both black and white politicians. Civil disorders—riots to some, rebellions to others—added to the challenge and the threat posed by the organized movement.

However, there was a fragmented grass-roots constituency for the antipoverty legislation of the 1960's. The Civil Rights movement was the most effective member of this antipoverty constituency in the early 1960's. But none of the groups or coalitions had sufficient power to persuade Congress and the bureaucracy to place all their financial bets on a particular solution to the problems of poverty. The antipoverty legislation was conceived in ambiguity and administered in contradictory, inconsistent ways. Advocates of conflicting viewpoints have claimed both victories and defeats since 1964.

Leaders of local black constituencies, especially those who had learned the politics of confrontation in the Civil Rights movement, were the most visible and successful spokesmen for the poor. Thus, although blacks constituted only about 30 percent of Americans below the poverty line, the mass

The March on Washington, 28 August 1963. Courtesy of Wide World Photos.

media, mayors of large cities, and congressmen responsive to city or Southern pressures regarded them as the focus of the antipoverty effort. Certainly blacks had always been disproportionately poor and concentrated in confined areas. Attention was paid to them now because black leaders skillfully dramatized black exploitation, demonstrated that, despite harassment, they could organize independent voting blocs, and fought for influence and patronage in local agencies and organizations disbursing antipoverty funds. The regulations and discretionary decisions of these federal agencies frequently provided leverage for black power seekers, though not as often as many black leaders wished. And, after 1967, there was increasing federal wariness of intervention in local political power struggles.

The ambiguous mandate for citizen participation in Community Action and Model Cities programs was an important lever with which leaders of the poor, and especially the black poor, gained influence over programs initially conceived and administered at the local level by the traditional public and private agencies. Participatory policy has shown much more than a "maximum feasible misunderstanding" on the part of naive social scientists and arrogant bureaucrats. The lack of attention paid in Congress and the Administration in 1964 to the participation clause of the Economic Opportunity Act suggests that the potential challenge of impatient blacks and other minorities was not fully appreciated. The protracted controversies over participation in subsequent years demonstrate the extent to which pressure for institutional change and redistribution of power—attacks on the causes of poverty—vied with the more cautious belief that public policy could only deal with the effects of poverty on individuals and families.

Yet the success of black leaders in becoming the public focus of antipoverty policies had political liabilities. Other groups with disproportionate numbers of poor citizens were angered because more funds, services, and jobs were flowing to blacks than to other needy Americans. Many Mexican-Americans, Puerto Ricans, Indians, Eskimos, and white Appalachians decided that black leaders were as much impediments to their own upward mobility as the people who exploited their labor, provided inadequate housing and services, and denied the validity of their culture. In many cities, minority groups fought viciously over the allocation of antipoverty services and dollars, often to the delight of political and civic leaders eager to preserve their own power and of federal officials anxious to avoid difficult and dangerous allocative decisions. It has proved impossible to build national constituencies of citizens affected by antipoverty policies across racial and ethnic lines. The major exception, the National Welfare Rights Organization, stands out in its isolation, and owes its success in large measure to the relative clarity and simplicity of its issues and the rigidity of its most determined opponents. In general, each minority group has created its own political pressure groups at the local, state, and national levels. And the white poor, though numerically dominant, do not view themselves as a single group, but rather identify with their regional or ethnic groups or organize around their status as farmers, miners, or the elderly.

This fragmentation of the potential antipoverty constituency has a double irony: not only do the funds allocated to meet the needs of all poor Americans remain woefully inadequate, but blacks have not received nearly as disproportionate a share of these funds as their potential allies believe. Certainly blacks have received more dollars and attention than other groups have. Clearly, civil disturbances, whatever their other effects, have dislodged funds from reluctant bureaucrats and legislators. But blacks remain the largest ethnic group of the American poor. Skillful politicians and administrators have responded to conflicting pressures for attention by developing allocation formulas that give geographical and demographic parity to contending groups.

This emphasis on the fragmentation of the antipoverty constituency and the suggestion that conflict among minority groups reduced the pressure for social change on behalf of the new poor of the 1960's are disputed by many observers. They argue that the war on poverty was a casualty of the war in Vietnam; that by 1967 the nation found it could not afford both guns and butter. The open question is, however, whether the war in Vietnam was cause or rationalization. Budgetary pressures were genuine. But subsidies for agriculture, highway construction, and commercial aircraft, for example, were not notably reduced in the late 1960's. Moreover, as early as 1965— before political rhetoric proclaimed the need to choose between solving foreign and domestic problems—strong pressure developed to curtail or stunt the amount spent on the poor, especially for Community Action programs. The effect of the war in Vietnam on antipoverty programs still requires further research, analysis, and debate. It is, however, a viable hypothesis that lack of cohesiveness in the potential antipoverty constituency reduced the political challenge of the poor. In this view, the war did not force a choice between guns and butter but rather helped create a political majority satisfied to meet the challenge of the poor with unbuttered bread.

An Uncertain Future

It is difficult and dangerous to predict the future of antipoverty politics and policies. On the one hand, there is some evidence of stronger alliances between low-income blacks and other citizens with similar problems: the welfare reform movement; the successful militancy of some unions of service employees—teachers, postal and hospital workers, for example; the growing constituency for national health insurance; and coalitions formed in support of candidates for public office. On the other hand, some blacks see increased group identity and solidarity as the key to upward mobility: continued pressure for community control of schools, housing, and social services, and greater emphasis on ghetto economic development.

The condition of the national economy will have a major effect on the mobility strategies pressed by leaders and constituents of low-income groups and their allies. The antipoverty programs of the 1960's were mounted in a period of spectacular national prosperity, in part a result, as in the past, of war and defense spending. It was possible, in a period of high economic growth, for instance, to reject the policy of government as employer of last resort and instead debate the merits of training workers for existing production or service jobs as opposed to training them to work in new, minority-controlled production or service enterprises. But if recession or worse characterizes the economy of the 1970's, feasible strategies and constituencies for antipoverty measures will change markedly: government-created employment, for example, may become both necessary and desirable.

There is, however, a broader issue: whether blacks, whatever their economic, social, and political condition, have more in common with one another than they do with other Americans. Blacks have benefited from deliberate and fortuitous changes in American society: New Deal programs, the accelerated mobility of World War II, the prosperity of the postwar years, the antipoverty policies and general economic escalation of the 1960's. But the unanswered question is whether racism, in all its various forms, will set a limit on fulfillment of the aspirations, even the basic needs, of blacks in our society. Finally at the center rather than at the edge of poverty's claim on the public interest, will the challenge of the black poor be met with increased opportunity or renewed resistance? The record of the first reconstruction, the years after the Civil War when black poverty challenged America's compassion, sense of justice, and resources, does not provide a hopeful analogy. Perhaps the second reconstruction will have different results.

4 SUGGESTIONS FOR FURTHER READING

Cahn, Edgar S., and Passett, Barry A., eds., *Citizen Participation: A Casebook in Democracy*. New York: Praeger Publishers, 1971. ▪ A collection of original essays on the relationship between federal policy and the potential anti-poverty constituencies in the 1960's.

Clark, Kenneth B., *Dark Ghetto: Dilemmas of Social Power**. New York: Harper, 1965. ▪ A provocative analysis of ghetto poverty.

Drake, St. Clair, and Cayton, Horace, *Black Metropolis: A Study of Negro Life in a Northern City**. New York: Harcourt, 1945. ▪ The classic sociological study of black urban life—a comprehensive survey of the Negro community in Chicago.

Du Bois, W. E. B., *The Philadelphia Negro**. Philadelphia: University of Pennsylvania Press, 1899. ▪ A well-written survey that is valuable for information on black urban life in the nineteenth century.

Fager, Charles, *Uncertain Resurrection: The Poor People's Washington Campaign**. Grand Rapids, Mich.: William B. Eerdmans Publishing, 1969. ▪ A vivid description of Resurrection City and its failures.

Glazer, Nathan, and Moynihan, Daniel P., *Beyond the Melting Pot**. Cambridge, Mass.: M.I.T. Press, 1963. ▪ A controversial examination of the role of ethnicity and race in New York City life.

Gosnell, Harold F., *Negro Politicians: The Rise of Negro Politics in Chicago**. Chicago: University of Chicago Press, 1935. ▪ A thorough study of black politics in Chicago in the early twentieth century.

Handlin, Oscar, *The Newcomers: Negroes and Puerto Ricans in a Changing Metropolis**. Cambridge, Mass.: Harvard University Press, 1959. ▪ A survey of urban minorities that maintains the experience of Negroes and Puerto Ricans is not essentially different from the experience of European immigrants.

---

*Available in paperback edition

Harrington, Michael, *The Other America: Poverty in the United States**. New York: Macmillan, 1962. ▪ A good profile of the poor in the United States that devotes special attention to racial discrimination as a cause of poverty among blacks.

Johnson, James W., *Black Manhattan**. New York: Alfred A. Knopf, 1930. ▪ A good description of the development of a Negro urban community.

Keil, Charles, *Urban Blues**. Chicago: University of Chicago Press, 1967. ▪ An engrossing analysis of the interplay of black religious and secular music.

Larner, Jeremy, and Howe, Irving, eds., *Poverty: Views from the Left**. New York: William Morrow, 1969. ▪ An interesting collection of articles from *Dissent* magazine, some of which focus on blacks and the politics of poverty.

McKay, Claude, *Harlem: Negro Metropolis*. New York: E. P. Dutton, 1940. ▪ An in-depth portrait of black Harlem in another day.

Marris, Peter, and Rein, Martin, *Dilemmas of Social Reform: Poverty and Community Action in the United States*. New York: Atherton Press, 1967. ▪ The most thorough analysis to date of the development of the antipoverty strategies of the 1960's.

Meier, August, and Rudwick, Elliott, eds., *The Making of Black America**, vol. 2. New York: Atheneum, 1969. ▪ An excellent series of essays that analyzes the black political and economic experience in the twentieth century.

Myrdal, Gunnar, *An American Dilemma**. New York: Harper, 1944. ▪ A controversial classic that remains valuable for the scope of its treatment of race relations.

Osofsky, Gilbert, *Harlem: The Making of a Ghetto, 1890–1930**. New York: Harper, 1966. ▪ An outstanding historical study, particularly strong in tracing patterns of ecological change in the city.

Record, Wilson, *The Negro and the Communist Party*. Chapel Hill: University of North Carolina Press, 1951. ▪ A very good account of black reaction to the Communist party and its effect on the black-white political relationship.

Ruchames, Louis, *Race, Jobs, and Politics: The Story of FEPC*. New York: Columbia University Press, 1953. ▪ A detailed study of the political struggle for fair employment.

Rudwick, Elliott, *Race Riot at East St. Louis, July 2, 1917**. Carbondale: Southern Illinois University Press, 1966. ▪ A good case study of one of the bloodiest of the World War I racial confrontations.

Scott, Emmett J., comp., "Letters of Negro Migrants of 1916–1918," *Journal of Negro History* 4 (1919): 290–340, 412–75. ▪ These first-hand accounts of black migration provide important insights into its causes and problems.

Silberman, Charles E., *Crisis in Black and White**. New York: Random House, 1964. ▪ A study that reflects the view that the problems Afro-Americans face are substantially different from the problems of white immigrants and stresses the urgency of America's racial problems.

Spear, Allan H., *Black Chicago: The Making of a Negro Ghetto, 1890–1920 **. Chicago: University of Chicago Press, 1967. ▪ A study of the dynamics of ghetto formation in Chicago, with emphasis on the internal leadership structure of the black community.

Sternsher, Bernard, ed., *The Negro in Depression and War: Prelude to Revolution**. Chicago: Quadrangle Books, 1969. ▪ An excellent collection of articles concerning the black experience in the "forgotten years," 1930–1945.

Stone, Chuck, *Black Political Power in America.* Indianapolis: Bobbs-Merrill, 1968. ▪ A good source for historical information, although primarily concerned with black politics in the 1960's.

Taeuber, Karl, and Taeuber, Alma F., *Negroes in Cities: Residential Segregation and Neighborhood Change**. Chicago: Aldine Press, 1965. ▪ The best recent sociological study of residential segregation patterns and the dynamics of ghetto formation.

Wade, Richard, *Slavery in the Cities: The South, 1820–1860**. New York: Oxford University Press, 1964. ▪ An important interpretive work on the ante-bellum origins of ghetto patterns.

Wilson, James Q., *Negro Politics: The Search for Leadership**. Glencoe, Ill.: Free Press, 1960. ▪ A discussion of the diversification and complexities of black politics.

Young, Whitney M., Jr., *To Be Equal**. New York: McGraw-Hill, 1964. ▪ An excellent statement on equal opportunity and the socioeconomic problems of the black community.

5

Toward a New Identity

Black Identity in the International Context

E. U. ESSIEN-UDOM

E. U. Essien-Udom is professor of political science at the University of Ibadan, Nigeria. He has written extensively on both African and Afro-American affairs and is the author of *Black Nationalism: A Search for an Identity in America* (University of Chicago Press, 1962). In the essay that follows, Mr. Essien-Udom discusses the African identity of black Americans. Noting the sense of homelessness that pervades their literature and folklore, he traces past efforts by black Americans to enlarge their ties with black Africa and gives a practical assessment of current international black unity and Third World concepts.

Afro-Americans are trying to achieve equality in American society while at the same time striving to maintain three overlapping identities —American in the broadest sense, black American in the sense of a unique American experience, and African in the sense of the land of their distant forebears. Their awareness of the African dimension of their identity, perhaps the most fragile, has progressively intensified since the late 1950's because of the attainment of political sovereignty by the majority of African countries. To these three dimensions should be added a more recent development among some Afro-Americans who tend to merge their aspirations for equality in America with the aspirations of exploited peoples of the Third World. This essay addresses itself primarily to the relationship between black Americans and Africa, but although this is singled out for discussion, the other aspects of black identity in America should be borne in mind constantly, lest the African dimension of the identity problem be grossly exaggerated.

We Are Americans

The degree of Afro-Americans' identification with Africa vis-à-vis America in the past is arguable. For example, the eminent Afro-American scholar (later Ghanaian citizen by naturalization) W. E. B. Du Bois observed:

From the fifteenth through the seventeenth centuries the Africans imported to America regarded themselves as temporary settlers destined to return eventually to Africa. Their increasing revolts against the slave system, which culminated in the eighteenth century showed a feeling of close kinship to the motherland and even well into the nineteenth century they called their organizations "African," as witness the "African unions" of New York and Newport, and The African Churches of Philadelphia and New York. In the West Indies and South America there was even closer indication of feelings of kinship with Africa and the East.[1]

In contrast, C. Eric Lincoln has remarked that, despite the feeling of kinship they felt toward Africa, "the vast majority of Negroes, slave or free, did not wish to leave America":

When emigration was made a condition of manumission, the typical slave accepted emigration against his preferences. By far, the prevailing sentiment was to remain in the country with which their lives and labour were inextricably identified, and to be *there* accepted as men. A resolution passed at one of the numerous Negro conventions of the pre-civil war era declared: "This is our home and this is our country. Beneath its soil lie the bones of our fathers; for it some of them fought, bled and died. Here we were born and here we will die."[2]

It should be emphasized at the outset that the repeated assertion by black Americans of their birthright as Americans has been made by successive generations of their leaders. For example, in his "Call to Rebellion" (1843), Henry Highland Garnet, while calling upon blacks "to think of the undying glory that hangs around the ancient name of Africa," equally urged them not to forget that they were "native born American citizens, and as such, you are justly entitled to all the rights that are granted to the freest."[3] Frederick Douglass, the celebrated nineteenth-century abolitionist leader, emphasized this point with greater force when he wrote in his weekly antislavery newspaper, the *North Star:*

It is idle—worse than idle, ever to think of our expatriation, or removal. . . . *We are here,* and here we are likely to be. To imagine that we shall ever be eradicated is absurd and ridiculous. We can be remodified, changed, and assimilated, but never extinguished. We repeat, therefore, that we are here; and that this is *our* country; and the question for the philosophers and statesmen of the land ought to be, "what principles should dictate the policy of

---

1 Speech made at the celebration of the second anniversary of the Asian-African (Bandung) Conference, 30 April 1957, quoted in John Henrik Clarke, "Book Review," *Freedomways* 2, no. 4 (1962): 499.

2 C. Eric Lincoln, "Color and Group Identity in the United States" (Paper presented at the Conference on Race and Color, Copenhagen, September 1965), p. 9.

3 The text of Garnet's statement is reproduced in Floyd B. Barbour, ed., *The Black Power Revolt* (Boston: Extending Horizons Books, 1968), p. 37.

action towards us?" We shall neither die out, nor be driven out; but shall go with these people, either as a testimony against them, or as evidence in their favour throughout their generations. . . . The white man's happiness cannot be purchased by the black man's misery. . . . It is evident that white and black must fall or flourish together.[4]

The essentially American identity of black Americans has often been stressed in other ways. James W. Ivy, for example, observed that:

> The Negroes of the United States are, along with New England Yankees and old-line Southerners, the most quintessential of Americans. They are biologically as much European as African and culturally more Europe-American than Afro-American. They have a Greek philosophy, an Anglo-Roman conception of law, a Judeo-Hellenic religion, and the American concept of free enterprise and the two-party system.[5]

This view is also emphasized by Margaret Just Butcher, who observes that the American "Negro has rarely set up separate cultural values or developed divergent institutional loyalties or political objectives."[6]

The black Americans' affirmation of their birthright as American citizens and their identification with America are indisputable. The most monumental testimony to their commitment to America is their protracted and untiring struggle for equality and dignity in American society. To achieve this measure of identity they have, in the words of James Weldon Johnson in his poem "Fifty Years," "more than paid the price."

However, the problem of black identity in America has not been eased by the simple fact that blacks are "the most quintessential of Americans" or by their repeated affirmation of their American citizenship. Unfortunately, their commitment to America has never been reciprocated in full measure by the white society, and throughout most of their history in the United States they have been rejected and treated like outcasts by the society they have so fervently declared their own.

A Long Ways from Home

Because of alienation from their African cultural and historical background and the failure of white society to treat them as equal fellow citizens, significant numbers of black Americans developed a deep-seated feeling that they

---

[4] Published under the heading "The Destiny of Colored Americans," *North Star,* 16 November 1849. See E. U. Essien-Udom, "The Nationalist Movements of Harlem," *Freedomways* 3, no. 3 (1963): 335–42.

[5] James W. Ivy, "The National Association for the Advancement of Colored People as an Instrument of Social Change," *Présence Africaine* (June-November 1956): 337.

[6] Margaret J. Butcher, *The Negro in American Culture* (New York: Alfred A. Knopf, 1957), p. 285.

were a homeless and powerless people. Psychologically America was not home in an unqualified sense because of white oppression of the blacks. The black subculture offered no shelter because from the point of view of both blacks and whites it had little prestige and probably because few black leaders cared to articulate the essence and meaning of their unique experience in America. Nor was Africa their "Zion," because of the continent's low prestige in the scale of white Christian civilization and because of the improbability that American blacks would return there either physically or wholly psychologically. All these factors have produced a psychological feeling of homelessness reflected in the frequent occurrence of the "home" theme in so many spirituals, which should be understood not only as religious inspirations but also as social testaments. The search for a home where one could be black and unashamed occurs in "Sometimes I Feel Like a Motherless Child," "Swing Low, Sweet Chariot," and "Deep River."

Coupled with the feeling of homelessness is the black American's profound awareness of having been irrevocably cut off from the mainspring of his origins. This is well conveyed in the poem "Outcast" by Claude McKay, one of the black poets of the Harlem Renaissance of the 1920's:

> For the dim regions whence my fathers came
> My spirit, bondaged by the body, longs,
> Words felt, but never heard, my lips would frame;
> My soul would sing forgotten jungle songs.
> I would go back to darkness and to peace,
> But the great western world holds me in fee,
> I may never hope for full release
> While to its alien gods I bend my knee.
> Something in me is lost, forever lost,
> Some vital thing has gone out of my heart,
> And I must walk the way of life a ghost
> Among the sons of earth, a thing apart;
> For I was born, far from my native clime,
> Under the white man's menace, out of time.[7]

The feeling that some vital thing has gone out of the lives of black Americans was conveyed to me by a member of the Nation of Islam, the Muslim movement led by Elijah Muhammad, when she explained why she joined the movement:

> All my life I was in darkness. I knew something was lost, I knew Solomon was black. I knew the Sphinx was in Egypt. I went to Church. I got nothing out of it. I saw Ethiopia in the Bible. I looked for the American Negro in the

---

[7] From Claude McKay, *Selected Poems of Claude McKay* (New York: Bookman Associates, 1953), p. 41. Reprinted by permission.

Bible. I could not find him there. I wondered why the American Negro had no customs, no traditions, nothing. . . . I wanted something to represent what was me.[8]

Black Americans have reacted in a variety of ways to the feeling of homelessness and loss of roots. Some have sought comfort in otherworldly religious promises, conveyed in the spiritual "City Called Heaven":

I am a poor pilgrim of sorrow.
I'm in this wide world alone.
No hope in this world for tomorrow.
I'm tryin' to make heaven my home.

Sometimes I am tossed and driven.
Sometimes I don't know where to roam.
I've heard of a city called heaven.
I've started to make it my home.[9]

Others, such as followers of Elijah Muhammad, have sought refuge in eschatological fantasy and racial mythology, believing that the blacks will inherit the earth when the Caucasian civilization is finally destroyed by Allah.[10]

The Invisible Humanity

Until recently few blacks realized that although something vital had gone out of their lives, something else, a uniquely black American "soul,"[11] had emerged in its place or was in the making. James Baldwin, the well-known black writer, has argued that a certain dimension was missing in Richard Wright's *Native Son*, "this dimension being the relationship that Negroes bear to one another, that depth of involvement and unspoken recognition of shared experience which creates a way of life":

What the novel reflects—and at no point interprets—is the isolation of the Negro within his own group and the resulting fury of impatient scorn. It is this which creates the climate of anarchy . . . which has led us all to believe

---

[8] E. U. Essien-Udom, *Black Nationalism: A Search for an Identity in America* (Chicago: University of Chicago Press, 1962), p. 96.

[9] From Langston Hughes and Arna Bontemps, eds., *The Book of Negro Folklore* (New York: Dodd, Mead, 1959), pp. 290–91. Reprinted by permission.

[10] Essien-Udom, *Black Nationalism*, Chapter 5.

[11] For a discussion of the implications of "soul," see Lerone Bennett, *The Negro Mood* (New York: Ballantine Books, 1965), and Stephen E. Henderson, "Survival Motion: A Study of Black Writers and the Black Revolution in America," in Mercer Cook and Stephen E. Henderson, eds., *The Militant Black Writer and His Roots in Africa and the United States* (Madison: University of Wisconsin Press, 1969), pp. 65–129.

that in Negro life there exists no tradition, no field of manners, no possibility of ritual or intercourse, such as may, for example, sustain the Jew even after he has left his father's house. But the fact is not that the Negro has no tradition but that there has yet arrived no sensibility sufficiently profound and tough to make this tradition articulate. For a tradition expresses, after all, nothing more than the long and painful experience of a people; it comes out of the battle waged to maintain their integrity or, put it more simply, out of their struggle to survive.[12]

Similarly, Ralph Ellison remarked that he felt a sense of obligation "to explore the full range of American Negro humanity and to affirm those qualities which are of value beyond *any* question of segregation, economics or previous condition of servitude":

The obligation is always there and there is much to affirm. In fact, all Negroes affirm certain feelings of identity, certain foods, certain types of dancing, music, religious experiences, certain tragic attitudes toward experience and toward our situation as Americans. You see, we do this all within the community, but when it is questioned from without—that's when things start going apart. Like most Americans we are not yet fully conscious of our identity either as Negroes or Americans. This affirmation of which I speak, this insistence upon achieving our social goal, has been our great strength and also our great weakness because the terms with which we have tried to define ourselves have been inadequate.[13]

By exploring the adventures of the main character in his play *Purlie Victorious,* Ossie Davis, as actor, as author, and as black man, discovered that the essence of his manhood lay in his "negroness":

Purlie told me my *manhood* was hidden within my *negroness,* that I can never find the one without fully, and passionately embracing the other. That only by turning again homeward, whatever the cost, to my own blackness, to my own people, and to our common experience as Negroes, could I come at last to my manhood—to my *Self!*[14]

The problem so eloquently stated by James Baldwin is now being tackled in many different ways: from the popular version of James Brown's unabashed assertion of black self-pride in his rhythm-and-blues song "Say It Loud—I'm Black and I'm Proud" to the penetrating analysis by LeRoi Jones of an aspect of the black American ethos[15] and to the poetry of young

[12] James Baldwin, *Notes of a Native Son* (Boston: Beacon Press, 1955), pp. 35–36.

[13] Ralph Ellison, *Shadow and Act* (New York: New American Library, 1966), p. 36.

[14] Ossie Davis, "Purlie Told Me," in John H. Clarke, ed., *Harlem, U.S.A.* (Berlin: Seven Seas Books, 1964), pp. 153–54.

[15] LeRoi Jones, *Home: Social Essays* (New York: William Morrow, 1966).

black writers[16] which blossomed during the 1960's. The challenge Ellison had earlier felt is now widely accepted by many black Americans working in different spheres of life. A provisional name for "the full range of American Negro humanity" is "soul." Lerone Bennett has described this specifically black American experience:

> The whole corpus of the tradition . . . is compressed into the folk myth *Soul*, the American counterpart of the African *Negritude*, a distinct quality of Negro-ness growing out of the Negro's experience and not his genes. *Soul* is a metaphorical evocation of Negro being as expressed in the Negro tradition. It is the feeling with which an artist invests his creation, the style with which a man lives his life. It is, above all, the spirit rather than the letter: a certain way of feeling, a certain way of expressing oneself, a certain way of being.[17]

We Are an African People

In the past, because of their legitimate desire for social equality in the United States, there was a tendency among black Americans to disregard the validity of their subculture, or their "soul." For a great many this disregard for or at best ambivalence toward their identity in America also affected their relation with Africa. In personal terms it led some to a dissociation from their African origin, others to a romanticization of Africa, and still others to an indifference toward Africa. However, to many who were deeply agitated about their identity in America, the route, if not the journey, to Africa was inescapable. But Africa was not "home," for something vital had been lost, though perhaps not forever, and it could not be fully regained. Nevertheless, some black Americans believe that their American identity need not preclude "our exploration of our identity as a minority of African descent and our recourse to the African heritage as a fructifying source of our creative endeavour."[18]

Although the controversy is rapidly becoming a matter of historical interest, there is no consensus among black Americans about the name by which they are to be known. Adelaide C. Hill has observed:

> Naming or nomenclature is a most important way of defining and *controlling* relations between people. "Native" and "foreigner" imply something quite different about the relations and status of the native from "native" and "Euro-

---

[16] See Clarence Major, ed., *The New Black Poetry* (New York: International Publishers, 1969), and Langston Hughes, ed., *New Negro Poets: U.S.A.* (Bloomington: Indiana University Press, 1966).

[17] Lerone Bennett, *The Negro Mood*, p. 89.

[18] Samuel W. Allen, "Negritude and Its Relevance to the American Negro Writer," in *The American Negro Writer and His Roots*, ed. John A. Davis (New York: American Society of African Culture, 1960), p. 14.

pean," for example. Also, as language is so important to our species, each communal group has generally named itself and in turn has been named by other groups. Depending on the character of the relationship, the names do not necessarily coincide. Even in the most modern context this is clear; we call ourselves Americans; foreigners call us Yanks.[19]

Hill believes that blacks in the United States have never been given an opportunity to name themselves. Whites have called them Africans (for a brief time in the North) and slaves. For a brief period after the Civil War they were called freedmen. Later they were called Negro, but this also had its variants and subtlety of meanings, encompassing "'nigger' meaning still slave and evil, 'niggrah' meaning still slave but compliant, 'negro' with a lower case 'n' meaning not slave or non-slave—but never citizen, or truly a free man —or even respected individual!"[20]

Groups of black Americans have in fact tried to give themselves a collective name, but they could not agree among themselves, and whites who controlled the communications media would not support any unconventional nomenclature. (The most the whites were prepared to concede was "Negro" with an upper-case *N*, in addition to "Colored.") However, it appears that disagreements and confusions about a collective name did not set in until after 1800; the name "African" was much in currency until the free blacks, fearing that they might be forced to leave the United States for settlement in Africa, sensed a danger in the continued use of the term.[21] But the issue did not rest there, and could not, for the question of their identity was closely related to the fact of their African origin. Thus, at the 1854 National Emigration Convention of Colored People at Cleveland, Ohio, the delegates resolved

> That no people . . . can ever attain to greatness who lose their identity. . . . That we shall ever cherish our identity of origin and race, as preferable, in our estimation, to any other people. That the relative terms Negro, African, Black, Colored and Mulatto, when applied to us, shall ever be held with the same respect and pride; and synonymous with the terms, Caucasian, White, Anglo-Saxon and European, when applied to that class of people.[22]

---

[19] Adelaide C. Hill, "What Is Africa to Us?" in Barbour, *Black Power Revolt,* p. 129.

[20] Ibid.

[21] St. Clair Drake, "Negro Americans and the African Interest," in John P. David, ed., *The American Negro Reference Book* (Englewood Cliffs, N.J.: Prentice-Hall, 1966), p. 662.

[22] "Platform: Or Declaration of Sentiments of the Cleveland Convention," in Herbert Aptheker, ed., *A Documentary History of the Negro People in the United States,* vol. 1 (New York: Citadel Press, 1962), p. 364. For a discussion of the Negro Convention movement, see John W. Cromwell, *The Early Convention Movement,* American Negro Academy, Occasional Papers, no. 9 (Washington, D.C., 1905), and Howard H. Bell, "The Negro Emigration Movement, 1849–1854: A Phase of Negro Nationalism," *Phylon* 20, no. 2 (1959).

Obviously the resolution was an untidy compromise reflecting a lack of agreement. In later years virtually all designations other than "Negro" and "Colored" were dropped. But use of the term "Afro-American" and its variants "Aframericans" and "Africans abroad" persisted among a small minority. However, by the late 1960's the terms "black" — previously the most despised — "black American," "Afro-American," and "African American" were widely in use.[23] Much change has occurred in the attitudes of black Americans toward themselves and Africa. A great many now proudly assert, "We are an African people," as in the caption of a popular 1970 calendar published by the Drum and Spear Press (Washington, D.C.) and in the assertion of John H. Clarke, associate editor of *Freedomways:* "Our place of origin was Africa, and no matter where we live on this earth we are an African people."[24]

The Avant-Garde

As early as the eighteenth century some black Americans in various ways defended the dignity of Africa and its peoples against white exploitation and the degrading image of their race propounded by Euro-American pseudo scientists and propagandists.[25] Most did so primarily through their writings. This avant-garde behavior is well illustrated by William Wells Brown, a physician who gave this as his reason for writing biographical sketches of leading black men:

> To meet and refute these misrepresentations, and to supply a deficiency, long felt in our community, of a work containing sketches of individuals who, by their own genius, capacity, and intellectual development, have surmounted the many obstacles which slavery and prejudice have thrown in their way, and raised themselves to positions of honor and influence.[26]

Martin R. Delany, another physician and a major in the United States Army during the Civil War, explained that the view that the African was inherently

---

[23] This radical change in attitude is partly accounted for by the spread of "nationalistic" ideas among the blacks and the independence of African states. It is reinforced by major black-controlled and white-controlled communications media. Significantly, the publisher of *Negro Digest,* established in 1945, changed the name of the periodical, beginning with the May 1970 issue, to *Black World.*

[24] John H. Clarke, "The Future of African Studies After Montreal," *Africa Report* 14, no. 8 (1969): 24.

[25] See Philip D. Curtin, *The Image of Africa* (London: Macmillan, 1965), and E. U. Essien-Udom, "The Relationship of Afro-Americans to African Nationalism: An Historical Interpretation," *Freedomways* 2, no. 4 (1962): 391–407.

[26] William Wells Brown, *The Black Man: His Antecedents and Achievements* (Savannah, Ga.: James M. Symms, 1863), Preface.

inferior had been inspired and motivated solely by the economic needs of those who profited from the slave system.[27]

In his attempt to encourage black American emigration to Liberia in the 1860's the West Indian–born Edward Wilmot Blyden also described the relation of black Americans to Africa in avant-garde terms:

> You will at once perceive that I do not believe that the work to be done by black men is in this country. I believe that their field of operation is in some other and distant scene. Their work is far nobler and loftier than that which they are now doing in this country. It is theirs to take themselves to injured Africa, and bless those outraged shores, and quiet those distracted families with the blessings of Christianity and civilization. It is theirs to bear with them to that land the arts of industry and peace, and counteract the influence of those horrid abominations which an inhuman avarice has introduced — to roll back the appaling [sic] cloud of ignorance and superstition which over-spreads the land, and to rear on those shores an asylum of liberty for the down-trodden sons of Africa wherever found. This is the work to which Providence has called the black men of this country.[28]

The missionary enterprise of black Christian churches and individuals during the nineteenth century was very avant-garde. Lott Carey and his friend the Reverend Collin Teague, reputed to be the first black American missionaries to Africa, went to Sierra Leone to serve their fatherland in 1820. The missionary efforts of the African Methodist Episcopal Church and the African Methodist Episcopal Zion Church are notable examples in this tradition.[29]

On the secular level, W. E. B. Du Bois thought of black Americans as "the

---

[27] Martin R. Delany, *The Condition, Elevation, Emigration, and Destiny of the Colored People of the United States, Politically Considered* (Philadelphia, 1852), p. 22. Of course, against such men as Delany and William Wells Brown, there were a few notable exceptions, such as George Washington Williams, who believed that "the Negro type is the result of degradation. It is nothing more than the lowest strata of the African race. . . . His blood infected with the poison of his low habitation, his body shrivelled by disease, his intellect veiled in pagan superstition, the noblest yearnings of his soul strangled at birth by the savage passions of a nature abandoned to sensuality, the poor Negro of Africa deserves more our pity than our contempt." George Washington Williams, *History of the Negro Troops in the War of the Rebellion, 1861–1865* (New York: Harper, 1888), quoted in Earl E. Thorpe, *The Mind of the Negro: An Intellectual History of Afro-Americans* (Baton Rouge, La.: Ortlieb Press, 1961), p. 24.

[28] Edward Wilmot Blyden, *Liberia's Offering: Being Addresses, Sermons, etc.* (New York: John A. Gray, 1962), p. 72. For Blyden's biography see Hollis R. Lynch, *Edward Wilmot Blyden: Pan-Negro Patriot, 1832–1912* (New York: Oxford University Press, 1967), and Edith Holden, *Blyden of Liberia* (New York: Vantage Press, 1966). Cf. Alexander Crummell, *The Relations and Duties of the Free Colored Men in America to Africa* (Hartford, Conn., 1861).

[29] Drake, "Negro Americans and the African Interest," pp. 667–73. George E. Shepperson, "Notes on Negro American Influences on the Emergence of African Nationalism," *Journal of African History* 1, no. 2 (1960): 299–312.

advance guard of the Negro people" and in 1897 surmised that "the 8,000,000 people of Negro blood in the United States of America . . . must soon come to realize that if they are to take their just place in the van of pan-Negroism, then their destiny is *not* absorption by the white Americans."[30] This belief was evident in the thinking of Marcus Moziah Garvey, leader of the Universal Negro Improvement Association (UNIA) and African Communities League,[31] and is subtly implied in Elijah Muhammad's notion of the Nation of Islam as the divinely appointed instrument of black liberation.[32] However, the avant-garde tradition is now virtually moribund and since the end of World War II has been overtaken by political developments in Africa.

The African Movement

W. E. B. Du Bois wrote in 1919:

> The African movement means to us what the Zionist movement must mean to the Jews, the centralization of race effort and the recognition of a racial fount. To help bear the burden of Africa does not mean any lessening of effort in our own problem at home. Rather, it means increased interest. For any ebullition of action and feeling that results in an amelioration of the lot of Africa tends to ameliorate the condition of colored people throughout the world.[33]

Before Du Bois wrote these words, Edward Wilmot Blyden had urged the necessity for black Americans to emigrate to Liberia, where they could "create an African power which would command the respect of the world and place in the possession of Africans, its rightful owners, the wealth which is now diverted to other quarters." He continued: "We need some African power, some great centre of the race where our physical, pecuniary, and intellectual strength may be collected. We need some spot whence such an influence may go forth on behalf of the race as shall be felt by the nations. We are now so scattered and divided that we can do nothing."[34] And from West Africa, J. E. Casely Hayford, the distinguished Gold Coast (now Ghana) lawyer and leading pan-African nationalist of his time, had written of black Americans in 1911:

> It is not so much *Afro-Americans* that we want as *Africans* or *Ethiopians,* sojourning in a strange land. . . . How extra-ordinary would be the spectacle

---

[30] W. E. B. Du Bois, *The Conservation of Race,* American Negro Academy, Occasional Papers, no. 2 (Washington, D.C., 1897), p. 10.

[31] Amy Jacques Garvey, comp., *The Philosophy and Opinions of Marcus Garvey,* 2nd ed. (New York: Humanities Press, 1968). Amy Jacques Garvey, *Garvey and Garveyism* (New York: University Place Book Shop, 1963). E. D. Cronon, *Black Moses* (Madison: University of Wisconsin Press, 1955).

[32] Essien-Udom, *Black Nationalism,* pp. 5–6.

[33] "The African Movement," *Crisis* 17 (February 1919): 166.

[34] Blyden, *Liberia's Offering,* p. 72.

of this huge Ethiopian race—some millions of men—having imbibed all that is best in Western culture in the land of their oppressors, yet remaining true to racial instincts and inspiration, customs and institutions, much as did the Israelites of old in captivity! When this more pleasant picture will have become possible of realization, then, and only then, will it be possible for our people in bondage "metaphorically to walk out of Egypt in the near future with a great and real spoil."[35]

The African movement is largely a loose configuration of ideas and sentiments as well as aspirations (all of which are not necessarily compatible) shared by African people in their different settings. And from time to time such ideas, sentiments, and aspirations have led to limited forms of collaboration at the international level. There are two aspects to this movement: one is cultural and is concerned with racial or "national" identity; the other is political or quasi-political and raises the issue of "black power" and solidarity. Both derive from historical, political, and economic forces which in modern times have conditioned the relations between the black world and the white world.

Black Identity

Apart from uninformed claims by white propagandists that Africans have no historical heritage worthy of serious consideration, it is well known that contacts between blacks and whites, between black culture and white culture, have had denationalizing effects on blacks in both Africa and the New World. The denationalization process and the reactions of blacks to it have engendered to an extent a common content in thought and sentiment that has tended to bind blacks internationally. Commenting on the effect of nonblack cultural contacts on the educated African, Blyden observed:

> He does not like to be odd. He is ashamed of everything that does not accord to the European standard or represent European conceptions. This is the inveterate condition to which he has been reduced.
> This is his most serious weakness and his most distressing stumbling block. God has made him odd, and he will do anything not to appear so. There is no other race on the face of the earth like him—"black skin and woolly hair." In America he tries to bleach his skin and straighten his hair. But this cannot alter his destiny. It is fixed. His work and his destiny are peculiar and unique. But, under the foreign training he has received, he is never satisfied unless he thinks he is imitating the white man. Observers, however, know that he is not imitating but only aping. The foreigners know and the uncontaminated native knows. Imitation implies an inward perception and approximation, a conformity in spirit as well as in action. Unless the

---

[35] J. E. Casely Hayford, *Ethiopia Unbound: Studies in Race Emancipation,* 2nd ed. (London: Frank Cass, 1969), p. 173.

black man can imitate the idiosyncracy of the white man he must remain an outsider, his attempt at imitation must be futile, and not only futile but ridiculous: for there must be many features in his model that will escape him.[36]

And from the Gold Coast, the Reverend Attoh Ahuma wrote in 1905:

We have fought valiantly for what we deemed were our Ancestral Rights in the past and would fight again, if those rights were menaced tomorrow — but the greatest calamity to West Africa that must be combated tooth and nail, we feel, is the imminent Loss of Ourselves. . . . Rather let men rob our lands if possible, but let us see that they do not rob us of ourselves. They do so when we are taught to despise our own Names, Institutions, Customs and Laws. . . . The days are coming, however, when not to stand by the nation and its true life shall mean the eternal forfeiture of all claim to respect and reverence. [37]

Although the black Africans in Africa were not physically removed from their cultural environment, their confrontation with white settlers, imperial agents, Christian missionaries, and merchants had the effect, though to a lesser extent than in the New World, of denationalizing them, especially the Western-educated elite. It should be recalled that in a colonial situation the alien power substitutes not only its political authority, its economic interests, and as far as possible its institutions for those of the colonized people but, wholly or partially, its values, ideology, and mystiques as well. Indeed, in a colonial situation the colonial authority tries to manipulate the attitudes and behavior of the colonized, to instill in them the belief that the institutions of the colonizing power as well as its morals, ethics, and aesthetic standards are superior to those of the colonized people. The language of the colonizer is substituted for that of the colonized; a new religion which claims superiority and universality is substituted, wherever possible, for that of the colonized people. By attempting to destroy and, where this failed, to degrade African belief systems, cultures, and institutions, the colonizers of Africa were in effect degrading and denationalizing the African. The Western-educated African's reactions to this situation are in many important respects similar to those of the blacks in the New World.[38] These reactions tend to heighten the African's sense of his identity not only as an African but also as a black man.

---

[36] Holden, *Blyden of Liberia,* pp. 766–67.

[37] S. R. B. Attoh Ahuma, *Memoirs of West African Celebrities* (Liverpool: D. Marples, 1905), pp. 2–3. Cf. Hayford, *Ethiopia Unbound,* and Okot p'Bitek, *Song of Lawino* (Nairobi, Kenya: East African Publishing House, 1966).

[38] Frantz Fanon, *Black Skin, White Masks,* trans. C. L. Markmann (New York: Grove Press, 1967); *Towards the African Revolution: Political Essays,* trans. Haakon Chevalier (New York: Grove Press, 1967), pp. 17–27. Katrin Norris, *Jamaica: The Search for an Identity* (London: Oxford University Press and Institute of Race Relations, 1962).

In the New World, Marcus Garvey, as Elijah Muhammad would later, deplored the process of denationalization among the blacks and asserted:

> So many of us find excuses to get out of the Negro Race, because we are led to believe that the race is unworthy—that it has not accomplished anything. Cowards that we are! It is we who are unworthy, because we are not contributing to the uplift and upbuilding of this noble race.[39]

The process of denationalization has produced both in Africa and the New World, in the words of Alioun Diop, founder of the cultural journal *Présence Africaine,* the need to affirm on an international level "the presence or ethos, of the black communities of the world, and to defend the originality of their way of life and the dignity of their culture."[40]

The need to affirm the essential human dignity of blacks has also given rise to a body of literature by black writers in Africa and the New World that celebrates the virtues of blackness. From West Africa R. E. G. Armattoe writes:

> Our God is black.
> Black of eternal blackness,
> With large voluptuous lips,
> Matted hair and brown liquid eyes . . .
> For in His image we are made.
> Our God is black.[41]

And the President of Senegal, Leopold Sedar Senghor, writes of the black woman:

> Naked woman, black woman
> Clothed with your color which is life, with your form which is beauty!
>
> .   .   .
>
> And your beauty strikes me to the heart like the flash of an eagle.[42]

From the Guyanan poet Léon Damas:

> Give me back my black dolls to play
> the simple game of my instincts . . .
> to recover my courage
> my boldness
> to feel myself myself

---

[39] Garvey, *Philosophy and Opinions of Marcus Garvey,* 1:6.

[40] Quoted in Colin Legum, *Pan-Africanism: A Short Political Guide* (New York: Frederick A. Praeger, 1962), p. 96. See also Claude Wauthier, *The Literature and Thought of Modern Africa: A Survey* (London: Pall Mall Press, 1966), and Jacob Drachler, ed., *African Heritage* (New York: Crowell-Collier, 1963).

[41] Quoted in Ras Khan, "The Poetry of Dr. R. E. G. Armattoe," *Présence Africaine* (February-March 1957): 39. Reprinted by permission.

[42] From the poem "Black Woman" from *Selected Poems* by Leopold Sedar Senghor. Translated and Introduced by John Reed and Clive Wake. Copyright © Oxford University Press 1964. Reprinted by permission of Atheneum Publishers, U.S.A.

a new self from the one I was yesterday
yesterday
without complications
yesterday
when the hour of uprooting came. [43]

And from the United States, Colin Legum has selected:

Black
As the gentle night,
Black as the kind and quiet night,
Black as the deep and productive earth.
Body
Out of Africa
Strong and black . . .
Kind
As the black night
My song
From the dark lips
Of Africa . . .
Beautiful.[44]

Some black writers are defiant in their reactions, knocking hard at the myths of white superiority and at white ethics and aesthetic standards. Out of the need to affirm the ethos of the black communities of the world and to defend the originality of their way of life emerge three related notions, "African personality," "negritude," and "soul," each emphasizing aspects of experience thought to be unique to the black world.

The notions of African personality and negritude have been popularized during the last two decades, although historically claims of the uniqueness of the black race are traceable to educated blacks such as Edward Wilmot Blyden,[45] whose ideas about the destiny of the races of mankind were much influenced by the absurd theory of the hierarchy of the races propagated by the Euro-American pseudo scientists and propagandists. Blyden, for example, believed that the "African is a spiritual and ministerial race" while the "European is an imperial and conquering race. He is by calling the statesman the soldier, the sailor, the policeman of humanity. The Negro is the protégé; the child, the attendant, the servant, if you like, of this dominant race."[46] However, those who speak or write about the African personality, negritude, or soul insist that these notions derive from black experience and not genes. The proponents of African personality have had a difficult task defining it.

[43] Quoted in Legum, *Pan-Africanism*, p. 19. Reprinted by permission.

[44] Quoted in Legum, *Pan-Africanism*, p. 18. Reprinted by permission.

[45] E. U. Essien-Udom, "God, Race and Nation-Building: The Social and Political Ideas of Edward W. Blyden," in E. A. Ayandele and A. Hussain, eds., *African Political Theory* (London: Longmans, forthcoming). Cf. Lynch, *Edward Wilmot Blyden*, Chapter 4.

[46] Holden, *Blyden of Liberia*, p. 699.

However, Alex Quaison-Sackey has explained that the proponents "are conscious of their ancient roots, and from this sense of tradition they gain their strength, in action, in the struggle toward individual emancipation and national realization."[47] But this is not sufficiently helpful, for it leaves unanswered these questions: What is it? Do all Africans have the same "personality"? In what crucial respects does the African personality differ from, say, the European and the Asian? Whatever the African personality may be, it is claimed that African people are bound together by a historical experience that they alone have had.

Negritude, like the concept of African personality, is an expression which, according to its proponents, Martinique poet Aimé Césaire and Leopold Sedar Senghor, is the unifying essence of black culture and experience throughout the world. But negritude is just as difficult to explain as African personality. Samuel W. Allen has said that for him it "is essentially a means toward achievement of a sense of full cultural identity and a normal self-pride in the cultural context."[48] Negritude then is the common denominator binding together soul, which is claimed to be the essence of black American humanity, and the African personality, said by Quaison-Sackey to be confined to the African continent.[49] However, a number of black Africans, especially in the former British territories, do not take the notions of the African personality and negritude seriously.[50]

In addition to the "brotherhood of the pen" and in spite of disagreements, black intellectuals have sought closer contacts through the forum provided by the Society of African Culture. This "International Association of Negro Men of Culture" was spearheaded by Alioun Diop.[51] Its first international conference, held in Paris in 1956, was attended by a large number of delegates from Africa, the West Indies, and the United States.[52] A second conference was held in Rome in 1959. In the final resolution at the Paris conference, the delegates noted, among other things, "the urgent necessity to rediscover the historical truth and revalue Negro cultures; these truths, often misrepresented and denied, being partly responsible for provoking a crisis in Negro culture and in the manner in which that culture relates to World culture." They rec-

[47] Alex Quaison-Sackey, *Africa Unbound* (New York: Frederick A. Praeger, 1963), p. 49. Cf. Mercer Cook, "African Voices of Protest," in Mercer Cook and Stephen E. Henderson, eds., *The Militant Black Writer and His Roots in Africa and the United States* (Madison: University of Wisconsin Press, 1969), pp. 3–62.

[48] Allen, "Negritude and the American Negro Writer," p. 14.

[49] Quaison-Sackey, *Africa Unbound*, p. 49.

[50] Ezekiel Mphalele, *The African Image* (New York: Frederick A. Praeger, 1962), pp. 40, 53.

[51] See "Final Resolutions," *Présence Africaine* (June-November 1956): 371.

[52] James Baldwin has given an interesting account of the conference in *Nobody Knows My Name* (New York: Dial Press, 1961), pp. 13–55. The American Society of African Culture is a branch of the Society of African Culture.

ommended "that artists, writers, scholars, theologians, thinkers and technicians participate in the historic task of unearthing, rehabilitating and developing those cultures so as to facilitate their being integrated into the general body of World culture."[53]

What the black writers and artists were urging at the Paris conference in 1956, black scholars such as Carter G. Woodson, William Leo Hansberry, J. E. Casely Hayford, and others in the United States, the West Indies, and Africa had long advocated in history, sociology, and related studies. In 1915, for example, five black Americans under the leadership of Carter G. Woodson founded in Chicago the Association for the Study of Negro Life and History, and in 1916 the association issued the quarterly *Journal of Negro History.* One of the stated objectives of the journal was to collect sociological and historical data on the "Negro" and "peoples of African blood." Woodson pioneered and urged what is now broadly called "black studies" in the United States. The establishment of institutes of African studies in nearly all African universities and at the University of the West Indies, and the African Heritage Association[54] recently organized by black scholars in the United States, all for the purpose of rediscovering black history and revaluing Negro cultures, suggest the commonality of need and similarity in response of the men of culture of the black world. But, as the poet Don L. Lee has written on the matter of survival:

> i ain't seen no poems stop a .38,
> i ain't seen no stanzas brake a honkie's head,
> i ain't seen no metaphors stop a tank.[55]

And thus the other face of the African movement is the need as well as the aspiration for power and unity of the black world.

Black Power

The question of "African power," or, in contemporary parlance, "black power," was first raised in 1862 by Edward Wilmot Blyden when he urged emigration of black Americans to Liberia. However, the first pan-African conference to deal directly with the question of African power was held in London in 1900. The conference was called by the West Indian barrister Henry Sylvester-Williams and was attended by thirty delegates, most of whom were from the United States and the West Indies. The conference was to serve as a forum of protest against colonialism, to foster closer relations between

---

[53] "Final Resolutions," pp. 370–71.

[54] For the background to the formation of the African Heritage Association, a breakaway group from the white-controlled African Studies Association (U.S.A.), see *Africa Report* 14, no. 8 (1969): 16–27.

[55] From Don L. Lee, "In the Interest of Black Salvation," *Black Pride* (Detroit: Broadside Press, 1968), p. 21. Reprinted by permission.

peoples of African descent throughout the world, to establish friendly relations between the black and white races, and to start a movement aimed at securing all African people living in civilized countries their full rights and promoting their business interests.[56] The delegates, having deliberated on the "situation and outlook of the darker races of mankind," declared:

> The problem of the twentieth century is the problem of the color-line, the question as to how far differences of race—which show themselves chiefly in the color of the skin and the texture of the hair—will hereafter be made the basis of denying to over half the world the right of sharing to their utmost ability the opportunities and privileges of modern civilization.[57]

The conference solemnly appealed to, and pleaded with, the great powers of the world not to allow color or race to be "a feature of distinction between white and black men, regardless of worth," not to sacrifice the "native of Africa . . . to the greed of gold, their liberties taken away, their family life debauched, their just aspirations repressed, and culture taken from them." It appealed to the British nation to "give, as soon as practicable, the rights of responsible government to the black colonies of Africa and the West Indies." It called on the United States to grant black Americans the right of franchise and ensure to them security of person and property. The conference pleaded with the great powers to "let the Congo Free State become a great central Negro State of the world" and to respect the integrity and independence of Abyssinia (Ethiopia), Liberia, Haiti, the "independent tribes of Africa," and the blacks of the West Indies and America.[58]

The conference idea was not revived until after World War I, although the need for racial solidarity and action against the predatory use of "white power" over black people throughout the world continued to be recognized. Two international efforts emerged after World War I. The first was the Pan-African Congress, spearheaded by Du Bois in 1919 with the financial assistance of the National Association for the Advancement of Colored People;[59] the second was the Garvey movement. Under Du Bois' leadership, five pan-African

---

[56] Alexander Walters, *My Life and Works* (New York: Fleming H. Revell, 1917), pp. 251–53.

[57] "Address to the Nations of the World by the Pan-African Conference in London, 1900," in V. B. Thompson, *Africa and Unity: The Evolution of Pan-Africanism* (London: Longmans, 1969), p. 319. This document was signed by Bishop Alexander Walters (President, Pan-African Association), Henry B. Brown (Vice-President), H. Sylvester-Williams (General Secretary), and W. E. Burghardt Du Bois (Chairman, Committee of Address).

[58] "Address to the Nations of the World," pp. 320–21.

[59] The National Association for the Advancement of Colored People financed the first and second congresses (1919 and 1921). Thereafter its support dwindled. The fourth congress, in New York in 1927, was supported largely by an interested group of black American women headed by Mrs. Addie W. Hunton and Mrs. Addie Dickerson. For a detailed account of the NAACP's interest in Africa, see James W. Ivy, "Traditional NAACP Interest in Africa as Reflected in the Pages of the *Crisis,*" in John A. Davis, ed., *Africa from*

congresses were held—the first in Paris in 1919 and the fifth in Manchester, England, in 1945, at which, in addition to Du Bois, Jomo Kenyatta (President of Kenya), Dr. Kwame Nkrumah (Former President of Ghana), and George Padmore (an outstanding pan-African activist) played prominent roles.[60] The post–World War I congresses continued the tradition of protest against colonialism and exploitation of the black world which the Pan-African Conference of 1900 had begun. From the need for racial solidarity and the desire for concerted protest against racial subordination emerged the idea of African unity. However, Du Bois, generally regarded as the father of pan-Africanism, observed:

> The idea of one Africa to unite the thought and ideals of all native peoples of the dark continent belongs to the twentieth century and stems naturally from the West Indies and the United States. Here various groups of Africans, quite separate in origin, became so united in experience and so exposed to the impact of new cultures that they began to think of Africa as one idea and one land.[61]

Du Bois' Pan-African movement was in membership essentially elitist and had no visible impact on the masses of the black population in either the New World or Africa. However, Marcus Garvey, Du Bois' bitter rival, took the message of international black solidarity and the idea of Africa united under one government to the masses, especially in the United States. Garvey was primarily concerned with the question of black power vis-à-vis white power. He was interested in establishing a powerful black empire in Africa. To this end he established in Jamaica in 1914 the Universal Negro Improvement Association (UNIA) and African Communities League[62] with the aim of "uniting all the Negro people of the world into one great body to establish a country and government absolutely their own." He moved from Jamaica to New York, where he established the UNIA in Harlem in 1916. The movement grew rapidly, and at its height in 1923 Garvey claimed a membership of six million scattered throughout North America and South America, the

---

the Point of View of American Negro Scholars (Paris: Présence Africaine, 1958), pp. 229–46. For a useful collection of documents indicating black American interest in Africa, see Adelaide C. Hill and Martin Kilson, eds., Apropos of Africa (New York: Humanities Press, 1969).

[60] For a detailed discussion of these conferences, see Thompson, Africa and Unity; George Padmore, Pan-Africanism or Communism?: The Coming Struggle for Africa (New York: Roy Publishers, 1956); Rayford W. Logan, "The Historical Aspects of Pan-Africanism, 1900–1945," in Pan-Africanism Reconsidered, ed. American Society of African Culture (Berkeley: University of California Press, 1962), pp. 37–52; and Legum, Pan-Africanism.

[61] W. E. B. Du Bois, The World and Africa (New York: Viking Press, 1947), p. 7.

[62] For a detailed discussion of the Garvey movement, see Cronon, Black Moses; Garvey, Garvey and Garveyism; Essien-Udom, Black Nationalism, pp. 36–43, 54–61; and J. A. Langley, "Garveyism and African Nationalism," Race 2, no. 2 (1969): 157–72.

Caribbean, and Africa. Apart from his idea of uniting the "three units" of the race (Africa, Caribbean, and North America and South America), one of Garvey's objectives was to establish a base in Africa (possibly in Liberia), and with carefully selected black colonists he hoped to give battle to the European colonial powers in Africa. Beginning in 1920, under the auspices of the UNIA, he convened several black international conferences, at which he urged the delegates to unite in the struggle for the emancipation of the African race. Twice the UNIA petitioned the League of Nations, pleading the cause of the black race. In its 1922 petition the UNIA observed that there was "a growing national, racial sentiment among the four hundred million Negroes of the world" and declared:

> We believe that as a people we should have a Government of our own, in our homeland — Africa; that we should be accorded the opportunity to demonstrate our ability for Government, even as the other races have been given such an opportunity by the League. We believe we are fully competent, and adequately equipped, to administer, in Africa, a Government of our own. Whilst we do not desire to establish a Government on the entire continent of Africa, we feel that certain sections of Africa should be returned to us, as a race, so that we may be able to develop a civilization of our own, among ourselves, as a distinct ethnic group, among the many independent groups comprising the human family.[63]

The petition of 1928 detailed the wrongs committed by whites against the African peoples "at home and abroad." The UNIA told the League:

> The entire regions of West Africa could be brought together as one United Commonwealth of Black Nations, and placed under the government of black men, as the solution of the Negro problem, both in Africa and the Western World; and we further believe that an amicable agreement could be reached between the United States, England, France and Belgium and the other nations concerned and the natives of Africa, their Chiefs and Kings, and the Negroes of the Western World, looking toward a solution of the vexed and dangerous problem that may lead to other consequences if not now adjusted on fair lines.[64]

In spite of his failings, Garvey emerges as the most important black leader during the 1920's; he strenuously sought to establish an international African movement and to "internationalize" the struggle for racial freedom and dignity. However, his movement had lost much of its fervor by 1927, when he was deported from the United States after serving a prison term for using the

---

[63] "Petition of the Universal Negro Improvement Association and African Communities' League to the League of Nations" (Presented at the Hague, September 1922).

[64] "Renewal of Petition of the Universal Negro Improvement Association and African Communities' League to the League of Nations . . . and to the Separate and Distinct Nations of the World, and Their Nationals and Peoples, on Behalf of the Hundreds of Millions of Black, Struggling and Oppressed People of the World" (Presented at the Hague, September 1928).

mail to defraud. After 1945 the Du Bois–inspired Pan-African Congress was overtaken by the movement for national independence in Africa, and the Manchester conference of 1945 decisively marked the end of the avant-garde tradition.

Nevertheless, the interest of black Americans continued, and a growing number began to raise the now familiar question posed by Countee Cullen:

> What is Africa to me
> Copper sun or scarlet sea,
> Jungle star or jungle track,
> Strongbronzed men, or regal black
> Women from whose loins I sprang
> When the birds of Eden sang?
> *One three centuries removed*
> *From the scenes his fathers loved,*
> *Spicy grove, cinnamon tree,*
> *What is Africa to me?*[65]

In the past the answers black Americans have given to this question have varied. But now, more than at any other period in their history, there is a growing awareness at all levels of the group that their struggle for equality and status in the United States bears some relationship to that of the African peoples in Africa and the Caribbean, nay, the peoples of the Third World. Similarly, in Africa there is a greater awareness than in the past of the international situation of blacks. This shared consciousness of the relative position of the African peoples in the world gives to the problem of black identity an international dimension.[66] But this general convergence of thought and feeling derives from common experience in the relationship of blacks to whites and the relative weakness of power of the former vis-à-vis the latter.

Politically the black world seems utterly powerless in its confrontation with the terrifying military and technological power of the white world. The former is conscious of the fact that in the past white power has been employed to suppress and exploit blacks. Against this background they face the future with apprehension, and many would agree with Garvey that "a race without authority and power is a race without respect." This lack of power becomes obvious when one considers that all the African states combined are unable to deal effectively with the racist governments of South Africa, Rhodesia, and the Portuguese colonies of Angola, Mozambique, and Guinea.

---

[65] The first stanza of "Heritage" in *On These I Stand* by Countee Cullen, Copyright, 1925 by Harper & Row, Publishers, Inc.; renewed 1953 by Ida M. Cullen. Reprinted by permission of the publisher.

[66] Locksley Edmonson, "The Internationalization of Black Power: Historical and Contemporary Perspectives," *Mawazo* 1, no. 4 (1968): 16–30; "The Challenge of Race: From Entrenched White Power to Rising Black Power," *International Journal* (Canadian Institute of International Affairs) 24, no. 14 (1969): 693–716.

Black Power and the Third World

The weakness of black power is manifest also among the independent African and West Indian states where blacks hold formal political power but where vital sectors of national life—intellectual, economic, and in some countries military—are either controlled by or heavily dependent upon the Western world. The clientage relationship of African and West Indian states with the West is in many ways similar to the situation of blacks in the United States in their relationship with white society. Understood against this background, the call for black power in the United States has some appeal for and makes a lot of sense to elements of black populations throughout the world. This general feeling also explains the view of some black power leaders, such as James Forman, that the struggle for equality in the United States is fundamentally linked with those in Africa, Asia, and Latin America:

> Our liberation will only come when there is final destruction of this mad octopus—the capitalistic system of the United States with all its life-sucking tentacles of exploitation and racism that choke the people of Africa, Asia, and Latin America.
>
> To work, to fight, and to die for the liberation of our people in the United States means, therefore, to work for the liberation of all oppressed people around the world. . . . While such a task may well be beyond our capacity, an aroused, motivated, and rebelling black American population nevertheless helps in our indivisible struggles against racism, colonialism, and apartheid.[67]

The Third World view is expressed by Eldridge Cleaver, an early Black Panther Party leader:

> The black man's interest lies in seeing a free and independent Vietnam, a strong Vietnam which is not the puppet of international white supremacy. If the nations of Asia, Latin America, and Africa are strong and free, the black man in America will be safe and secure, and free to live in dignity and self-respect. . . . The only lasting salvation for the black American is to do all he can to see to it that the African, Asian, and Latin American nations are free and independent.[68]

However, it was Malcolm X who not only emphasized this point of view but, through his Organization of Afro-American Unity, his travels in Africa and the Middle East, and an appeal to the heads of state attending the summit

---

[67] James Forman, "1967: High Tide of Black Resistance" (New York: SNCC International Affairs Commission), p. 11. See also "The Indivisible Struggle Against Racism, Apartheid and Colonialism: Position Paper—SNICK," mimeographed (Lusaka, Zambia: International Seminar on Apartheid, Racial Discrimination and Colonialism in Southern Africa, 24 July–4 August 1967). Cf. Kwame Nkrumah, "The Scepter of Black Power," *Africa and the World* 4 (January 1968): 9–12.

[68] Eldridge Cleaver, *Soul on Ice* (New York: McGraw-Hill, 1968), p. 125. Cf. James Boggs, *Manifesto for a Black Revolutionary Party* (Philadelphia: Pacesetters Publishing House, 1969), p. 25.

meeting of the Organization of African Unity in 1964, sought to international-ize the black freedom movement in the United States.[69] After the death of Malcolm X in 1965, Stokely Carmichael more or less succeeded Malcolm X as a roving ambassador, traveling, lecturing, and calling for black solidarity and the violent overthrow of the capitalist-imperialist system which impedes the freedom of the Third World.[70]

Although there is a general awareness that some relationship exists be-tween the struggle of black Americans and that of all nonwhites, the vast majority of black Americans probably share Martin Luther King's view that though they have been abused and scorned, "our destiny is tied up with the destiny of America. In spite of the psychological appeals of identification with Africa, the Negro must face the fact that America is now his home, a home that he helped to build through 'blood, sweat and tears.'"[71] King rejected as frivolous the argument that the freedom of black Americans is fundamen-tally linked with that of the people of the Third World:

> Arguments that the American Negro is a part of a world which is two-thirds colored and that there will come a day when the oppressed people of color will violently rise together to throw off the yoke of white oppression, are beyond the realm of serious discussion. There is no colored nation, including China, that now shows even the potential of leading a violent revolution of color in any international proportions. Ghana, Zambia, Tanzania and Nigeria are so busy fighting their own battles against poverty, illiteracy and the sub-versive influence of neo-colonialism that they offer little hope to Angola, Southern Rhodesia and South Africa, much less to the American Negro.[72]

Essentially, King was arguing in part against Frantz Fanon's thesis (shared by radical blacks) that violent confrontation alone holds promise for the op-pressed people of the earth.[73] Nevertheless, he reached a conclusion not so dissimilar to the one he was attacking: "The hard cold facts today indicate that the hope of the people of color in the world may well rest on the American Negro and his ability to reform the structure of racist imperialism from within and thereby turn the technology and wealth of the West to the task of liber-

---

[69] See Ruby M. and E. U. Essien-Udom, "Malcolm X: An International Man," in John H. Clarke, ed., *Malcolm X: The Man and His Time* (New York: Macmillan, 1969), pp. 235–67; George Breitman, ed., *By Any Means Necessary* (New York: Pathfinders Press, 1970); and Malcolm X, *Malcolm X Speaks,* ed. George Breitman (New York: Grove Press, 1966). See also Malcolm X and Alex Haley, *The Autobiography of Malcolm X* (New York: Grove Press, 1965).

[70] For example, Mr. Carmichael made such a call in a public lecture at Trenchard Hall, University of Ibadan, Nigeria, on 10 February 1970. See also Lawrence P. Neal, "Black Power in the International Context," in Barbour, *Black Power Revolt,* pp. 136–46.

[71] Martin Luther King, Jr., *Chaos or Community?* (London: Penguin Books, 1969), p. 57.

[72] King, *Chaos or Community?,* pp. 60–61.

[73] Frantz Fanon, *The Wretched of the Earth,* trans. C. Farrington (London: Penguin Books, 1967).

ating the world from want."[74] One suspects that this belief had earlier inspired the formation of the American Negro Leadership Conference on Africa, of which King was a founder. At its inaugural meeting at the Arden House campus of Columbia University in 1962, the conference noted that the "struggle for freedom and equality is world wide":

> The American Negro Community in the United States has a special responsibility to urge a dynamic African policy upon our government. Although we have a serious civil rights problem which exhausts much of our energy, we cannot separate this struggle at home from that abroad. . . .
>
> We rededicate and reaffirm our ethnic bond with and historic concern for the peoples of Africa and our complete solidarity with their aspirations for freedom, human rights and independence . . . and we call upon the entire Negro community in the United States to join with us in this commitment to the end that our total influence as a group will be used to aid Africans in their march towards freedom.[75]

The conference urged the United States government to "review its economic aid to Africa" and suggested that it "develop programs comparable in scope and magnitude to those programs administered in Europe."

Problems of race and color undoubtedly disturb the international community. They are a subject of continuing debate at the United Nations and at other international gatherings. They touch the international community in many ways, from the problem of apartheid in South Africa and apprehension over China's steady march to full membership in the "nuclear club" to the participation of groups or states in international sports. The problem of racial discrimination featured prominently in the resolutions of the Afro-Asian Solidarity Conference, held at Bandung, Indonesia, in 1955; and, at the instigation of Malcolm X, the 1964 summit conference of the Organization of African Unity declared it was "deeply disturbed . . . by continuing manifestation of racial bigotry and racial oppression against Negro citizens of the United States of America." The summit reaffirmed the OAU's "belief that the existence of discriminatory practice is a matter of deep concern to member states of the OAU" and urged "the government authorities in the United States of America to intensify their efforts to ensure the total elimination of all forms of discrimination based on race, color, or ethnic origin."[76]

Problems of race and color in the international community are complicated by the superior economic and technological positions of the developed (white)

---

[74] King, *Chaos or Community?*, pp. 60–61.

[75] *American Negro Leadership Conference on Africa Resolutions* (Harriman, N.Y., 23–25 November 1962), Preamble. The conveners of the conference were Roy Wilkins (NAACP), Whitney Young, Jr. (National Urban League), Martin Luther King, Jr. (SCLC), A. Philip Randolph (Brotherhood of Sleeping Car Porters, AFL-CIO), Dorothy I. Height (National Council of Negro Women), and James Farmer (CORE).

[76] Quoted in Malcolm X, *Malcolm X Speaks*, p. 92.

nations. This situation engenders a feeling of insecurity and a need for solidarity among the Third World countries. In this connection, Leopold Sedar Senghor has compared the estrangement of the peoples of the Third World with the alienation of the nineteenth-century proletariat in Europe. Commenting on the Bandung conference of 1955, Senghor observed:

> If the Congress of the Federation of Communists, held in London in November 1847 was, with the publication of the *Communist Manifesto,* the most significant event in the nineteenth century, the Bandung Conference of 1955 can undoubtedly be considered its counterpart in the twentieth century. Analysis reveals in both instances a similar alienation. The proletariat of the nineteenth century was estranged from humanity. The colonised people of the twentieth century, colored peoples, are estranged even more seriously. To economic alienations, others are added: political, social, and cultural. The result is physical and moral suffering, poverty, and uneasy conscience, the latter stemming from a feeling of frustration. Thus, in both instances, revolt and struggle serve "to abolish present conditions" and "transform the world" by re-establishing the natural equilibrium. Where coloured people are concerned, one has accurately spoken of a "revolt against the West."[77]

The dissatisfaction of have-not nations with current international economic arrangements was underscored by the establishment in 1964 of the United Nations Conference on Trade and Development (UNCTAD), comprising most of the African, Asian, and Latin American countries. The failure of the developed countries to respond positively to the demands of the have-not nations for equitable trade arrangements has led UNCTAD's general secretary, Dr. Raul Prebisch, to warn:

> If we do not succeed in effective and rigorous economic development the alternatives are clear. The deteriorating situation in the have-not countries will demonstrate that the extremists are right. Black Power—now merely a U.S. phenomenon—will become brown, yellow and black power on a global scale.[78]

Although there are many ties that bind and there has always been much talk about black unity, neither the black world nor the Third World is monolithic. In Africa blacks belong to several hundred ethnic groups which speak hundreds of different languages. The African peoples outside Africa are scattered throughout the Western Hemisphere, with large emigrant groups in Great Britain. They belong to different nations and live under various systems of government. They speak a variety of languages and experience different cultural and religious influences. In each country blacks are divided into social classes, and internationally they include sophisticated and rela-

---

[77] Leopold S. Senghor, *Nationhood and the African Road to Socialism,* trans. Mercer Cook (Paris: Présence Africaine, 1962), p. 21.

[78] "The Haves and Have-Nots," *Newsweek,* 22 April 1968.

tively opulent New Yorkers and illiterate peasant farmers in Africa and the Caribbean. Moreover, blacks are at different stages of economic development. These differences tend to preclude any meaningful political action on the international level. Blacks have not succeeded in establishing and sustaining an international structure for cooperation or for tackling common problems. They have not evolved a political organization remotely resembling that of the Zionist movement or an economic organization comparable to the modern international cartels. Without an international structure, black unity, let alone the unity of the Third World, exists largely in feeling, cultural expression, and poetic imagination.

In his attempt to affirm his humanity, the black American has necessarily turned to his roots. In his attempt to find his roots, he encounters Africa and the Third World. And he sees that his predicament in America is reflected in the crisis of Africa and the Third World. The problems that confront Africans today—the crisis of identity, lack of power, and lack of unity—though by no means identical,[79] are in many ways similar to the problems blacks face in America. Insofar as blacks in Africa and in the New World are unable to come to terms with their crisis of identity and remedy their lack of power, the need for international black solidarity and the desire for Third World solidarity will persist.

---

[79] Cf. Tom Mboya, *The Challenge of Nationhood: A Collection of Speeches and Writings by Tom Mboya* (London: Andre Deutsch, 1970), pp. 222–32.

Black Nationalism
Since Garvey

JOHN H. BRACEY, JR.

John Bracey is assistant professor of history at Northern Illinois University. With August Meier and Elliott Rudwick, he is coeditor of *Black Nationalism in America* (Bobbs-Merrill, 1969). In the following essay, Mr. Bracey analyzes the forms and intensity of black nationalism in the United States since the 1920's. Presenting the conceptual framework for that analysis, he begins by defining the types of activities he feels are indicative of nationalist feeling. Mr. Bracey's essay puts stress on the relationship between black nationalist activity and economic class and, viewing the black experience in America as similar to the colonial experience of Africans, finds that the resurgence of black nationalism during the 1960's was a sign of decolonization.

Domestic Colonialism and Black Nationalism

Despite the beliefs, if not the desires, of most historians, black and white, black nationalism has deep roots in American history. Black nationalism as a body of ideas and a pattern of behavior stemming logically from the colonial relationship of Black America to White America is both a response to colonial subordination and an affirmation of the existence of an alternative nationality and set of values. As Harold Cruse has remarked in his discussion of domestic colonialism: "It is not at all remarkable then that the semi-colonial status of the Negro has given rise to nationalist movements. It would be surprising if it had not."[1]

The black experience in America can be viewed as similar to the colonial experience of blacks in Africa, the West Indies, and Latin America. The historical process in these areas — colonization, resistance, accommodation, nationalism, decolonization, nationhood — is operable in Black America. The corresponding historical continuum in America, then, is colonialism (slavery), 1619–1865, colonialism (imperialism), 1865–1963, and decolonization, since

---

[1] Harold Cruse, *Rebellion or Revolution?* (New York: William Morrow, 1968), p. 77.

1963.[2] This essay proceeds from the assumption that Black America is an internal or domestic colony and that an understanding of black nationalism is central to understanding the history of race relations in the United States.

A further assumption is that socioeconomic status or class is of crucial importance in understanding the varying complexities and intensities of black nationalism in America. Black people, or the black community, are not and have never been a social and economic monolith. Black nationalism has exhibited greater strength and persistence in the minds and institutions of lower-class blacks than among the black upper classes and intelligentsia. Thus, in discussing nationalist ideologies and movements, it is necessary to specify the social origins of a particular spokesman or movement and whose interests are being spoken for or represented.

Further prelude to the rendering of a historical account of black nationalism since Garvey is settlement on a definition and typology of black nationalism. In American history, "black nationalism" has most often been used to describe a body of social, cultural, and political thoughts and actions ranging from ethnocentrism to pan-Africanism and embracing varying and complex forms in between. E. U. Essien-Udom states:

> The concept of nationalism . . . may be thought of as the belief of a group that it possesses, or ought to possess, a country; that it shares, or ought to share, a common heritage of language, culture and religion; and that its heritage, way of life, and ethnic identity are distinct from those of other groups. Nationalists believe that they ought to rule themselves and shape their own destinies, and that they should therefore be in control of their social, economic, and political institutions. Such beliefs among American Negroes, particularly among the followers of Muhammad, are here called black nationalism.[3]

---

[2] Recent discussions and applications of the colonial analogy are Robert Allen, *Black Awakening in Capitalist America: An Analytic History* (New York: Doubleday, 1969); James Boggs, *Racism and the Class Struggle* (New York: Monthly Review Press, 1970); Harold Cruse, *Rebellion or Revolution?* (New York: William Morrow, 1968); and Ernie Mkalimoto, *Revolutionary Nationalism and the Class Struggle* (Detroit: Black Star Publishers, 1970). Harry Haywood's *Negro Liberation* (New York: International Publishers, 1948) and "Two Epochs of Nation-Development: Is Black Nationalism a Form of Classical Nationalism?" (*Soulbook* 1, no. 4 [Winter 1965–1966]: 257–66) are still valuable. Article-length treatments include Robert Blauner, "Internal Colonialism and Ghetto Revolt," *Social Problems* 16 (Spring 1969): 393–408; Charles V. Hamilton, "Conflict, Race and System-Transformation in the United States," *Journal of International Affairs* 23, no. 1 (1969): 106–18; Albert and Roberta Wohlsetter, "'Third Worlds' Abroad and at Home," *Public Interest,* no. 14 (Winter 1969): 88–107; and several included in "Colonialism and Liberation in America," *Viet-Report* 3, special issue nos. 8–9 (Summer 1968).

[3] E. U. Essien-Udom, *Black Nationalism: A Search for an Identity in America* (New York: Dell Publishing, 1964), p. 20.

Black nationalism manifests itself in a number of different ways and at a number of different levels. The typology of black nationalism that I will follow is substantially that offered by two coeditors and myself in a documentary study of the subject.[4] The simplest or least intense form of racial or ethnic feeling that can be called black nationalism is *racial solidarity,* or the belief that black people, bound to each other by their common color and condition of oppression, should utilize their group strength to alleviate their oppression.

A more complex expression than racial solidarity is *cultural nationalism,* or the belief that black people in the United States and elsewhere share a culture, style of life, aesthetic standard, and world view distinct from that of white Americans and Europeans. The degrees of intensity of this belief range from the mere assertion that in a culturally pluralistic America there is a black subculture to the assertion that Afro-American culture is superior to American culture, and generalized black culture has more value than Western civilization.

Similar in form and complexity to cultural nationalism is *religious nationalism,* or the belief in a distinct black religion, church, or denomination. Black Christians have established both their own churches and their own denominations. Some have proclaimed that God, Mary, and Jesus were black and that blacks are "God's chosen people." Some blacks have become orthodox Muslims, while others have founded their own varieties of Islam, such as the Moorish American Science Temple and the Nation of Islam. Some blacks adhere to the tenets of several varieties of Judaism, of West African religions, and of a myriad of Oriental mysticisms and cosmologies.

Economic nationalism embraces the full spectrum of economic thought from pre-industrial African communalism to Marxian socialism. Black bourgeois nationalists or black capitalists advocate either gaining control over the black sector of the American market or establishing a completely black capitalist economy parallel to American capitalism. More radical than the bourgeois nationalists are those who view the formation of producer and consumer cooperatives within the basic framework of American capitalism as a solution to black economic problems. To the left of these are the black nationalist socialists who contend that only with the abolition of private property and the establishment of a socialist society can all black people be liberated. (These socialists should be distinguished from socialists like Bayard Rustin and A. Philip Randolph, who advocate a policy of integration.) At the opposite end of the spectrum are those nationalists who wish to re-establish pre-industrial and precapitalist African communal forms. Generally speaking, black nationalists who are socialists tend also to be revolutionary nationalists who apply Marxist theories to the experience of Afro-Americans,

---

[4] John H. Bracey, Jr., August Meier, and Elliott Rudwick, eds., *Black Nationalism in America,* American Heritage Series, vol. 89 (Indianapolis: Bobbs-Merrill, 1970).

whereas those who favor pre-industrial African forms tend to be cultural nationalists as well.

Politically, black nationalism at its mildest is merely *black ethnic politics* based on liberal reformist assumptions. Advocates of such a view assume that politically the United States is pluralistic and that liberal values and a democratic political process are still operative. Demands for more black representation and for black political and administrative control over local areas where blacks predominate are manifestations of this view. A left-wing variant also based on liberal assumptions is the advocacy of the formation of an all-black political party. At its most radical, political black nationalism is *revolutionary nationalism,* which advocates the overthrow of existing political and economic institutions as a prerequisite for the liberation of black Americans.

A significant variety of black nationalism, more important historically than during the period covered in this essay, is *emigrationism.* Emigrationism (sometimes called Black Zionism) posits the solution to the problems of blacks in the United States in a return to Africa, the ancestral homeland. *Territorial separatism* is that variety of emigrationism which advocates establishing a sovereign black political entity—town, state, or nation—within the present territorial limits of the United States. Milder forms of territorial separatism merge with the concepts of ethnic politics and black control of the black community.

At its most comprehensive and sophisticated, black nationalism is *pan-Africanism* (sometimes called pan-Negroism). Pan-Africanism, historically and in its broad ideological sense distinct from the more restrictively political pan-Africanism of the new African nations, asserts that people of African descent throughout the world share certain cultural characteristics and social conditions as a result of their African origins: their political oppression and economic exploitation by Europeans and Americans, and their stigmatization by the racial attitudes, theories, and behavior of Western civilization.

These varieties of black nationalism are in reality often not as sharply delineated as they are presented here, nor are they mutually exclusive. Human existence is no less complex when black folk are involved, so one should not be surprised to find within the mind of any individual or group a number of combinations of black nationalism. There is no unanimity as to what black nationalism is or is not; therefore it is openly acknowledged that the definitions offered here are tentative.

Black Nationalism During the Depression and the New Deal

The proliferation of nationalist movements and ideologies in the 1920's was followed by a period in which nationalism as a significant theme in black thought was at a low ebb. During the thirty-year period from the 1930's to the 1960's, Negro organizations, dominated by the goals and outlook of the Negro middle class, with few exceptions stressed interracial cooperation, civil rights, and racial integration. Among other reasons for the temporary eclipse of nationalism were the effects of the Depression, and the consequent necessity of relying on the New Deal for survival, and the influx into the black communities of white trade unionists and Communists seeking allies. The principal ideological concerns of black intellectuals such as E. Franklin Frazier, Ralph Bunche, and Abram Harris were the practical aspects of the Negro's relationship to the New Deal, the role of trade unions in the advancement of the race, and the relevance of Marxism to the problems of Afro-Americans.

The onset of the Depression ended virtually all effective support for the Garvey movement, which was already in decline after Garvey's deportation in December 1927. Only a few small groups carried on Garvey's ideas. The UNIA, of course, continued in various stages of health in a number of cities. A number of splinter groups, located primarily in New York, Chicago, and Detroit, exist to the present.[5]

Religious nationalism persisted in the day-to-day activities of the myriad of black churches with few overtly nationalistic ideologies being expressed. One Christian movement which manifested its own peculiar variety of nationalism, however, was Father Divine's Peace movement. Father Divine, whose exact origins and early life are unknown, attracted wide attention during the early 1930's by the insistence of his followers that he was God. Father Divine, through the organization of the collective efforts of his followers, was able to provide food, work, clothing, and shelter for a large number of blacks whose condition was not being measurably improved by the New Deal. His "kingdoms" across the nation were places of refuge, and, despite his insistence upon celibacy, sexual segregation, and the renunciation of worldly goods (money), his followers numbered in the tens of thousands. The nationalistic implications of a short black American Negro being worshiped as God were not lost on lower-class blacks nor on several students of the movement. Essien-Udom, who classifies Father Divine's movement as religiously separatist, concludes that "independence of white control, rejection of the traditional Christian concept of God, denial of the power of the dominant society, and differentiation of his followers from the Negro subculture and society are policies which Father Divine shares with the black nationalists."[6] Sara Harris, in her biography of Father Divine, says:

---

[5] Discussions of the Garvey splinter groups and several new Garveyite groups can be found in Essien-Udom, *Black Nationalism,* pp. 44–66; Arna Bontemps and Jack Conroy, *Anyplace But Here* (New York: Hill & Wang, 1966), pp. 208–11; and John Henrik Clarke, "The New Afro-American Nationalism," *Freedomways* 1 (Fall 1961): 285–95.

[6] Essien-Udom, *Black Nationalism,* p. 45.

He went a step beyond what even Marcus Garvey, the most aggressive Negro chauvinist of recent years, had ever dared to say. Where Garvey had said that black was basically superior and white was basically inferior, the Messenger Father Divine exemplified that statement. He said, I am a Negro and God dwells in me. You are a Negro and you are like unto me. Therefore, you are superior to white.[7]

As for the presence of whites in the movement, Claude McKay concludes, at least for the New York area, this:

All of the followers belong to the same type. They are emotionally-inspired congregations of brown and black Americans with a leaven of Negroid Spanish-Americans and West Indians. They are flecked with whites just as ardent. But despite the spirit of abnegation and general fellowship before their God, the Father, the whites appear to the penetrating eye more like slightly uncomfortable visitors. They give one an impression of the missionary type, the God servants who resolutely mingle with the minister to natives of a colony.[8]

Other manifestations of religious nationalism during the 1930's were Noble Drew Ali's Moorish-American Science Temple and Elijah Muhammad's Nation of Islam. Noble Drew Ali was a self-proclaimed Muslim prophet who founded the Moorish-American Science Temple in Newark, New Jersey, in 1913. During the period between 1913 and his arrival in Chicago in 1925, he also founded temples in Pittsburgh and Detroit. Drew Ali believed that American blacks were actually descendants from the Moors of northern Africa and were Asiatic in origin. Noble Drew Ali died under peculiar circumstances in the spring of 1929 after violent conflict arose surrounding a challenge to his leadership. The movement then fragmented, with a number of followers proclaiming themselves the rightful spiritual heir.

One such follower was W. D. Fard, who founded the Nation of Islam in Detroit in 1930. By 1933 Fard had gathered an estimated 8,000 followers into an organization which proclaimed that whites were devils and that the "Asiatic Black Man" was the original and rightful inhabitant of the earth. Fard also organized the Fruit of Islam, the all-male defense group, and the University of Islam, where the children of members could be educated. Fard disappeared mysteriously around 1934, and the leadership of the movement was taken over by Elijah Muhammad.

Muhammad proclaimed that Fard was actually Allah come to earth and that he, Muhammad, had been personally designated "Messenger of Allah" and "Allah's Prophet." Throughout the rest of the 1930's and 1940's the Nation

---

[7] Sara Harris, *Father Divine: Holy Husband* (New York: Doubleday, 1953), p. 27.

[8] Claude McKay, *Harlem: Negro Metropolis* (New York: E. P. Dutton, 1940), p. 39.

of Islam grew slowly, drawing its strength primarily from the black lower classes and particularly from prison inmates. In 1942, Muhammad was sent to federal prison for three years for refusing to respond to the draft. After Muhammad's release, the Muslims continued their steady but unspectacular growth until Malcolm X joined the movement after his release from prison in 1952.[9]

A number of ex-Garveyites joined religious movements such as that of Father Divine, while others went into the new industrial labor unions. Some of the cultural nationalists of the Harlem Renaissance responded to the appeals of the Communist party and subordinated their nationalist instincts to the class struggle.

During the Depression, nationalist tendencies were also manifested in the realm of economics. Bourgeois economic nationalism provided the ideology of the "Buy Black" and "Don't Buy Where You Can't Work" campaigns. The purpose of the "Buy Black" campaigns was obvious; the boycott and picketing campaigns sought more jobs, chiefly for the middle and upper classes, in white-owned businesses located in black communities. Organizations such as the New Negro Alliance in Washington, D.C., and the Future Outlook League in Cleveland were typical.

One activist who did not conform to the pattern was Sufi Abdul Hamid of Chicago's South Side. Sufi Abdul Hamid was a black American living in Chicago who, before his boycott activities, had engaged in various forms of mysticism and occultism, styling himself an "Oriental philosopher" and going by the name of Bishop Conshankin. In 1930, with the aid of other community leaders, Sufi began his efforts to secure more jobs for blacks. He was quite successful and moved to Harlem to initiate a similar campaign.

In Harlem in 1933, Sufi organized jobless black white-collar workers into the Negro Industrial and Clerical Alliance (later the Afro-American Federation of Labor) and launched a boycott and picketing campaign. Plagued by intracommunity factionalism, attacked by the white Left, and bogged down in legal squabbles over extraneous issues (such as defending himself against charges of anti-Semitism and being a black Nazi), Sufi discontinued his work in 1934, having achieved mixed results.

Also expressing concern for the economic needs of the black masses was W. E. B. Du Bois, the race's leading scholar and protest leader, who was not immune to the social forces at work in both the black community and the nation at large. Returning in 1934 to an idea that had long held an attraction for him, Du Bois advocated that blacks form economic cooperatives, both consumer and producer, in order to ensure the survival and well-being

---

[9] For a detailed discussion of these movements during this period see Bontemps and Conroy, *Anyplace But Here,* pp. 204–08, 216–25; and Essien-Udom, *Black Nationalism,* pp. 45–48, 55–57.

of the race under the conditions that prevailed during the Depression. Du Bois said:

> What then can we do? The only thing that we not only can, but must do, is voluntarily and insistently to organize our economic and social power, no matter how much segregation it involves. Learn to associate with ourselves and to train ourselves for effective association. Organize our strength as consumers; learn to co-operate and use machines and power as producers; train ourselves in methods of democratic control within our own group. Run and support our own institutions.[10]

This view conflicted with the integration-at-any-cost outlook of the NAACP, and in 1934 Du Bois resigned his post as editor of that organization's publication, the *Crisis.* In 1940 in his autobiography, *Dusk of Dawn,* Du Bois restated in greater detail his idea of a black group economy.

The drive by blacks to relieve their economic situation in this period culminated in A. Philip Randolph's March on Washington movement of 1941. Randolph, former editor of a socialist magazine, the *Messenger,* and founder of the Brotherhood of Sleeping Car Porters, organized the March on Washington movement to protest discriminatory hiring practices in the new and expanding wartime industries. He proposed to bring ten thousand blacks to Washington to pressure President Roosevelt to ensure equal employment opportunities. Roosevelt yielded to the threatened march and in June 1941 issued an executive order establishing the Fair Employment Practices Commission. Randolph then called the march off.

Randolph himself was not a nationalist and took great pains to make this clear to any and all concerned. He was, however, attuned to the needs and wishes of lower-class blacks and offered their need for self-reliance as reason for the exclusiveness of his movement. The disbanding of the March on Washington movement marked the virtual disappearance of significant nationalist movements and ideologies among American blacks until the 1960's.

Black nationalist movements and ideologies during the Depression and New Deal were not aggressive in their confrontations with white society. The principal concerns were those of the masses of lower-class blacks during a period of serious crisis. Survival was the issue, and the black community itself was both the force to be organized and the focus of all action. Black nationalism was clearly on the defensive.

Alternatives to Integration

From the end of World War II through the early 1960's integration was the dominant ideology among Negro protest movements. A few nationalist

---

[10] W. E. B. Du Bois, "Segregation in the North," *Crisis* 41 (April 1934), quoted in Bracey et al., *Black Nationalism in America,* p. 291.

groups, such as the UNIA splinter groups and the Nation of Islam, persisted but could arouse little mass support. The predominance of the integrationist ideology can be traced to a number of factors. First, the goals of integration and equal rights coincided with the interests of the new Negro middle class that was developing as a result of the rise in trade union and low-level white-collar jobs produced by an expanding postwar economy and the growth of federal, state, and local bureaucracies. This generation of clerks, teachers, and postmen had achieved a sufficient degree of economic security to be able to direct their attention to issues such as integrated education, open housing, and free access to public accommodations, and they had the financial resources to support organizations like the NAACP, the Urban League, and the numerous local human relations committees that acted in their behalf. This group of blacks was making social and economic progress, and so far as they were concerned that meant *all* blacks were making progress.

Second, the publication of Gunnar Myrdal's *An American Dilemma* in 1944 set an ideological tone accepted by both black and white social scientists, who played important roles in protest movements and on human relations committees. *An American Dilemma* emphasized integration as a goal and asserted that the black community and its institutions were pathological in nature and should be done away with and replaced by "normal"—that is, integrated —ones. Myrdal, with an eye on maintaining social stability accompanied by gradual, carefully defined changes, was opposed to an expansion in the size of the black population and, most of all, to the masses of blacks organizing themselves along racial lines.[11] To justify such a view, the notion that most Americans believed in the American creed of equality of opportunity and in reward for individual merit was evoked as the framework within which blacks must carry out their struggle. The guilt feeling engendered in the white mind because of the gap between the rhetoric of the American creed and the reality of racial oppression would act as the prime motivating force.[12]

Liberals—integrationists—black and white agreed with these views, as did middle-class black radicals who believed that the solution to the race problem lay in the black and white working-class struggle manifested in the new industrial unions. Thus, having lost support from the middle classes, the black lower classes were left virtually without political and intellectual leadership.

As has happened before, lower-class blacks channeled their nationalistic

---

[11] Gunnar Myrdal, *An American Dilemma* (New York: Harper, 1944), pp. 167, 169, 178, 853.

[12] Myrdal, *An American Dilemma,* pp. 3–25. The inadequacies in Myrdal's approach are analyzed in greater detail in my "An American Dilemma: A Nationalist Critique." This paper was presented at the fall 1969 convention of the Southern Historical Association (Washington, D.C., 1 November 1969) and is part of a larger study now in progress.

impulses along cultural lines, and the period was an exciting and fruitful one, artistically if not financially, for black musicians—jazz, gospel, and rhythm and blues—and for black dances and dancers.[13]

The 1954 Supreme Court decision *Brown v. Board of Education of Topeka,* which stated that separate schools for blacks were inherently unequal (or, as Floyd McKissick once remarked, "You mix black with black and you get stupidity"), climaxed a long and successful legal campaign by the NAACP and signaled to middle-class blacks that the black man's day of freedom was nigh. In the mid-1950's, the Montgomery bus boycott initiated a ten-year period of nonviolent direct action protests. Throughout the rest of the black world—in Africa and the West Indies—black nations, under the leadership of individuals every bit as middle-class as those in the NAACP and the Urban League (in many cases educated at the same universities), were coming into existence, sparking a growing interest in and identification with Africa. Significant numbers of Afro-Americans took up residence in or made extended visits to the new African nations.[14]

Outstanding among the repatriates were the pioneering but shamefully ignored Africanist William Leo Hansberry, who went to Nigeria in 1961 to head the newly established Hansberry Institute for African Studies at the University of Nigeria, and W. E. B. Du Bois, who took up citizenship in Ghana in 1961. Of course, Du Bois had maintained his interest in pan-Africanism during the period covered by this essay; he served as honorary president of the Pan-African Congress held in Manchester, England, in 1945 and wrote two books on colonialism and African history—*Color and Democracy* (1945) and *The World and Africa* (1947). In "Ghana Calls," a poem published in 1962 in *Freedomways,* a black journal on political and cultural developments, Du Bois turned his back on America and the West, having found in Africa a land where he could carry on his life's work:

> Here at last, I looked back on my Dream;
>   I heard the Voice that loosed
>   The long-locked dungeons of my soul
>   I sensed that Africa had come
>   Not up from Hell, but from the sum of Heaven's glory.[15]

---

[13] For discussions of these developments see Rolland Snellings, "Keep on Pushin': Rhythm & Blues as a Weapon," *Liberator* 5 (October 1965): 6–8; Larry Neal, "Black Art and Black Liberation," *Ebony* 24 (August 1969): 54–62; A. B. Spellman, "Revolution in Sound," *Ebony* 24 (August 1969): 84–89; and Phyl Garland, *The Sound of Soul* (Chicago: Henry Regnery, 1969).

[14] St. Clair Drake, "Negro Americans and the African Interest," in John P. David, ed., *The American Negro Reference Book* (Englewood Cliffs, N.J.: Prentice-Hall, 1966), pp. 691–700.

[15] From W. E. B. Du Bois, "Ghana Calls." Reprinted from *Freedomways* magazine, Winter 1962. Published at 799 Broadway, New York City. Reprinted by permission.

In 1960 black college students in the United States became actively involved in the integrationist Civil Rights movement and the struggle for equal rights continued. However, the activities of two men kept the question of black nationalism from being totally ignored. The men were Robert Franklin Williams and Malcolm X. Robert F. Williams was an ex-Marine who, after returning to his home town of Monroe, North Carolina, joined its moribund NAACP chapter in 1955, became its president in 1957, and began to involve it in direct action campaigns to secure the desegregation of public accommodations.[16] Williams organized a defense group that protected the community and the protest leaders against Ku Klux Klan intimidation. Continuous harassment and attempts at repression provoked Williams to declare in May 1959 that blacks must defend themselves by "meeting violence with violence" and if necessary "stop lynching with lynching." Williams was promptly suspended as president of his NAACP branch by Roy Wilkins, executive secretary of the national association. At a trial held on June 3 in New York City before the NAACP's committee on branches, Williams was given a six-month suspension from the organization. At the organization's annual convention in New York in July, Williams successfully proposed a resolution in which the NAACP affirmed the right of individuals and groups to defend themselves against illegal assaults, but he failed to have the final months of his suspension rescinded.

In the summer of 1961, Williams rescued from a racist mob a contingent of freedom riders who had come to Monroe to show that nonviolence could still work. In the confusion that ensued, Williams was accused of kidnapping a white couple who had somehow wandered into the black community. Caught between the Ku Klux Klan and the state and local governments, who were determined to defeat him at all costs, he had to flee with his family to prevent a massive attack on the entire community.

Williams first went to Canada and then to Cuba, where he continued to publish his newsletter, the *Crusader.* In 1966, he took up residence in China, where he remained until he returned to the United States in 1969 as the president of the Republic of New Africa (a territorial separatist group). Williams has since resigned this position and is currently residing in Detroit, fighting extradition to North Carolina on the 1961 kidnapping charges.

Williams' words and actions during the period 1959–1961 were signif-

---

[16] Williams' story can be found in Truman Nelson, *People with Strength: The Story of Monroe, North Carolina* (published privately), and in Robert F. Williams, *Negroes with Guns* (New York: Marzani & Munsell, 1962). Other sources of interest are George Lavan, *The Monroe Story* (New York: Committee to Aid the Monroe Defendants, 1961), and Harold Cruse, *The Crisis of the Negro Intellectual* (New York: William Morrow, 1967), pp. 351–62, 368–99. Not readily available but of great interest in following Williams' ideological development are issues of the *Crusader,* published in Monroe, N.C., Cuba (1962–1965), and China (1966–1968).

icant for a number of reasons. First, during a period when the tactic of nonviolence was rapidly achieving the status of a philosophy, Williams reasserted
the need for the tactical flexibility necessary for the success of any social
movement. Second, his movement showed once again that a cohesive, well-
organized black organization could be just as effective in achieving civil
rights goals as an interracial one. Third, Williams organized young and lower-
class blacks — laborers, farmers, domestic workers — many of whom, as one
observer of the movement put it, "were surprised to learn that they could
join the NAACP." Williams' goals were equal rights and integration, but
his methods and the nature of his NAACP branch clearly set him apart not
only from the NAACP but from CORE, SNCC, and the SCLC as well.

Organizationally, Williams inspired the Deacons of Defense, a self-defense
group formed in Louisiana to protect civil rights workers, and several North-
ern-based revolutionary nationalist movements, the most important of which
was the Revolutionary Action Movement (RAM). RAM was made up of ghetto
street youths and college-trained blacks who "decided there was a need for
a 'Third Force' or movement that would be somewhere between the Nation
of Islam (Black Muslims) and SNCC."[17]

RAM openly called for a world-wide black revolution to overthrow Western
imperialism:

> RAM philosophy may be described as revolutionary nationalism, black
> nationalism or just plain blackism. It is that black people of the world (darker
> races, black, yellow, brown, red, oppressed peoples) are all enslaved by the
> same forces. RAM's philosophy is one of the world black revolution or world
> revolution of oppressed peoples rising up against their former slavemasters.
> Our movement is a movement of black people who are co-ordinating their
> efforts to create a "new world" free from exploitation and oppression of
> man to man.[18]

Because it expressed such views both orally and in a theoretical journal
called *Black America,* and because it attempted to form an organization that
would carry them through, RAM was persistently harassed by government
authorities, who arrested a number of RAM leaders in 1967, breaking up
and silencing the organization.

The second figure of importance during the late 1950's and early 1960's
was Malcolm X, Minister of the Nation of Islam.[19] Malcolm was also an

---

[17] Max Stanford, "Towards Revolutionary Action Movement Manifesto," *Detroit Correspondence* (March 1964), p. 3. The views of Williams and his followers have been critically analyzed by Harold Cruse in *The Crisis of the Negro Intellectual,* pp. 375–99.

[18] Stanford, "Towards Revolutionary Action Movement Manifesto," p. 3.

[19] The details of Malcolm's life are presented in Malcolm X and Alex Haley, *The Autobiography of Malcolm X* (New York: Grove Press, 1965), one of the outstanding human
documents of the twentieth century.

inspiration to RAM; much of its ideology was a secularized version of the revolutionary but religious nationalism preached by Malcolm. Malcolm's keen mind, quick wit, oratorical brilliance, and charismatic appeal soon made him a figure of national importance.

Throughout most of his years of national prominence, Malcolm X expounded the views of Elijah Muhammad. In contrast to the doctrines of integration, nonviolence, and civil rights, Elijah Muhammad and the Muslims advocated separatism, self-defense, and self-determination. Muslims repudiated many of the values of Western society, warned blacks against intermarriage with whites, and looked forward to the day of Armageddon, when Allah would wreak divine retribution upon the West for its years of oppressing black people. A key Muslim demand was for land to build a nation.

Programmatically, the Muslims duplicated Garvey's bourgeois nationalism in setting up businesses such as dry cleaners, grocery stores, and restaurants. They also owned and operated truck and dairy farms and bakeries. The University of Islam, the Muslim school, extended from elementary school through high school. The weekly newspaper *Muhammad Speaks,* carrying accounts of the activities and struggles of black people in this country and throughout the world, remains the most widely read black newspaper in the country.

Malcolm X left the Nation of Islam in March 1964 because of differences with Elijah Muhammad. He formed the Muslim Mosque, Inc., and then the Organization of Afro-American Unity (OAAU), largely inspired by the Organization of African Unity. The program of the OAAU was black nationalism at its broadest, embracing pan-Africanism, self-defense, political nationalism, bourgeois economic nationalism, and cultural nationalism. Malcolm traveled widely in Africa and the Middle East during 1964. He was assassinated on February 21, 1965, at the Audubon Ballroom in New York. Malcolm's image has assumed legendary proportions since his death, and his influence on black ghetto youth is unmatched by that of any other figure.

Decolonization and the Revival of Black Nationalism

During the era of integrationist sentiment from 1945 to 1963, with the exceptions already discussed, the black middle class and intelligentsia defined the struggle of blacks against white oppression in ways that adhered to and even celebrated the professed ideals of American democracy. Like a colonial elite, the black middle class was inclined to try to get the colonizer to grant status to those of the colonized who adhered most closely to the cultural and social values of the colonizer. This generally involved the attempt to avoid any extensive cultural and social ties with the masses of blacks, who had as a necessary instrument for their survival a set of cultural and social values different from those of the colonizer and the colonial elite. What happened in the United States around 1963 was the convergence of a number of social factors, resulting in a redefining of the relationship between Black America and White America. Many black Americans began to subscribe to the view that theirs was a situation similar to that of oppressed peoples throughout the world and that what was needed was a shift in social and political power from White America to Black America—in a word, decolonization. The current demands for black power and the many manifestations of black nationalism in the late 1960's can best be understood when viewed in this perspective.

One influential factor was that interest in Africa had been rising among black Americans throughout the 1960's; even more important, it was being reciprocated by Africans who spoke out in the United Nations and elsewhere about the plight of their black brothers in the United States. The blacks who disrupted the U.N. proceedings in 1961 to protest the murder of Patrice Lumumba represented the feelings of a large number of black Americans. Abdulrahman "Babu" Muhamud, a pan-Africanist from Zanzibar, maintained a cordial rapport with Harlem black nationalists. Oginga Odinga, a cabinet minister in the Kenya government, toured the American South to observe civil rights activities and was the inspiration of a song, bearing his name, written by the SNCC Freedom Singers. African nations such as Ghana, Guinea, and Tanzania invited protest figures such as Malcolm X to make official visits.

An influential second factor was that the expectations of the young middle-class civil rights workers had been kindled by early successes and by the need to have hope to sustain themselves in their dangerous activities. In such an atmosphere, defeats and repression became hard to take, and a search began for new methods to solve the problems of the black rural poor in the South and the black ghetto poor in the North. Bourgeois political movements such as the Freedom Now party and ACT were attempts to give new direction to the Civil Rights movement. The Freedom Now party, launched in 1963 during that year's March on Washington, was short-lived, gaining its most notable successes in Michigan state elections in 1964. ACT was a national confederation of black groups and individuals who attempted to bridge the gap between civil rights protest and black nationalism by asserting that an all-black organization was necessary for blacks to achieve equal rights.

Many civil rights workers in SNCC and CORE began to turn their backs on nonviolence and integration after a series of shocks that included the deaths of four black girls in the bombing of a Birmingham church in 1963, the many beatings, jailings, and killings of civil rights activists, and the rejection of the delegation of the Mississippi Freedom Democratic party from the Democratic party's 1964 presidential convention. The Harlem ghetto rebellion in the late summer of 1964 provided an inkling of the new mood of Black America and gave civil rights activists something else to ponder.

A third factor became evident in 1965. The Watts rebellion of August signaled the end of the nonviolent integrationist movement and the active involvement once again of large numbers of lower-class blacks in the struggle for freedom. Throughout the late 1960's, ghetto rebellions occurred in black ghettos across the nation. The most significant ones, in addition to that in Watts, were those in Newark and Detroit in 1967 and the 1968 nationwide outburst sparked by the assassination of Martin Luther King, Jr.

The strength that the rebellions demonstrated forced the black middle class and intelligentsia to respond. Within a year after Watts, CORE moved to oust whites from positions of leadership, and SNCC elected Stokely Carmichael its new chairman as it too converted to an all-black membership. SNCC formed the Lowndes County, Alabama, Freedom Democratic Organization (informally called the Black Panther Party) and made plans to execute a political take-over of the areas in the South where blacks constituted a majority of the population. Struggle and experience forced SNCC to consider necessary in 1966 a strategy that had been thought absurd when proposed in 1948 by Harry Haywood in his book *Negro Liberation.*

In the summer of 1966, on the continuation of a march through the South begun by James Meredith, Stokely Carmichael and Willie Ricks raised the slogan "Black Power," which came to symbolize the new ideological outlook and unity of Black America. Ignored in the hysterical responses that followed were previous uses of the phrase, such as the title of Richard Wright's book about Ghana, *Black Power* (1954), the conference called in the summer of 1965 to establish the Organization of Black Power, and Adam Clayton Powell's speech before Congress and his Howard University baccalaureate address in the spring of 1966.

"Black power" soon came to have a wide variety of meanings, ranging from a revolutionary overthrow of the "white power structure" to increased benefits for blacks from the existing social and economic system. Harold Cruse saw the slogan as an umbrella to cover up the retreat of those civil rights activists who refused to admit the inadequacies of their ideology and tactics. Robert Allen saw it as an ideology designed to cloak the transition from Black America as a colony to Black America as a neocolony, and he presents impressive evidence to show that white economic and political leaders have effectively used the slogan to thwart the goals of blacks.[20] CORE interpreted black power to mean a wide variety of things, including the development of political power through the support of black candidates, the cultivation of a more positive black self-image, the command of a greater share of federal resources, and the development of black capitalism.

After an initial period of vagueness, SNCC, under the leadership of Stokely Carmichael (chairman in 1967) and H. Rap Brown (chairman in 1968), interpreted black power to mean the black solidarity necessary for a black rev-

---

[20] Cruse, *The Crisis of the Negro Intellectual,* pp. 544–65. Robert Allen, *Black Awakening in Capitalist America* (New York: Doubleday, 1969), Chapter 2.

olution. SNCC began to abandon its Southern base and to direct its attention in two new directions. James Forman, in the pan-African tradition of Du Bois, traveled throughout Africa attempting to solidify ties between the liberation struggles of black Americans and Africans. Forman was successful in gaining SNCC representation at U.N. conferences, performing a unique service until he shifted his attention in 1969 to the churches and subsequently delivered his Black Manifesto. Carmichael led the return of SNCC workers to the college campuses, where from 1966 through 1968 they played a significant role in converting middle-class students to a black power outlook.

Black student organizations came into existence on virtually every campus where there were black students. Militant action such as building take-overs and disruptions of university functions to gain a hearing or to achieve a list of demands became common. The specifics of the demands varied with the peculiar circumstances of each school, but a look at the demands made by FMO (For Members Only) and the Afro-American Student Union at Northwestern University in Evanston, Illinois, in the spring of 1968 will reveal some common concerns. The Northwestern demands called for the enrollment of a larger number of black students (in this case 10 to 12 percent of each freshman class), at least half to come from inner-city schools; the granting of greater financial assistance to black students; the establishment of separate living units for those blacks who desired to use them; a black student social and cultural center; the hiring of black counselors; and the establishment of a committee, on which black students would have substantial representation, to oversee the implementation of the other demands. The hiring of more black faculty and the "blackening" of existing curricula by the establishment of black studies programs or black studies departments are now truisms in most large colleges and universities.

Despite revolutionary rhetoric and militant action, the reformist nature of many black power demands could lead one to conclude that perhaps black power is a ploy on the part of the black middle class to achieve integrationist goals while still maintaining the necessary support of the lower classes. Middle-class blacks are gaining in numbers and influence within the two-party system. Blacks are more visible in the middle levels of government and private industry and in the mass media than ever before. More black students are on predominantly white college campuses—North and South, public and private—than ever before. These gains have resulted primarily from influential whites' increased awareness and fear of rebellions by ghetto blacks and from the pervasiveness of the rhetoric of black consciousness among blacks. The black power conferences held in Newark in 1967 and in Philadelphia in 1968 were attended by nationalists of all social classes and of varying perspectives but were dominated by middle-class blacks espousing bourgeois nationalism and black capitalism.

Since 1966 a wide spectrum of black nationalist ideologies and organizations has developed. Cultural nationalism has fostered the founding and growth of journals such as *Black Dialogue, Black Theatre,* and the *Journal of Black Poetry.* Mass-distributed black periodicals such as *Ebony* now devote much attention to cultural nationalist developments, and *Ebony* has shifted substantially from its gradualist integrationist stance of previous years. *Negro Digest,* renamed *Black World,* provides a forum for the prose and poetry of both new and established black writers and thinkers. Many black communities now have cultural organizations or centers where black artists gather to work cooperatively and to present their art to a black audience. LeRoi Jones's Spirit House Movers in Newark and the Organization of Black American Culture are two such organizations. Black poetry, art, and literature are widely known and enjoyed for the first time since the Negro Renaissance period. Africa is a prominent inspiration to cultural nationalism, with many blacks adopting African names, wearing African-styled clothes, and learning to speak African languages. (The natural hair style is so widely accepted and worn that it has lost much of its early ideological implication. To paraphrase Rap Brown, there are a lot of natural hairdos covering up "processed" minds.)

Journals of political and social thought such as Daniel Watts's *Liberator* (New York) and Nathan Hare's *Black Scholar* (San Francisco) are presenting the writings of black thinkers on the problems of strategy and direction faced by Black America. At various locations throughout the country, groups of black scholars are gathering on permanent and semipermanent bases to try to develop ways to serve Black America. Atlanta's Institute of the Black World and Washington, D.C.'s New School of Afro-American Thought are two such groups.

Religious nationalism has reached new intensities. In addition to the older bedrock lower-class black churches and the Nation of Islam, there are new separatist developments—Christian, African, and mystical. The Reverend Albert Cleage, a nationalist minister in Detroit active in the Freedom Now party, has renamed his church the Shrine of the Black Madonna and has installed in its main auditorium a wall-size portrait of a black Madonna and Child painted by Glanton Dowdell, a nationalist artist. Cleage has presented the essentials of his black theology in *The Black Messiah* (1969). Many blacks have become converted to Islam, adopting Muslim names and adhering rigorously to its doctrines and practices. Some have taken up African religions such as those of the Yoruba. An increasingly large number of blacks—primarily lower-middle-class and middle-class in status—have turned to various forms of mysticism and practice the rituals of a number of Eastern and pre-Christian cults or express great faith in astrology and other cosmic sciences.

Territorial separatism has, in addition to the Nation of Islam, a new host of advocates. Robert S. Browne, an economics professor at Fairleigh Dickinson University, presented a resolution at the Newark black power conference asking that "a national dialogue be initiated on the feasibility of establishing a separate homeland in the United States for Black People."[21] The Republic of New Africa, supported by some of the older nationalist groups and by numbers of ghetto youth, seeks independence from the United States, the founding of a new nation consisting of Mississippi, Alabama, Georgia, Louisiana, and South Carolina, and $400 billion in reparations from the federal government. The Nation of Islam, using normal procedures, is currently attempting to secure land in the South to establish a land base for their movement. Territorial separatism is not dead by any means.

Emigrationism is not as strong an impulse as in earlier periods of nationalist ferment, but in 1967 the Al-Beta Israel Temple, a group of black Jews based in Chicago, acquired land and founded a community in Liberia. In 1969 some members of this group migrated to Israel, where they were admitted as Jewish citizens and allowed to establish communities. In the spring of 1969 Robert Nix, a black congressman from Pennsylvania, introduced a bill calling for federal financial and administrative assistance for those black Americans who wished to repatriate to Africa. At present there are approximately 2,000 black Americans residing in Africa.

Revolutionary nationalism has been adopted as the ideology of an increasing number of organizations with ghetto constituencies. The Republic of New Africa and RAM have endorsed the idea of the necessity of armed struggle to achieve a separate nation. SNCC spokesmen Stokely Carmichael and H. Rap Brown have spoken often of the need for revolution to secure black liberation. Two of the most important groups espousing revolutionary nationalism, however, are the Black Panther Party and the League of Revolutionary Black Workers. The Black Panther Party, borrowing its name from SNCC's political experiment in Alabama, was formed in Oakland, California, in October 1966 by Huey P. Newton and Bobby Seale. Newton was a graduate of Merritt College in Oakland, California, where he had been active in organizing black students. Seale, an ex-G.I., met Newton at Merritt; together they formed the Black Panther Party for Self-Defense and wrote its initial platform and program. In 1967 Eldridge Cleaver, recently paroled from San Quentin and author of *Soul on Ice,* gave the Panthers the link to the white Left that later was to assume great importance. Although he has lived in exile in Algeria since 1969, Cleaver is still listed as an editor on the staff of *Ramparts.*[22]

By 1969 the Panthers had repudiated much of their early nationalist

---

[21] Browne explained his reasoning in greater detail in subsequent writings, most notably in "The Case for Black Separatism," *Ramparts* 6 (December 1967). He also served as an adviser at the Black Government Conference held in Detroit in the summer of 1968, at which the Republic of New Africa was founded.

[22] For accounts of the brief history of the Black Panther Party see Gene Marine, *The Black Panthers* (New York: New American Library, 1969), and two books by Panther leaders: Robert Scheer, ed., *Eldridge Cleaver: Post-Prison Writings and Speeches* (New York: Random House, 1969), and Bobby Seale, *Seize the Time* (New York: Random House, 1970).

rhetoric and adopted a version of Marxism-Leninism in which a socialist revolution to free oppressed peoples in the United States regardless of race took precedence over the national liberation of Black America. The violent conflict between the Panthers and US, a West Coast cultural nationalist group headed by Ron Karenga, caused the Panthers to take a rigid position against cultural nationalism, which cost them some black support. The misunderstanding in 1967–1968 concerning a proposed Panther merger with SNCC, which resulted in bad feeling between the two groups (personified in the verbal warfare that has been going on between Eldridge Cleaver and Stokely Carmichael ever since), further limited the potential of the Panthers for organizing mass support. A proposed alliance with the League of Revolutionary Black Workers has never been consummated.

The Panthers have been subjected to tremendous repression, both violent and legal, and most of the national leadership is in jail (Bobby Seale), released on bond (Huey Newton), or in exile (Eldridge Cleaver). Local police forces were apparently given a go-ahead by the national government to destroy the Panthers and killed or wounded a number of them in raids on Panther offices across the country in late 1969 and early 1970. The survival of the Black Panther Party as a viable political organization will depend on whether it can maintain past levels of recruitment, break off debilitating ties to the white Left, and regain its early nationalistic appeal.

The Panther platform demands an end to the many ways by which black people in the United States are oppressed and cites the Declaration of Independence as sanction for carrying out an armed revolution if Panther demands are not met. The party publishes a weekly newspaper, the *Black Panther.* Panthers train black youth in the arts of self-defense and in military discipline. In a number of cities, they have instituted breakfast-for-children programs which provide free hot meals to underfed ghetto youngsters. Recently, most of their energies have had to go into legal defense activities to protect themselves against further repression.

A most significant variety of revolutionary nationalism is that of the black workers who have formed caucuses and movements to challenge the racism of both industry and the trade union movement. One such group is the League of Revolutionary Black Workers, a confederation of "revolutionary union movements" in Detroit, the largest of which is the Dodge Revolutionary Union Movement (DRUM). DRUM was started in 1968 by a group of young black automotive workers. The response to the formation of a union group to address itself specifically and militantly to the problems of black workers was so great that a number of groups were formed in other automobile plants and even in nonrelated occupations such as clerical and hospital work. At the union level, the League fights to achieve and maintain safe and secure working conditions for black workers, to end on-the-job harassment by white union representatives, to gain political control over locals where black workers constitute a majority, and to secure black community control over the expenditure of union funds. The League has made such an impact on union politics that at a recent UAW local's election even the most moderate slate included a few black candidates.

The League actively involves itself in the community at every level, from supporting the organization of high school students and parents' groups to challenging repressive law-and-order legislation in the local government to supporting militant black candidates for public office. The League takes a revolutionary position on foreign affairs, supporting the liberation struggles of the Vietnamese and other Third World peoples. A leaflet containing DRUM demands called for an equalization of the hourly wage rate in Chrysler plants throughout the world, including those in South Africa.

Unlike the Panthers, whose members are primarily high school, college, and ghetto street youth, and unlike the primarily middle-class black caucuses in the professions—teachers, social workers, scholars—the League of Revolutionary Black Workers consists of workers employed in strategically significant sectors of the American economy and therefore has a kind of leverage that few black groups have been able to obtain. The continued growth of such groups in black communities across the nation will be a key factor in determining the direction of social change in Black America.

Stokely Carmichael's return from Guinea in early 1970 after living and working for a year with Kwame Nkrumah, the exiled President of Ghana, has once again made pan-Africanism a live issue among many blacks. In speeches, interviews, and a journal article,[23] Carmichael stressed that black Americans are Africans and should learn to consider themselves such and that white Americans are Europeans and should be called such. Carmichael's key emphases are first on the necessity for a land base from which to launch a revolution to liberate all of Africa and end the oppression of all Africans throughout the world and second on the need for a strong leader for this pan-Africanist revolution. Carmichael sees Ghana as the land base and Nkrumah as the leader; therefore, his first priority in terms of action is to work to reinstate Nkrumah as head of the Ghanaian government. Despite some passing remarks about the necessity for struggle within the United States, it is crystal clear that Carmichael, like Garvey before him, has chosen Africa as the battleground where the destiny of Black America will be determined.

Conclusion

Black nationalism remained a force in Black America after the decline of the UNIA despite its temporary eclipse during the 1940's and 1950's. The revival of black nationalism at a higher level than ever before was a hallmark of the late 1960's. Cultural nationalism, territorial separatism, religious

---

[23] Stokely Carmichael, "Pan-Africanism—Land and Power," *Black Scholar* 1 (November 1969).

nationalism, bourgeois nationalism, revolutionary nationalism, and pan-Africanism all had their advocates. This revival continues to manifest several characteristics that distinguish it from the earlier periods when black nationalism was the dominant ideology: the depth and intensity of nationalist feeling, the pervasiveness of black-consciousness ideologies among all classes of blacks, the willingness of influential economic and political leaders to grant the legitimacy of black nationalism, the sharing of ideologies with some African nations, the large number of blacks, especially among the youth, who reject the legitimacy of American values and institutions, and the acceptance of the right of armed self-defense and retaliation.

These characteristics indicate that Black America has successfully completed the ideological shift from a belief in integration and individual success to a belief in the importance of political and economic power and in collective responsibility. One can no longer justify leaving the ghetto and rejecting the values and culture of the lower classes by saying that one is "setting an example" or reflecting "credit on the race." Now a middle-class black has to justify his individual success by such collective criteria as, "Is it relevant?" "Does it serve the black community?" "Does it help the brothers on the block?"

Viewing the recent history of Black America in a larger context, one can see that the revival of black nationalism in the 1960's indicates the onset of decolonization. For the first time in the history of the United States, there is a full-blown black nationalism with nationalist leadership and nationalist ideologies and organizations. It is true that most of the leaders are still middle-class and that bourgeois nationalism and cultural nationalism predominate. But all strata of Black America and the political and economic leaders of White America realize that blacks must have a larger measure of self-determination if the nation as presently constituted is to survive. The attainment of specific black nationalist goals—whether a separate nation, black capitalism, or the overthrow of the West—lies in the future if it is to occur at all. Black America, now aware and confident, will no longer tolerate a colonial status. The rallying cry for blacks from Jesse Jackson's Operation Breadbasket to revolutionary nationalists and pan-Africanists is "It's Nation Time." The history of black nationalism since Garvey is the history of their coming to this awareness and their gaining this confidence.

Prospects for the Future

ST. CLAIR DRAKE

St. Clair Drake, professor of sociology at Stanford University, is coauthor with Horace R. Cayton of *Black Metropolis: A Study of Negro Life in a Northern City* (Harcourt, 1945). His many writings on the socioeconomic life of black Americans will soon be augmented by the publication of *Black Diaspora*, a comparative study of Africans throughout the New World. In the essay that follows, Mr. Drake explores the courses America's racial situation may take in the coming years. Suggesting that the emphasis of black action changed substantially in 1964, he analyzes racial developments in the last two decades with a focus on the events of the late 1960's and early 1970's and weighs the ends and means black Americans may adopt in the future.

No American, black or white, can escape the haunting presence of the Dream. Dr. Martin Luther King, possessed by it as he was, stirred the hearts of tens of thousands in the summer of 1963 during the March on Washington. That ritual of reaffirmation culminated before the shrine of a martyred President who himself had harbored serious doubts as to whether the ex-slaves he had helped to free should allow themselves to dream the Dream. A century later, those assembled before his statue still dreamed it: eloquently and passionately, Dr. King evoked the prospect of a day to come when white children and black children would walk hand in hand over the hillsides of Alabama, happy and secure in their friendship, oblivious to the social appraisal that previous generations had made of the differences in the color of their skins, the texture of their hair, and the cut of their features. But, less than five years later, those whom Southern-born novelist Lillian Smith had called the Killers of the Dream killed King. Even before the assassin's bullet cut him down, some black leaders warned that his dream was a mirage. After his death only a few black leaders continued to speak out openly in favor of the Dream. Was the Dream, like the great dreamer, *dead?* Or had it just become, in the words of poet Langston Hughes, a "dream deferred"?

Integration, Separation, or Pluralism?

The National Advisory Commission on Civil Disorders, in its report to the President on the underlying causes of the ghetto disturbances of 1967, expressed alarm over what it perceived as a dangerous drift toward two separate societies, one white, one black.[1] Since the members of the commission must have known that there never was a time in American history when there were *not* two separate societies, they were probably reacting to expressions of black skepticism and cynicism with regard to what was usually referred to as integration. During the decade of rapid desegregation of public facilities in the South (1955–1964), many people, black and white, spoke and acted as though they thought the Dream was about to be realized. A mood of euphoria had been created among interracial groups; they marched together and went to jail together, singing "We Shall Overcome"—and some died together.

However, it was evident by 1967 that large groups of Afro-Americans and some very influential black leaders had lost faith in either the validity of the Dream or the possibility of its realization. The rate of desegregation had been so slow; discrimination remained so persistent, even in some areas of life where segregation had been eliminated; and social and economic problems were so critical that black Americans had begun to question the desirability of a major expenditure of their time and effort in pursuit of the Dream.

Alternative dreams had always been a part of the black experience in the United States: Back to Africa visions presented by Paul Cuffee, Martin R. Delany, and Marcus Garvey; "exoduster" hopes from "Pap" Singleton's Kansas expedition to Mr. Muhammad, calling upon the government to give land to "the Lost-Found Nation in this Wilderness of North America"; or the Marxist version of integration within some future socialist Utopia.[2] The number of Afro-Americans responding to the charismatic leader who espoused such dreams depended upon the general state of race relations and socioeconomic conditions of the specific period. Only in the years immediately following World War I did a genuine mass movement arise as Garvey called upon "the beloved and scattered millions" to unite around the slogan "Africa for the Africans, at Home and Abroad!" Then, from the mid-1920's to the 1950's, the masses seemed immune to dreams.

From the late nineteenth century to the outbreak of World War II most black Americans accepted the doctrine "separate but equal" as the best of a bad bargain. The United States government had adopted it as an official

---

[1] *The Report of the National Advisory Commission on Civil Disorders* (New York: Bantam Books, 1968), p. 1.

[2] For a brief, comprehensive discussion of emigrationist sentiment and some of the associated movements and personalities, see August Meier, *Negro Thought in America, 1880–1915* (Ann Arbor: University of Michigan Press, 1963), pp. 271–74.

policy.[3] Afro-Americans continued to give allegiance to their own families and churches, and to voluntary associations that emphasized faith in education, hard work, and quiet pressure as the means by which their separate status would gradually become somewhat less unequal.

In 1954, the Supreme Court declared that enforced segregation in public educational institutions was a denial of the principle of equality. Then, in 1955, Southern black people chose a single issue upon which they were prepared to challenge law and custom in their region. They began to use nonviolent civil disobedience and the economic boycott to destroy patterns of segregation and discrimination in places of public accommodation and in public transportation. The National Association for the Advancement of Colored People (NAACP) had concentrated its efforts primarily upon securing favorable decisions before the Supreme Court. Now, new organizations emerged in the civil rights struggle. Leading what came to be called the Movement were the Southern Christian Leadership Conference (SCLC) and the Student Nonviolent Coordinating Committee (SNCC). Dr. Martin Luther King provided the Movement with an ideology and inspired his followers, black and white, with his own faith in an ultimate victory that would go far beyond mere desegregation. For the first time since Marcus Garvey stirred the black masses after World War I, a leader who symbolized a dream secured a large, disciplined, loyal following. This time, however, the dream was integration, not separation. For ten action-filled years, Afro-Americans seemed to display faith in the possibility of a future without segregation and discrimination, and perhaps even in an era of the brotherhood of man.[4]

By 1964, the desegregation of public facilities in the South had been virtually accomplished and members of the Movement began to focus upon another short-term issue of immediate concern to them—the removal of all obstacles to registration and voting. With the passage of the Voting Rights Act of 1965 the most urgent task became mobilizing to reap the fruits of the victory. The belief that in-group solidarity, not integration, was necessary for the maximization of political strength became widespread after 1964 when the Democratic national convention refused to seat the Mississippi Freedom Democratic party. Young militants who had been active in SNCC now raised the slogan "Black Power," and Stokely Carmichael lent assistance to leaders in Lowndes County, Alabama, in organizing a political party with the black panther as its symbol.[5]

---

[3] The decisive Supreme Court decision was *Plessy v. Ferguson* (1896), which upheld the legality of segregation in public transportation if equal accommodations were provided.

[4] For an account of the period that captures the mood as well as providing a graphic description of the action and Dr. King's role in it, see Louis E. Lomax, *The Negro Revolt* (New York: New American Library, 1962).

[5] The first systematic statement of the black power concept was made in Stokely Carmichael and Charles V. Hamilton, *Black Power: The Politics of Liberation in America* (New York:

Dr. King felt that this separatist emphasis was inconsistent with the goals visualized in the Dream and began to give his primary attention to organizing the poor, irrespective of their race, creed, or color, for a massive demonstration in Washington, D.C., to call attention to their needs. He plunged into the campaign against the War in Vietnam, too, because he felt the war was both a denial of the Dream and a barrier to concentration of national effort on behalf of the poor. He was assassinated during this period of reorientation of his efforts.

The new black power emphasis had wide appeal in the South but was usually placed within a context of the "dream deferred," as a necessary step in the movement toward it. The concept also won acceptance in the North, where the low-income population of the ghettos had never been gripped by enthusiasm for the Dream, having been much more sympathetic to the views of the Black Muslims and of Malcolm X even while the Movement was winning substantial victories in the South.[6] The Southern Civil Rights movement had brought them no surcease of police brutality or of exploitation by landlords and merchants. A few nonviolent attempts to integrate neighborhoods and schools adjacent to black communities only accelerated the flight of white people to the suburbs. The ghettos grew larger and larger and the public schools within them more and more unsatisfactory. Unemployment rates, especially for the young, remained high. Black consciousness was heightened among a large segment of the youth throughout the 1950's as a "cult of Africa" grew up, one aspect of a vicarious identification with Africans who were struggling for independence. This cult was eventually assimilated into the much more widespread "cult of soul" that had as its defiant slogan "Black Is Beautiful."[7] Ghetto leaders began to transform black consciousness into black power with movements for community control of economic and political institutions, the schools, and the police.

The news media had a tendency to equate the black power demand with violence and to associate it with the ghetto outbursts in Harlem, Philadelphia,

---

Random House, 1967). It was a moderate, low-keyed appeal for black solidarity. See especially pp. 98–121.

[6] See Elijah Muhammad, *Message to the Blackman* (Chicago: Muhammad Mosque of Islam No. 2, n.d.), pp. 217–18, and Archie Epps, ed., *The Speeches of Malcolm X at Harvard* (New York: William Morrow, 1969), pp. 127–31.

[7] See Ulf Hannerz, "The Rhetoric of Soul: Identification in Negro Society," in August Meier and Elliott Rudwick, eds., *The Making of Black America* (New York: Atheneum, 1969), pp. 481–92. Evidence of the restricted penetration of the cult of Africa is suggested in a recent poll, in which only 45 percent of respondents reported liking Afro natural hair styles and only 35 percent, *dashikis;* on the other hand, 54 percent felt Afro-Americans have a "special soul." (*Newsweek,* 30 June 1969, p. 22.) An analysis of the psychological changes among segments of the black population in the North that led to the acceptance of black power ideology is presented with insight by Larry Neal in "New Space: The Growth of Black Consciousness in the Sixties," in Floyd B. Barbour, ed., *The Black Seventies* (Boston: Porter Sargent, 1970), pp. 9–31.

and Rochester in 1964, Watts in 1965, and in cities throughout the country during the "hot summer" of 1967. But these were spontaneous eruptions, not a new ideological thrust. Influential members of the American "Establishment," however, recognized the historic significance of the black power upsurge and were quick to accept a moderate version of it in an attempt to co-opt the movement for nonmilitant ends, such as the development of black capitalism.[8] Some philanthropic foundations proceeded to fund organizations seeking community control of ghetto schools or to encourage voter registration and community development. The National Advisory Commission on Civil Disorders, on the other hand, not only expressed concern over the more militant expressions of the black power idea but even seemed to deplore the most moderate interpretations of it:

> The Black Power advocates of today consciously feel that they are the most militant group in the Negro protest movement. Yet they have retreated from a direct confrontation with American society on the issue of integration and, by preaching separatism, unconsciously function as an accommodation to white racism. Much of their economic program, as well as their interest in Negro history, self-help, racial solidarity and separation is reminiscent of Booker T. Washington. The rhetoric is different, but the programs are remarkably similar.[9]

A report of another government commission, released in 1970, makes a more accurate assessment of the black power thrust, an orientation that will continue to affect race relations in the 1970's:

> The notion that advocates of black autonomy have "retreated from a direct confrontation with white society on the issue of integration" is misleading. It ignores both the fact that the decline of the goals of the early civil rights movement came about as the direct result of societal, and especially governmental, inaction, and that blacks may be expected to modify their tactics after decades of such inaction. It also fails to appreciate the fact that black protest now aims, at least in theory, at a transformation of American institutions rather than inclusion into them. . . . This is not separatism, nor is it racism. Militant leaders from Malcolm X to Huey P. Newton have stressed the possibility of coalitions with white groups whose aim is radical social change. . . . For the most part the new black stance is better described as a kind of militant

---

[8] The first national black power conference was convened in Newark in the summer of 1967 under the leadership of an Episcopal minister with financial support from white industrialists. One of the participants, Chuck Stone, subsequently published *Black Political Power in America* (Indianapolis: Bobbs-Merrill, 1968).

[9] *Report of the National Advisory Commission,* pp. 232–35. In sections labeled "Black Power," "Old Wine in New Bottles," and "The Meaning," this study noted that, "having become a household phrase, the term generated intense discussion of its real meaning, and a broad spectrum of ideologies and programmatic proposals emerged."

pluralism, in which not whites, but traditional politics and politicians of both races, are rejected.[10]

As perceptive as this comment is, it obscures two facts. First, some groups advocating black autonomy *are* separatist—the conservative Black Muslims and the militant Republic of New Africa, for instance, both demand territory within which to build the black nation. The Black Panthers, on the other hand, feel that blacks, Mexican-Americans, Puerto Ricans, and poor whites should organize separately but work together closely for a revolution resulting in a socialist society in which individuals and groups will have free choice as to whether they do or do not wish to retain ethnic and racial solidarities. Second, a concept of pluralism exists among black Americans that is not of the Panther revolutionary variety, and that is likely to be more significant during the next decade than either black nationalist separatism or a pluralism that rejects conventional politics.

As the 1970's began, the black power emphasis was being included in a concept of pluralism that could evolve into a satisfying compromise between total integration (for which few Americans, black or white, express any enthusiasm) and complete ethnic and racial separatism. Pluralism involves positive acceptance of the fact that many members of ethnic groups may wish to preserve their sense of ethnic identity and to share in some aspects of their subculture carried by families, churches, and voluntary associations composed of ethnic members only, without necessarily wanting the concentration of all group members in separate geographical areas. While complete cultural assimilation to the white majority's norms and values would not be expected, structural integration on a basis of complete equality into the nation's economic and political system would be an important goal. Discrimination or forced segregation in public accommodations and institutions would not be tolerated. Persons who wished to participate in interethnic and interracial friendship groups and associations or to intermarry would be free to do so, these being defined as private matters and individual rights. Some individuals would choose to play roles in both their group of racial and ethnic origin and in interracial or interethnic groups.[11]

Such a concept of pluralism is consistent with the aspirations of the major-

---

[10] Jerome H. Skolnick, *The Politics of Protest: A Report Submitted by the Task Force on Violent Aspects of Protest and Confrontation of the National Commission on the Causes and Prevention of Violence* (New York: Simon & Schuster, 1970), pp. 169–70. Chapter 4 presents a comprehensive analytical study of militancy within Afro-American communities since 1960.

[11] A discussion of pluralism between Ralph Ellison, J. Saunders Redding, Oscar Handlin, Talcott Parsons, and Everett Hughes is presented in the transcript of the American Academy Conference on the Negro American (Boston, 14–15 May 1965), in "The Negro American," *Daedalus* 95, no. 1 (Winter 1966): 402–15.

ity of Afro-Americans and would probably eventually win acceptance from all but the most racist minority of whites. It falls far short of the kind of society envisioned in the Dream but is a movement in that direction and away from the separate-but-equal model that never assured any measure of equality. It also makes possible the organization of broad united fronts within black communities involving separatist Black Muslims as well as NAACP integrationists and electoral campaigns such as that which elected a black mayor in Newark, New Jersey, and it may portend the crystallization in the South of large pockets of black power organized into varied kinds of coalitions with whites. Small militant black groups will, of course, continue to operate outside this framework, and some of them will not be nonviolent. "Taking care of business" assumes many forms.

"TCB"—Taking Care of Business [12]

After widespread violent outbursts of anger following Dr. King's assassination, black communities settled down to taking care of business on the local level. With two martyred charismatic leaders in their graves—Malcolm and Martin—other types of leaders became dominant. The first few years of the 1970's are likely to be devoted to consolidating the gains of the previous two stormy decades rather than to dramatic mass movements. Black theoreticians in 1970 were insisting that the integration versus separation dichotomy poses a spurious issue that could seriously divide the black community, and were forming united fronts that included Black Muslims as well as NAACP leaders in pursuit of limited local goals. To them, the issue is liberation. [13] Maximizing the high black power potential in the South and rehabilitating Northern ghettos assume priority. A mood of optimism prevails within the ranks of virtually all black Southerners and among the 70 percent of Northern ghetto dwellers who are above the poverty line. There is wide consensus as to what is necessary if conditions are to continue to get better, as most Afro-Americans seem convinced they inevitably will. Certain goals are clear: [14]

1. Achievement of parity with whites in occupation and income
2. Access to adequate housing within or outside black neighborhoods, to reduce the high proportion of blacks now living in poverty areas

---

[12] Stokely Carmichael devotes a chapter to this concept (or slogan) in Carmichael and Hamilton, *Black Power.*

[13] See *Ebony*'s special issue "Which Way Black America? Integration, Separation, Liberation?" (August 1970).

[14] A 1969 Gallup poll reported that 3 out of 5 black Americans felt that their jobs and their children's opportunities had improved since 1964. Over 50 percent had secured better housing. Two-thirds expected things to be "still better" during the next five years. Only 22 percent were "satisfied," and nearly 60 percent thought the pace of change was too slow.

3. Closing of the educational gap, as measured by median years of schooling for both sexes and the proportion of youths completing high school, four years of college, and graduate schooling
4. Drastic reduction of differentials in morbidity and mortality rates
5. Strengthening of the entire black institutional structure—family, church, schools, voluntary associations, and businesses
6. Maximization of the present black power potential, both economic and political
7. Improvement of the reputation of the ethnic group

These are interlinked objectives that feed back on each other.

Seen from the black perspective, the primary task in the struggle for liberation during the decade 1970–1980 is to move as far as possible toward achieving group parity with white fellow citizens in median income and proportion of men and women employed and firmly established above the poverty line. Attainment of this goal involves getting at least a proportionate share (11 to 12 percent) of jobs within the major occupational categories, at the same pay as whites, or concentrating upon movement into selected well-remunerated fields. With money in their pockets, Afro-Americans can take care of other kinds of business themselves. Achievement of this goal depends upon two interrelated processes: (1) utilizing economic and political pressure to force access to jobs and training for jobs where the opportunity is now denied, and (2) overcoming handicaps imposed by inadequate formal schooling—including improving predominantly black educational institutions at all levels, taking advantage of opportunities provided in integrated schools, and inspiring, motivating, and retooling those who have been crippled by inferior schooling or the direct or indirect impact of a racist society upon their lives. Most black Americans assume that these tasks can be carried out within the system, but only as the system is drastically reformed in the process.[15]

Leaders were suggesting during 1970 that the liberation process involves a mix of integration and separation, depending upon time, place, and circum-

---

Jobs, education, and housing were pinpointed as problems for future action in that order of priority. ("Report from Black America," *Newsweek,* 30 June 1969, p. 19.) A Harris poll the next year reported 64-percent agreement that "things are getting better than they were four to five years ago." ("Black America 1970," *Time,* 6 April 1970, p. 29.)

[15] A surprising 63 percent in the 1970 Harris poll agreed that "the system is rotten and has to be changed completely for blacks to be free." It is doubtful, however, that the overthrow of the democratic free enterprise system was what they had in mind, but rather the system of race relations as they perceived and experienced it. Over 90 percent felt that "real progress" would come from "getting more blacks better educated," "starting more black-owned businesses," and "electing more blacks to public office." But 80 percent also did not believe that local police "apply the law equally," two-thirds believing that "police are against blacks" and three-fourths that local police are "dishonest." On the other hand, the federal judiciary received a high vote of confidence. (*Time,* 6 April 1970, p. 28.)

stance. They were reminding Black America that neither Stokely Carmichael nor Malcolm X repudiated total integration as a long-term goal; both simply insisted that the immediate problem was one of how to maximize group solidarity in order to "TCB."[16] The separation versus integration dichotomy is misleading in another sense, too, for "integration" is a word used with multiple shades of meaning. Sometimes it refers to cultural assimilation and sometimes to social relations. If confined to the latter context, it is obvious that the extent of integration varies from one extreme—that of the economic system, where it has always been the rule—to the other—that of family and kinship structure, where it has been virtually tabooed by the white majority. Residential integration has, until recent decades, been more acceptable in the South than in the North, while political integration has been acceptable in the North but not in the South. The significant problems are how, when, where, and under what conditions Afro-Americans and white Americans are integrated, and in what sectors black Americans will in the future demand more of it and fight for it as one aspect of their struggle for liberation.

Integration with full equality is the only acceptable kind of integration. Black Americans have always been integrated in work situations, although not on a basis of full equality. When most black Americans work in factories, offices, homes, and warehouses, on docks, trains, and boats, and in numerous other situations, they are in constant interaction with whites. But the general pattern has been one in which they occupy positions subordinate to those occupied by whites. It is certain that the pressure for more and better jobs and for dignity on the job will not be relaxed. The issue was joined in 1941 when A. Philip Randolph organized the March on Washington that resulted in President Roosevelt's issuance of the executive order establishing the Fair Employment Practices Commission. Thirty years of experience have proved that employment victories can be won. The most dramatic changes came in the North during the 1950's and 1960's when a massive breakthrough into the white-collar sector occurred, laying the economic base for a new middle class: youthful, self-confident, and competent, moving with ease in the white world of work; resentful over barriers to the rental and purchase of housing in a free and open market; and on the whole quite unconcerned about integration into white church, family, and associational structures

---

[16] It is significant that while most Afro-Americans told the Gallup pollsters mentioned in footnote 14 that they approve of racial solidarity, black capitalism, and the mystique of "soul," at least 7 out of 10 respondents said they "would rather send children to an integrated school" and would "rather live in an integrated neighborhood." A similar proportion said they did *not* think "Negroes will make more progress by running their own schools, businesses, and living in their own neighborhoods." Less than 1 in 4 approved of a separate nation. (*Newsweek*, 30 June 1969, p. 20.) Conceding the possibility of some bias in the sample, and taking into account differences by age and region, the integrationist wish is still probably stronger than most black nationalists consider desirable. It is, however, the "dream deferred" and not something to assign highest priority to.

—yet insistent upon the right of any individual who wished to associate across racial lines in these areas to do so. No comparable changes at the white-collar level occurred in the South, so the 1970's are likely to see increased pressure for an expansion of such opportunities there, especially for black women, who are now disproportionately represented among domestic and personal servants. It is inconceivable that a vigorous fight will not be launched by Southern black youth to attain economic parity with black people in other regions.

An appetite has been whetted for the higher-status and higher-paid jobs, and this is reflected in greatly expanded enrollment in high schools, community colleges, and universities. Only in the construction industry has serious direct confrontation been necessary to win entry into specific occupations, although undoubtedly the ghetto explosions between 1964 and 1969 spurred on "merit employment." There is a tendency now to think in terms of targets of 10 to 20 percent—of fighting for the expected or porportionate share of employment in every occupational category within specific local areas.

One result of the new occupational roles played by Afro-Americans during the 1960's was a rise in median income and a reduction in the proportion of individuals and families below the poverty line. By 1970, about three-fourths of all Afro-Americans were above the poverty line, but below it was a restive 25 percent determined not to endure its lot in silence and developing a more explosive potential than it has in the past. Within its ranks was a core of unemployed and subemployed youth, educated usually through a few years of high school. Programs such as Upward Bound, Higher Horizons, and Job Corps were constantly feeding the more ambitious and disciplined individuals into a system of formal education inculcating middle-class consumption standards and status goals. Black males were finishing high school in the same ratio as black females. Black Americans will certainly resist any attempts by conservative, economy-minded politicians to close these channels of mobility.

One optimistic assessment of the future made by the black member of the Federal Reserve Board, Andrew Brimmer, notes that between 1960 and 1970 the proportion of employed Afro-Americans in professional and technical pursuits increased from 6 percent to 10 percent and is likely to increase to 12 percent by 1980, leaving only a 3-percent differential between them and their white counterparts. The overwhelming majority of these people are now in, and will be in, integrated work situations. Only 3 percent of employed blacks were managers, proprietors, and officials in 1970, and Brimmer foresees only a slight increase in this proportion, with a 12-percent differential persisting between blacks and whites in these roles.[17] Only an

---

[17] Andrew F. Brimmer, "The Economic Outlook and the Future of the Negro College" (Memorandum prepared for a conference sponsored by *Daedalus*, "The Future of Predominantly Black Colleges," Boston, 2–3 October 1970), pp. 17–21.

expansion of the black institutional structure is likely to change this forecast. A steady decline in the proportion of the self-employed is likely, however, raising the serious question of whether the emphasis upon encouraging *small* black business does not lead into a blind alley except in very highly specialized areas. Brimmer's projections are based upon the assumption that the economy will continue to expand, stimulated by a population increase that will generate an increasing demand for services—medical, educational, recreational, and welfare-related—but require a decreasing proportion of blue-collar workers. It is in these service fields that individuals from among those now in high school are most likely to move upward if they can secure the training. Brimmer also assumes a rational approach to postwar adjustment. A more pessimistic perspective is presented by Arnold Schuchter in his critical analysis of James Forman's Black Manifesto, for he assumes that the military-industrial complex has so distorted the economy that projections based upon assumptions of "normality" may be illusory.[18]

The expansion of economic opportunity in the North has been related only in part to the private sector. The first significant white-collar gains after World War I were made in social work, school teaching, post office and city hall positions, and other occupations where either political patronage was involved or political power could enforce some degree of fairness in civil service appointments. The wielding of political power involved an intricate balancing of separation and integration: a high enough concentration of black voters for them to get into a bargaining position and an insistence that precinct and ward positions must go to blacks only; then the use of the "clout" to elect blacks to "mixed" legislative bodies and to demand positions in integrated segments of the political machine. Occasionally a black candidate won by an appeal to a mixed constituency, but this was not the rule.

During the 1960's, however, several significant victories—the election of a black senator in Massachusetts and of black mayors in Cleveland and Newark—portended new possibilities. Most prestigious of the posts held by black Americans are those of Supreme Court Justice Thurgood Marshall and Federal Reserve Board Governor Andrew Brimmer. Such appointments were "political" in the sense that they were certainly made in the hope of impressing the black electorate, although they were not patronage payoffs and the men selected were eminently well qualified. Throughout the moderately high levels of the federal government other appointed black men and women were engaged in tasks that ranged from race relations work to expert services that had nothing to do with racial matters at all, such as the ambassadorship to Sweden. Black congressmen, while primarily responsible to black constituencies, also assumed wider responsibilities. For instance, Adam Clayton Powell was chairman of the House Committee on Labor and Education, and

---

[18] Arnold Schuchter, *Reparations: The Black Manifesto and Its Challenge to White America* (Philadelphia: J. B. Lippincott, 1970), pp. 115–41.

Congressman William L. Dawson was chairman of the powerful Government Operations Committee. Senator Edward Brooke, on the other hand, although not elected by a predominantly black constituency, has felt some responsibility to play the role of spokesman for the race. A similar pattern was becoming manifest in metropolitan areas, North and South. Black mayors in Newark and Cleveland were "integrated" mayors, not black power mayors, and the black head of the school board in Atlanta served the whole city. At any tier above the ward and precinct level, *shared* power, not black power, is mandatory; serving the general welfare, not blacks alone, must be the norm.

The most urgent necessity in the South is to use the opportunities opened up by the Voting Rights Act of 1965 to acquire black power at local levels —in some instances, entire towns or counties. In early 1971, blacks controlled only 4 of the 101 Southern counties with black voting-age majorities, and they held only 40 of the 1,805 state legislative seats, although they make up about 20 percent of the population in the South. The Alabama elections of 1971 indicate the possibilities latent in independent political organization. The black National Democratic party of Alabama captured control of Greene, Macon, and Lowndes counties and elected one person to the state legislature; yet 15 of the state's 67 counties are black. As more and more local pockets of black power are consolidated, they will become the bases from which political leaders can bargain for a share of power at the state level (no state has a black majority). The socially conscious young black electorates will increasingly demand more than "jobs for the boys" from these black politicians. They will expect progressive leadership on a wide variety of social issues.

The desire to maximize black power is inconsistent with a vigorous effort to deconcentrate the black population, to foster residential integration. "Electing more blacks to public office" was rated by 92 percent of respondents to a Harris poll in 1970 as "necessary for real progress," yet 74 percent of the individuals in a Gallup poll sample the previous year had said they would "rather live in an integrated neighborhood." There is no pressure to reconcile this attitudinal inconsistency, however, for whatever the subjective wishes of blacks may be, white behavior shows no changes that would seem to lead toward residential desegregation. Washington, D.C., Atlanta, Gary, and Newark had become over 50 percent black by 1970. A score of cities will probably cross over the 50-percent line during the 1970's.[19] White America watches with apprehension as the unintended consequences of its own preferences and prejudices based upon race and class work themselves out relentlessly and inexorably in metropolitan areas. The white middle class has drifted to the suburban "ring" and left the inner city to the poor and the minorities. In 1970 over half of all Americans were living in suburbs. White America cannot have its cake and eat it too. There is no evidence of a will to

---

[19] See *Report of the National Advisory Commission,* pp. 390–92. Some of the cities involved and some implications of the shift toward a black majority are discussed.

solve this contradiction. If America wants residential exclusiveness it will get ghettos. Ghettos will inevitably generate black power—political and economic. Black Americans have decided to maximize that power as their most effective instrument in transforming ghettos into livable communities.

By Any Means Necessary?

The integration-separation antithesis does not reflect the contemporary American reality or the probable direction of movement, nor does the violence-nonviolence dichotomy. Except for Dr. King, a minority of his most devoted followers, and some of the members of CORE, few black Americans in the Civil Rights movement had a religious or ethical commitment to absolute nonviolence. (Although Garrison and Thoreau held such views, there is no record of any prominent black abolitionist who did. Most of them preferred to trust the "lightning of His terrible swift sword," and John Brown and Nat Turner, as well as the black men in blue, were cherished as the instruments of liberation.) It is a tribute to King's personal qualities that he was able to keep young militants of SNCC within the framework of the nonviolent movement from 1960 until he was assassinated, for they accepted the method only as a tactic, not as an ethical principle. It is not surprising, therefore, that they later proclaimed the principle "Any Means Necessary," which most Afro-Americans have always really believed in: tempered of course by the caveat that the means have some chance of getting results without bringing down disaster upon them.

Dr. King insisted that those in his movement not destroy property nor become participants in fights, the throwing of objects, or the use of firearms, but he did *not* refuse to accept governmental armed force to protect his nonviolent demonstrators or to coerce his opponents. Nor did he denounce the Deacons for Defense, though he stated his own personal aversion to their protecting him. With him it seemed to be a matter of how "legitimate" the violence was.

The street people of the Northern ghettos seemed to take the position that nonviolence so defined might be a proper and adequate technique for the South, but not for them—if it included a ban on destruction of property. They showed how they felt during the "hot summers" of 1964, 1965, and 1967, as well as in their reaction to King's death.

King's method did achieve its objective in the South: desegregation. The wholesale destruction of property and the looting in the North achieved something, too. It made the nation face up to the facts of ghetto life. By 1969, however, the Northern masses themselves seemed to have decided, at least temporarily, that it was to their advantage to "cool it." Meanwhile, some black militants had begun to experiment with other violent forms of attack such as sniping and bombing.

It would be hazardous to speculate about possible patterns of violence in the future. One can only say with assurance that there is no evident widespread revulsion in black communities against those who are alleged to be developing guerrilla warfare tactics, and there is a firm belief that both violence and nonviolence have been factors in bringing about favorable changes during the 1960's. This attitude must be taken into account.

A 1970 Harris poll reported that 77 percent of the black respondents in the sample felt that continuous pressure must be kept up to complete the work of black liberation in America, but 58 percent felt that the ultimate victory could be won without violence. (Age made little difference in the responses.)[20] Yet 40 percent of those interviewed in 1969 felt that riots had helped more than they had hurt, and an even larger proportion seemed to feel they were inevitable, 2 out of 3 respondents saying they "expected more riots in the future." The overwhelming majority, however, stated that they did not expect to participate themselves.[21]

In view of the recent shift in patterns of violence away from mass outbursts toward incipient urban guerrilla warfare, it is significant that over two-thirds of the black respondents in 1970 agreed with the statement "Panthers give me a sense of pride." Only one-fourth, however, said they agreed with Black Panther ideology. It is unlikely that many of these respondents were familiar with the details of the neo-Marxian analysis that Panther para-intellectuals are developing, a view that assigns the vanguard role in the American socialist revolution to the black *Lumpenproletariat*—the chronically unemployed, the criminals and ex-criminals, the street gangs and the juvenile delinquents— after they have become politicized. Those whom Marx rejected the Panthers say they will organize.[22] It is precisely their success in giving a sense of social concern to some of the people in this stratum that appeals to their black middle-class admirers, who also vicariously identify with the Panthers for their boldness and reckless courage. But insofar as the middle classes are even vaguely aware of the full implications of the Panther critique of the social order they must oppose the ideology. The Panthers assail black capitalists as being as reprehensible as white capitalists, and black preachers and politicians are defined as corrupt misleaders. Pride in the Panthers will likely evaporate quickly should they ever decide to bring pressure to bear upon established black community leaders and their organizations.

Admiration of the Panthers is also related to the automatic acceptance by black Americans of the legitimacy of the peculiarly American pattern of inducing social change. A certain amount of violence is viewed as a normal

---

[20] *Time,* 6 April 1970, pp. 28–29.

[21] *Newsweek,* 30 June 1969, p. 20.

[22] See Philip S. Foner, ed., *The Black Panthers Speak* (Philadelphia: J. B. Lippincott, 1970), pp. 108–16. Eldridge Cleaver wrote in the *Black Panther,* 6 June 1970, "Essentially what Huey [Newton] did was to provide the ideology and the methodology for organizing the Black Urban Lumpenproletariat. . . . Huey transformed the Black lumpenproletariat from the forgotten people at the bottom of society into the vanguard of the proletariat."

reaction to oppression, and liberals use it, or the probable outbreak of it, to shake the conservatives and the indifferent out of their smugness or complacency so that they will sanction reforms within the system.[23] The Panthers may think of their violence as leading toward revolution, but others see them only as a minority necessary to scare "Whitey." Such a view always takes into account the possibility of backlash and assesses the point at which violence may become counterproductive. There was widespread discussion within black communities during the late 1960's and throughout 1970 over the possibility of repressive measures being taken toward such groups as the Panthers and the Revolutionary Action Movement (RAM), but even moderate leaders had a tendency to oppose attempts to wipe out such groups by police violence or suspected legal frame-ups. This tolerance could, of course, disappear.

Alternatives and Perspectives

The Black Panthers visualize a future socialist America in which racism will no longer exist, a society to be brought into being by a violent revolution in which black people, Mexican-Americans, Amerindians, Puerto Ricans, and the white poor will participate. The Panthers comprise one small segment of the country's alienated youth, most of whom are not committed to violent revolution, but many of whom feel that radical social change will only come after a period of right-wing repression that, from their perspective, has already begun. During the late 1960's and the early 1970's white liberals were fearful that the excesses of the youth subculture and the violence of some left-wing groups would inevitably bring on such repression. They, unlike many of their black counterparts, also felt that if the government ever became convinced that Afro-Americans were serious when they spoke of "Any Means Necessary," the danger from the Right would increase. Negroes were prepared to risk it; whites weren't. White liberals urged the revival of the labor-liberal coalition, allied with disadvantaged minorities, to stop what they visualized as a drift toward fascism.

These fears were not the fantasies of political paranoids, for the emphasis of the Nixon-Agnew-Mitchell administration upon "law and order," its strategy of building a coalition upon those elements that constitute what they call Middle America—involving a "Southern strategy" that ignores the wishes of the black electorate—does have fascist potential. There is also an element of self-fulfilling prophecy in the behavior of militant activists, for if they escalate urban guerrilla warfare, they invite repressive legislation and provide a legitimate excuse for the right wing to take actions that have ends other

---

[23] See St. Clair Drake, "Urban Violence and Social Movements," in Robert H. Connery, ed., *Urban Riots: Violence and Social Change,* Columbia University, Proceedings of the Academy of Political Science, vol. 29, no. 1 (New York, 1968), pp. 13–24.

than the mere restoration of "law and order": the muzzling of criticism of imperialistic plundering at home and abroad; the enforcement of cultural conformity; and the preservation of entrenched power and privilege throughout the social system.

The process of disengagement from the war in Vietnam will test the strength of democratic institutions in the United States. If it involves widespread unemployment due to an unwillingness on the part of the federal government to plan carefully for peacetime reconversion and full employment; if federal aid to states and cities for welfare needs is not increased; if black ex-soldiers are subjected to employment discrimination and other forms of humiliation, then vigorous and violent expressions of discontent are likely. If such violence escalates and assumes political implications, it is not inconceivable that the federal government will resort to measures so extreme as to warrant the designation "fascist."

However, it is very unlikely that a consolidation of right-wing power (by what President Eisenhower once called the military-industrial complex) at the national level or in Northern and Western states would be explicitly anti-Negro. Even in the South, expressions of racism would be muted by the new codes of speech and conduct that became institutionalized during the 1960's, though more overt racism would be expressed there than in the North. In all regions, however, it is highly probable that an attempt would be made to make sure that all blacks (and members of other minorities) do not gravitate to the liberal left end of the political spectrum.

It is likely that at the nation's capital and in Northern states the power structure of a repressive right-wing government would install a token representation of conservative blacks in some high-level posts in army units, police forces, administrative cadres, and the judiciary. Attention had been given, by 1970, to strategies for incorporating some blacks into the milieu and mystique of Middle America. For instance, it is significant that when Daniel Patrick Moynihan made his widely publicized statement advocating "benign neglect," it was embedded in a position paper that emphasized the point that enough black Americans had now reached a middle socioeconomic level to build a new black-white coalition that would isolate black extremists. The Nixon administration's emphasis upon black capitalism was explicitly defined as an attempt to create a stratum that would have a stake in the system. The defense of "no-knock laws" and similar legislation is put in terms of protection for blacks, who suffer more from criminal depredations than do whites.

Most black leaders would probably oppose a repressive right-wing national government, but there are likely to be some who would feel that their own best interests would be served by it. The leaders of the black middle class in the North are in the position to make some profitable trade-offs with the Right. The tiny stratum that has become integrated into the upper levels of politics and business (and even into some suburban neighborhoods) can maintain its status and privileges by a clear, open repudiation of radicalism in all its forms and by its high visibility lend this country legitimacy and credibility in the eyes of the world. These Afro-Americans would be invaluable showpieces for a nation that cannot ignore its international relations, however right-wing it might be. That segment of the black middle class populating the inner cities in metropolitan areas such as Newark, Washington, Cleveland, and Chicago, among others, would be in a position to win merit and economic rewards for cooperating in the rounding up and detention of black militants whose pressure they would be feeling and resenting. Facing the fact that black capitalism will always be dependent on white industrial and commercial institutions, black businessmen could bargain for a larger "cut" through more franchises, deposits in local banks, and partnerships in ghetto enterprises. Ghetto politicians, in alliance with the police, could guarantee a good investment climate and function as agents of indirect rule, as tribal chiefs did in British colonies in Africa. Prosperous churches and voluntary associations within ghettos, as well as modest guaranteed family incomes, could create a level of personal satisfaction that would take the pressure off white suburbia. Black community control in middle-class hands would have its payoff to both blacks and whites, but would require rigid control of "militants" and "criminals." Black police and judges, instead of white officials, might be used to do the job, however, thus relieving white consciences.

Many black militants are convinced that they would be "ripped off first" during a period of severe repression, and that a policy of genocide would then be carried out against the entire black population, except for a few collaborators. They see nothing improbable in the bizarre, disastrous end depicted in the King Alfred extermination plan in John A. Williams' novel *The Man Who Cried I Am.* But to believe, as they do, that the ghettos will be cordoned off and masses of black men and women herded into vans en route to gas chambers in the deserts, or that mass executions will take place in Southern forests, swamps, and bayous, is to assume that what white Americans find easy to do in Southeast Asia they could also bring themselves to do on their own soil, and that they could get away with it. But even when race riots and lynchings were frequent genocide was never the goal.[24] The need for black labor, the basic American value structure, and the web of interpersonal ties between black and white people are likely to prevent such

---

[24] From the end of the Civil War until the outbreak of World War II, however, there was the hope and expectation in some circles that disease and constitutional debility would eliminate the black population. Thus, one prominent statistician, writing about thirty years after the end of the Civil War, expressed a prevalent point of view:

> The Negro is subject to a higher mortality rate at all ages, but especially so at the early age periods. . . . The natural increase in the colored population will be less from decade to decade and in the end a decrease must take place. It is sufficient to

wholesale slaughter in the future, even to provide a scapegoat during some national disaster. Genocide has become a convenient propaganda term, too loosely used, for very real evils that fall far short of the precise meaning of the term—persecution of the Black Panthers, the attack on the Jackson State College dormitory in 1970 by Mississippi state police, or indiscriminate shooting during ghetto rebellions. A roundup of the militant black minority is entirely possible, but this would not be genocide. The deliberate extermination of over twenty million black Americans is inconceivable.

Concern with the possibility of a right-wing drift was voiced by major television newscasters during the acrimonious election campaign of 1970. Over a year before such Establishment spokesmen used the term publicly, the Black Panthers had convened an "antifascist" conference, and members of both the old and new Left had begun to revive memories of the 1930's by supporting this Panther initiative. The present generation of concerned black college students will have to make the decision whether they wish to join such a coalition or to develop initiatives of their own, looking toward a coalition with the new breed of liberal—though not radical—white students as a means of preventing a victory for the Right. Students will not decide the issue, although they may play a crucial role during elections when liberal leaders are trying to mobilize support, in organizing progressive blocs within the two major political parties, or in forming new political parties.

It is not inconceivable that black individuals and black institutions will actually play a vanguard role in some future antifascist united front, not the role that the Black Panthers hope they will play in a future revolution. The willingness of whites to follow black leadership in a liberal coalition has been shown in the cases of Julian Bond and Charles Evers in the South and Ron Dellums in northern California. Arnold Schuchter, in suggesting an alternative to James Forman's concept of a black-led Marxist revolution, has outlined a bold plan for carrying out a program of reparations that he prefers to call redress. It includes suggestions for "Building New Communities in Negative Urban Space," "Transfer of Slum Ownership," "Breaking White Union Barriers," and "Redress [of] Financing Mechanisms." Central to the preparation of the public for such innovations is his concept of "Centers of National Reform." As he visualizes them, they would involve the building of a coalition of black and white students, with blacks as leaders. He states the main purposes of the centers as follows:

---

know that in the struggle for race supremacy the black race is not holding its own; and this fact once recognized, all danger from a possible numerical superiority of the race vanishes. (F. L. Hoffman, quoted in S. J. Holmes, *The Negro's Struggle for Survival* [Berkeley: University of California Press, 1937], pp. 15–16.)

In 1930, Dr. Raymond Pearl, a biologist, spoke of an "absolutely definite. . . . final extinction." (Raymond Pearl, quoted in Holmes, *The Negro's Struggle for Survival,* p. 16.)

(1) to prepare conversion plans and guidelines, operating in effect as "think tanks" for a reparations program in a peace economy; (2) to watch government policies and operations that support militarization at the expense of conversion to a peace economy; (3) to educate blacks and whites in changing the dominant institutions of our society in accordance with the goals of redress, with a special focus on universities; (4) to prepare plans for new cities and towns as well as for the renewal of existing urban communities, with an initial focus on opportunities in the South; (5) to play a key role in political mobilization and education in the South aimed at accelerating black acquisition of political power; (6) to attract the largest possible number of scientists, engineers and technicians displaced by a contracting war economy to teach in black colleges, to assist in preparing realistic conversion plans, new communities and the renewal of cities; (7) in general, to upgrade dramatically the cultural and educational opportunities of black colleges, in part for the purpose of attracting talented white students committed to the goals of redress; (8) to educate clergy from all religious denominations so that they can return to their churches as missionaries for the goals of redress; and (9) to provide a setting in which whites and blacks from diverse backgrounds, from the Black Panthers to Wall Streeters, can exchange ideas on national conversion policies and the innumerable problems involved in making American society livable for blacks and whites.[25]

In 1970 models for future action like Schuchter's had a very limited appeal to black Americans, for they were inclined neither to cast themselves in the role of trying to help America to save itself, nor to accept the degree of white leadership implied. They were concerned with what Vincent Harding, director of the Institute of the Black World, calls a Black Agenda, with taking care of business for themselves. Yet, the most broadly based movement in existence in 1970, the Southern Christian Leadership Conference, and the most highly publicized one, the Panthers, were both, however dissimilar they were in other respects, committed to the ultimate realization of the Dream as King dreamed it. And both held out an invitation to poor whites to join in the struggle for the goal, though very few accepted it. In fact, nearly all Afro-Americans, except for the most extreme black nationalists, have accepted the necessity of coalition formation after black groups are sure they have "defined themselves for themselves" and have "got themselves together." The determination of with precisely whom coalitions are formed involves a matter of principle, but the decision to form coalitions is primarily a matter

---

[25] Schuchter, *Reparations,* p. 150. This book was written in an attempt to suggest an alternative to James Forman's clear call for a Marxist solution to American difficulties, with black radicals in the vanguard—a statement made in the preamble to his Black Manifesto (adopted at the National Black Economic Development Conference, Detroit, 26 April 1969).

of timing. Being a numerical minority dictates the need for coalition politics. It does not necessarily imply acceptance of a Messianic vanguard role.

The working out of cooperative relations with white groups, on terms defined by blacks, was already becoming a trend in the early 1970's. However, structuring satisfactory relationships with any white Americans, after decades of insult and subordination to most of them, is a complex process. Sharpening boundaries is crucial for increasing group solidarity, but if pushed to a point that makes coalition politics impossible, it becomes self-defeating. It is also difficult to draw the line between the personal and the political, as current controversies over the acceptability of interracial marriage, dating, and even friendship indicate. The danger of psychological co-optation is ever present, and some of the revulsion against school desegregation and the frequent demands for a measure of separatism on predominantly white college campuses are rooted in this fear. Since the cults of Africa and soul have been made salable commodities by the opinion makers of the press, film, radio, television, and the record industry, and since black Americans now function in a diversity of new occupational roles and work settings, old derogatory stereotypes are rapidly disappearing, thus preparing white Americans for a new black modus vivendi. For the first time, black Americans may be able to decide how much integration they desire. One of the ongoing processes during the 1970's will be the evolution of new patterns of interracial behavior consistent with a pluralism that preserves group identity without destroying freedom of association and collaboration across ethnic lines.

The demand for black solidarity will continue as long as racism manifests itself in American society. There is increasing empirical evidence, however, to indicate that impermeable boundaries between blacks and whites cannot be maintained except within cults and sects with which only a small portion of the black population is ever likely to be affiliated. Both the economic system and the political system impose a high degree of integration in work situations, in occupational and professional associations, in conferences and public meetings connected with coalition politics, and in social and quasi-social extensions of these contacts. The line may hold in the more intimate relations of family, recreational associations, and religious congregations, but it will continuously be broken in economic and political situations, as it has been forcibly broken in transportation and public accommodations and in educational institutions at all levels in both the North and the South. It is likely, however, that the black caucus pattern will become the institutionalized expression of a group *presence* and will be considered normal in so-called integrated situations.

The internal structure of black communities underwent profound changes between 1950 and 1970 due to a dramatic rise in educational level, access to a wider range of occupations, and the growth of black consciousness. Whether viewed in terms of social class or of life style, the choices facing individuals became more complicated.[26] The conflict between wanting to get ahead as an individual and a sense of obligation to the black community has posed problems for ambitious and fortunate individuals. One social process among Afro-Americans that began in the 1950's will certainly continue on into the 1970's: the black population will remain split into a majority group above the poverty line and a smaller group that exhibits a poverty dependency syndrome. The black middle class has always been concerned about the fate of the black lower class, even when it showed its fear of that stratum by dissociating itself from it (as all upwardly mobile Americans have done with respect to lower strata whose life styles differ from theirs). The most effective way the professional classes can pay their dues is not by artificial and strained attempts to relate socially, but by the use of their power and influence as leaders in coalition with whites to mobilize public pressure: for a guaranteed annual income that will be no less than the annual median; for a comprehensive plan of free medical care; for low-cost housing and experimental cooperatives fitted to the needs of black communities. There was much talk of community development during the 1960's, but it often boiled down to planning for black capitalism as a panacea. In the long run that road is more likely to lead to the same kind of action against the black middle class that was visited upon "Whitey" in the ghettos during the 1960's.

The process of social differentiation has thrown up a small stratum of almost completely integrated Afro-Americans and will continue to do so. This is one of the results of tokenism at the top levels of industrial, commercial, and governmental bureaucracies. This group will have to be written off as black leaders, though they do bring prestige to the Afro-American ethnic group and function as pioneers on new frontiers. Many of them are in roles where their first concern must be for general interests rather than black interests (though these are not necessarily antithetical).

The elections in the fall of 1970 suggest that an increasing number of black individuals will be finding themselves in such a position. In California, a distinguished black educator was elected Secretary of Public Instruction in a state administration headed by a conservative governor. He, like Senator Brooke of Massachusetts, finds himself responsible to a broad interracial electorate and not primarily responsible to the black community. Another black candidate barely missed appointment as Secretary of State. A militant black leader won a congressional seat through the energetic work of white liberals and radicals, as well as black supporters. These electoral victories may portend a future situation in which the white public will respond to

---

[26] See St. Clair Drake and Horace R. Cayton, *Black Metropolis* (New York: Harcourt, 1970), for a social class conceptualization, and William McCord, John Howard, Bernard Friedberg, and Edwin Harwood, *Life Styles in the Black Ghetto* (New York: W. W. Norton, 1969).

black leadership as it has to Jewish leadership in the past—that is, choose an individual in whom they have confidence despite their prejudiced attitudes toward the ethnic group from which he comes, but remain disinclined to have any intimate social relationships with him or members of his ethnic group. This trend toward election of black leaders responsible to integrated constituencies may imply a need to develop a parallel group of equally competent leaders whose primary concern would be for the welfare of the black community, and a need to strengthen the black institutional structure, which can support them as adequately as the broader structure does the "integrated" Negroes.

Integrated blacks are always suspected of being bought off or co-opted, or of having sold out. Among them are a few executives of large corporations, professionals and administrators in the educational system, judges, ambassadors, foreign service career officers, mayors of Northern cities, and denominational representatives of "white" churches. There has been a widening of the area of interracial social participation through the friendship groups and voluntary associations associated with these occupations. Black professionals find new opportunities to take up residence outside ghettos in areas deemed appropriate for persons of their status, and some families do not pass up the chance to live in such a setting. Ironically, the expansion of this segment of the black upper class is taking place during a period when pressure from within the black community against integration is stronger than it has ever been. It is unlikely, however, that this attitude will deter many black Americans who have the chance to accept the rewards of that limited integration from doing so. What it is doing, and will continue to do, however, is to pressure those who have moved into these circles to give some attention to paying dues—finding ways to relate to the basic institutions of black communities. Most will respond positively, since except for the tiny minority who can pass for white, they are well aware that when the chips are down in this society, they are still black.

The interracial dynamics of the future will continue to be what they have been in the past, an ongoing process of restructuring *social* relationships between individuals and groups defined as white and black. For over two hundred years, the basic cleavage was between white masters and black slaves, but by the end of that long time span there were 500,000 free Negroes in interaction with about 4,000,000 slaves and various classes of whites other than the slaveholders. The second phase of the black experience extended over the eighty-five years between 1865 and 1950 during which relations between blacks and whites in the South were organized by a caste system while in the North a system of institutional racism[27] became a firmly

---

[27] Louis L. Knowles and Kenneth Prewitt, eds., *Institutional Racism in America* (Englewood Cliffs, N.J.: Prentice-Hall, 1969).

entrenched feature of an ethnic class system.[28] For the past two decades the system of race relations has been undergoing rapid and profound transformation. By the end of the 1960's the caste system in the South had been broken and institutional racism in the North was under persistent attack. New values and new social structures are in the making in both the North and the South. These basic changes were initiated by Afro-Americans themselves, who had determined to tolerate caste and institutional racism no longer and were willing to suffer and sacrifice in order to destroy the old order. The 1970's will be characterized by an intensified process of restructuring race relations.

The future grows out of a present that has been shaped by the past. The fate of black Americans during the 1970's will involve the development of trends that were very evident in the 1950's and 1960's as well as the unfolding of events whose seeds have already been sown but whose results are only barely discernible. A stream of technological innovations continuously generates changes in social relations and values as well as in the economic system. Changes in fertility, birth, and death rates have long-term repercussions on relations between ethnic groups and races.[29] These basic factors affecting relations between black and white Americans are reflected in the evanescent rhetoric of militants, right and left, but, amidst the flux and flow, great dreams remain as constants in the historic process, never being realized, but pulling mankind onward. The voices that evoke images associated with the dreams, inspiring men and leading them onward, pass away—but the dreams never die. Martin Luther King's dream was one of these. It will be an integral part of the American future.

---

[28] For an empirical study of what is here defined as an ethnic class system, see W. Lloyd Warner and Leo Srole, *The Social Systems of American Ethnic Groups* (New Haven, Conn.: Yale University Press, 1946). See also St. Clair Drake, "The Social and Economic Status of the Negro in the United States," *Daedalus* 94, no. 4 (Fall 1965): 771–72.

[29] The demographers' predictions referred to in footnote 24 were not realized, of course, and a population expert indicates why and projects a trend:

> Between 1940 and 1960, the birth rates of both whites and nonwhites rose with the postwar baby boom. Nonwhite fertility increased by 90 percent . . . while white fertility rose by 88 percent. . . . The great increase in nonwhite birth rates represents an astonishing reversal and occurred, interestingly enough, even while the Negro was becoming rapidly urbanized and metropolitanized. . . . The phenomenal increase in nonwhite fertility is a result of the striking rise in nonwhite urban fertility, largely because of the decrease in childlessness brought about by improved health, including reduction in venereal and debilitating diseases. . . . The nonwhite rate of population growth in 1960, if sustained, would double the Negro population in a little over thirty years. In contrast, the continuation of the 1960 white rate would require over fifty years before doubling the population. (Philip M. Hauser, "Demographic Factors in the Integration of the Negro," *Daedalus* 94, no. 4 [Fall 1965]: 848.)

5 SUGGESTIONS FOR FURTHER READING

Allen, Robert, *Black Awakening in Capitalist America: An Analytic History.* New York: Doubleday, 1969. ▪ An examination of the changing relationship between Black America and White America in the late 1960's.

Barbour, Floyd B., ed., *The Black Power Revolt**. Boston: Extending Horizons Books, 1968. ▪ A useful collection of documents and essays on the development and unification of the several kinds of black power.

"The Black Revolution," *Ebony* 24 (August 1969). ▪ A special issue devoted to summarizing the social and economic changes in black life in the 1960's.

Bracey, John H., Meier, August, and Rudwick, Elliott, eds., *Black Nationalism in America**. Indianapolis: Bobbs-Merrill, 1970. ▪ A volume of documents that reviews black nationalist movements and ideologies from 1787 to the present era.

Breitman, George, ed., *By Any Means Necessary**. New York: Pathfinders Press, 1970. ▪ A collection of the speeches and writings of Malcolm X.

Carmichael, Stokely, and Hamilton, Charles V., *Black Power: The Politics of Liberation in America**. New York: Random House, 1967. ▪ A discussion of the meaning of the slogan "Black Power" and the early impact of the movement.

Clarke, John Henrik, ed., *Malcolm X: The Man and His Times.* New York: Crowell-Collier, 1969. ▪ A volume of essays by black writers evaluating the importance of Malcolm X; includes some of his speeches and articles.

Cleage, Albert B., Jr., *The Black Messiah**. New York: Sheed & Ward, 1969. ▪ A black clergyman's call for black power Christianity.

---

* Available in paperback edition.

Cook, Mercer, and Henderson, Stephen E., eds., *The Militant Black Writer and His Roots in Africa and the United States.* Madison: University of Wisconsin Press, 1969. ▪ The best scholarly attempt to define and compare the phenomena of "soul," "negritude," and "African personality" as they appear in the writings of blacks in Africa, the United States, and the Caribbean.

Cruse, Harold, *The Crisis of the Negro Intellectual**. New York: William Morrow, 1967. ▪ A controversial interpretation of the aspirations of black intellectuals from the 1920's to the late 1960's.

Draper, Theodore, *The Rediscovery of Black Nationalism**. New York: Viking Press, 1970. ▪ A study that sees history as an argument against present-day black nationalists.

Essien-Udom, E. U., *Black Nationalism: A Search for an Identity in America**. Chicago: University of Chicago Press, 1962. ▪ The classic account of the Nation of Islam by a Nigerian scholar, who studies the movement with both sympathy and insight.

Fanon, Frantz, *Black Skin, White Masks**, trans. Charles Lam Markmann. New York: Grove Press, 1967. ▪ A discussion of the psychological problems that arise from denationalization.

Hill, Adelaide C., and Kilson, Martin, eds., *Apropos of Africa: Sentiments of American Negro Leaders on Africa from the 1800's to the 1950's.* New York: Humanities Press, 1969. ▪ An excellent collection of documents that reflect the attitudes black Americans have taken toward Africa.

Jones, LeRoi (Ameer Baraka), and Neal, Larry, eds., *Black Fire: An Anthology of Afro-American Writing**. New York: William Morrow, 1968. ▪ An anthology that provides a good sampling of the prose and poetry being produced by the new wave of black writers.

Killian, Lewis M., *Impossible Revolution: Black Power and the American Dream**. New York: Random House, 1968. ▪ An analysis that sees little chance for a reconciliation of the black socioeconomic thrust and the American ideal.

King, Martin Luther, Jr., *Where Do We Go From Here: Chaos or Community?**. New York: Harper, 1967. ▪ The late leader's call for peace in the midst of crisis.

Lincoln, C. Eric, *The Black Muslims in America**. Boston: Beacon Press, 1961. ▪ A sociologist's first-hand account of the internal structure of the Black Muslims and their influence on the black community.

Lynch, Hollis R., *Edward Wilmot Blyden: Pan-Negro Patriot, 1832–1912**. London: Oxford University Press, 1967. ▪ A scholarly biography of one of the most outstanding pan-African nationalists.

Malcolm X, *The Autobiography of Malcolm X**. New York: Grove Press, 1965. ▪ The classic narrative by Malcolm X of his life story (as told to Alex Haley).

Oppenheimer, Martin, *The Urban Guerrilla**. Chicago: Quadrangle Books, 1969.
▪ A unique look at the possibilities and limitations of armed domestic conflict in the United States.

Thompson, Vincent B., *Africa and Unity: The Evolution of Pan-Africanism.* New York: Humanities Press, 1969. ▪ An excellent historical and analytical discussion of pan-African efforts.

"Which Way Black America? Separation? Integration? Liberation?" *Ebony* 25 (August 1970). ▪ A vital discussion of the alternative goals of future action.

Index

Ohio, clientage politics in, 172–73
Oklahoma, 111–12, 115
Operation Breadbasket, 279
Organization of African Unity, 271
Organization of Afro-American Unity (OAAU), 254–55, 256, 271
Organization of Black American Culture, 275
Organization of Black Power, 273
Osofsky, Gilbert, 158
Ottley, Roi, 153
"Outcast" (McKay), 236

P

Padmore, George, 251
Pan-Africanism (Pan-African movement), 104, 105, 120, 249–51, 253, 260, 262, 268, 271, 274, 278, 279
Pan-Negroism, 262
Peculiar Institution, The (Stampp), 133
Pennsylvania, 176
Peonage laws, 77
People's party. *See* Populist party
Philadelphia, 154, 161–62, 176, 183, 185
  black power conference in (1968), 274
  clientage politics in, 174
  leadership in, 165
  machine politics in, 183–84, 186, 187, 188
  race riot in, 283
Phillips, Ulrich B., 7
Pickens, William, 128
Pittsburgh, 162, 176
Plantations, 51, 72, 73
  and Black Codes, 75
  desertion of, by ex-slaves, 50, 51, 75
Plessy v. Ferguson, 19*n.,* 85, 282*n.*
Pluralism, 211, 281, 285–86, 299
Polish-Americans, 192, 203, 204, 210
Political participation, among blacks, 95–96
  election gains in 1960's, 206, 286, 290, 291, 300–01
  during Reconstruction, 16–17, 77–78, 82
  see also Disfranchisement
Politics, 81, 84, 97, 108, 110, 262
  black-white coalitions in, 297–99, 300–01

clientage, 171–74
Democratic national convention's refusal to admit Mississippi Freedom Democratic delegation, 272, 282
machine, 182–89, 191, 208, 214
Nixon administration's "Southern strategy," 294
and poverty, 212–26
and racism, 81, 182–84
Population, 6, 93, 94, 126, 129, 134, 175–76, 203
  cities 50-percent black, 291
  increase in the South, 80–81
  increase of Negro, in cities, 83, 116, 161–62
  increase of Negro and white, in Northern cities, 1910–1920, 175, Table 2
  Negro urban and rural, by region, 1900–1930, 175, Table 1
Populist party, 51, 81, 82, 84, 163
  failure of, 215
  and racism, 82, 109
Port Royal experiment, 13
Powderly, Terrence, 63–64
Powell, Adam Clayton, Jr., 179–80, 273, 290–91
Prebisch, Raul, 257
Présence Africaine, 246
Presidential elections, voting in, by ethnic groups in Chicago, 190, Table 4
Price, Sam, 137
Progressive era, 19, 68, 214
Protective Benevolent Mutual Aid Association, 62
Protest movements, 129, 130, 132, 133, 144
  NAACP emphasis on legalism, 131
Pryor, Henry, 36
Puerto Ricans. *See* Spanish-speaking Americans
"Purlie Victorious" (Davis), 238

Q

Quaison-Sackey, Alex, 248
Quillin, Frank U., 172–73

R

Race, 160, 195, 196, 247
  and pluralism, 285–86, 299